Materials for Interior Environments

Materials for Interior Environments

Corky Binggeli, ASID

John Wiley & Sons, Inc.

Library of Congress Cataloging-in-Publication Data:

Binggeli, Corky.
    Materials for interior environments / Corky Binggeli.
        p.   cm.
    Includes bibliographical references and index.
    ISBN 978-0-470-11428-5 (cloth)
        1. Building materials—Handbooks, manuals, etc.   2. Interior decoration.   I. Title.
    TA403.4.B56   2007
    729–dc22
                                                                    2007022258

Printed in the United States of America

10 9 8 7 6 5 4 3 2

Contents

Acknowledgments   x
Preface   xi

Chapter 1 Finish Selection and Specification   1
   Health and Safety Codes   2
   Human Factors and Material Selection   4
   Accessible and Universal Design   6
   Other Design Criteria   9
      Budgetary Criteria   9
      Functional Criteria   10
      Environmental Criteria   12
   Energy Use   14
      Fossil Fuels   14
      Greenhouse Gases   14
   The LEED System   15
      Water Use   17
      Recycling   17
      Indoor Air Quality (IAQ)   19
   Historic Preservation, Restoration, and Adaptive Reuse of Materials   22
   Conclusion   27

Chapter 2 Concrete and Cement-Based Materials   29
   Cement   29
      Historical, Cultural, and Architectural Context of Cement   29
      Types of Cement   30
      Environmental and Health Impacts of Cement   30
      Cement-Based Materials and Applications   31
      Grout   32
      Terrazzo   34
      Installing Terrazzo   35
      Cement-Based Overlays   36
   Concrete   37
      Historical, Cultural, and Architectural Context of Concrete   37
      Physical Properties, Characteristics, and Types of Concrete   38
      Aesthetic Qualities of Concrete   40
      Materials Sources and Manufacturing Processes for Concrete   43
      Environmental and Health Impacts of Concrete   45
      Interior Applications for Concrete   46
      Finishes for Concrete   47

Chapter 3 Stone, Masonry, and Concrete Masonry Units   53
   Stone   53
      Historical, Cultural, and Architectural Context of Stone   53
      Physical Properties, Characteristics, and Types of Stone   55
      Aesthetic Qualities of Stone   55
      Manufacturing and Fabrication of Stone   55

Environmental Impact of Stone   60
Interior Applications of Stone   60
Installation and Maintenance of Stone   62
Brick   62
Historical, Cultural, and Architectural Context of Brick   63
Physical Properties, Characteristics, and Types of Brick   65
Aesthetic Qualities of Brick   66
Materials Sources and Manufacturing Processes for Brick   66
Environmental and Health Impacts of Brick   69
Interior Applications for Brick   69
Specifying Brick   69
Cost Factors for Brick   71
Installation and Maintenance Practices for Interior Brick   71
Finishes for Brick   72
Concrete Masonry Units   73
History, Types, and Characteristics of CMUs   73
Environmental and Health Impacts of CMUs   74
Specifying CMUs   74
Cost Factors for CMUs   75
Installation and Maintenance of CMUs   75

Chapter 4 Glass and Ceramics   77
Glass   77
Historical, Cultural, and Architectural Context of Glass   77
Physical Properties, Characteristics, and Types of Glass   80
Aesthetic Qualities of Glass   83
Manufacturing Process for Glass   83
Environmental and Health Impacts of Glass   84
Interior Applications for Glass   85
Specifying Glass   90
Cost Factors for Glass   92
Installing Interior Glass   95
Finishes for Glass   95
Ceramics   97
Historical, Cultural, and Architectural Context of Ceramics   97
Physical Properties and Types of Ceramics   97
Manufacturing Process for Ceramics   98
Environmental and Health Impacts of Ceramics   98
Interior Applications for Ceramics   98
Maintenance and Disposal of Ceramics   100

Chapter 5 Wood and Wood Products   101
Wood   101
Historical, Cultural, and Architectural Context of Wood   101
Physical Properties, Characteristics, and Types of Wood   105
Aesthetic Qualities of Wood   108
Manufacturing Processes for Wood   108
Environmental Impact of Wood   111
Interior Applications for Wood   111
Finishes for Wood   113
Wood Veneer   113
Wood Veneer Grades   113
Cost Factors for Veneers   115
Manufacturing Wood Veneer   115

        Construction and Installation Practices for Wood Veneer 117

        Finishes for and Maintenance of Wood Veneers 118

    Interior Applications for Wood Panel Products 118

        Plywood 119

        Composite Panels 119

        Specifying Wood Products 122

Chapter 6 Plaster and Gypsum Board 125

    Plaster 125

        Historical, Cultural, and Architectural Context of Plaster 125

        Aesthetic Qualities of Interior Plaster 130

        Manufacturing Gypsum Products 130

        Environmental and Health Impacts of Gypsum and Plaster 130

        Installing and Maintaining Plaster 131

        Finishes for Plaster 138

    Stucco 138

        History and Aesthetics of Stucco 138

        Manufacturing Stucco 138

        Installing Stucco 139

    Gypsum Board 140

        Physical Properties, Characteristics, and Types of Gypsum Board 140

        Environmental and Health Impacts of Gypsum Board 140

        Specifications for Gypsum Board 141

        Installing Gypsum Board 141

        Discarding and Recycling Gypsum Board 145

    Glass-Fiber-Reinforced Gypsum (GFRG) 146

Chapter 7 Metals 149

        Historical, Cultural, and Architectural Context of Metals 149

        Aesthetic Qualities of Metals 151

        Sources and Manufacturing for Metals 152

        Finishes for Metals 152

    Ferrous Metals 156

        Iron 156

        Steel 156

        Iron Ore 157

        Environmental Impact of Ferrous Metals 158

        Costs Associated with Ferrous Metals 159

        Joining Processes for Ferrous Metals 159

        Maintenance of Ferrous Metals 160

        Forms of Ferrous Metals 161

    Nonferrous Metals 162

        Aluminum 162

        Bronze and Brass 164

        Chromium 166

        Copper 167

        Lead 169

        Magnesium 170

        Manganese 170

        Nickel 170

        Tin 171

        Titanium 172

        Zinc 173

Chapter 8 Synthetics   175

History of Synthetic Materials   175

Physical Properties, Characteristics, and Types of Plastics   177

    Thermoplastics   177

    Thermoset Plastics   179

Aesthetic Qualities of Synthetic Materials   181

Environmental and Health Impacts of Synthetic Materials   181

Cost Factors for Synthetic Materials   183

Interior Applications for Synthetic Materials   183

    Architectural Resin Panels   183

    Plastic Laminates   185

    Plastic Lumber Products   186

    Solid Surfacing Materials   187

    Synthetic Fibers   188

    Finishing and Maintenance for Synthetic Textiles   192

Leather   193

Chapter 9 Finish Flooring Comparisons   195

Hard Floor Coverings   195

    Tile Flooring   195

    Concrete and Cementitious Floors   200

    Poured Floorings   201

    Wood Flooring   202

    Laminate Flooring   209

    Bamboo Flooring   210

Resilient Flooring   211

    Cork Flooring   212

    Linoleum Flooring   212

    Rubber Flooring   213

    Vinyl Flooring Products   214

Soft Floor Coverings   216

    Carpets   216

    Rugs   220

Chapter 10 Wall and Window Finishes Comparisons   223

Fire-Resistance Ratings   223

Plaster   223

Gypsum Wallboard   224

Glass-Fiber-Reinforced Gypsum   226

Plywood Paneling   227

Solid Wood Paneling   228

Wood Veneers   228

Prefinished Panels   228

Ceramic Wall Tile   230

Stone Facing   231

Flexible Wallcoverings   232

    Vinyl Wallcoverings   232

    Wallpaper   234

    Textile Wallcoverings   235

    Upholstered Wall Systems   236

    Fiberglass Wallcoverings   236

    Natural Fiber and Recycled-Content Flexible Wallcoverings   237

    Wood Flexible Wallcoverings   237

    Paints, Coatings, and Custom Finishes   237

Moldings and Trims   240
Glass and Glazing   244
Window Films   244
Window Treatment Selection and Installation   244

Chapter 11 Ceiling Finishes Comparisons   247
Ceiling Forms   249
Exposed Ceiling Treatments   250
   Exposed Wood Structure   251
   Exposed Concrete Structure   251
   Exposed Metal Decking   252
Wood Ceiling Treatment   253
Illuminated Ceilings   255
Plaster and Drywall Ceilings   255
Acoustical Ceiling Tiles   256
Metal Ceilings   257
Suspended Ceiling Systems   258
   Acoustical Panels   259
   Linear Metal Ceilings   260
   Perforated Metal Pans   261
   Suspended Decorative Grids   262
Stretched Ceiling Systems   262
Banner Materials   263

Chapter 12 Millwork, Furniture Materials, and Textile Comparisons   265
Cabinets   265
Countertops   269
   Sink Installation   276
Manufactured Toilet Partitions   277
Demountable Partitions and Office Systems   278
Furniture Materials   278
Upholstered Furniture   281
Textiles   284
   Textile Selection   285
   Textile Appearance   286
   Textile Fibers   287
   Textile Fiber Sources   287
   Fabric Finishes   295
   Basic Weaves and Fabrics   297
   Dyeing and Printing   299

Appendix: Woods Used in Interiors   303

Index   327

Acknowledgments

The structure of *Materials for Interior Environments* began with the organization of the materials course I taught with Rachel Pike, ASID, at Wentworth Institute of Technology, Boston. Rachel's extensive knowledge and formidable organizational skills helped me put this very broad range of subject matter into usable form. I am also indebted to Rachel and WIT for allowing me to photograph teaching samples from their materials collection.

Paul Drougas, my editor at John Wiley & Sons, encouraged me to take on this project and helped smooth my path. I would also like to thank Lauren LaFrance and Raheli Millman for their support and quick responses to questions. Copy editor Janice Borzendowski patiently and wisely helped me follow a consistent format, and senior production editor Alda Trabucchi guided the book through to publication. The support of the Wiley team made it possible for me to meet an aggressive schedule while keeping many other balls in the air.

Dorothy Deák, who is finishing her master's in interior design thesis as I write this, helped me acquire and organize the illustrations. Dorothy joined us for long days spent assembling the final manuscript, and her cool head and seemingly infinite patience helped us persist to the end.

There is no way that I could have produced *Materials for Interior Environments* without the help of my husband, Keith Kirkpatrick. He is an author's dream, working late nights and weekends proofreading, scanning, and copying images—even cooking meals to keep me going. Thank you, Keith.

Preface

The materials used in interior environments—their composition, forms, characteristics, cost, uses, and effects on human health and the environment—encompass an immense, diverse, and constantly changing body of knowledge. *Materials for Interior Environments* was written as a guide to learning about these materials, with the emphasis on clarity and comprehensiveness.

The enormous amount of detail needed to describe interior finish materials can be daunting, not only to the student but to the teacher as well. The organization of this book draws on my own and my colleagues' experience teaching materials and construction methods to interior design and facilities management students. It also benefits from my work designing commercial spaces such as restaurants, college facilities, health clubs, and offices.

The book begins with a discussion of the considerations involved in selecting interior materials, by surveying the constraints of codes, the parameters of physical accessibility, and the impact on the environment. This first chapter introduces how we describe materials, their functional properties, and their environmental impact. It also considers the role of interior materials in historic buildings.

Chapters 2 through 8 each look at one basic group of materials: concrete and cement; stone and masonry; glass and ceramics; wood; plaster and gypsum wallboard; metals; and synthetics. The information for each material includes a brief review of its history and aesthetic properties, description of its varieties and characteristics, and impact on human health and the environment. These chapters also include brief descriptions of each material's interior uses.

Chapters 9 through 12 guide the reader in comparing different materials with one another in respect to a given application. Chapter 9 looks at all the materials used for finish flooring, Chapter 10 examines window and wall materials, and Chapter 11 covers ceiling materials. Chapter 12 compares material selections for millwork and cabinets, furniture, and textiles.

When used in a course, *Materials for Interior Environments* both serves as an introduction to each of the different types of materials and provides the information needed to compare alternatives. Students will find suggestions for materials to explore in design projects. For the professional designing interior spaces, it serves as a reference for information on properties, environmental impact, and human health and safety, and as a source of suggestions for design solutions.

As an experienced educator and design professional, I have answered many of my own questions while researching and writing *Materials for Interior Environments*, and I hope that you will enjoy reading it and, ultimately, benefit from doing so.

Corky Binggeli, ASID
Arlington, Massachusetts

Finish Selection and Specification 1

There are thousands of products available for use in interior environments, and each has its assets and disadvantages. More interior materials come into the market every day, while others are dropped from the list of possibilities. These factors can make the process of selecting the right interior material for the job bewildering and—sometimes—perilous. The purpose of this book is to aid designers in this process, to serve as a guide to learning about, evaluating, and selecting materials that will look good, work well, and respect human and environmental needs.

As interior designers select finishes for projects and present them to clients, they assess each alternative for its aesthetic contribution to the design concept. In addition to a material's surface appearance, they consider its tactile appeal, acoustic properties, light reflectance, and even its scent. Shape, texture, proportion, and scale are related to the balance and symmetry of the space and the harmony of the design. Whether a material transmits light influences how it can be used to open or enclose a space. Each selection becomes part of complex relationships between unity and variety, rhythm and repetition, and emphasis and hierarchy. The way a material expresses its function is also part of its aesthetic quality.

The selection of materials is restrained by codes and regulations that have been instituted to ensure the public's safety. Interior materials can either contribute potential fuel to a fire or resist ignition and flame spread, for example. The materials that line the paths to exits—the means of egress—are especially important.

Interior materials also often affect human health and well-being, so designers must:

- Review materials for their ability to prevent slips and falls and to cushion surfaces from impact.
- Check details of product manufacture and installation for exposed sharp edges and shatter resistance.
- Select electrically conductive materials where built-up static electricity is likely to be released as painful shocks.
- Insulate from contact materials that are likely to become very hot or cold.
- Design materials to protect both surfaces and people in spaces where potentially dangerous chemicals are in use.
- Avoid materials that expose people to harmful chemicals or unsafe conditions during their manufacture, delivery, installation, use, or disposal, or that degrade *indoor air quality* (IAQ).

Designers also must consider how a material will perform under the conditions of the project. They rate materials for durability, colorfastness and fading, and stain and water resistance, and evaluate them for ease of maintenance. Materials may be tested and labeled by the manufacturer for light, moderate, or heavy use. Designers rely both on their education and experience to select materials with solid reputations, and constantly investigate and screen new products for evidence of reliability.

Sustainable, local, and recycled sources for materials reduce depletion of resources and energy use. The manufacture, shipping, and installation processes for materials that have received certification as environmentally friendly have been reviewed for energy and water use and for production of potentially damaging by-products. Demolition, construction waste, and eventual disposal of the material are examined to conserve and reuse resources.

A material's availability during a project's schedule is related to manufacturing schedules and shipping and warehouse arrangements. Custom-ordered items often require longer lead times and additional paperwork. Special government conditions apply to the export or importation of rare and antique materials.

Designers weigh a material's cost against its durability and useful life. They consider delivery, maintenance, replacement, and disposal costs. Energy costs are also a factor in material selection, production, and installation, and during use. Materials that help to reduce heat loss, decrease the need for air-conditioning, help in the collection and use of nonpolluting energy sources, and adjust to changes in climate all lower building energy costs.

HEALTH AND SAFETY CODES

Before starting to select the finishes and furniture for a project, a designer determines which codes are applicable. Recent changes in the organization of building codes are reflected in local jurisdictions. The three main building code organizations in the United States have now merged into the International Code Council (ICC), which publishes the International Codes (I-Codes). Although many jurisdictions use the I-Codes, some retain what are now referred to as *legacy codes*. An alternative set of codes, published by the National Fire Protection Association (NFPA), is called the C3-Codes. Some jurisdictions also use NFPA publications, including the *Life Safety Code* and the *National Electrical Code*.

 Note: Code information in this text is meant for general reference only; designers must check which codes apply to a given project.

The Codes Guidebook for Interiors, 3rd edition (John Wiley & Sons, Inc., 2005), by Sharon Koomen Harmon, IIDA, and Katherine E. Kennon, AIA, has more comprehensive information on applying codes to interior projects. The major areas that affect interior design projects are listed in Table 1-1.

Most interior projects are required to be accessible to all, and accessibility requirements are included in most building codes. Many codes reference the ICC/ANSI accessibility standard ICC/ANSI A117.1. Federal law requires the use of the *ADA Accessibility Guidelines (ADAAG)* in many projects; these guidelines, published July 23, 2004, are still being incorporated into the work of government agencies.

Interior wall finishes that are subject to code provisions include most of the surfaces applied over fixed or movable walls, partitions, and columns. Interior finishes for ceilings (including suspended ceiling grids and coverings applied to fixed or movable ceilings, soffits, and space frames) are covered in codes. Coverings applied over finished or unfinished floors, stairs (including risers), and ramps are also included.

The ADAAG are available free from the United States Access Board at www.access-board.gov.

Table 1-1 Code Sections

Code Section	International Building Code (IBC) Chapters	NFPA 5000 Building Construction and Safety Code Chapters
Use or Occupancy Classification	Chapter 3: Use or Occupancy	Chapter 6: Classification of Occupancy, Classification of Hazard of Contents, Special Operations. Chapter 16–13, on different occupancy classifications
Special Use or Occupancy Requirements	Chapter 4: Special Detailed Requirements Based on Use and Occupancy	Chapter 31: Occupancies in Special Structures Chapter 33: High-Rise Buildings Chapter 34: High Hazard Contents
Types of Construction	Chapter 6: Types of Construction	Chapter 7: Construction Types and Height and Area Requirements
Fire-Resistant Materials and Construction	Chapter 7: Fire-Resistance-Rated Construction	Chapter 8: Fire-Resistive Materials and Construction
Interior Finishes	Chapter 8: Interior Finishes	Chapter 10: Interior Finishes
Fire Protection Systems	Chapter 9: Fire Protection Systems	Chapter 55: Fire Protection Systems and Equipment
Means of Egress	Chapter 10: Means of Egress	Chapter 11: Means of Egress
Accessibility	Chapter 11: Accessibility	Chapter 12: Accessibility
Interior Environment	Chapter 12: Interior Environment	Chapter 49: Interior Environment
Plumbing Systems	Chapter 29: Plumbing Systems	Chapter 53: Plumbing Systems

Building and fire safety code requirements affecting furnishings include exposed finishes found in furniture and window treatments (fabrics, wood veneers, and laminates) as well as nonexposed finishes, such as the foam in seating and the linings in draperies. This encompasses whole pieces of furniture and upholstered seating, as well as panel systems.

Although the codes are much stricter for commercial projects, deaths occur more often in residential fires. Therefore, all wall and ceiling finishes for a residence—except for trims and materials less than 1/28 inch (0.9 mm) thick, wallpaper, and paint—are required to meet the testing requirements set forth in ASTM E84, issued by the American Society for Testing and Materials. Some finishes, such as wood veneer and hardboard paneling, must conform to other standards as well. Finishes in showers and bath areas are also regulated; they must be smooth, hard, and nonabsorbent, such as fiberglass, vinyl, or ceramic tile.

HUMAN FACTORS AND MATERIAL SELECTION

The selection of materials and furnishings involves considering which are culturally and age-appropriate, as well as designed to fit a variety of human sizes and shapes. Our need to maintain appropriate social distances and to have control over personal space affects the use of materials in interiors. However, the way space is defined and demarcated varies across cultures. In some, for example, spaces are divided according to gender, and domestic spaces are treated differently than public spaces.

Figure 1-1 Islamic buildings often include sheltered views that preserve privacy for interior spaces.

Interior materials intended to create privacy are used to screen views. Materials intended to provide security are often designed to do so unobtrusively, to avoid the perception of being watched.

Researchers have identified four levels of interpersonal space:

- *Intimate space* allows physical contact, and any invasion by a stranger can cause discomfort.
- *Personal space* allows friends to come close, and possibly to penetrate the inner limit briefly; conversation is carried on at low voice levels.
- *Social space* is where informal, social, and business transactions take place at normal to raised voice levels.
- *Public space* accommodates formal behavior and hierarchical relationships, and louder voice levels with clearer enunciation are used.

Intimate interior spaces invite the use of precious or delicate materials. Small-scale and intricate detail are best appreciated with close observation and personal attention. Maintenance of intimate spaces may be more refined than for more public spaces.

Personal interior spaces reflect the character of their owners. Therefore, materials are selected with attention to individual taste and personal history. And because access to personal spaces is ordinarily limited, materials can be selected to support specific lifestyles and maintenance requirements.

Social spaces must accommodate varied activities, and materials are chosen that will suit the intended group of users. The materials used in an office workspace, for example, will be subject to spilled coffee and rolling desk chairs; the materials in a day care center must respond to the safety and durability needs of small children. Materials for hospitality spaces and restaurants, in contrast, demand a high level of aesthetic discrimination, matched with heavy use requirements. Health care facilities, too, have special needs, for cleanliness, maintenance, and durability.

Materials used in public spaces, naturally, must withstand a higher level of abuse than those intended for private use. Larger-scale interactions in public spaces suggest a larger scale of interior material treatment. Issues of public security and safety require materials to be durable, securely fastened, and vandalproof. (See color plate C-2 for finishes in a public space.)

Our body dimensions and the way we move through and perceive space also are determining factors for interior design. Dimensional requirements will vary according to the nature of the activity and the social situation, from how we reach for something on a shelf to how we sit at a table, walk down a set of stairs, or interact with other people.

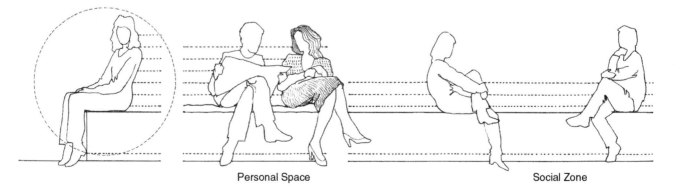

Personal Space   Social Zone

Figure 1-2 Intimate, personal, social, and public spaces. Reproduced with permission of the publisher from Francis D. K. Ching and Corky Binggeli, *Interior Design Illustrated*, 2nd ed. (Hoboken, NJ: John Wiley & Sons, Inc.), © 2005 by John Wiley & Sons, Inc.

When specifying and designing the details for materials, certain dimensions are particularly important to interior designers. These include, in order of importance:

1. Height
2. Weight
3. Sitting height
4. Buttock–knee length (the length from the buttock to the back of the knee)
5. Breadth across elbows and hips when seated
6. Knee front and back heights
7. Thigh clearance and heights

 Note: Design for the most common body sizes generally omits extremes at both ends of the range.

When selecting materials, designers consider what will be within reach of the user. For example:

- Materials used overhead are generally out of reach, but may be handled to access equipment above the ceiling.
- A corridor floor must withstand traffic patterns as well as people leaning against the walls.
- The edges of counters are rubbed against and sometimes picked at.
- Chairs are scraped on floors, rubbed against walls, and turned onto tabletops for cleaning.
- Cleaning equipment bumps into walls and furnishings.

All these possibilities have to be considered and factored into the long-term cost of a material.

ACCESSIBLE AND UNIVERSAL DESIGN

Accessible design addresses the requirements of a single group within the larger population, specifically, people with disabilities. There are differences between appropriate accessible design for public facilities and the best approach for private, custom,

Figure 1-3 Important dimensions for furniture and built-in seating design.

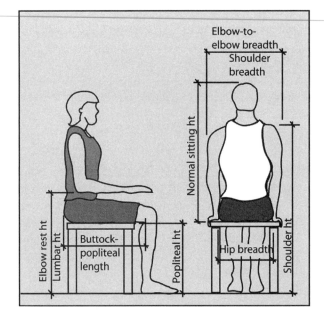

Figure 1-4 The ability of people to reach up and out varies greatly.

Figure 1-5 Shelves must be within the reach of most users. Drawers and files need additional space in front for the user.

accessible projects. When designing for a broad range of users, it is important to ensure that the design meets the needs of the targeted population. For example:

- Materials are selected to eliminate irregularities and avoid slipping on walking surfaces.
- Surfaces are protected from contact with wheelchairs.
- Wall-mounted materials are limited as to height and extension from the wall.
- Changes in finishes indicate changes in location. Carefully chosen materials help users find their way through interior spaces.

Universal design is based on principles that include:

- Equitable use
- Perceptible information
- Flexibility
- Tolerance of error
- Simple and intuitive use
- Low physical effort

Universal design is inclusive of all people with respect to human factors issues. It differs from accessible design in that it addresses as widespread a group as possible. Providing securely braced grab bars in all bathtubs, for use by children as well as older people—by anyone who might slip—is an example of universal design. Provisions for universal design do not have to be institutional in style, and can add to the beauty, function, and safety of an interior design.

Materials that accommodate the majority of users and include those with special needs also enable people to continue to use an interior as their physical needs change.

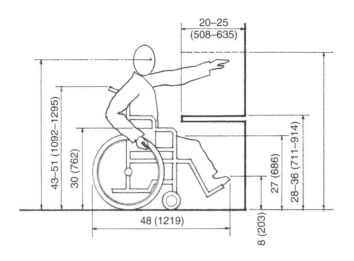

Figure 1-6 Wheelchair footrests are likely to come in contact with doors and walls. Kickplates and durable finishes help prevent damage.
Reproduced with permission of the publisher from Francis D. K. Ching and Corky Binggeli, *Interior Design Illustrated,* 2nd ed. (Hoboken, NJ: John Wiley & Sons, Inc.), © 2005 by John Wiley & Sons, Inc.

Figure 1-7 Universal design kitchen at Seniors Residence, Weston, Massachusetts. This kitchen is in the shared common area for the use of residents and guests.

The increasing mobility of a growing child, for instance, is taken into account in selecting finishes for a bedroom or play space. A family home can be designed to accommodate the needs of the parents as they age. Commercial and public interior spaces that employ universal design make business, government, and recreation open to all.

In the case of children, their needs change as they grow, as does how they perceive and use objects and spaces. Very young children will be unable to read signs, for example, and so will need to rely on graphic symbols for guidance. Design options such as attractive yet durable finishes that are located at a child's eye and hand level also will help to create welcoming spaces. (See color plate C-3 for a space designed for children.)

 Note: The ADAAG cites special considerations for spaces used by children; materials selected for use in these spaces must address the health and safety needs of all children.

In the case of older people, they typically become less active and move more slowly, and design must accommodate these changes. Aging does not, however, inevitably lead to disability, and interior spaces that are designed to be both accessible and efficient allow older people to retain their independence. Many of the same features that make an interior convenient for the general population also work for seniors. Handrails and nonslip flooring promote safety and independence. (See color plate C-4 for a space designed for older people.)

Code requirements, human factors, and accessibility are all very important to the selection of materials for interior spaces. Three other design criteria are budgetary, functional and environmental considerations.

OTHER DESIGN CRITERIA

Budgetary Criteria

To respect a client's budget, a designer should provide guidance as to where money can be spent wisely—and where it makes sense to economize. Creativity need not be limited by financial constraints, however, and interior designers who find creative solutions without breaking the budget are highly prized.

One of the most important budgetary considerations for interior designers is the *life-cycle cost* of a product. The life-cycle cost of a material includes its purchase cost, as well as costs for transportation from its source, maintenance, replacement, and disposal or recycling. Interest rates on invested money are also factors.

Figures are available in published and software forms and on the Internet for estimating the cost of interior design materials and labor. Note, however, these sources are based on figures for a specific year and, therefore, must be adjusted for inflation if not for the year in which construction will take place.

Many energy-efficient designs may have a higher initial cost, but show savings in energy costs over time.

An estimate generally includes the cost to purchase and install interior improvements to a space. Depending on the project, the estimate may include furniture, window treatments, accessories, cabinets and millwork, and installation of specified furnishings and equipment. Some sources include information on adding allowances for profit, overhead, and shipping.

Many interior design projects involve elements of building construction or modification. Consequently, some estimating data sources include information in assembly form (cost to build a standard handicapped accessible bathroom, for example) and/or broken down into components (individual plumbing fixtures, finishes, wall construction, etc.). The cost of interior design and construction work will vary from region to region and country to country. The cost of local materials and local labor will affect the estimate, as will the currency exchange rate. And, of course, the cost of a project will vary according to size. When economies of scale are taken into account, the cost of improving a single room will be higher than the cost per room of a project with 100 rooms.

Scheduling affects costs as well, with aggressive timelines typically increasing the cost. Likewise, work in occupied buildings may have to be done at night or on weekends, adding to labor costs. When work has to be done during a contractor's busy season, the contractor may ask for more money than if the work is taken on during a slow season. Similarly, prices may be higher in a booming economy than in a slow one.

A number of other design factors have budgetary ramifications:

- Designs that are highly detailed and include unusual or unique features may be more expensive to build than conventional designs.
- A design that takes advantage of stock material sizes and uses materials efficiently is generally less expensive to build.

- Materials that are difficult to acquire, rare, or unusual tend to increase overhead as well as materials costs.
- The level of refinement that the designer specifies will also affect costs. A project that demands perfect surfaces and impeccable detailing takes more skill and usually more time to produce than one that is intended to be a bit rough. An experienced designer can create designs that achieve aesthetic and functional goals while simplifying the fabrication process.

Functional Criteria

The basic functional qualities of major materials categories suggest their appropriate uses. These include safety, durability, comfort, ease of care, fire resistance, and acoustic properties.

Safety

Safety issues for interior materials include toxicity, health effects, slip resistance, and shatter resistance. Not only should designers select a material to be safe for use as intended, but they should also consider the unexpected; for example, wired glass will not break when hit by water from a fire hose (its intended function), but will break if struck by a strong fist, causing cuts and bleeding. It is important to keep in mind that safety concerns change over time. A case in point is asbestos: when introduced to prevent the spread of fire, its effect on human health was not clearly understood, or was not considered.

Durability

Durability involves evaluating a material for its ability to stand up to its intended use. Materials are rated for their resistance to abrasion, exposure to sun, and freeze/thaw cycles. Some materials will melt when they come in contact with a heat source; others will deteriorate from contact with alcohol or acetone (nail polish remover). Water will damage or weaken some materials, while others will dry out in low humidity. The preparation of the substrate (for example, a clean, smooth surface) for installation of the material and the use of proper installation procedures affect the durability of a material, as does its finish.

Comfort

Comfort is a functional criterion for interior materials that come in contact with the human body. A sturdy but hard chair may encourage short visits in a food court; in contrast, a cozy, large one will induce lingering. Materials that carry heat away from the human body may be welcome in a tropical climate but will feel unpleasantly cold to the touch elsewhere. The texture of a floor may not be important for someone passing through a space one time, but it becomes critical for those who spend their workday on their feet in the same space.

Ease of Care

Ease of care affects a material's continued performance over time. A material that can be used in a carefully controlled environment with excellent maintenance procedures may not withstand exposure to unsupervised users and less diligent maintenance. Products with frequent, complex, or expensive maintenance requirements often fail to retain their initial appearance, especially if untrained personnel, rather than skilled labor, are performing the maintenance.

Fire Resistance

Fire resistance is such an important topic that designers often limit their initial materials selections to those that meet the requirements of fire codes. Codes consider not only the ability of a material to ignite and burst into flame, but also how much smoke it will produce and whether fire will quickly spread across its surface. When exposed to fire, some materials produce toxic chemicals that may be odorless and produce no smoke or flame.

Acoustic Properties

Acoustic properties of materials make a big difference in how that space will function. Interior materials affect the acoustic quality of a space by absorbing or reflecting sound within a space, and by transferring sound from one space to another.

Within a space, a sound generated from one location will spread out and away from its source; this is referred to as *diffusion*. It continues to spread and gradually becomes weaker, which is called *attenuation*, until it is either absorbed or reflected by an intervening material. In some spaces, a designer will want sound to be *reflected* and bounced around. In other interiors, a high level of sound absorption will keep noise at an acceptable level. Within a single interior space, there may be areas of relative quiet and noise.

The materials chosen for the ceiling surface usually have the greatest impact on *sound absorption*. Next in importance are the surfaces behind the source of the sound. The surfaces in front of the sound source are also important. In terms of sound absorption, the flooring material is generally the least important. However, the sound of footfalls and chairs scraping on a hard-surfaced floor can add a considerable amount of noise to a space.

Impact sound—the sound made by one object striking another, such as a shoe on a floor—will reflect into the room where it originates but may also pass through the building structure to another location. For example, sometimes footfalls are more audible to people in a room below than in the room of origin.

Some materials tend to block the transfer of sound. These include large amounts of sound-absorbent material and massive materials. Other materials are considered to be acoustically transparent, allowing sound waves to pass directly through to the other side; open-weave fabrics and perforated panels are used this way. Some materials will pick up the vibration of a sound wave and amplify it, much like the head of a drum.

Figure 1-8 Reflected sound

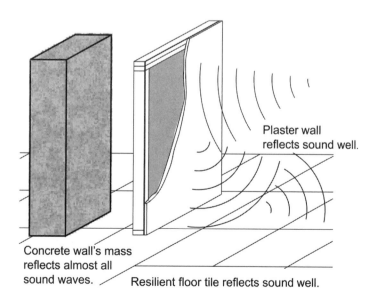

Plaster wall reflects sound well.

Concrete wall's mass reflects almost all sound waves.

Resilient floor tile reflects sound well.

Environmental Criteria

The indoor air quality (IAQ) of a space depends on three factors:

- Introduction and distribution of adequate ventilating air
- Control of airborne contaminants
- Maintenance of acceptable temperature and humidity

Although these are usually considered mechanical systems issues, the decisions made by interior designers play a substantial role in ensuring clean indoor air. By selecting materials that avoid adding contaminating chemicals to the air and that do not encourage the growth of molds or bacteria, interior designers contribute to the environmental quality of the interior.

Sustainable materials are renewable or regenerative materials that can be acquired without ecological damage and used at a rate that does not exceed the natural rate of replenishment. Manufacturers wishing to attain environmental certification for materials must inform the certifying organization of the reasons the materials should be certified, and in which category. Products accepted for evaluation go through extensive testing by accredited laboratories before meeting standards for environmentally friendly design.

Closed-loop models for the use of materials treat waste material as raw material for new products. Thus, a closed-loop recycling process is one in which a manufactured product is recycled back into the same or a similar product without significant deterioration of quality of the product. Steel and other metals, glass, and some types of plastic are examples of materials that can be recycled in a closed-loop process. This *cradle-to-cradle approach* is economically sustainable, and does not rely on nonrenewable resources. William McDonough and Michael Braungart employ cradle-to-cradle design to create products and systems that contribute to economic, social, and environmental prosperity. Their

Figure 1-9 Cushioning a floor with carpet and pad is one of the best ways to reduce impact sound.

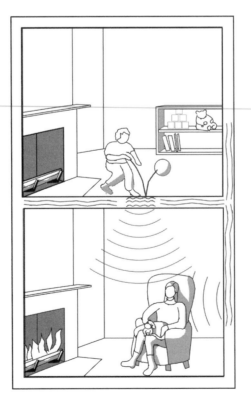

innovations are revolutionizing the production of what are often called "green" interior finish materials.

Environmentally preferable products (EPPs) are defined by U.S. federal government Executive Order 13101 as products that have "a lesser or reduced effect on human health and the environment when compared to competing products that serve the same purpose." EPPs are not necessarily fully sustainable, but are considered better than other readily available materials.

Green products are those considered to be environmentally preferable or to have a low impact on the environment. This is an informal designation that is applied to products that promote IAQ, usually through reductions of *volatile organic compounds* (VOCs) such as formaldehyde. It is often used for durable materials with low maintenance requirements. Green products often incorporate recycled content, such as postconsumer and/or postindustrial materials. However, the term's use is not regulated, and "green" is sometimes used for products with minimal environmental benefits.

Material Safety Data Sheets

Material Safety Data Sheets (MSDS) are forms that contain data on the properties of particular substances. They are intended for workers and emergency personnel as part of workplace safety programs, rather than for general consumer information. An MSDS contains information regarding potentially significant levels of airborne contaminants. These forms are supplied by manufacturers of products containing hazardous chemicals.

The search for accurate information about green materials requires research, critical evaluation, and common sense. A designer preparing an evaluation of environmentally preferable materials would, for example, collect information on critical performance criteria; available environmental products; MSDS information on potential hazards associated with installation, use, and disposal; maintenance expectations for the material or system; and the corporate environmental policy statements from manufacturers under consideration.

Designs by Anne Beetz

Climatex Lifecycle

Pattern	6694 Summit
Color	13 Blue Ridge
Width	54 inches
Repeat	7/8″ length, 2 1/2″ width
Content	76% Wool, 24% Ramie
Uses	Upholstery, Panels
Flame Retardancy	Passes California Bulletin 117
Origin	Switzerland
Durability	No wear after 30,000 double rubs

Eco-Info
- *No pollutants during manufacture*
- *All waste scrap recycled*
- *Compostable after useful life*
- *More info under swatch*

These products have been developed under license from Design Tex, and McDonough Braungart Design Chemistry, LLC.

Carnegie (800) 727-6770
www.carnegiefabrics.com

Printed on recycled paper

©copyright 1999, Carnegie Fretric

Figure 1-10 McDonough Braungart fabric protocols. This fabric is designed for minimum environmental impact.

ENERGY USE

The source and amount of energy used to produce a material, as well as its effect on the environment, should be major concerns for the interior designer. *Embodied energy* is energy that is used to obtain, process, fabricate, and transport a unit of building material. For example, the embodied energy for wood includes the sunlight used for its growth, the fuel needed to cut, transport and process wood products, and to install them at the site. Embodied energy calculations can also include the material's impact on building heat gain or loss, and energy used for disposal.

By choosing to reuse existing interior materials, a designer saves energy and lowers disposal costs. *Selective demolition*—the dismantling of reusable building parts for reuse—adds to the availability of low-cost construction materials and helps keeps waste out of landfills.

Fossil Fuels

Our most commonly used energy sources—coal, oil, and gas—are fossil fuels that are not renewable. Often, energy from fossil fuels is used to obtain and process raw materials, to manufacture products, and to transport them to distributors and then to building sites. Additional energy is used to install and finish materials, and to maintain, repair, and ultimately replace and dispose of materials. Even recycled materials use energy for transportation, separation and processing, and manufacturing.

Greenhouse Gases

Human activities are adding *greenhouse gases*, pollutants that trap the earth's heat, to the atmosphere at a rate faster than at any time over the past several thousand years. A warming trend has been recorded since the late nineteenth century, with the most rapid increase occurring since 1980, raising the global temperature and changing our planet's climate at an unprecedented rate. As greenhouse gases accumulate in the atmosphere, they absorb sunlight and infrared (IR) radiation and prevent some of the heat from radiating back out into space, trapping the sun's heat around the earth.

A global rise in temperatures of even a few degrees could result in the melting of polar ice and the ensuing rise of ocean levels, and would affect all living organisms. Energy from fossil fuels used to produce and transport materials add to greenhouse gas buildups.

The nonprofit U.S. Green Building Council (USGBC) has created a comprehensive system for sustainable design methods called LEED, short for Leadership in Energy and Environmental Design. LEED provides investors, architects, designers, construction personnel, and building managers with information on environmentally preferred

THE LEED SYSTEM

Table 1-2 Green Product Standards

Organization	Standard	Content
Carpet and Rug Institute	Green Label program for carpets	Certifies that product has been tested by independent lab and has very low chemical emissions.
EcoLogo	Canadian third-party certification program examines available research and life-cycle assessments, but does not typically carry out primary research.	Covers environmental, health, and safety issues; resource and energy consumption; contains market data on the product and industry sector, and socioeconomic data.
Environmental Building News	*GreenSpec* Directory (6th ed.) third-party evaluations	Evaluates building materials.
Forest Stewardship Council (FSC)	Third-party certification program	Lists certified or sustainably harvested wood products obtained from well-managed forests.
Green Seal	Third-party certification program considered a mark of environmental responsibility	Uses standards and research by others.
Oikos Green Building Source, from Iris Communications	Publisher of books on environmental issues	Provides a gallery of environmentally responsible building materials.
Rainforest Alliance	Certification and rating program for wood products and paper	Monitors products from rain forests.
Scientific Certification Systems	Third-party certification; auditing and testing services; standards	Recognizes highest levels of performance in food safety and quality, environmental protection, and social responsibility.
U.S. Environmental Protection Agency (EPA)	Executive Order 13101–Greening the Government Through Waste Prevention, Recycling, and Federal Acquisition	Addresses green standards in federal agency procedures.
	Executive Order 13123–Greening the Government Through Efficient Energy Management	Covers standards for government buildings.

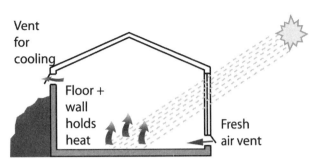

Figure 1-11 Floor and wall materials with high thermal capacity store the sun's heat, thereby containing solar energy.

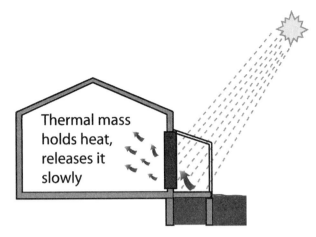

Figure 1-12 Materials with high thermal capacity can block unwanted solar heat from entering a building directly and store it for later use.

Table 1-3 Greenhouse Gases

Type of Gas	Sources
Carbon dioxide (CO_2)	Burning fossil fuels for transportation, electrical generation, heating, and industrial purposes.
Methane	Human production of fossil fuels, livestock and manure, rice cultivation, biomass burning, and waste management account for about 60 percent of global methane emissions. Natural sources of methane include wetlands, gas hydrates, permafrost, termites, oceans, freshwater bodies, nonwetland soils, and other sources such as wildfires.
Carbon monoxide (CO)	Internal combustion engines burn CO to produce CO_2. Human-produced sources include unvented kerosene and gas space heaters; leaking chimneys and furnaces; backdrafting from furnaces, gas water heaters, wood stoves, and fireplaces; gas stoves; generators, and other gasoline-powered equipment; automobile exhaust from attached garages; and tobacco smoke.
Hydrofluorocarbons (HFCs)	Refrigerants, propellants, and cleaning solvents. HFCs have been banned by the Montreal Protocol on Substances That Deplete the Ozone Layer. Although being phased out, off-gassing still occurs from foam building insulation.
Perfluorocarbons (PFCs)	Aluminum smelting and semiconductor manufacturing.
Chlorofluorocarbons (CFCs)	Polyurethane foams used for insulating homes and other buildings. Some have dissolved into the oceans and will eventually come out into the atmosphere. Current decline is due to a ban by the Montreal Protocol.
Sulfur hexafluoride	Insulating gas used in electrical equipment
Nitrous oxide (NOx)	Naturally emitted by bacteria in soils and oceans. Agriculture: soil cultivation, nitrogen fertilizers, animal waste handling. Production of nylon and nitric acid. Burning of fossil fuel in internal combustion engines.
Tetrafluoromethane	Refrigerant. Slowly being phased out.

building techniques and strategies. LEED also certifies buildings that meet the highest standards of economic and environmental performance, and offers professional education, training, and accreditation. LEED professional accreditation recognizes an individual's qualifications in sustainable building.

The LEED green building rating system is based on overall performance criteria for entire buildings. LEED evaluates buildings for performance in five categories:

- Sustainable sites
- Water efficiency
- Energy and atmosphere
- Materials and resources
- Indoor environmental quality

Further, the LEED system establishes criteria for the use of reused materials, recycled-content materials, local or regional materials, rapidly renewable materials, certified wood, and low-emitting materials.

Interior designers are among those becoming LEED-accredited by passing the LEED Professional Accreditation Examination, which establishes minimum competency in much the same way as the National Council for Interior Design Qualification and other professional exams. The LEED Rating System for Commercial Interiors (LEED-CI) is now in use. In order to meet LEED-CI standards, an interior space must be located in a LEED-certified building or in a building that takes advantage of brownfield redevelopment, water management, renewable energy, and/or community density and connectivity measures. New LEED residential standards for single and multifamily residences with three or fewer habitable floors define features of a green home and provide a consistent rating system with third-party verification and on-site inspections.

Water Use

Ninety-nine percent of the earth's water is either saltwater or glacial ice. One-quarter of the solar energy reaching the earth is employed in constantly circulating water through evaporation and precipitation in a process known as the *hydrologic cycle*. The most accessible sources of water for human use are precipitation (rain and snow) and runoff. These provide a very large but thinly spread supply of relatively pure water that, when absorbed into the ground as *groundwater*, makes up the majority of the water supply.

The manufacturing process uses large amounts of water. In closed-loop manufacturing, water is repeatedly circulated and reused. Wastes are prevented from polluting the water supply downstream and, ideally, are turned into useful products.

Recycling

The best way to conserve materials and energy is to retain existing materials in new designs. Reducing the amount of new material is the second most effective method. Using recyled materials or new materials with recycled content is a third way to support sustainable design. Recycled materials almost always require additional energy for manufacture or transportation.

There are three major categories of recycled materials:

- *Postconsumer recycled material* is defined as a reclaimed waste product that has already served a purpose to a consumer and has been diverted or separated from waste management collections systems for recycling. An example would be used newspaper that has been made into cellulose building insulation.
- *Preconsumer recycled material* takes waste removed from production processes, including scrap, breakage, and by-products, and reuses it in another process

before consumer distribution. One example is mineral (slag) wool, a by-product of the steel blast furnace process, which is used for mineral fiber in acoustical ceiling panels.
- *Salvaged material* such as used brick is collected from existing or demolished buildings for reuse.

Interior designers play a key role in the reuse of nonstructural interior building components when they consider which elements can be reused in a new design or salvaged for another project. Demolition by hand salvage produces useful building components, and even some architectural gems. The dismantling of a building generates reusable roof boards, framing lumber, and tongue-and-groove wood flooring. Doors, windows, bathroom fixtures, plywood, siding, and bricks all can be reused, as can furniture, equipment, and appliances.

Interior designers work with contractors to ensure that materials removed during renovation and the waste generated by construction have a second life; recycling

LEED Project Credits

LEED-CI (commercial interiors) project credits are given for:
- Site Selection: Space in a LEED-certified building or in a building located so as to take advantage of brownfield redevelopment, water management, renewable energy, and community density and connectivity measures.
- Water Use Reduction: 20 percent and 30 percent decreases.
- Energy and Atmospheric Measures:
  - Energy-efficient and nonpolluting lighting power and controls, HVAC systems, equipment and appliances
  - Green power sources
  - Energy use, management, and payment accountability
- Materials and Resources:
  - Storage and collection of recyclables
  - Long-term tenants
  - Reuse of nonstructural interior building components
  - Construction waste diversion from landfills
  - Resource reuse of furniture and furnishings
  - Recycled content of materials
  - Use of regional materials
  - Rapidly renewable materials
  - Certifiable wood
- Indoor Environmental Quality:
  - IAQ performance minimums, environmental tobacco smoke controls, outside air delivery monitoring, and increased ventilation.
  - IAQ management during construction and before occupancy
  - Low-emitting materials: adhesives and sealants, paints and coatings; carpet systems; composite wood and laminate adhesives; systems furniture and seating.
  - Indoor chemical and pollutant source controls
  - Lighting, temperature and ventilation controls
  - Thermal comfort compliance and monitoring
  - Daylight and views
- Innovation and Design Process including use of LEED-accredited professional

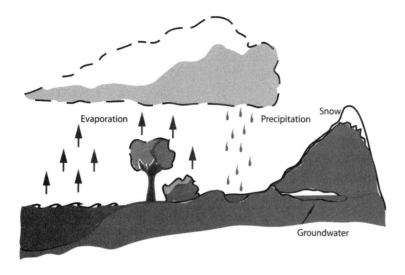

Figure 1-13 *Hydrologic cycle. Continual evaporation of water into the environment distills the earth's limited supply. This clean water is then returned to Earth as rain or snow.*

requirements are now commonly included in demolition specifications. Asphalt, concrete, bricks, and metal are routinely recycled to meet market demands. Shingles, carpet, wallboard, doors, windows and other pieces of demolished homes and offices can be diverted into the resale and recycling market. Concrete and masonry can be crushed and used as aggregate for road building. Glass can be recycled into "glassphalt" road-surface reflectors. Chopped-up wood becomes mulch or helps the composting of sludge at sewage treatment facilities. Manufacturers that take back used carpet grind it up for attic insulation or recycle it into new carpet. Plate glass becomes fiberglass insulation, and used acoustic tiles are recycled into new ones.

The disposal of drywall, or gypsum wallboard, can pose an environmental danger. Many landfills today won't accept gypsum wallboard scrap because it produces toxic hydrogen sulfide gas when buried. Fortunately, it can be recycled, with up to 85 percent of the material reused for new drywall. Unpainted drywall can also be composted, replacing lime in the soil.

Indoor Air Quality (IAQ)

Air pollution problems can start with a building's materials and finishes, followed by the construction methods used to build or renovate the building. Interior designers play a major role in specifying materials that potentially contribute to indoor air pollution; they are key players in the renovation of buildings for new uses and to accommodate new ways of working.

To improve indoor air quality and prevent contamination by pollutants, a building's architect, engineers, and interior designer must work together. The interior designer can specify appropriate materials, products, and equipment, and evaluate the amount and toxicity of emissions given off during installation or use, especially where the surfaces of potentially polluting materials are exposed to the air and to people.

Maintenance requirements for cleaning processes, stain-resistant treatments, and waxing that emit pollutants may contribute to poor IAQ. When construction is complete, the interior designer should provide the building's management, users, and owners with appropriate information about maintenance requirements.

Volatile organic compounds (VOCs), chemicals that tend to evaporate at room temperature and normal atmospheric pressure (thus, are volatile) and contain one or more carbon atoms (therefore, are organic compounds), are invisible fumes or vapors. Some VOCs have sharp odors, while others are detectable only by sensitive equipment. VOCs commonly evaporate from plywood, plastic, fibers, varnishes, and coatings;

from cleaning chemicals, solvents used in paints, waxes, and petroleum fuels; and from some consumer products. Some products will off-gas VOCs for a limited period—during which the space must be ventilated—and then revert to a safe state.

 Note: Not all VOCs are dangerous. Consider the scent of a rose, which is the off-gassing of a volatile organic compound.

Formaldehyde

Formaldehyde, a common VOC, is a colorless, strong-smelling gas used in the manufacture of synthetic resins and dyes, and as a preservative and disinfectant; it is present in pressed-wood products. After exposure, healthy people may have difficulty breathing, and may cough, wheeze, and feel tightness in their chests. At high levels, formaldehyde causes tearing, burning, and stinging eyes; sneezing and a tingling sensation in the nose; and soreness and dryness in the throat. The irritation persists even after removal of the source, and can temporarily heighten sensitivity to other contaminants. Formaldehyde may also increase the risk of cancer in humans, and has been clearly demonstrated to have negative effects on people with chemical sensitivities.

Formaldehyde is found in particleboard, interior laminated panels, glues, fabric treatments, and paints. Interior-grade plywood, particleboard, medium-density fiberboard (MDF), insulation, and some textiles emit it. Its effects are most severe when products are new, but they can last anywhere from a few hours to many years after installation. Fortunately, alternatives to particleboard are becoming more readily available. When formaldehyde-bearing products are used, however, they should be sealed with laminates or a liquid sealer formulated especially for formaldehyde reduction, including edges, backs, under desks or tabletops, and inside cabinets and drawers.

Table 1-4 Federal Guidelines for Recycled Content of Interior Materials

Interior Material	Recycled Material	Percent of Material's Composition
Carpet—polyester	Postconsumer Polyethylene Terephthalate (PET)	25–100%
Cement and concrete	Coal fly ash	0–40%
	Ground, granulated blast furniture slag	25–50%
Dividers: restroom and shower	Postconsumer plastic	20–100%
	Postconsumer steel	16%
Fiberboard—structural	Recovered	80%
Floor tiles	Recovered	80%
Paint	Reprocessed latex (white, pastel)	20% postconsumer
	Reprocessed latex (gray, dark)	50–99% postconsumer
	Consolidated latex	100% postconsumer
Paperboard—laminated	Postconsumer	100%
Patio blocks	Postconsumer rubber	90–100%

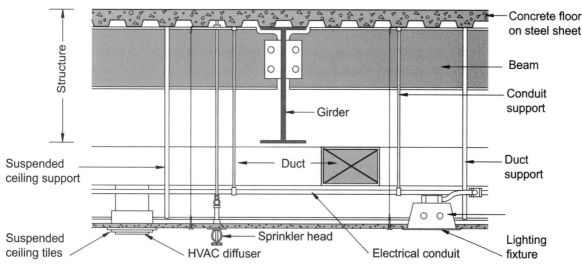

Figure 1-14 Floor/ceiling plenum

Materials Stability

The stability of materials has an impact on interior air quality over an extended period. Interior design finishes that do not produce or retain dust, and designs that limit open shelving or areas that collect dust help control VOC retention. Durable materials, such as hardwoods, ceramics, masonry, metals, glass, baked enamels, and hard plastics are generally low in VOC emissions; low-VOC paints are readily available as well. Fibers like cotton, wool, acetate, and rayon have low VOCs, but their dyes and treatments may release toxic chemicals.

The period immediately following the finishing of the building's interior is critical for VOC exposure. Aging materials before installation may help release some of the VOCs outside the space. If possible, occupancy should be delayed to allow for off-gassing from adhesives, paints, and other materials and finishes. The re-release of VOCs that have been absorbed by furnishings can be controlled by using the maximum amount of outside air ventilation possible during and following the installation of finishes and furnishings. Installed materials can be protected from collecting VOC emissions from other products by sealing them in plastic vapor barriers. Newly occupied buildings should be operated at the lowest acceptable temperatures to slow VOC emissions.

Asbestos

The inhalation of asbestos fibers over a long period of time can cause cancer, fluid in the lungs, and asbestosis, a fibrous scarring of the lungs. Asbestos is white, light gray, or light brown, and looks like coarse fabric or paper; it may appear as a dense, pulpy mass of light gray, stuccolike material applied to ceilings, beams, and columns. Up until 1975, asbestos was widely used for steam pipe and duct insulation and in furnaces and furnace parts. Before 1980, acoustic tiles and fiber-cement shingles and siding contained asbestos. Vinyl floor tiles made from the 1940s to the 1980s contain asbestos, as does their adhesive. Asbestos fibers may still be found in existing construction, especially in the insulation on heating system components and other equipment, in acoustic tiles, and in drywall joint-finishing material, and textured paint purchased before 1977. Some sprayed and troweled ceiling-finishing plaster installed between 1945 and 1973 also contains asbestos.

Most asbestos can be left undisturbed, as long as it does not emit fibers into the air. If it is not crumbling, it can be sealed with a special sealant and covered with sheet metal.

If it remains in place, it must be dealt with later during renovation or demolition. The interior designer should avoid drilling holes, hanging materials onto walls or ceilings, causing abrasion, or removing ceiling tiles below any material containing asbestos. Wrapping can repair asbestos-covered steam lines and boiler surfaces, but asbestos in walls and ceilings usually cannot be repaired, as it is difficult to keep airtight. It is possible to enclose asbestos in areas with low ceilings or small areas that are unlikely to be disturbed or damaged by water, or where the asbestos is unlikely to deteriorate. Encapsulation may cost more than removal. Removal is the only permanent solution, but if done improperly, can be more dangerous than leaving the asbestos in place. If removal is required, it should be done by a properly certified and licensed expert. Areas from which asbestos is being removed must be isolated using airtight plastic containment barriers, and kept under negative pressure with special high-efficiency particulate air (HEPA) filtration. The work site should be inspected and its air quality tested after the work is done.

Lead

Lead was present in most paint in the United States until it was banned in 1978 by federal law (it had been banned in most other countries decades earlier). Until 1985, pipes and solder also contained lead, as did gasoline, and it was commonly found in dust and soil near roads.

Lead is a neurotoxin that is especially damaging to fetuses, infants, and young children, and can cause learning disabilities, nausea, trembling, and numbness in the arms and legs. Children ingest and inhale lead-based paint chips or dust by playing on floors and other dusty surfaces and then putting their hands in their mouths or noses. Lead particles are suspended in the air or settle on surfaces such as carpets, which can release the particles back into the air when disturbed. Lead accumulates in the body over time, and lead poisoning has become the number-one health hazard to children under the age of seven. Lead exposure has been implicated in attention deficit disorder, impaired hearing, reading and learning disabilities, delayed cognitive development, reduced IQ scores, mental retardation, seizures, convulsions, coma, and death. In adults, lead exposure can cause high blood pressure; and occupational exposure has been implicated in kidney disease.

Houses built prior to 1950 are likely to contain paint with high levels of lead. Lead-based paint is in three-quarters of U.S. homes built prior to 1975, amounting to nearly 60 million private homes. The woodwork and walls of many homes were painted with lead-based paints. This residential exposure accounts for 80 to 90 percent of total lead exposure; therefore, it is critical that old lead paint be identified and removed, or sealed in an approved manner. Old pipes and solder should also be replaced.

An interior designer is in a position to advocate for the proper handling and disposal of lead paint by a licensed contractor. If the lead-based painted surfaces are clean and intact, and there is no cracking, peeling, blistering, or flaking, they can sometimes be encapsulated with a coating applied in liquid form that provides a flexible, impact-resistant barrier. Encapsulation is the most economical and simplest procedure, and does not require hazardous waste removal or the relocation of building occupants.

HISTORIC PRESERVATION, RESTORATION, AND ADAPTIVE REUSE OF MATERIALS

By keeping older buildings in usable condition and protecting their original use or finding a new one, communities create a sense of continuity and cultural richness. While the exterior appearance of a building in many communities is regulated by law to maintain a prescribed historic appearance, the interior is permitted to be changed to accommodate new uses and evolving tastes. In these cases, the interior designer has the option of working with existing interior elements or installing a totally new interior into the historic building shell.

The following four approaches to the preservation of historic buildings are regulated in the United States by government entities, including the Secretary of the Interior, the National Historic Preservation Fund, and the *National Register of Historic Places*.

- *Preservation* focuses on retaining and repairing as much of an existing property as possible. The subject of a preservation effort is often a building, or parts of a building, with significant historical value. Details from more than one historic period may be preserved, showing how the building has changed over time. Existing materials are preserved wherever possible by cleaning and, sometimes, by coating surfaces. Paints are matched to original colors, although modern formulations are used. The interior designer's role in preservation involves conducting careful historic research and providing expert advice. The accuracy of the preservation is a major concern, as the client is often a museum, a preservation society, or a private owner of a valuable landmark property.

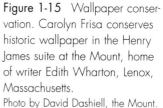

Figure 1-15 Wallpaper conservation. Carolyn Frisa conserves historic wallpaper in the Henry James suite at the Mount, home of writer Edith Wharton, Lenox, Massachusetts.
Photo by David Dashiell, the Mount.

- *Restoration*, in contrast, seeks to depict a specific period of time. The focus is on the period of greatest cultural, historical, and architectural significance. Original components from the desired period are either uncovered or accurately copied, and details from other periods are removed. The goal is an accurate depiction of the building at a specific moment in history. (See color plate C-1, Paint color restoration.)
- *Reconstruction* supplements original elements from a specific historical period, with new construction imitating the original. New methods and materials may be used to re-create a historically significant period. Reconstruction often seeks to maintain, with historic accuracy, a neighborhood that reflects a period from the past.
- *Rehabilitation* attempts to retain elements of a building's history, cultural environment, and architectural character while altering or expanding the existing property to accommodate new needs or uses. Repairs, alterations, and additions compatible with contemporary use are permitted, such as accommodations for ductwork or an elevator. Rehabilitation, it is important to point out, runs the risk of altering subtle but important relationships of proportion and detail.

Figure 1-16 The Earle Theatre, Washington, DC. Now known as the Warner Theatre, this performance space was thoroughly documented with photographs and drawings for its restoration in 1992.

Rehabilitation of Historic Building Interiors

Focus on:
- Portions significant to its historic, architectural, and cultural values
- Floor plans and interior spaces that define overall historical characteristics
- Size, configuration, relationships, and proportion of rooms and corridors
- Relationships of special features to spaces

Avoid:
- Dividing historically important spaces
- Making new cuts in floors and ceilings
- Dividing spaces horizontally with new floors or mezzanines
- Dropping ceilings below ornamental ceilings
- Changing room proportions
- Furring out perimeter walls for insulation
- Removing paint and plaster from traditionally finished surfaces
- Painting previously unpainted millwork
- Using destructive paint removal processes
- Using harsh cleaning agents

Retain, preserve, and repair:
- Columns, doors, fireplaces, and mantels
- Cornices, baseboards, paneling, hardware, and flooring
- Lighting fixtures and elevator cabs
- Stair locations and configurations
- Wallpaper, plaster, paint, stenciling, marbling, graining
- Visible building mechanical system elements
- Use of period colors
- Deteriorated decorative plasterwork

Figure 1-17 The actual composition of a wall in an existing building is sometimes unknown until demolition begins, as is the case here. Discrete removal of outer layers can provide a glimpse of what is behind.

Figure 1-18 Adaptive reuse of mill building, Lowell, Massachusetts. The steel columns, heavy wood beams, brick floor and walls, and wood plank ceiling of this building can be incorporated into designs for a variety of new uses.

In contrast to those four approaches, *renovation* and *adaptive reuse* of existing buildings are less concerned with historic accuracy.

- Buildings are renovated for many reasons, but principally to correct existing problems of structure or use. Design elements may be inconsistent with the historic period, and new materials may be used. Renovation may strive to create a period style while accommodating current needs and methods. Many upgrades of existing buildings fall into this category, which is not considered to be historic by government agencies.
- Adaptive reuse seeks to change the function of a building into something not intended for the original structure. Many times, buildings that have become obsolete are slated for adaptive reuse in order to extend their useful lives. The key elements of adaptive reuse are (1) the change from the building's original function and (2) adaptation to a new use. By adapting an existing structure to a new use, demolition is unnecessary.

According to "Rehabilitating Interiors in Historic Buildings" (Preservation Brief 18, National Park Service, U.S. Department of the Interior), by H. Ward Jandl, the process of historic interior preservation begins with the identification, retention, repair, and protection of a building's floor plan, the arrangement of its spaces, its features, and the applied finishes that define its historical character and purpose. After assessing the alterations that have already been made, as well as any deterioration the building has undergone, the degree of change appropriate to a project can be determined. Existing fabrics and original floor plans may reveal which alterations were added and where historical features are covered up but not destroyed. Identifying which walls and architectural features have been removed helps to establish the history of the building. Greatly altered spaces might not be worth returning to their original condition. If a building's history is important and well recorded, it may be possible to reconstruct its interior. The documentation of existing conditions includes photographing interior features and preparing measured floor plans prior to beginning any rehabilitation.

Historically preserved buildings must comply with contemporary building, life safety, and fire codes. However, when compliance would damage distinctive interior features, it may be possible to obtain a code compliance variance. The entire process benefits from close cooperation with code officials, building inspectors, and fire marshals.

Historic preservation construction usually involves a team of highly skilled, experienced, and specialized workers. State historic preservation officers and local preservation organizations can help a designer locate workers with established reputations. Information on preservation techniques can be found in the Association of Preservation Technology's *APT Bulletin* and in *The Old House Journal*.

CONCLUSION

Interior designers share in the responsibility to use resources wisely, to create buildings that support human and environmental health and safety, and to respect the architectural history of the buildings on which they work. Whether a project is very large or quite small, the interior designer benefits from an awareness of the impact it will have on the environment, the welfare of its users, and the nature of the community of which it is part.

Concrete and Cement-Based Materials 2

oncrete and cement-based (*cementitious*) materials have been widely used throughout history for architectural structures. Concrete and cement products are used to build interior bearing and nonbearing walls and to prepare interior surfaces for finishes; they are also used as finishes.

 Note: *Terrazzo*, a cement-based product with stone chips, is included in this discussion; some concrete applications are discussed here as well. Interior concrete floors are covered in Chapter 9, and walls in Chapter 12; concrete countertops also are discussed, in detail, in Chapter 12.

Cement is made of finely pulverized clay and limestone and used as an ingredient in concrete or mortar. Cement is calcined, that is, heated to a high temperature without melting or fusing. It acts as a *binder*, a substance that sets and hardens independently and can hold other materials together; in concrete, it binds aggregates into a strong, solid mass.

 Note: The term *cement* is frequently used incorrectly for *concrete*.

CEMENT

Historical, Cultural, and Architectural Context of Cement

Cement can be formed naturally; evidence from Yiftah El in Israel dates the use of natural cement made of limestone and oil shale to 7000 BCE. Man-made concrete has been found in a hut floor from 5600 BCE at Lepenski Vir in Serbia. Pyramids in Egypt were being made with gypsum and lime mortars in 3000 BCE.

By 300 BCE, the Romans were using pozzolana cement, a pink, sandlike material from Pozzuoli near Mount Vesuvius in Italy, to build the Appian Way, public baths, and the Coliseum. They employed lightweight concrete embedded with bronze reinforcing bars for the roof of the Pantheon.

The Industrial Revolution led to the development of natural and artificial cements in England, France, and the United States. Stonemason Joseph Asdin invented portland cement in 1824 by heating finely ground limestone and clay on his kitchen stove, then grinding the mixture to a powder. Portland cement contains calcium, silicon, aluminum, and iron. It is made of limestone shells or chalk mixed with shale, clay, sand, or iron ore. The basic materials are usually mined in a quarry near a plant where they are crushed.

 Note: Portland cement is named for its resemblance to stone quarried on the Isle of Portland off the British coast.

Cured cement is a hard, dense solid with a rough texture that cracks and crumbles readily. The uniform gray or white texture of cement combines with the color and texture of aggregates in concrete. Cement lacks the durability of concrete.

The cement business is seasonal, with most work taking place in the warmer months. It tends to be regional, as well, as the cost of shipping heavy materials is lower when they are purchased from local sources. In the United States, most of the transportation is by truck, with small amounts shipped by barge or rail.

Types of Cement

Hydraulic cement is any cement that hardens with the addition of water. Today's portland cement is a hydraulic cement made by burning a mixture of clay and limestone in a rotary kiln fired by powdered coal or natural gas, and pulverizing the resulting clinker into a very fine powder.

The American Society for Testing and Materials (ASTM) Specification C150 describes five major types of portland cement, along with several subtypes. Interior floors and precast concrete products are made with Type I, normal portland cement, which is available in white or gray. White portland cement is similar to gray cement, but is made of materials with low levels of magnesium and iron oxides, and used for white or colored concrete or mortar. Blended hydraulic cements are made of portland cement with other cementitious materials such as ground granulated blast-furnace *slag* (a by-product of manufacturing iron), *fly ash* (produced in coal-fired electric generating plants), natural volcanic ash, and silica fume, a by-product of the production of silicon. Cements made with fly ash, or with natural volcanic ash, are referred to as *pozzolans*.

Environmental and Health Impacts of Cement

The raw materials in cement are generally common in nature and environmentally inert. The calcium in cement comes from limestone, marl (lime-rich mudstones), and chalk. Silicon is found in clay, sand, or shale; fly ash can also be added for its silicon content. Iron and aluminum in cement comes from iron ore and bauxite (consisting of aluminum ore with iron oxides and clay). The distance from the point of use and the quality of the sources have an impact on energy use. The water and gravel used to make

Figure 2-1 Cement plant, United States Pipe & Foundry Company, Bessemer, Alabama.

cement are quite abundant. A significant amount of water is used for washing these materials.

The making of cement and concrete is one of the most energy-intensive industrial manufacturing processes, with most of the energy expended to operate rotary cement kilns. Fossil fuels and electricity generated by coal provide the power for machinery during mining and transportation. The burning of coal results in the emission of high levels of carbon dioxide, nitrous oxide, sulphur, and other pollutants. Cement also can be produced using waste fuels such as used motor oil, spent solvents, printing inks, paint residue, cleaning fluids, and scrap tires. Cement kilns burn at extremely high temperatures, resulting in very complete combustion of these waste products, and very low emission levels.

Carbon dioxide is emitted by the cement industry in significant amounts, accounting for approximately 5 percent of man-made carbon dioxide emissions globally. About half of carbon dioxide emissions result from the manufacturing process used to convert limestone to calcium oxide, and then into cement clinker. It is chemically impossible to do this without producing carbon dioxide, which is currently emitted to the atmosphere. Between the combustion of fossil fuels to operate the cement kiln and the process of turning limestone into lime, each ton of cement releases 1.25 tons of carbon dioxide into the atmosphere. Attempts at reducing carbon dioxide emissions have, so far, seen little development since the 1990s.

Air pollution from cement plants includes sulphur dioxide, nitrous oxides, and smaller amounts of sulphuric acid and hydrogen sulfide. The lime used in a cement kiln acts as a *scrubber*, an industrial pollution control device, that absorbs some of the sulphur.

The process of making cement produces a great deal of dust from cement kilns, handling of raw materials, grinding cement clinker, and packaging and loading finished cement. It is difficult but possible to collect and recycle dust at the cement plant. Dust is controlled through water sprays and the use of enclosures, hoods, curtains, and covered chutes. Cement dust can be used for agricultural soil treatments or used as landfill on-site.

Workers are exposed to cement dust when they open bags, and sand, cut, or grind concrete. Cement can cause an allergic skin reaction or respiratory allergy in some people. Sensitivity to the ingredients in cement may develop suddenly after years of exposure, and can continue to worsen throughout the sufferer's lifetime. Cement dust in the eyes can cause irritation, and even chemical burns and blindness. Therefore, individuals exposed to cement dust should wear protective clothing and glasses, and wash off dust thoroughly with clean water.

Cement-Based Materials and Applications

The cementitious materials most often used in building interiors are mortar and grout. *Mortar* is used to assemble masonry units and as a bed for tiles. *Grout* is placed in the openings in masonry walls and is visible in the spaces between ceramic tiles.

Mortar

Cement mortar consists of portland cement, sand, and water. Its relative stiffness, as compared to concrete, facilitates handling with a trowel when it is spread on masonry units, and allows it to support the weight of masonry units without squishing out between courses. Unlike the water in concrete, which becomes chemically bonded as hydration occurs, excess water in mortar is absorbed into adjacent masonry units, where it helps to create a bond.

Weathered joint

Concave joint

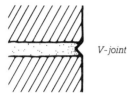

V-joint

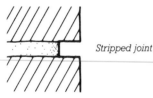

Flush joint

Raked joint

Stripped joint

Struck joint

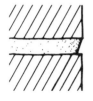

Figure 2-2 Joint profiles
Reproduced by permission of the publisher from Edward Allen and Joseph Iano, *Fundamentals of Building Construction: Materials and Methods,* 4th ed. (Hoboken, NJ: John Wiley & Sons, Inc.), © 2004 by John Wiley & Sons, Inc.

Lime mortar, a mixture of lime, sand, and water, is rarely used today because of its slow rate of hardening and low compressive strength. Cement-lime mortar is a cement mortar to which lime is added to increase its plasticity and water retention.

Masonry cement is a proprietary mix of portland cement and other ingredients, such as hydrated lime, plasticizers, air-entraining agents, and gypsum. Masonry cement requires only the addition of sand and water to make cement mortar.

Specifications for mortar indicate the type of mortar to be used, the mixing procedure, and types of joint profiles.

- High-strength mortar is used for masonry construction.
- Type O mortar is low-strength mortar suitable for use in interior, nonload-bearing walls and partitions.
- Type K mortar is very low-strength mortar suitable only for use in interior nonload-bearing walls, where permitted by the building code.

Mortars come in many shades and textures. Some suppliers keep stockpiles of sands from a variety of beaches (each with its own color) for mixing custom mortar colors.

Mortar Construction and Installation Practices

Mortar is used on brick, concrete block masonry, gypsum plaster and gypsum board, concrete slabs, and plywood. It can be applied to open stud framing and furring with metal lath, and is used to bond masonry units and for tile beds. Mortar for repointing masonry in historic buildings is mixed using special formulas.

Mortar is usually visible only at joints between masonry units, but these can be prominent design elements in brick or stone. Mortar joints vary from 1/4 to 1/2 inch (6 to 13 mm) thick but are typically 3/8 inch (10 mm) thick. The type of joint used determines the appearance of the shadow line that gives texture to masonry walls.

Tooled joints are mortar joints compressed and shaped with any tool other than a trowel. Concave and V-joints are common tooled joint profiles. Tooling protects mortar against forced water penetration by compressing the mortar and forcing it tightly against the adjacent surfaces. Troweled joints, which are finished by striking off excess mortar with a trowel, include weathered joints—the most effective at shedding water—as well as struck and flush joints. Raked joints, which are made by removing mortar to a given depth with a square-edged tool before hardening, are used exclusively on interior applications.

Cracks in mortar permit water infiltration, and crumbling mortar loses its strength. Mortar is maintained by repointing (also called pointing) joints using mortar that is compatible with the existing materials. Differences in hardness can cause older (pre-1930s) masonry units to break down as the installation expands and shrinks. To repoint a joint, a mason removes the existing mortar with a chisel to a depth of about one inch. The joint is then cleaned of mortar dust (which would keep new mortar from sticking), and packed with new mortar. Tuck pointing, applying new mortar over old without chiseling, is even less expensive but may weaken or widen the joint.

Grout

Grout has the same ingredients as concrete, but is much more fluid in its initial state.

Grout for Masonry Walls

Grout is placed in the cells of hollow masonry units and in relatively narrow spaces in brick walls; it must be fluid enough to fill the spaces and joints between masonry units without clumping or leaving airspaces. Grouted masonry walls have all interior joints

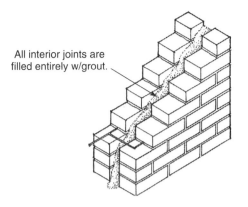

All interior joints are filled entirely w/grout.

Figure 2-3 Grouted masonry wall
Reproduced by permission of the publisher from Francis D. K. Ching and Cassandra Adams, *Building Construction Illustrated*, 3rd ed. (New York: John Wiley & Sons, Inc.), © 2001 by John Wiley & Sons, Inc.

filled entirely with grout as the work progresses. Fluid grout with portland cement consolidates adjoining materials into a solid mass. Low-lift grout installation methods add grout as the wall is being built, to a maximum of 5 feet in height at a time. High-lift grout installation is completed one story at a time.

ASTM C476 covers the specification of masonry grout, including type, mixing procedures, and joints. Dark-colored grout is often specified for floors; lighter grout is typically specified for walls. Grout specifications include whether it is to be mixed at the plant or in the field, the size of the crew needed, consolidation practices, the speed of placement, and whether a demonstration panel is to be built before installation.

Grouts are classed as fine or coarse, depending on aggregate size. Newer self-consolidating grouts (SCGs) use admixtures called polycarboxylates that create a very fluid but stable mix. SCGs can be installed faster than standard grouts with smaller crews.

Mortars and Grouts for Ceramic Tile Installation

Ceramic tile is either set in a bed of mortar or attached to the substrate with adhesive. Both cementitious mortars and noncement-based mortars are used with ceramic tiles, and will be discussed below. Grout is used to fill the spaces between ceramic tiles after they have been set. The specific type of tile, mortar, and grout must be selected to be compatible.

Three classes of cementitious mortars are used with ceramic tile.

- *Dry-set mortar* with sand and other additives is the most common type, used over concrete and other hard surfaces and valued for its moisture and impact resistance.
- *Portland cement* mortar is always used for thickset tile installation; it consists of portland cement, sand, and water.
- *Latex portland cement mortar* is a flexible mortar used in dry applications of porcelain tiles; it can take weeks to dry.

Noncement-based mortars are generally more expensive than cementitious mortars. Epoxy mortar has good chemical resistance, high bond strength, and impact resistance, and is resistant to high temperatures. Modified epoxy emulsion mortars also have high bond strength, but are easier to apply. Furan resin mortar is used in laboratories and industrial applications where high chemical resistance is important.

Grouts for ceramic tiles include both cementitious and noncementitious types. Cementitous types include:

- Portland cement grout: dense, with good water resistance and uniform color
- Sand portland cement grout: mixed at the job site

- Dry-set grout: used for floors without difficult conditions
- Latex portland cement grout: latex helps the grout to cure, and reduces absorption

Noncementitious grouts include:

- Epoxy grout: good chemical resistance; used with epoxy mortar
- Furan resin grout: very expensive; used for difficult conditions
- Silicone rubber grout: very expensive; temperature resistant; not used near food preparation areas

(See color illustration C-8 for tile grout colors)

Terrazzo

Terrazzo is a dense, extremely durable smooth flooring with a speckled appearance. It is composed of marble or other stone chips, set in a cementitious resinous matrix, and ground and polished when dry. The underbed is the mortar base on which the terrazzo topping is laid. When a latex, polyester, or epoxy binder is combined with stone chips, the terrazzo topping is especially resistant to chemicals and abrasion. The size and colors of the aggregate and the color of the binder determine the final coloring. The matrix acts as a binder to hold the chips in place. The three basic types of matrices are cementitious, modified-cementitious, and resinous.

Specifying Terrazzo

It is difficult to duplicate the physical specifications of terrazzo precisely, as marble and other aggregates vary in color, size, and denseness, and granules are not always uniform. Cement shades also vary. Local supplies of certain marble colors may not match some standard colors, so it is best to expect minor variations.

Rocks like marble that can be ground and take polishing well are used for terrazzo aggregates. Quartz, granite, quartzite, and silica pebbles are used for nonpolished surfaces such as rustic terrazzo.

Standard terrazzo is a ground and polished terrazzo finish consisting mainly of relatively small stone chips. Venetian terrazzo contains large stone chips, with smaller chips filling the spaces between. Rustic terrazzo for exterior use has a uniformly textured finish produced by washing the matrix before it is set to expose the chips, which are not ground smooth. Palladiana is a mosaic terrazzo finish consisting of cut or fractured marble slabs set by hand in the desired pattern, with smaller chips set into the spaces between. Conductive matrix terrazzo eliminates static buildup in areas with explosive hazards. The conductive material, carbon black, produces a black matrix.

Terrazzo guide specifications, details, and technical data are available for copy and use from the National Terrazzo and Mosaic Association(www.ntma.com).Online images and paper samples are available from the National Terrazzo and Mosaic Association, but these are limited by the color-rendering properties available. Actual physical samples from the terrazzo contractor should be used for final color approval.

Table 2-1 Terrazzo Matrices

Cementitious matrix	Portland cement	White, gray, or tinted with mineral color pigments; marble chips
Modified cementitious matrix	Polyacrylate modified cement	Thinset applications
Resinous matrices	Epoxy or polyester	Two-part thermal setting for thinset applications

Terrazzo can be customized for unusual shapes and contours, either as precast or on-site applications. Precast terrazzo is available as steps, treads and risers, bases, planters, wall panels, windowsills, thresholds, and outdoor furniture. Some standard shapes are available, and custom designs are possible. Terrazzo for precast pieces is poured into molds and then moisture cured, ground, polished, or otherwise finished. It is installed with temporary wood strips, which are replaced by a fluid-applied sealant. (See color plate C-9, Precast Terrazzo.)

The cost of terrazzo installations increases with the use of larger chips, as in Venetian and Palladiana terrazzos. Intricate or complex divider strip layouts also increase costs, as does the use of a complex specialized formula. Larger proportions of rare or expensive marble chips cost more than standard mixes, and extremely hard chips such as granite and quartz add to grinding costs. Additional transport costs apply to chips shipped from locations away from their use. Color pigments in the matrix material also add to the cost, but only slightly. White portland cement terrazzo matrix is somewhat more expensive than gray. (See color plate C-10, Terrazzo samples.)

Terrazzo formulations are labeled with the initial letter of a descriptive term. Standard (S) terrazzos are available with either resin or cement-based binders. More expensive Designer (D) and Exotic (E) mixtures are available only with epoxy resin binders, and use specialty aggregates. Venetian (V) and Rustic (R) formulations usually use portland cement binders. SF in a terrazzo designation refers to special finish techniques, which cost more due to additional labor and materials requirements.

Installing Terrazzo

Terrazzo is constructed in thinset, monolithic, bonded or sand-cushion installations.

- *Thinset terrazzo* is lightweight (weighing only 4 pounds per square foot), comes in a full range of colors, and can be used both horizontally and vertically for restoration work. Its resin matrix resists chemical spills, making it suitable for labs, hospitals, and manufacturing facilities.
- *Monolithic terrazzo*, which is poured in one step directly onto a concrete base, is the most economical installation, and so is ideal for large areas such as shopping malls, schools, and retail stores. The performance of monolithic terrazzo depends on the quality of its substrate. Long, narrow strips of terrazzo should be avoided. Monolithic terrazzo weighs 7 pounds per square foot.
- *Bonded terrazzo* is installed as a portland cement topping and underbed totaling at least 1–3/4 inches (45 mm) in thickness. Chemically bonded terrazzo has a similar topping installed over a smooth-finished slab with a chemical bonding agent. Bonded terrazzo is used in both interior and exterior projects to fill recessed depths from 1–3/4 to 2–1/4 inches. It is used for floors, bases, walls, and any vertical surface. The relatively thin installation weighs 18 pounds per square foot.
- *Sand-cushion terrazzo* is a system for controlling cracking when structural movement is expected. The entire installation is about 3 inches thick and weighs 30 pounds per square foot. Sand-cushion interior installations are used on the lower and ground levels, as well as in multistory buildings. Considered the best cement terrazzo technique, it is ideal for designing patterns and using with multiple colors.

Metal or plastic-tipped divider strips are placed every 20 feet to localize shrinkage cracking and serve as construction joints where the terrazzo is installed over isolation or expansion joints in the subfloor. Divider strips are used to separate different colors of a floor pattern; most styles are available in both zinc and brass. Heavy top strips, which

Recycled materials such as glass have been introduced in newer terrazzo products.

give a clean line to separate parts of a design, are made of zinc, brass, or plastic, on bases that are usually zinc-coated steel. Aluminum divider strips may be used with epoxy terrazzo systems, but not with cement-based products.

Terrazzo sealers are used to improve appearance and maintenance. A penetrating sealer is applied to the surface of a portland cement-based terrazzo immediately after its final polish. Water-based acrylic sealers are usually specified with a slip-resistance coefficient of friction of at least 0.5. Solvent-based sealers may discolor and be difficult to strip.

Most terrazzo installations in public buildings are dust-mopped daily to remove tracked-in dust and grit. Terrazzo is cleaned with a gentle neutral cleaner in clean water that is left on the floor for several minutes and then rinsed with clear water. Cleaning up spills immediately prevents stains. Sweeping compounds containing oil should not be used, as they can penetrate and permanently stain the floor; they are also a fire hazard and usually contain sand, which abrades the floor and diminishes its shine.

Cement-Based Overlays

Over time, concrete and other floors can become uneven or damaged. Cement-based overlays are used to smooth and level uneven or spalled (chipped or scaled) concrete surfaces and to resurface interior floors. Linoleum or vinyl flooring and carpet are removed first, along with residual adhesives. Overlays are available pretinted or with a mix-in liquid coloring agent; overlays of different hues produce surfaces with color variations. (See color plate C-5, Cement-based floor finish overlay.)

Figure 2-4 Thinset terrazzo installation.
Reproduced by permission of the publisher from Francis D. K. Ching and Cassandra Adams, *Building Construction Illustrated*, 3rd ed. (New York: John Wiley & Sons, Inc.), © 2001 by John Wiley & Sons, Inc.

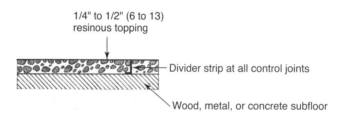

1/4" to 1/2" (6 to 13) resinous topping

Divider strip at all control joints

Wood, metal, or concrete subfloor

Figure 2-5 On concrete stairs, a 5/8-inch (16-mm) terrazzo topping is set on a 7/8-inch (22-mm) underbed.

Many cement-based overlays blend cement, sand, and additives to improve performance, wear resistance, and appearance. Overlays can be applied in layers from very thin to several inches thick without delamination or failure. They adhere well to existing concrete, and resist damage from salt, chemicals, ultraviolet ray (UV) exposure, cycles of freezing and thawing, and abrasion. Costs in the United States for labor and materials to install cement-based overlays run around $1 to $3 per square foot.

Costs are provided for comparison only.

Cement-based overlays are installed quickly on a structurally sound concrete substrate that does not have cracks wider than a hairline, severe delamination, or an unstable subbase. Cement-based overlays are often sprayed on evenly with an air-powered hopper gun. A splatter coat can be added for a textured slip-resistant finish, or the surface can be troweled down to a smooth finish.

Paper or adhesive stencils are used to produce decorative borders and medallions, tile patterns, and embossed or inlaid motifs. Reusable stencils that became available in the 1980s pressed a light design into a fresh cement overlay or concrete topping. Newer adhesive-backed vinyl stencils can be used on existing hard cement and concrete surfaces, but are limited to a single use per stencil. Stampable overlays, which involve less time and labor-intensive installation than stamped concrete, are applied as a uniform 1/4- to 3/4-inch thick wet topping, and then are imprinted with semiflexible stamping mats or texturing skins.

Microtoppings are applied with a trowel or squeegee in very thin layers—a minimum of 20 mils (0.02 inch) thick. Microtoppings are finished very smooth, and can have a featheredge that blends into the existing surface.

CONCRETE

Concrete is made by mixing cement and various mineral aggregates such as gravel with water. Adding the right amount of water causes the cement to set and bind the entire mass. Although concrete is inherently strong in compression, steel reinforcement is required to handle tensile and sheer stresses. Heavy-normal reinforced concrete weighs 150 pounds per cubic foot—pcf (2400 kg/m^3).

Historical, Cultural, and Architectural Context of Concrete

Concrete floor and wall fragments from around 100 CE found at Teotihuacan, Mexico, were made with volcanic gravels. Mayan stone buildings from 250 to 900 CE at Piedras Negras, Uaxactun, and Tzimin Kax, and at Chichen Itza (built 800–1000 CE) were constructed with flat lime concrete roofs more than an inch (30 cm) thick, built on top of crossed wood beams. Smaller sticks filled the spaces between the beams; and when the concrete dried and contracted, the beams were retied, a method still used in Yucatán, Mexico.

The Romans embedded bronze bars in the concrete of the Pantheon as reinforcing around 125 CE; but because bronze expands and contracts at a different rate than concrete, this application caused spalling. Reinforced concrete was attempted again following the publication of *The Encyclopedia of Cottage, Farm and Village Architecture*, by J.C. Loudon (London, 1834), which included a description of a roof composed of a lattice of iron rods embedded in concrete. An 1854 patent application for an improvement in the construction of fireproof dwellings, warehouses, and other buildings was submitted by William Wilkinson of Newcastle. A French lawyer named Jean-Louis Lambot exhibited a boat made of iron rods covered with fine concrete at the Paris Exhibition of 1855.

Physical Properties, Characteristics, and Types of Concrete

Concrete is plastic and malleable when newly mixed and can be formed into almost any shape. It is also strong and durable in compression when hardened and becomes stronger with time. Its tensile strength can be improved by the addition of steel reinforcement. Concrete is inherently fire-resistant, and accepts a wide variety of surface finishes and textures.

As previously mentioned, concrete is made of cement plus aggregate and water, which undergo a chemical reaction and become hard (set). Aggregates, including sand, gravel, or other mineral materials, make up 60 to 80 percent of concrete by volume, and add strength, weight, and fire resistance. A typically well-proportioned mix is 10 to 15 percent portland cement, 60 to 75 percent aggregate, and 15 to 20 percent water. Mixes may include between 5 and 8 percent entrained air, which is intentionally mixed into the concrete to improve its performance when frozen and thawed. The cement and water are mixed into a paste that coats the surface of the aggregates. High-quality concrete keeps the ratio of water to cement as low as possible without reducing workability of fresh concrete too much. A chemical reaction called *hydration* hardens the paste and makes the concrete strong. Not enough paste compared to aggregates produces rough honeycombed surfaces and porous concrete. Too much cement paste is easy to place and flows to a smooth surface, but is likely to shrink more and is ultimately less economical.

Ready-mixed concrete makes up around three-quarters of all concrete used. It is delivered to the site by a truck with a revolving drum, where it may be remixed or have materials added; it sets more rapidly if remixed. Ready-mixed concrete is good for small quantities or intermittent placing, and for large jobs in tight spaces. The three categories of ready-mixed concrete include central-mixed concrete completely mixed at the plant; transit-mixed, or truck-mixed, concrete made in small batches on the way to the site; and shrink-mixed concrete partly mixed at the plant.

Precast concrete products are cast in a factory for better quality control and waste management, and can be used in construction in all types of weather. Specialty products can be designed specifically for a single project. Precast building elements are very durable and may be reused after their original purpose is done.

Precast products used in interiors include concrete bricks and paving stones and structural components. Precast concrete sandwich panels have insulation placed between two layers of concrete for energy efficiency. In addition to its structural uses, precast concrete is used for planters, seating, and other objects. Concrete masonry units (see Chapter 3) are also a form of precast concrete.

Note: Materials costs for precast concrete are higher than for site-poured concrete, but these may be offset by savings in labor and scheduling efficiencies.

Reinforced concrete combines steel, for high tensile strength, and concrete, for great compressive strength, making it strong in both compression and tension. Reinforcement

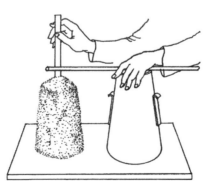

Figure 2-6 Mixed concrete is rated by the amount it will slump when formed into a cone and deposited on a flat surface. Reproduced by permission of the publisher from Francis D. K. Ching and Cassandra Adams, *Building Construction Illustrated*, 3rd ed. (New York: John Wiley & Sons, Inc.), © 2001 by John Wiley & Sons, Inc.

Figure 2-7 Once water is added, concrete must be continually mixed or it will set; even so, the time it can be kept in a fluid state is limited. Concrete trucks mix the concrete while transporting it to the site.
Reproduced by permission of the publisher from Francis D. K. Ching, *A Visual Dictionary of Architecture* (New York: John Wiley & Sons, Inc.), © 1995 by John Wiley & Sons, Inc.

consists of steel bars, strands, or wires. Reinforced concrete absorbs tensile, shearing, and sometimes compressive stresses in a concrete member or structure. Steel reinforcement also ties vertical and horizontal elements together, and reinforces edges around openings. It helps to minimize cracking that occurs during concrete shrinkage, and controls thermal expansion and contraction.

Reinforcing bars are steel sections hot-rolled with ribs or other deformations for better mechanical bonding to concrete. The bar number refers to its diameter in eighths of an inch (e.g., a #5 bar is 5/8 inch (16 mm) in diameter).

Welded wire fabric, which consists of a grid of steel wires or bars welded together at all points of intersection, is typically used to provide temperature reinforcement for concrete slabs. Heavier gauge welded wire fabric can also be used to reinforce concrete walls. The fabric is designated by the size of the grid in inches followed by a number indicating the wire gauge or cross-sectional area.

Reinforced concrete construction results in thinner concrete slabs, which use less material. This decreases the weight of the building's structure and allows for less massive foundations. Thinner structural members take up less space between one floor and the next, making possible higher interior ceilings. Smaller, lighter buildings have less exposed building exterior, making heating and cooling savings possible.

Prestressed concrete structural units are given compressive stresses by high-strength steel tendons before loads are applied. These compressive forces are balanced by tensile stresses when loaded. The technique makes possible lighter, shallower concrete structures without sacrificing strength. Prestressed concrete is used for roofs, floors, and walls with longer unsupported spans. Prestressed concrete may be either pretensioned or posttensioned.

Pretensioning steel reinforcing is stretched before the concrete is poured into molds and cured. When the concrete cures to the required strength, the stretching force is released, causing the steel to try to return to its original, shorter length; this produces compressive stress in the concrete. *Pretensioned concrete* is used for roof slabs, piles, and wall panels.

Concrete is cast around but not in contact with posttensioned steel that is stretched after the concrete hardens, putting the concrete in compression. *Posttensioned concrete* is used for cast-in-place concrete, large girders, floor slabs, shells, roofs, and pavements. Commercial buildings, shopping centers, school auditoriums, gymnasiums, and cafeterias employ posttensioned steel for long spans.

Tilt-up concrete walls are cast horizontally, tilted to vertical, and moved into place with mobile cranes. The panels are cast close to their intended location, often on the concrete floor slab of a building. Reinforced steel, a vapor seal, insulation, door and window frames, electric conduit, and outlet boxes are prepositioned. This quick, efficient, and economical method for individually designed reinforced concrete structures can use locally available material and relatively unskilled labor. Pieces can be mass-produced, and changes in panel heights and lengths are easily accommodated.

Figure 2-8 Reinforcing bars improve the tensile performance of concrete.

Tilt-up concrete can be colored, textured, and shaped. Finishes include paint, brick facing, curved surfaces, and exposed aggregates. Tilt-up construction is used for single-story commercial buildings including warehouses and office buildings, condominiums of 2 to 4 stories, and hotels to 10 stories.

Aesthetic Qualities of Concrete

The development of concrete buildings by the Romans introduced new aesthetic possibilities, beyond those possible with cut stone or post-and-beam structures. Concrete's great strength allows spans in the form of arches, vaults, and domes. The flexibility of its molded form could easily imitate the details of laboriously carved stone.

Starting around 200 BCE, the Romans faced what they considered unsightly cores of concrete walls with slabs or mosaics of tufa, a soft volcanic stone found in central Italy, or kiln-dried bricks. Facing materials could be finished with a *veneer* (thin surface layer) of stucco or plaster that was molded, patterned, or painted, sometimes to

resemble marble. Luxurious and expensive finishes of marble were used to create decorative pilasters or half-columns on concrete walls. The Romans eventually accepted a utilitarian concrete aesthetic, with brick-covered concrete used for functional buildings in Rome and Ostia, including high-rise tenements (*insulae*), commercial buildings, warehouses, and markets.

In the early twentieth century, the introduction of concrete reinforced with steel created a new aesthetic. Concrete slabs cantilevered beyond their supports and allowed exterior walls to become nonstructural screens. Open-plan interior spaces could be defined with nonload-bearing partitions that responded to functional uses rather than structural requirements.

The design of the Villa Savoye (1929–1930) in Poissy, France, by Swiss-born designer Le Corbusier epitomized the possibilities of design with reinforced concrete. The building's low rectangular body was raised on slender concrete pillars (*pilotis*). The open floor plan, long horizontal strip of windows, and flat roof terrace defined the clean Modernist lines of what came to be known as the International Style.

Le Corbusier used concrete's sculptural freedom of form to great effect in the Chapel of Notre-Dame-du-Haut at Ronchamp, France (1950–1955). The massive, soaring curves of the roof rest on thick walls punctured by small rectangular windows that give color to shafts of light inside. The appearance of the walls is deceiving: the roof is actually supported by reinforced concrete columns inside the walls. Interior walls are finished with a 4-centimeter-thick coating of concrete sprayed onto expanded wire mesh.

Today, the appearance of concrete surfaces are modified by changing the size, shape, texture, or color of the coarse and fine aggregates, and by exposing varying amounts of the aggregate on the surface. Concrete can be made with either gray or white cement. The texture or pattern of the surface can be altered by the design of the form. The use of form liners simulating wood, brick, stone, and other textures, and the application of rustication strips at joints in textured liners modify the aesthetic effect. The choice of edge treatments for joints between forms is another expressive tool. Concrete surfaces can be treated or tooled after curing.

Figure 2-11 The three tiers of classical columns on the Coliseum are decorative rather than structural. The building itself is a concrete structure.

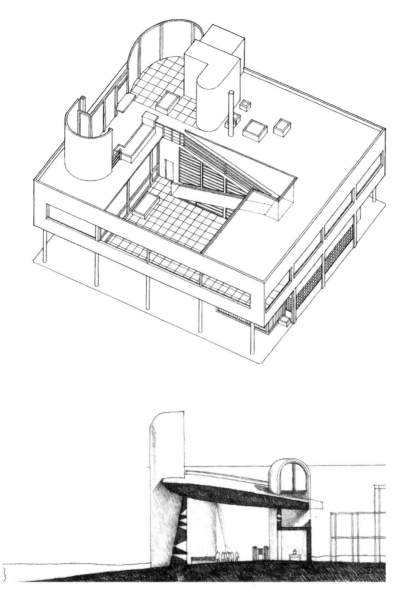

Figure 2-12 Villa Savoye, Poissy, Paris, France. The planar concrete forms are raised above the ground on concrete columns. Reproduced by permission of the publisher from Francis D. K. Ching, Mark M. Jarzombek, and Vikramaditya Prakash, *Global History of Architecture* (Hoboken, NJ: John Wiley & Sons, Inc.), © 2007 by John Wiley & Sons.

Figure 2-13 Section, Notre-Dame-du-Haut at Ronchamp, France. The massive quality of concrete is expressed by the sweeping roof and thick walls. Reproduced by permission of the publisher from Francis D. K. Ching, Mark M. Jarzombek, and Vikramaditya Prakash, *Global History of Architecture* (Hoboken, NJ: John Wiley & Sons, Inc.), © 2007 by John Wiley & Sons.

Materials Sources and Manufacturing Processes for Concrete

The amount of concrete that the industry produces is tied to the overall activity of the construction industry. China is the world's largest producer of concrete, followed by India and the United States.

Water used to make concrete is usually potable (drinkable) water with no pronounced taste or odor, although some water not safe for drinking can also be used. Excessive impurities in water affect concrete's setting time and strength, and may cause *efflorescence* (a white, powdery deposit), staining, or corrosion of reinforcement. Poor-quality water results in volume instability and reduced durability.

Aggregates for concrete are dug from gravel pits or along rivers, or crushed from larger rocks. They are selected by size (graded), durability, particle shape and surface texture, abrasion and skid resistance, unit weights and voids (which affect the amount of cement used), and absorption of surface moisture. Aggregates are graded to be appropriate for the intended use. Relatively thin concrete building elements use small coarse aggregates. Ideally, there is a consistent gradation of particles from the smallest to the largest acceptable size.

Figure 2-14 Exposed aggregated concrete finish.
Reproduced by permission of the publisher from Edward Allen and Joseph Iano, *Fundamentals of Building Construction: Materials and Methods,* 4th ed. (Hoboken, NJ: John Wiley & Sons, Inc.), © 2004 by John Wiley & Sons, Inc.

Recycled concrete is often used as aggregate in new concrete. Concrete aggregates are available in many types and colors. Ceramic materials added to concrete as aggregates come in many brilliant and varied colors.

Chemical admixtures are added to concrete just before or during mixing to modify its properties when hardened. Chemical admixtures include:

- Air-entraining
- Water-reducing
- Retarding (slows down hydration in hot weather)
- Accelerating (speeds up hydration in cold weather)
- Plasticizers and superplasticizers to increase workability for up to one hour at site

Hydration takes place after aggregates, water, and cement have been combined, when the mix starts to harden through a chemical reaction with water, causing cement particles to link together with the aggregates. The mix builds up progressively as it stiffens, hardens, and becomes stronger. The concrete mix must be placed in forms before it becomes too stiff. As concrete is placed, it is consolidated (compacted) within forms to eliminate honeycombs and air pockets.

Curing begins after the exposed surfaces of concrete are hard enough to resist marring. Hydration and strength gain continue during curing. Concrete is cured by sprinkling it with a water fog, or by covering it with moisture-retaining fabrics like burlap or cotton mats. Evaporation can also be prevented by sealing surfaces with plastic or special sprays called curing compounds. The longer concrete is kept moist, the stronger and more durable it becomes. The rate of hardening depends on the composition and fineness of the cement, the proportions of the mixture, and the conditions of moisture and temperature. Most of the hydration and strength gain takes place in the first month, but it continues at slower rate for many years.

Concrete is normally specified according to the compressive strength it will develop within 28 days after placement. High-early-strength concrete is specified according to the compressive strength it will develop within seven days. In a slump test, which

Table 2-2 Aggregate Color Selection

Aggregate	Color Selection
Marble	Green, yellow, red, pink, gray, white, and black
Quartz	Naturally clear, white, yellow, green, gray, light pink or rose
Granite	Range from white, pink, and red to gray, dark blue, and black
Basalt and other fine-grained igneous rocks	Gray, black, and dark green
Limestone	White and gray
Expanded lightweight shale	Soft, dull surface colors in reddish-brown, gray, or black
Miscellaneous washed and screened gravel	Brown or reddish-brown
Riverbed gravels	Yellow ochre, umber, and buff shades, as well as pure white

determines consistency and workability, freshly mixed concrete is poured into a conical mold and tamped. When the cone is removed, the slump is measured in vertical inches of settling. A compression test determines the compressive strength of a concrete batch by using a hydraulic press to measure the maximum load that a test cylinder 6 inches (150 mm) in diameter and 12 inches (305 mm) high can support in an axial compression before fracturing.

Environmental and Health Impacts of Concrete

The concrete industry considers water pollution from washout water to be the main environmental issue associated with concrete, because the water used to wash the insides of concrete trucks, tools, and related equipment is highly alkaline, and toxic to fish and other aquatic life. Concrete companies are increasingly adopting closed-loop water recycling procedures at plants, and collecting and properly disposing of water from rinsing of trucks and chutes at building sites.

Concrete and cement make up the largest and most visible component of construction and demolition waste; currently, only a low percentage of concrete is recycled. During new construction, partial loads of concrete are dumped on the site. The use of admixtures to retard setting allows leftover concrete to be taken back to the plant and either made into another product, such as concrete masonry units, or reactivated for use within a couple of days. Precast concrete eliminates this on-site problem and offers better control of water used for mixing and washing.

The dust produced in the production and transportation of concrete includes that from sand and aggregate mining, material transfer, wind erosion of stored piles of material, mixer loading, and concrete delivery, including dust from unpaved roads. Concrete dust can be controlled through the use of water sprays, enclosures, hoods, curtains, and covered chutes.

In addition to its use in manufacturing cement, fly ash is used to make concrete, using up a waste material and reducing overall energy use. Fly ash content is required by the U.S. Environmental Protection Agency in concrete buildings receiving federal funding. It is also used for autoclaved cellular concrete.

Hazardous materials in wet concrete and mortar include alkaline compounds such as lime (calcium oxide) that are corrosive to human tissue. Trace amounts of crystalline silica are abrasive to skin, and can damage lungs. Some workers experience allergic reactions to trace amounts of chromium.

The most common problem is the caustic, abrasive and drying properties of concrete in contact with the skin. Short-term exposure followed by washing with fresh water is usually not a problem; continuous contact and skin penetration can cause first-, second-, and third-degree burns or skin ulcers that may take several months to heal, and could involve hospitalization and skin grafts.

Workers are advised to wear protective clothing while working with concrete. However, some problems originate when wet cement gets inside of, or is absorbed by, protective clothing. Cement dust dispersed during bag dumping becomes a caustic solution when combined with water from sweat or wet clothing.

Once hardened, concrete is a generally safe, inert material appropriate for designs for chemically sensitive people. Its durability extends its useful life, and its heat storage capabilities and thermal mass have passive solar applications.

Some additives to concrete can be a problem. Workability agents that contain formaldehyde compounds could possibly off-gas small quantities of formaldehyde, and should be avoided, used in minimal quantities, and sealed in spaces occupied by people with chemical sensitivities. Other products used with concrete, such as asphalt-impregnated expansion joint fillers, curing agents, and special oils used on concrete forms, also may generate chemical sensitivity problems.

Concrete floors and walls with moisture problems may support the growth of mold and mildew. Moisture in concrete surfaces usually wicks through the concrete from surrounding soil; proper drainage and exterior surface protection will help prevent this problem. Moisture within a building can condense on cold concrete surfaces, a problem that is solved by adding insulation to the surfaces.

Interior Applications for Concrete

Concrete fireplace surrounds are fire-resistant with good heat retention and the ability to be molded into virtually any form. They are specified from accurate measurements of the fireplace opening, including its width and height, as well as any details that may limit the design of the mantle or hearth. Precast concrete fireplace surrounds are available that can be cut to fit unique shapes. Many fireplace surrounds are made of *glass-fiber-reinforced concrete (GFRC)*, which saves time and money. GFRC offers many style options in a durable material that is lighter in weight than precast concrete.

Concrete sinks and vessels can be made in any shape, and concrete companies offer their own sink lines. Vessel sinks resemble a bowl set on a countertop. Integral sinks are available in a variety of designs, including a wave sink with a pair of slot drains in its center, sinks cast with a front apron, and wall-mounted sinks for a floating effect. Other options include a ramp countertop sink and a multiple-trough sink that is custom-cast with two to four faucets. Concrete sinks adapt to standard rough-in plumbing.

Concrete countertops are durable; however, they need to be sealed before use. Concrete countertops are somewhat heavier than granite, but can usually be supported by standard base cabinets. See Chapter 12 for more details.

Concrete water features and faux rock are molded, textured, and colored for the specific application. They are built on-site of strong but lightweight polymer-modified or

Figure 2-15 Concrete fireplace surround.
Courtesy of Advanced Concrete Enhancement.

glass-fiber-reinforced concrete, and are installed in interiors as well as outdoors. Compared to moving and cutting large rocks, durable concrete features are easier and quicker to install and can conceal plumbing. (See color plate C-7 for concrete furniture.)

Finishes for Concrete

Various colors and textures, including exposed aggregate and pattern-stamped surfaces, are available for site-cast concrete. The simplest finish is strike-off and screeded, a process of cutting off excess concrete to bring the surface of the slab to the desired grade: a straight-edge is moved across the concrete with a sawing motion and advanced a short distance with each movement. The concrete can be scored with a broom before it is fully hardened.

Jointing eliminates random cracks by making construction joints with a hand groover or by inserting strips of plastic, wood, metal, or preformed joint materials into unhardened concrete. The concrete is then floated with a wood or metal hand float or a finishing machine with float blades; this eliminates high and low spots and embeds large aggregate particles. Finally, an installation can be steel-troweled for a smooth, hard, dense surface.

Concrete acid staining is used on new, old, plain, or previously colored concrete surfaces. Metallic salts in an acidic water-based solution react with hydrated lime (calcium and hydroxide) in hardened concrete to produce translucent permanent stains. The basic color groups for acid stains are black, brown, and blue-green; light tans, greens, and browns; and tans, browns, terra cottas, and soft blue-greens. A black wash

Figure 2-16 A wave sink has an appealing form with a central drain.
Courtesy of Advanced Concrete Enhancement.

is a combination of stain and water used to reduce the contrast between colors. The acid opens the top surface of the concrete so that the metallic salts reach free lime deposits. The water in the solution continues to produce the reaction for around a month. The results of acid staining concrete are affected by the type and amount of cement and aggregate used, concrete finishing methods, concrete air and moisture content, as well as weather conditions when the stain is applied, and the presence of efflorescence. Cements with large amounts of calcium hydroxide during hydration accept more stain color, and higher cement content leads to more intense colors. Concrete acid-stained finishes are very easy to clean and maintain and are used for concrete countertops, sinks, and showers, and plaster stucco walls. (See color plate C-6, Acid-stained concrete.)

Concrete dyes are very fine coloring agents that penetrate the concrete surface but do not react chemically with the concrete. They are available in almost any color. Water-based dyes produce soft pastel tones and subtle earth tones. Solvent-based dyes are used for bolder red, blue, yellow, green, purple, orange, and other colors. They can be used to achieve a variegated layered color on an acid-stained floor. Concrete dyes are usually packaged in concentrated form and used full strength or diluted with water or solvent. They are mixed at the job site and applied with a sprayer, roller, or brush. They dry in about one minute and require minimal cleanup. The concrete surface should be tested first, however, as results vary with the application method used, the

Figure 2-17 Broom finish
Reproduced by permission of the publisher from Francis D. K. Ching,
A Visual Dictionary of Architecture (New York: John Wiley & Sons, Inc.),
© by 1995 John Wiley & Sons, Inc.

Figure 2-18 Float finish
Reproduced by permission of the publisher from Francis D. K. Ching,
A Visual Dictionary of Architecture (New York: John Wiley & Sons, Inc.),
© 1995 by John Wiley & Sons, Inc.

Figure 2-19 Trowel finish
Reproduced by permission of the publisher from Francis D. K. Ching,
A Visual Dictionary of Architecture (New York: John Wiley & Sons, Inc.),
© 1995 by John Wiley & Sons, Inc.

Figure 2-20 Swirl finish
Reproduced by permission of the publisher from Francis D. K. Ching,
A Visual Dictionary of Architecture (New York: John Wiley & Sons, Inc.),
© 1995 by John Wiley & Sons, Inc.

age and porosity of the concrete, and the cleanliness of the surface; dense nonporous surfaces do not accept dyes well.

Dyed concrete surfaces are protected with a topical sealer or wax; most water-based, solvent-based, or urethane-based sealers are compatible with dyes. Indoor surfaces can be protected with one coat of solvent-based acrylic with a topcoat of water-based acrylic, and maintained with additional coats of water-based acrylic sealers or waxes. Concrete color samples are available from local concrete contractors. Samples in standard colors cost about $25 to $50 per sample; custom color samples cost $75 to $150 and up.

Prices for stained concrete floors are relatively expensive, similar to high-quality ceramic tile installations. For example, simple stains with cleanup, final sealer, and minimal slab preparation cost $2 to $4 per square foot. Larger projects are less expensive than smaller. Sandblasted stencil work runs about $1 to $25 per square foot in the stenciled area.

New and old concrete floor surfaces can be ground to a high-gloss finish, with no waxes or coatings needed. Spreading a commercial polishing compound in the final step produces a shiny, clean, dirt-resistant surface. An impregnating sealer that sinks in and is not visible on top is applied during polishing. A partial polish uses two grinding steps to expose the aggregate and then seal the surface. A *honed finish* has some surface shine

Table 2-3 Concrete Topical Sealers

Concrete Sealer Type	Advantages	Disadvantages
Acrylic	UV stable; inexpensive; easy application and reapplication.	Softer surface requires more maintenance. Finish dries and stays on surface.
Solvent-based acrylic	Wet look enhances color finishes. Solvent bonds repairs better.	Moderate heat resistance.
Epoxy	Water-based epoxies bond well to concrete. Much harder surface than acrylics.	Not UV-resistant. More difficult to apply and reapply. Clear, nonporous finish does not release trapped moisture.
Urethane	Most abrasive resistance; stain- and heat-resistant.	Very expensive; reapplication expensive. Does not bond well to concrete, applied over water-based epoxy.
Wax	UV stable; easy to apply and reapply.	Not very scratch- or stain-resistant.

and is smooth and easy to maintain. The designer and client can review the surface at intermediate polish levels before deciding whether to continue to a higher polish.

Dry polishing is done with machines that have dust-containment systems that eliminate almost all of the mess; it is normally used for initial grinding. The messy slurry produced by wet polishing requires collection and disposal. New concrete must be cured a minimum of 28 days before polishing. Existing floors must be clean, with coatings removed. Wavy floors, those in need of extensive patching, and extremely porous floors do not polish well. A good polished shine will last for years; should it dull in high-traffic areas, it can be buffed with a commercial polishing compound or be lightly repolished with a fine-grit abrasive.

Dusting removes grit from polished concrete, and a damp mop with a neutral cleaner enhances the shine. Some specialized cleaners leave a dirt-resistant film, and can be applied with a mop or auto scrubber; no buffing is needed.

Concrete engraving uses special tools and equipment to cut patterns and designs into existing concrete, which can be stained first so that the engraved surface shows in contrast. The concrete is cleaned and acid etched, if necessary, for a stain bond. Small hairline cracks may be repaired or kept for texture. Cost for concrete engraving is about $3 to $6 per square foot; small jobs cost more, as do complex patterns.

Concrete self-leveling overlays are fluid polymer-modified toppings that will form a level surface without troweling. The overlay is poured or pumped onto a surface and distributed with a spreader. The end result is seamless except at control joints or saw-cut or engraved designs. The overlay can be poured level with the tops of decorative wood, or metal strips can be attached to the base concrete. Concrete self-leveling overlays can be stained or dyed. They are also used as an *underlayment* for tile, carpet, and other floor coverings.

Figure 2-21 Engraved concrete
Photo courtesy of Engrave-A-Crete, Inc.

Color is added to concrete overlays in several ways. Dry-shake color hardeners produce a durable, dense, and abrasion-resistant surface with brighter or unusual colors. Dry-shake color hardeners are broadcast into freshly laid concrete, which is then troweled. The dry-shake hardeners do not color the concrete throughout. They are often used with stamping, then sealers are applied to accentuate color. Colored liquid or powdered release agents can be used with stampable overlays. Other options for coloring concrete overlays include dyes, chemical or acrylic-based stains, and tinted sealers. Overlays can be seeded with decorative aggregates, color chips, or recycled glass.

Insulating concrete forms (ICFs) are used for wall systems in residential construction. They are essentially a variation on poured-in-place concrete. The polystyrene forms used to shape the concrete remain in place as insulation on the concrete structure. The use of ICFs is a very efficient way to provide insulation and save time. They are increasingly used to build walls, and eventually may have attached floors.

Stone, Masonry, and Concrete Masonry Units 3

The term *masonry* refers to stone, brick, concrete, or tile building units that are usually mortared together. Masonry is used for building structures, and may be left visible on the exterior or interior. These materials are also used as interior finish materials.

Masonry materials tend to be strong in compression and blocklike rather than planar. The units themselves are often produced in standard sizes for modular construction. The modular units for standard bricks and concrete masonry units are compatible.

Rock is stone before it is moved from where it is found. Stone is rock removed from its bed for use. After a rock is taken from a quarry and mechanically *dressed*—squared and shaped on one or more surfaces—it is referred to as *dimensional stone*.

STONE

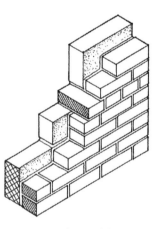

Figure 3-1 The modular units for standard bricks and concrete masonry units are compatible. Reproduced by permission of the publisher from Francis D. K. Ching and Cassandra Adams, *Building Construction Illustrated*, 3rd ed. (New York: John Wiley & Sons, Inc.), © 2001 by John Wiley & Sons, Inc.

Historical, Cultural, and Architectural Context of Stone

In addition to being used as a structural material throughout human history, stone has been an important interior material. The huge, closely packed stone columns of the temple at Karnak in Egypt (begun 1505 BCE) support stone lintels over relatively small spans. They are covered with hieroglyphics and scenes of religious practices and royal achievements, combining decoration with communication.

The thick windowless walls of houses in ancient Greece were of impermanent sun-dried brick over rubble, sometimes finished with plaster and paint inside. Floors of compacted earth were sometimes finished with plaster, paint, paving stone, or mosaics of pebbles, glass, or stone set in mortar.

The Byzantine Church of Hagia Sophia in what is now Istanbul, Turkey, was designed by two mathematicians, Anthemius of Tralles and Isidore of Miletus, between 532 and 537 CE. Hagia Sophia's interior was embellished with marbles in many colors, and purplish-red porphyry, reddish-brown carnelian, multicolored onyx, mother-of-pearl, and ivory inlays.

The Romanesque style that arose in Italy and southern France during Charlemagne's reign owed much to Roman architecture; buildings often used fragments from Roman ruins. The Roman-style rounded arches and vaults replaced earlier fire-prone wood roofs. Workers recycled marble columns into decorative disks, and reused stone, glass, and gold mosaic tesserae in rich colors. Designs with lions and eagles, and columns with spiral-twisted shafts were popular.

Gothic churches are stone structures with complex metal grilles and gates, and carved stone screens, altars, and tombs. Gothic ornament emphasizes the vertical, with columns clustered into piers, surface ribs, and long, thin sculptured figures, as seen on the Chartres Cathedral portals. Sculptures of saints, royalty, and grotesque human and animal forms abound, with symbolic motifs helping the public identify religious figures. Grotesques and gargoyles were intended to amuse or frighten, as well as to serve as water spouts.

Early Islamic stone and mud brick architecture preserved older structures within new construction, or built new buildings with parts of old ones. As in early Christian

and Byzantine architecture, relatively plain, massive exterior forms contrast with interiors full of color and energy. Structural elements are often hidden by interior ornamentation and copied in nonstructural stucco, plaster, and woodwork. The Great Mosque of Córdoba, called the Mezquita, built in 785, is known for its unusual arch pattern, with the lower of the double-height arches bracing the taller arches. Each arch is made of alternate red brick and white stone, for a striped effect that extends into complex vaults of intersecting ribs. The interior of the Mezquita incorporated as many as 850 pillars of jasper, porphyry, and marble from an earlier Christian church, from older Roman buildings in Spain or North Africa (Carthage), and from Constantinople. These recycled columns were too short for their new home, so rectangular piers were placed on top to support semicircular arches. These arches in turn held up the roof.

Great Zimbabwe (1050–1450) at its peak was a wealthy inland center trading gold with the Swahili coastal center on Kilwa. More than 200 huge, carefully laid dry stone walls circling living compounds (called *zimbabwe*) make up Great Zimbabwe. The massive 30-foot-high stone walls of the Great Enclosure are 20 feet thick at their base, and follow flowing curves over and around huge granite boulders. Royal families lived in stone buildings, while the common people occupied traditional thatch houses outside the stone compounds.

The Incan stonework of Cuzco and Machu Picchu in Peru is built of local granite laid without mortar but with such precision that much of it remains standing today. Each block—some of which weighed as much as 200 tons—was individually fitted perfectly to its neighbors.

After 1450, wealthy Italian merchants build palaces (*palazzi*) three to four stories high in the city and suburban villas in country towns. Thick stone walls with doors and windows in deep untrimmed reveals were topped with flat lintels or arches, and kept the cool air of the evening inside during the heat of the day. Semicircular arches with architrave molding would spring from one classical column to another to create arcades between interior and exterior spaces.

When Indian architects transferred their freestanding architecture from wood to stone, they retained post-and-beam construction, with stone lintels spanning openings and corbelled vaults. Orissa in North India is the home of many ornate stone temples built from 600 to 1300 CE. The Rajarani Temple is constructed of tightly fitted russet and ochre sandstone. Temple carvings of vases overflowing with foliage, lions eating strands of pearls, and sensuous maidens and couples symbolize abundance.

The Taj Mahal (1648) in Agra, India, was built by emperor Shah Jahan as a mausoleum for his wife Mumtaz Mahal, who died in childbirth in 1631. The Taj Mahal is approached along marble paths through gardens, fountains, and waterways. The surface of gleaming white marble is inlaid with *pietra dura*, inlays of precious and semiprecious stones in floral sprays, arabesques, and Islamic calligraphy. (See color plate C-13, Taj Mahal *pietra dura* inlays.)

The U.S. Customs House (1833–1842) in Washington, DC, now called Federal Hall, was designed by the architectural firm of Ithiel Town (1784–1844) and Alexander Jackson Davis (1803–1892) as a stone building with Doric porticoes front and back.

The interiors by John Frazee (1790–1852) include a rotunda within a circle of Corinthian columns and pilasters that support a coffered dome under the main gable roof.

American architect Henry Hobson Richardson (1838–1886) designed Trinity Church (1877) in Boston with a rich palette of ruggedly finished stone. Richardson also designed the Marshall Field Wholesale Store in Chicago (1885; since destroyed), a seven-story building a block long.

Physical Properties, Characteristics, and Types of Stone

Stone is classified by its origin as igneous, sedimentary, or metamorphic rock.

Igneous rock is formed by the cooling and crystallization of molten magma (lava). The grain and texture of igneous rock is related to how quickly the lava cools. Coarse-grained granite has cooled slowly, whereas glassy obsidian is the result of rapid cooling. Igneous rocks are generally hard, strong, and resistant to chemicals.

Sedimentary rock is formed from sediment deposited under water. Sand, shells, minerals, and bone sink to the bottom and are slowly compacted into layers called strata by the weight of the water. Sedimentary rock may reveal fossil shells and bones when it is split. (See color plate C-12, Sandstone with embedded fossil.)

Metamorphic rock is made when igneous, sedimentary, or even other metamorphic rock is subjected to extreme pressure and high temperature. Physical and chemical changes occur that make the rock harder and more crystalline in structure. Metamorphic rock often includes mineral intrusions and veins.

The hardness of stone is related to its composition: igneous granite is hard; metamorphic marble is softer; and sedimentary sandstone even softer than that.

- *Fieldstone* is rounded stone left by receding glaciers that is used as it is found. The irregular shapes in fieldstone walls are usually held in place with large amounts of mortar, much of which is visible in the finished wall.
- *Rubble* consists of quarried stone of varied shapes and sizes with irregular mortar joints.
- *Ashlar* is the term used for stone that has been dressed to rectangular shapes. Ashlar walls may contain stones of uniform or varied sizes, with regular mortar lines.

Aesthetic Qualities of Stone

Stone expresses permanence and timelessness. The weight and massiveness of the material suggests immovability. When stone such as alabaster or onyx is used as a thin, transparent material, its ability to allow light to pass seems almost miraculous.

Stone carries records of its place and time of origin. Carrera marble, for example, is identified by the name of the location where it is quarried. Sandstone and other rocks carry embedded fossils. Geologists use the composition and placement of rock layers to understand the history of the earth.

Some stones are prized for their beauty. Semiprecious and precious gemstones are cut and polished to reveal intricacies of color and light. From massive mountains to grains of sand on a beach, stones teach us about scale and color.

Manufacturing and Fabrication of Stone

Stone is quarried from the earth by drilling, sawing, and splitting into large blocks and thick, broad slabs or other pieces. Whether stone is cut parallel, perpendicular, or at a 45-degree angle to the layers of its bed affects its appearance. A cut perpendicular to the vein is called an across-the-bed or vein cut; one parallel is called a with-the-bed, or Fleuri cut. (See color plate C-11, granite quarry.)

Table 3-1 Igneous Stone

Stone	Sources	Characteristics	Color and texture	Workability	Form	Uses
Granite: mostly quartz, feldspar, and mica	India, China, Brazil, Scotland, Suriname	Hard, durable, strong; resists weather and chemicals, staining, scratching. Poor resistance to fire; crumbles when exposed to intense heat.	Consistent color and texture. Coarse grained. More than 200 colors. Dense grain.	Polishes very well to lasting shine. Cuts and shapes without secondary flaws. Yields long and thin slabs.	Slabs	Floors, counters, wall cladding, fireplaces, shower and tub surrounds
					Tiles	Floors, fireplaces, bartops, countertops, tub and shower surrounds
					Stone bricks	Paving walls and hard-surfaced floors
					Stone blocks	Furniture
					Stone steps, treads, risers	Interior or exterior stairs
					Stone circles, medallions	Decorative flooring
Malachite	Congo, Nambia, Russia, Australia, United States	Moderately hard; opaque, dull luster	Bands of light to dark green	Reasonably workable	Veneer	Highly polished for decorative objects.
Obsidian: volcanic lava cooled quickly in water	Italy, Mexico, Scotland, United States	Semiprecious stone; vitreous, translucent	Dark green to black with a bright luster; glassy texture; various sheens	Softer than quartz. Used for ornamental carvings.		Ornamental uses; also used for surgical knife blades.
Onyx: a form of agate, chalcedony quartz	Brazil, India, California, Uraguay	Warm, waxy luster. Some parts are translucent. Heating intensifies its color. Dyes easily with black or bright, unusual colors.	Black and white banded, often layered. Sardonyx is a variety of onyx that is reddish-brown with white and lighter reddish bands.	Carves well.	Slabs	Lighting fixtures, furniture, stair treads
					Veneer	Intaglio (inlaid decoration)
Serpentine: magnesium iron silicate hydroxide	Italy, Russia, Switzerland, United States, Canada	Luster is greasy, waxy, or silky. Massive or fibrous. Asbestos is a flexible, fibrous form of serpentine.	Yellow-green or olive; also golden, brown, or black	Polishes and carves well	Veneer	Interior decorative facing

Table 3-2 Metamorphic Stone

Stone	Sources	Characteristics	Color texture	Workability	Forms	Uses
Marble: Crystallized limestone. Carrara marble is a white or blue-gray marble from Tuscany.	Spain, Italy, India, Australia, Namibia, China, United States	Glassy, highly reflective; strong; resistant to fire and erosion Red wine and other materials may stain marble.	White, pink, green, black, shaded, striped, brown. Purest calcite marble is translucent white. (See color plates C-20 and C-21.)	Takes a high polish.	Slabs Stone treads and risers Large blocks	Floors, walls, countertops, furniture Poured flooring
Quartz: silicon dioxide	Most common mineral on earth; varieties widespread	Luster is glassy to vitreous as crystal; other forms usually waxy to dull. Transparent to translucent; some forms opaque.	Clear, milky quartz (white or cloudy), amethyst (purple), rose quartz (pink), smoky quartz (gray, brown to black)	Very good workability; used for sculpture and building.	Slabs, blocks, tiles Ground	
Quartzite: mostly quartz; derived from sandstone	Widely available worldwide	Compact, granular; very hard; barely weathers	Many colors, usually light; often has a sugary appearance.	Building and heat-resistant materials	Crushed aggregate Tiles, slabs	Flooring Walls, floors
Slate: formed by compression of sediments including clay or shale.	Many locations worldwide	Dense, fine-grained; low porosity; weather-resistant, and resists cracks, scratches, burns and watermarks	Dark to light gray, red, brown, green, black, gray, blue (See color plates C-22 and C-23.)	Good cleavage along parallel planes	Slab Tiles	Blackboards, floors, countertops, fireplaces Floors, walls
Soapstone (also called steatite): high proportion of talc	Widely available	Massive, soft rock. Very dense, nonporous, nonstaining	Naturally shades of gray	Mineral oil enhances darkening	Stone steps, treads, and risers	Hearths, tabletops, and carved ornaments. Stone medallions

Table 3-3 Sedimentary Stone

Stone	Sources	Characteristics	Color and texture	Workability	Form	Uses
Bluestone: claylike sandstone	Great Britain, United States, Australia	Dense, fine-grained	Gray stone appears blue when wet or freshly broken.	Splits easily along bedding planes to form thin slabs.	Slabs	Flooring and cladding, fireplaces and interior walls
Brownstone: type of sandstone	United States, Germany	Term also used for nineteenth-century row houses in U.S.	Reddish-brown	(See sandstone.)	Slabs	Flooring, cladding, fireplaces, and interior walls
Limestone: calcium carbonate from shells and coral	Readily available	Durable; very heavy. Damaged by acid rain. Hard, impervious, compact; not very water-absorbent	White or almost white, blue, green, brown, desert yellow, black.	Easily cut into blocks and carved.	Slab	Countertops, floors, cladding, pavement.
				Ground to make lime.	Stone bricks	Paving walls and hard-surfaced floors.
					Stone blocks	Garden furniture, structural stone
Sandstone: sand, (quartz), silica, clay, calcium carbonate	Rajasthan in India, Scotland, Algeria.	Low porosity; highly resistant to acids, alkalis, thermal impact.	Red, green, yellow, gray, white, blue, brown, desert yellow, black	Easily cut in blocks and carved	Slabs vary in size, shape	Exterior cladding
						Flooring, wall cladding, fireplaces
					Tiles: polishes well	Countertops, floors, sinks, interior and exterior wall cladding, paving, masonry heaters
					Stone bricks	Hard-surfaced floors
Travertine: variety of limestone deposited by cold or hot spring waters	Italy, Croatia, Afghanistan, China, Guatemala, Turkey. May be sold as marble.	Holes formed by gas escaping during formation. Smooth, durable; stains; thin pieces translucent. (See color plate C-18, Unfilled travertine.)	Soft cream blue, white, pink, yellow, brown. Luster dull to pearly.	Holes can be filled with matching portland cement, colored epoxy, polyester resins (See color plate C-19, Filled travertine.)	Tiles	Paving, wall finishes, floors, carvings
					Aggregate building stone	

Figure 3-3 A polished stone finish is shiny and reflective.

Sedimentary stone can be difficult to cut and so is often split, or *cleft,* along its natural layers; the resulting surface may vary as much as 1/8 inch (3 mm) in thickness. Stone tiles are sawn from larger blocks and are usually made of granite, marble, sandstone, or limestone. (See color plate C-17 for carved limestone.)

Stone slabs are sent to mills for finishing. Stone may be given a quarry face, a machine finish, or a hand finish. Quarry face is the surface of the stone as it comes from the quarry, showing the marks of its removal. Machine finishes include sawn, milled, polished (ground and buffed to a glasslike surface), honed (a smooth surface with little or no gloss), and flamed. Flamed finish, also referred to as thermal finish, is produced by superheating the surface to cause small chips to split off. Stone can also be hammered or chiseled by hand.

Figure 3-4 A honed stone finish is smooth but has noticeable texture.

Table 3-4 Relative Costs for Stone*

Stone	Finish or Use	Cost
Slate, imported	Cleft finish	$3–$6 per sq ft
Engineered stone, installed	Adhered to wall	$19.01 per sq ft installed
Granite	Polished or honed finish	$7–$14 per sq ft
	Flamed or other finish	Add $1–$2 per sq ft
Limestone	Polished or honed finish	$5–$12 per sq ft
Marble	Polished or honed finish	$5–$12 per sq ft
Natural thin stone (2 in.)	Adhered to wall	$23.59 per sq ft installed
Split fieldstone	4 in. wall, installed	$41.40 per sq ft installed

*Costs are for comparison purposes only; actual costs will vary with time and location. Shipping costs are significant.

Stone slabs can be impregnated with resin to make them stronger. This makes it possible to market slabs that have been otherwise rejected for brittleness or other problems.

Environmental Impact of Stone

Stone's great thermal mass makes it ideal for passive solar design: large areas of stone will collect the sun's heat slowly and later release it to cooler surrounding air.

The amount of embodied energy in processed stone relates to how difficult it is to remove from the earth and how far it must be transported. Loose stones near the surface are acquired with less energy, while those extracted from within the earth embody more. The use of stone from local sources reduces the amount of embodied energy, as does the use of local finishing, cutting, and manufacturing facilities. By writing stone specifications to allow for dimensional variation in size and thickness, and by specifying rougher stone finishes, less energy is used to finish the stone.

Interior Applications of Stone

Interior designers specify stone for the tops, bases, and panels of furniture. Stone panels and tiles are used for floors and walls. Stair treads, toilet partitions, countertops, columns, and other architectural features are also made of stone. (See color plate C-16 for ancient stone furnishings.)

Solid stone steps express stability and durability over time. Because of their weight, interior steps are often made of thinner stone treads and risers. These are specified to be structurally sound, flat, dry, clean, and smooth. Their dimensions must be regular and uniform. They are affordable, durable, very hard wearing, and easy to use, and are available with flamed and polished surfaces. Treads and risers are most commonly granite, with marble also widely used, as well as sandstone and limestone.

Note: Stone tiles are discussed in detail in Chapters 9 and 10.

Stone circles are decorative designs made either as solid disks or graduated diameters of circles assembled from precut flags (flat paving stones, usually from sedimentary rocks). Commercially manufactured stone circles are supplied with a squaring-off kit that fits the circular stone design into a rectangular space. Strong and long-lasting

Figure 3-5 The heat-produced stone texture in a flamed stone finish is more pronounced.

circles in a variety of designs are available in sandstone, granite, limestone, and slate. (See color plate C-14, Stone medallion.)

Tumbled stone is smoothed and polished. Rocks are loaded in a rubber barrel with abrasive grit—usually silicon carbide—and a lubricant, which is usually water. The barrel is placed on slowly rotating rails and turned to polish the stones. Tumbled stones are one of several types of finishes: natural tumbled, with rounded edges; honed tumbled, with a smooth matte look; polished tumbled, which are highly glossy; and antique tumbled, which have a slightly rustic look.

Tumbled stone is used for nonslip floors, shower and tub surrounds, bathroom counters and borders, and custom tiles. Tumbled marble has softly rounded edges and is used for floors and walls. Tumbled limestone has a dull, porous surface that does not show wear, and so is popular for backsplashes, countertops, tabletops, and small floors. Tumbled slate is very durable; water repellant; and resistant to acid, frost, stain, and fire. It is a very practical finish for floors, walls, and fireplaces.

Riverbed pebbles are round or partially round rock or mineral fragments from 0.08 to 3 inches (2 to 75 mm) in diameter. They are found along riverbanks and running through sand deposits. Pebbles are, ideally, round or elliptical and relatively flat. They are durable, functional, and low maintenance. Marble pebbles come in pink, white, black, yellow, and brown. Limestone pebbles are available in gray, black, white, and buff. Granite pebbles are usually in shades of red or pink. Riverbed pebbles of varied colors are used in gardens and landscaping. Interior applications include decorative borders, in aquariums and water features, and dry garden beds. They can be used to surface cement pavers, swimming pool decks, and patios.

Pebble tile can be used for floors, walls, fireplaces, walkways, and decorative accents. It is produced with a mesh backing and is affixed with tile glue and then grouted. Because pebbles are natural products, no two sheets of tile are the same and variations in patterns are common.

Engineered composite stone products are formulated from stone aggregate and synthetic resin matrix materials. They are available in sizes ranging from tile units to large panel sheets for horizontal and vertical applications. Composite stone characteristics

Figure 3-6 Durable granite steps contrast with adjacent rock wall.

include strength, nonporosity, durability, and flexibility. Polished finishes predominate. Colors range from natural stone tones to vibrant colors. Thicknesses vary, and due to the strength of the composite material, can sometimes be thinner than natural dimension stone. Typical sheet sizes are 3/4 inch (2 cm) or 1–1/8 inch (3 cm). Installation for sheet panels is similar to natural stone. Tile units are installed with the same thinset methods as ceramic tile. (See color plate C-15, Engineered composite stone.)

Installation and Maintenance of Stone

Natural stone is laid in mortar, much like clay and concrete masonry units, to make both bearing and nonbearing walls, or used as a facing veneer tied to a concrete or masonry backup wall. To prevent discoloration of stone, only nonstaining cement and noncorrosive ties, anchors, and flashing should be used. Copper, brass, and bronze may stain under certain conditions.

Stone tiles are 3/4 inch (19 mm) thick or less, and from 4 inches (10 cm) square to 3.28 feet (1 m) square. Stone with distinctive texture and markings such as some marble can be arranged into specific patterns:

- A *blend pattern* is when panels of the same variety of stone but not necessarily from the same block are arranged at random.
- A *side-slip pattern* uses panels from the same block placed side by side or end to end in sequence, to ensure a repetitive pattern and blended color.
- In an *end-match pattern*, adjacent panel faces are finished, and one panel is inverted and placed above the other.
- *Book-match pattern* is similar to end-match, but with one panel next to the other.

Wire-tie anchoring systems with plaster or mortar spots are traditional methods for installing interior stone facing. Wire ties are anchored to gypsum board, masonry, or concrete wall.

BRICK

A brick is a rectangular masonry unit made of clay that has been hardened by drying in the sun or baking in a kiln. Common brick, made for general use, is not treated for

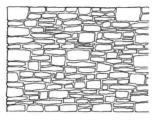

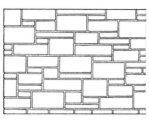

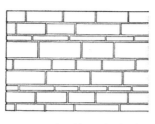

A Squared rubble is a masonry wall built of squared stones of varying sizes and coursed at every third or fourth stone.

B Random ashlar is built with stones in discontinuous courses.

C Coursed ashlar is built of stones having the same height within each course, but with courses varying in height.

D Broken rangework is ashlar masonry laid in horizontal courses of varying heights, any one of which may be broken at intervals into two or more courses.

Figures 3.7 A-D are reproduced by permission of the publisher from Francis D. K. Ching and Cassandra Adams, *Building Construction Illustrated,* 3rd ed. (New York: John Wiley & Sons, Inc.), © 2001 by John Wiley & Sons, Inc.

color or texture. Facing brick is made in special colors and textures for surfacing a wall.

Sun-dried and kiln-fired bricks are linked to human concepts of home and hearth, warmth and protection. Brick materials provide shelter from excessive heat, and keep warmth within an interior. Brick, adobe, and related materials are tied to specific places and times.

Historical, Cultural, and Architectural Context of Brick

Traditionally, brick has served as both a structural material and as a finish material. People learned to make brick from mud and clay wherever stone and wood were not easily obtained. Where sun-dried bricks were used, fewer buildings have survived the ages.

The rectangular wood frame and mud-brick homes and shrines of Çatal Höyük in Anatolia (now Turkey) occupied between 6500 and 5700 BCE, are around 20 feet (6 m) long by 15 feet (4.5 m) wide, with rooms, hearths, and doorways built to standard sizes.

Between 5700 and 5300 BCE, rectangular houses of mud bricks with thatched roofs appeared at the walled village of Sesklo in central Greece. This classic freestanding rectangular megaron house was the basis for later development in both Cyprus and Greece.

The seven square dwellings at Skara Brae in the Orkney Islands off Scotland, occupied between 3500 and 2400 BCE, were built closely together of sun-dried mud bricks. Walls tapered and curved in as they rose from their 6-foot (2-m) thick bases and were surrounded by protective mounds of earth.

In the Indus valley civilization around 2300 to 2000 BCE, all bricks were made in the ratio of 4:2:1, which is considered an optimal relationship for a good brick bond today. Houses, stores, and workshops for Mohenjo Daro's population of around 40,000 were organized into grids of streets with nearly identical rectangular brick houses.

The Sumerian city of Uruk's mud-brick buildings were decorated with mosaics, sculpture, relief carving, and cast metal. The ziggurat, or tower, with spiraling stairways at Ur, built by King Ur-Nammu around 2100 BCE, had a covering of fired bricks set in bitumen, the black oil tar that oozes up out of ground locally.

Etruscan buildings were generally built with mud-brick walls, sometimes faced with sheets of bronze. The Romans operated mobile kilns, which their military units took

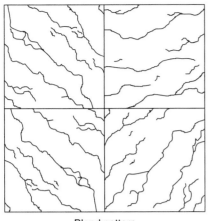

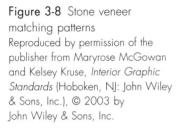
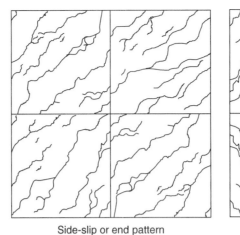

Blend pattern

Side-slip or end pattern

End-match, book-match, or quarter-match pattern

Figure 3-8 Stone veneer matching patterns
Reproduced by permission of the publisher from Maryrose McGowan and Kelsey Kruse, *Interior Graphic Standards* (Hoboken, NJ: John Wiley & Sons, Inc.), © 2003 by John Wiley & Sons, Inc.

with them throughout the empire. Roman bricks in southern and western Germany reflect the traditions that the Roman architect Vitruvius had written about. When bricks from northern Italy were introduced into twelfth-century Germany, a style called brick Gothic, built almost entirely of bricks, spread to Denmark, Germany, Poland, and Russia.

In Africa, the thirteenth-century Great Mosque at Djenne in southwest Mali, rebuilt around 1835 and again in 1906, is made of puddled clay and sun-dried adobe bricks. Wooden poles support plasterers for annual replastering.

Adobe construction of sun-dried brick had been used in Spain since the time of the Moors, and was brought to colonial America. Walls from 3 to 6 feet thick sometimes included brick masonry, lintels of stone or wood, and arches, windows, and doorframes of fired brick. Although sizes varied, most bricks were 10 inches (25.4 cm) square and only 1–1/2 to 2 inches (38-51 cm) thick, like those in Spain and Mexico.

During the Renaissance and the Baroque period, brickwork was usually covered with plaster; until the mid-eighteenth century, this was the case throughout Europe. Brick was valued for its fire resistance, ease of construction, and low cost.

When Christopher Wren was put in charge of rebuilding the city of London after the great fire of 1666, he chose brick and stone. Nineteenth-century cities such as Boston and New York became known for their locally made bricks. The tremendous heat of the Chicago fire in 1871 attacked brick mercantile buildings; the bricks withstood the heat, but the mortar dissolved, collapsing masonry walls.

Daniel Burnham's design for the Monadnock Building in Chicago (1889) and H.P. Berlage's Amsterdam Stock Exchange (1903) used brick in load-bearing wall construction for simple, relatively unornamented surfaces. Since the late nineteenth century, brick's tradition of simultaneous use as both a structural and a finishing material has given way to an independent structure of steel or reinforced concrete, to which a facing of brick is attached; in many cases, the exterior appearance obscures the structural material. The steel or reinforced concrete structure allows much greater heights and spans than were achievable in brick. Factory buildings had flat brick surfaces and internal structures of heavy timber or cast-iron. The Fagus Works factory in Alfeld an der Leine (1911) and the model factory, Werkbund exhibition, Cologne (1914), by Walter Gropius and Adolf Meyer—both brick-clad buildings—combined elements of classical form with a Modern appearance.

Many of Frank Lloyd Wright's early projects that appeared to be load-bearing brick, including the Larkin Building in Buffalo (1904), the Robie House in Oak Park, Illinois (1909), and the Imperial Hotel in Tokyo (1916), were filled with hidden steel and

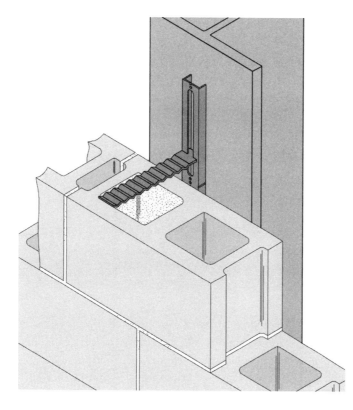

Figure 3-9 Tie anchor
Courtesy Hohmann & Barnard, Inc.

concrete elements. By midcentury, brick returned to a structural role in Le Corbusier's pair of houses, the Maisons Jaoul at Neuilly-sur-Seine (1955), which consisted of brick load-bearing walls supporting concrete-covered brick-faced vaults. Brick was used against exposed steel or concrete structural members in several projects by Louis Kahn, including the Phillips Exeter Academy Library in Exeter, New Hampshire (1972), and the Indian Institute of Management at Ahmedabad, India (1974). Alvar Aalto, in his Baker House dormitory at MIT in Cambridge, Massachusetts (1949), and Säynätsalo Town Hall in Finland (1952), used brick's texture and its historical associations for expressive purposes.

The Guild House in Philadelphia (1963), by Robert Venturi, used an obviously nonstructural brick arch. In the early 1970s, the architectural group SITE played with brick as both a construction system and as a material that ages over time.

Physical Properties, Characteristics, and Types of Brick

The physical properties of brick include compressive strength and durability. The American Society for Testing and Materials (ASTM) specification for brick assigns a grade of severe, moderate, or negligible weathering to accommodate varying climates and applications of brick. The strength of a brick construction depends on the compressive strength of the brick unit as well as its durability, combined with the strength of the *bond*, or pattern, in which it is laid. Most bricks currently produced have strengths ranging from 3,000 pounds per square inch (psi) to over 20,000 psi, averaging around 10,000 psi.

Significant amounts of water cannot pass directly through a brick unit; leaks in brick walls happen through separations or cracks between the brick units and the mortar. Brick units that develop a complete bond with mortar offer the best moisture resistance. Brick walls are routinely built so that any water that gets in can drain or evaporate back out.

Figure 3-10 These kilns near Tucson, Arizona, are made of sun-dried adobe.

Aesthetic Qualities of Brick

Although standard building brick is widely used, there are many colors, textures, and sizes of brick available. The level of refinement produced by uniform brick assembled with accuracy contrasts with bricks made to look older, rougher, and even as though they had been burnt in a fire. Antique salvage bricks are used for a historic or rustic appearance. Walls can intentionally be built with irregularities and curves that are more organic in form than a flat, rectilinear brick wall.

The size of a brick establishes the scale of the wall. Because fewer large units than smaller units are required to build a wall of a given size, labor costs are generally less for larger bricks.

Brick color is determined by raw materials and firing temperatures. Colors range from reds and burgundies to whites and buffs, with many manufacturers producing more than 100 colors. Many light and dark color variations are determined during the firing process by temperature variations and the order in which the units are stacked in the kiln. Sand, slurry, or ceramic glazes can be applied to the surface to achieve colors not possible with some types of clay. When combining units of contrasting colors in bands or other patterns, sample panels aid color selection.

Textures of brick include smooth, wire-cut (velour), stippled, bark, or brushed. Mortar can get into the spaces in rough-textured brick and make cleaning more diffi-cult. Both the brick's texture and the profile and depth of mortar lines enhance the play of light and shadow.

Materials Sources and Manufacturing Processes for Brick

Clay is one of the most abundant natural mineral materials on earth. Primarily, bricks are made of *kaolin* (a soft, earthy, usually white clay) and shale clays. Small amounts of other materials are blended with the clay to produce different shades. Many other additives have been used in brick, including by-products from papermaking, ammonium compounds, wetting agents, flocculents (which cause particles to form loose clusters), and deflocculents (which disperse such clusters). Some clays require the addition of sand or grog (preground, prefired material such as scrap brick).

Clays used in the production of brick must have enough plasticity to be shaped or molded when mixed with water. Sufficient wet and air-dried tensile strength allows them to maintain their shape after forming. Clay particles must fuse together when subjected to heat. Oxides of iron, magnesium, and calcium influence the color of the

Figure 3-11 Johnson Wax Building, Racine, Wisconsin, 1936. Horizontal mortar lines are emphasized over vertical ones in Frank Lloyd Wright's sensuous use of interior brick.

finished fired product. Even though manufacturers mix clays from different locations in the pit, the end result is not uniform.

To create a typical coating, sand is mechanically mixed with some type of colorant. Sometimes a *flux* is added to lower the melting temperature of the sand so it can bond to the brick surface. *Frit* (a glass containing colorants) is added to produce surface textures. Other materials, including graded fired and unfired brick, nepheline syenite (a pale gray or pink rock similar to granite), and graded aggregate can be used as well.

Some American brick manufacturers are making brick by mixing sewage sludge with clay, resulting in attractive and strong brick. Petroleum-contaminated soils, when combined with clay and fired at very high temperatures, yield brick that is free from hydrocarbon contamination.

Figure 3-12 Brick construction

Building brick is used in both structural and nonstructural masonry, typically as a backing material. Facing brick is used where appearance is important. Hollow bricks are identical to facing brick, but have a larger core area. Paving bricks are used for walkways and light vehicle traffic. Ceramic glazed bricks have a ceramic glaze fused to the body and are used as facing brick. Thin brick veneer units are fired clay units with normal face dimensions, but a reduced thickness. They are used in adhered veneer applications.

Modern bricks are usually not solid, for speedier firing and less weight. Some are pressed into shape with a frog, or depression, on their top surface. Salt glazing—the adding of salt during the burning process—yields a highly impervious and ornamental surface. A *slip*, a glaze material into which the bricks are dipped and subsequently reheated in the kiln, fuses into a glazed surface integral with the brick base.

Brick is made by forming clay into a rectangle, and hardening it by firing in a kiln or drying in the sun.

- Soft-mud, sand-struck, and water-struck bricks are made by pressing wet clay into a mold.
- In the stiff-mud process, stiff but malleable clay is extruded through a *die* (a tool used to form a manufactured item). The extruded material is cut to length with wires before firing.
- Sharp-edged and smooth-surfaced dry-press bricks are molded from relatively dry clay under high pressure.
- Bricks made from dampened clay are formed in molds with a great deal of pressure, usually applied by a hydraulic press; they have a dense facing surface that is highly resistant to weathering.

The shaped clay is then dried and fired to achieve the desired strength, usually while moving slowly through a continuously fired kiln on conveyors, rails, or kiln cars.

Environmental and Health Impacts of Brick

Brick manufacturing uses raw materials efficiently, typically close to their source. Clay depletion is generally not an environmental concern. Mined areas, including open pits, are reclaimed by replacing overburden and topsoil.

Processed clay and shale removed in the forming process prior to firing are returned to the production stream. Culls after firing are ground and used as grog with the prepared material to reduce shrinkage or crushed for use as landscaping materials.

Nonhazardous waste products from other industries are sometimes used as materials in brick manufacturing. Examples include bottom- and fly-ash from coal-fired generators, other ceramic materials used as grog, and sawdust. Recycled glass powder can be added to the clay mixture. This allows reduced firing temperatures and lower emissions, as well as increased compressive strength and frost resistance.

Air emissions are minimized with controls installed on kiln exhausts. Dust in plants is controlled through the use of filtering systems, vacuums, additives, and water mists.

Clay bricks have relatively low embodied energy. The majority of kilns in the United States use gas as a fuel source, though a third of the brick currently produced is fired using solid fuels such as sawdust and coal. Biomass is being introduced as a fuel for brick making.

Antique bricks are often reclaimed in massive quantities from commercial buildings that have outlived their original purpose, such as abandoned textile mills, warehouses, and manufacturing facilities. The market for these recycled bricks continues to grow, and hundreds of thousands, and sometimes millions, of bricks are reclaimed from a demolition site; the mortar is cleaned off each brick by hand. The bricks are being reused in gardens as pavers or for walls, as façades on new homes, and for interior walls in restaurants and other businesses.

Interior Applications for Brick

Inside buildings, brick floors are durable and strong and have a relatively maintenance-free surface. Mortarless installations reduce joints between bricks to fine thin lines. Mortarless brick flooring may be placed on a concrete slab or wood flooring system. See Chapter 9 for more information.

A brick fireplace can be hand-built or supplied in a kit form. A large number of designs are available for brick fireplaces, ranging from classic through inglenooks that extend the treatment to adjacent walls. Numerous brick finishes and styles are available for a brick fireplace.

Brick interior walls may be either load-bearing or nonstructural. Interior walls faced with brick often have another material behind. A serpentine wall is a brick wall that follows a curving, S-shaped path, rather than a straight line. Because a serpentine wall is more resistant to toppling than a straight wall, it may be made of a single thickness of unreinforced brick, and despite its longer length, it may be more economical than a straight wall.

Specifying Brick

Brick selection is based on aesthetics, physical properties (compressive strength and absorption, both of which affect durability), application (moisture penetration, movement of materials and structural loads), cost, and availability.

Bricks are usually laid flat; as a result, the effective limit on the width of a brick is set by the distance that can conveniently be spanned between the thumb and fingers of one hand, normally about 4 inches (102 mm). In most cases, the length of a brick is

Figure 3-13 Brick pavers

about twice its width, around 8 inches (20 cm). When specifying the size of units, dimensions should be listed by thickness, then by height, and, last, by length. The dimensions given should be specified, not nominal, dimensions.

Standards for brick construction applicable to interiors include ASTM Standard Specifications for Brick, Mortar, and Applicable Testing Methods for Units. Bricks are laid in *bonds* to increase stability and strength.

In the United States, the nominal dimensions of standard bricks are 4 × 2–2/3 × 8 inches (102 × 68 × 203 mm). The actual bricks are smaller, and the nominal dimensions add an allowance for the mortar joint. Three standard bricks with mortar total 8 inches (203 mm) vertically. In Britain, the usual (work) size of a modern brick is 215 × 102.5 × 65 mm (about 8.5 × 4 × 2.5 inches). With a nominal 10-mm mortar joint this forms a *coordinating*, or fitted, size of 225 × 112.5 × 75 mm (i.e., a ratio of 6:3:2).

Figure 3-14 Efflorescence on brick Reproduced by permission of the publisher from Edward Allen and Joseph Iano, *Fundamentals of Building Construction: Materials and Methods,* 4th ed. (Hoboken, NJ: John Wiley & Sons, Inc.), © 2004 by John Wiley & Sons, Inc.

The condition known as efflorescence occurs when water dissolves certain elements (salt is among the most common) in exterior sources, mortar, or the brick itself. The residual deposits of soluble material produce surface discoloration. Improper cleaning may cause the salt deposits to become insoluble; the efflorescence worsens, and extensive cleaning is required. This, as well as weathering, is not as problematic with interior uses.

Cost Factors for Brick

Bricks are usually priced per thousand units; pavers are usually priced per square foot or per thousand. Material selection is often based on initial cost only; however, although initial cost is important, life-cycle cost is a better tool for making critical decisions. The selling price of brick is governed by many factors, including manufacturing methods, size, and appearance of the unit. Shipping costs vary significantly with the distance between the manufacturing plant and the job site. Large increases in brick costs do not result in concomitant increases in wall costs; better mason productivity may actually lower in-place costs.

Installation and Maintenance Practices for Interior Brick

Relevant standards for brick masonry mortar include ASTM C270-02 Standard Specification for Mortar for Unit Masonry. Colored mortars are produced through the use of colored aggregates or suitable pigments. White sand, ground granite, marble, or stone usually have permanent color and do not weaken the mortar. For white joints, white sand, ground limestone, or ground marble with white portland cement and lime is used.

Most pigments that conform to ASTM C979, Standard Specification for Pigments for Integrally Colored Concrete, are suitable for mortar; requirements are generally met by metallic oxide pigments. Carbon black and ultramarine blue have also been used successfully as mortar colors. Organic colors and, in particular, those colors containing Prussian blue, cadmium lithopone, and zinc and lead chromates, as well as paint pigments, may not be suitable for mortars. The minimum quantity of pigments that will produce the desired results should be used; excess amounts may seriously impair strength and durability.

For more uniform color, cement and coloring agents are premixed in large, controlled quantities. Color uniformity varies with the quality and amount of mixing water and moisture content of the brick when laid. The time and degree of tooling and cleaning techniques will also influence final mortar color.

Thin, fired clay units, often referred to as *thin brick*, are used as interior or exterior wall coverings. Thin brick veneer is formed from shale and/or clay and kiln-fired. These thin brick units resemble facing brick (ASTM C216), but are only 1/2 to 1 inch (13 to 25 mm) thick. ASTM C1088, Thin Veneer Brick Units Made from Clay or Shale, covers two grades defined as Exterior and Interior.

Thin brick placed into forms and cast integrally with concrete form an architectural precast concrete panel. Thin brick can also be bonded to a 16 inch × 48 inch (406 mm × 1220 mm) substrate for a small, lightweight, easy-to-install modular panel. These can be installed using ceramic tile techniques.

Thin brick is used as an architectural wallcovering that has the maintenance-free benefits of conventional brick masonry. In comparison to conventional brick masonry, thin brick will have less fire resistance, sound resistance, structural strength, thermal mass, or insulation properties. Thin brick in panels can be used to create complex wall shapes with returns, soffits, or arches, by using jigs, forms, and templates; repetitive usage of these shapes can lower costs appreciably. The panels weigh approximately 35 pounds (16 Kg), which is light enough for one person to handle easily.

Glazed brick is generally installed in the same manner as face brick. Type N or S mortar is recommended for most installations following the guidelines in ASTM C270. A 3/8-inch (10 mm) joint size is typical; the mortar joints should not be sealed.

Wall ties should be placed at least every 24 inches (61 cm) vertically and 36 inches (91 cm) horizontally, or every 4–1/2 square feet (.42 square meters) in a staggered pattern. Expansion joints should be located on each side of a corner at 4 feet to 10 feet (1.22 meters to 3 meters) from the corner; however, on straight walls, the expansion joints need only be spaced at 3/4 inch (19 mm) per 100 feet (30.5 meters) of wall. Flexible anchors are used to connect to columns and beams.

Exposed, untreated interior brick is cleaned by first removing loose dirt by vacuuming the surface well, followed by wiping with a chemically treated dry sponge, unless the surface is especially rough. Deep cleaning requires scrubbing water and an alkaline solution or degreaser into the brick, allowing it to soak in and loosen dirt deep within the porous surface before blotting with an absorbent cloth.

Finishes for Brick

Bricks have integral and durable color and, when properly constructed, are resistant to rain penetration. Colorless coatings are generally applied to interior walls to facilitate cleaning or provide a gloss; water repellency and breathability are generally not concerns. A film-forming product such as a waterborne acrylic (acrylic emulsion) or urethane can be used to improve gloss and ease of cleaning. Both are durable in applications with no UV exposure.

Interior brick walls may be painted to increase light reflection or for decorative purposes. More information on painting brick walls is found in Chapter 10.

A colorless coating can decrease the slip resistance of an interior brick floor. Coated floors or pavements should be evaluated for slipperiness, for safety reasons, especially in public access areas and in areas where water may contact the floor or pavement. The slip resistance of a coating can be measured using ASTM D2047, Test Method for Static Coefficient of Friction of Polish-Coated Floor Surfaces as Measured by the James Machine. Acrylics can be particularly hazardous; epoxy-based coatings may perform better. Film-forming coatings may separate from the brick paving and turn cloudy if moisture migrates through the brick floor.

Concrete masonry units (CMUs) are precast of portland cement with fine aggregate and water and molded into various shapes. Technically, the term *concrete masonry unit* includes blocks made of cinder concrete (cinder blocks or breeze block), hollow tile, and ordinary concrete blocks. Cinder and tile blocks are used as a structural core for veneer brick or are used alone, where they are sometimes finished with stucco or a surface-bonding cement for added strength. They are used as low-cost structural elements and are often covered with other interior finishes. CMUs can be faced with ceramic or be glazed or polished.

 Note: Concrete blocks are often referred to as cement blocks, but this is incorrect.

History, Types, and Characteristics of CMUs

Hand-molded concrete blocks were first made in 1882, and were commercially manufactured in the United States from cement, sand, and water by 1900. These 20 × 20 × 8 inch (508 × 508 × 203 cm) blocks were heavy and unmanageable, and were made at the job site. Today, blocks are made in standard sizes that facilitate handling and simplify their use with other materials. Any type of CMU structure can be reinforced by fully grouting the voids or inserting reinforcing bars vertically into grout-filled voids.

Concrete blocks have excellent structural strength and fire resistance, and maintenance requirements are minimal. A standard common concrete masonry unit is nominally 8 × 8 × 16 inches (20 × 20 × 41 cm), usually manufactured with two hollow cores to reduce weight and make handling easier. Filled cell insulation added to the cores improves thermal and acoustic properties. Concrete blocks are manufactured as either lightweight (under 105 pounds per cubic foot) or normal (medium) weight units (105 to 125 pounds per cubic foot). Solid load-bearing concrete blocks are more than 75 percent solid and are used for veneer-faced walls, cavity walls, and multiwythe reinforced walls.

Standard integral colors produced by mineral oxide pigments are buff, red, brown, and yellow. The type of aggregate used and the water content during molding determine the texture of concrete blocks. Smooth-surfaced blocks vary between denser closed textures and very porous and open ones. The face textures of split face and striated (scratch) face blocks are mechanically created. Glazed CMUs expand the color options and add a glossy finish.

Whether painted or left bare, CMUs present a practical, durable, no-nonsense surface. Their unit sizes and mortar lines establish a scale for an interior space—designers can quickly measure the size of a room by counting CMUs.

Figure 3-15 Concrete blocks

In addition to architectural CMU types, screenwall block and concrete paving units are available. Screenwall blocks have an open web pattern that admits air and light for solar control, garden walls, and fences. Concrete masonry paving units are used on steep embankments to prevent soil erosion, and for paving driveways, walks, patios, and floors on grade. Concrete masonry paving units come in a range of shapes and colors and are easy to handle and install. Grass grid units are useful as for paving that allows water to drain back into the ground.

Environmental and Health Impact of CMUs

CMUs have good fire resistance and acoustic performance. Their high thermal mass allows them to retain their temperature for a long time, helping to reduce heating and cooling costs and moderating indoor temperatures. They are made from readily available local raw materials and manufactured close to construction cites, and have lower embodied energy than brick.

CMUs can be made using recycled aggregates and cementitious materials. They can be used without a painted finish, which reduces the amounts of volatile organic compounds (VOCs) on the job site. They do not support the growth of mold.

Specifying CMUs

Concrete masonry units are graded for compressive strength and intended use. Grade N is a load-bearing CMU, used both above and below grade in walls that are exposed to moisture or weather. Grade S is also load-bearing, but limited to use above grade, in exterior walls with weather-protective coatings, or in walls not exposed to moisture or weather.

Concrete Block Shapes

These are some of the many configurations of concrete masonry units available.
- Stretcher blocks: Most common type; two or three cores; nominal dimensions of 8 × 8 × 16 inches (20 × 20 × 40 cm). Also available 4 inches, 6 inches, 10 inches, and 12 inches (10, 15, 25, and 30 cm) wide.
- Corner blocks: Solid end face for a neat end or corner of a wall.
  - Corner-return blocks: Modified in shape to allow a wall to appear to maintain horizontal coursing with full and half-length units as it turns a corner.
  - Double-corner blocks: Solid faces at both ends.
- Coping blocks: Used at the top or finishing course of a masonry wall.
- Sill blocks: Sloped to shed rainwater from a sill.
- Sound-absorbing masonry units: Solid on top and have slots on face; sometimes filled with a sound-absorbing material.
- Lintel blocks: U-shaped in section to allow reinforcing steel to be embedded in grout for extra strength; used to span door and window openings.
- Split-face blocks: Split lengthwise by a machine after they are cured to produce a rough, fractured face texture.
- Faced blocks: Have special ceramic, glazed, or polished finishes on their primary face.
- Scored blocks: Have one or more vertical grooves that appear to be joints.
- Shadow blocks: Have a face shell with a pattern of beveled recesses.
- Screen blocks: Admit air and diffuse sunlight through a decorative pattern.
- Concrete brick: Solid rectangular CMU the same size as a standard clay brick; are also available 12 inches (305 mm) long.

CMUs are also specified by types, determined by moisture content: the lower the specified limit of moisture, the less the CMU shrinks during drying, and the less likely it will be to crack. Type I is a concrete masonry unit manufactured to a specific limit of moisture content. Type II CMUs do not have a specified limit.

Cost Factors for CMUs

Concrete masonry units are generally inexpensive; costs will vary with location, availability, and project schedule. The figures given here are meant for comparison only.

- Standard concrete blocks average around $1.30 per block, or $1.46 per square foot.
- Split-faced concrete block costs about $2.30 per block, or around $2.59 per square foot.

Masons sometimes charge an additional $1.00 per square foot for laying visibly exposed block with extra care. Four-inch-high split-face block resembles brick, and competes favorably with the price of brick veneer.

Installation and Maintenance of CMUs

A standard 3/8-inch (10-mm) mortar joint is used between concrete masonry units, as with brick; CMU actual dimensions are consequently 3/8 inch less than the nominal dimension. Except for the first course of hollow units, mortar is applied only to the edges of the faces of the block, but in sufficient quantity to ooze out when the block is pressed into place; the excess is then cut off with a trowel. Joints are compressed and shaped with a special tool. Concrete masonry units can be left unfinished or painted. Finishes appropriate for precast masonry can be used with CMUs. Where the block is left unfinished, the mason is required to take extra care to leave a clean and neat wall face.

Maintenance of concrete masonry units is the same as for other precast concrete products. CMU walls require very little routine maintenance; dust can be wiped or vacuumed off the extremely durable surfaces.

CMUs can be recycled by selective demolition, much like bricks, although breakage is more of a problem. Crushed CMUs can be used as aggregates in concrete.

Glass and Ceramics 4

Some sources classify glass as a form of noncrystalline ceramic, while others make a distinction between the two related materials. Glass is shaped by casting when fully melted, or by blowing or other methods while in a partly molten state. When heat treatments that cause partial crystallization of the glass are applied later, the resulting product is called a *glass-ceramic*.

Glass is a hard, brittle, noncrystalline substance made by melting silica, a white or colorless crystalline compound found in quartz, sand, and other materials, with various oxides (oxygen products).

Many types of glass are used in building interiors:

- The most common is *float glass*, used in windows and skylights.
- *Foamed or cellular glass* is used as rigid, vaporproof thermal insulation.
- *Glass fibers* are used in textiles and for material reinforcement; spun fibers are known as *glass wool*, which is used for acoustical and thermal insulation.
- *Glass block* controls light, glare, and solar heat.

Historical, Cultural, and Architectural Context of Glass

Archaeological evidence of glass has been found dating to around 3000 BCE. Core-formed and cast-glass vessels were first produced in early Egypt and Mesopotamia. Egyptian craftsmen making glass pots around 1500 BCE dipped a molded core of compacted sand into molten glass and turned it to distribute the glass. The glass-covered mold was then rolled smooth on a stone slab, where a patterned stone embossed a design. The Egyptians developed clear glass of crushed quartz or sand, with minerals added for blue, green, red, gold, black, opaque, and white glass, and later on, purple and lemon-yellow. Sophisticated glass fabrication techniques include core forming, cold cutting, molding, and lost wax.

Sometime after 27 BCE, the process of blowing glass through a long, thin metal tube was discovered, probably by craftsmen from Syria. Shortly after, the ancient Romans began blowing glass inside molds, and spread the technique from Italy throughout the empire. Mass-production methods reduced costs, making glass available for ordinary use; eventually, glass was shipped as far as China, along the Silk Road.

The techniques for making clear glass through the addition of manganese oxide was developed in Roman-ruled Alexandria, Egypt, around 100 CE. Cast-glass windows were used in Roman baths and in villas in Herculaneum and Pompeii in Italy. Large window openings filled with translucent glass introduced natural light while keeping weather out.

By the time of the Roman Republic (509–27 BCE), glass tableware and containers for expensive oils, perfumes, and medicines were common in the area that is now Tuscany and in parts of southern Italy. Roman glassmaking techniques improved quality, increased quantity, and offered greater variety for both commercial mold-blown and custom-blown pieces. Roman glass was made into multicolored *tesserae* (small, usually square pieces) for elaborate floor and wall mosaics, as well as lining pools and niches.

The beauty of Byzantine interior mosaic decoration is due to the use of smaller tesserae than in their Roman or early Christian counterparts and to the bonding of the reflective glass squares to gold leaf, silver, or mother-of-pearl. Romanesque buildings reused stone, glass, and gold mosaic tesserae in rich colors.

Byzantine influence encouraged glassmaking on the Venetian island of Murano in the latter half of the fifteenth century, and soda lime glass, also known as *cristallo*, was developed. The delicate and graceful glass produced by Venice's glassblowers was unique; eventually, their secret technology spread throughout Europe.

Techniques for making sheets of glass were developed in the eleventh century by German craftsmen, and further developed in thirteenth-century Venice. A hollow glass sphere would be blown and swung to produce a cylinder approximately as long as 9 feet (3 meters) and up to 1–3/4 inch (45 cm) wide. The ends of the molten cylinder were cut off and the cylinder was cut lengthwise and opened up flat. Crown glass also produced flat glass for use in windows.

Glazed windows were luxury items until the late Middle Ages, when stained-glass windows became increasingly popular in public buildings, inns, and homes of the wealthy. The hundreds of castles built in England by the Norman conquerors after 1066 usually had small windows with leaded-glass panes. The radiant color of Gothic stained glass transformed the interior of cathedrals. Colored glass was blown or cast in small pieces and joined with H-shaped leading into patterns and images set into stone tracery.

Glass was used for windows and glass mosaics in early Islamic buildings. Mosques were often lit with glass oil lamps. By the ninth and tenth centuries, cold-cut glass in complex relief and incised patterns modeled on Roman and Sasanian glass appear in the Mediterranean and Iran. *Rock crystal*, a colorless, transparent quartz found in Morocco, East Africa, Afghanistan, and Kashmir was highly polished, producing cut facets that reflected light brilliantly.

The windows of Renaissance churches brought in bright light through lightly colored glass to illuminate painted altarpieces, triptychs, and easel paintings illustrating religious themes. During the Iconoclastic Revolt in 1566, churches were stripped of Gothic sculpture, painting, and other decoration; their interiors were painted white, and light from clear glass windows replaced stained glass.

English glassmaker George Ravenscroft (1618–1681) patented the process for making lead crystal in 1674, producing a brilliant and highly refractive glass used for deep cutting and engraving. In France, in 1688, a new process for making mirrors by pouring molten glass onto a specially designed table and rolling it flat was developed. The cooled glass was ground with rotating cast-iron disks and progressively finer abrasive sands, and then polished with felt disks. The resulting flat glass with good optical qualities became a mirror when coated with a reflective metal on one side. The Palace of Versailles is an elaborate complex set in landscaped gardens, and includes the famous Galerie des Glaces (Hall of Mirrors). Mirrors on the gallery's inner wall echo garden windows.

Colonial style in North America often included a door surmounted by a fixed transom of small glass panes and flanked by two windows on each side with rectangular panes. The windows were double-hung, but only the bottom sash was operable.

The immense Crystal Palace, designed by Joseph Paxton for London's Great Exhibition of 1851, was built from prefabricated glass and iron sections that were assembled on-site. Although it was intended as a temporary building, it was reassembled in southeast London after the Exhibition, where it stood until it was demolished by fire in 1936. The technology used in the Crystal Palace was remarkably innovative, a quality that, ironically, many of the pieces exhibited inside it lacked.

In France, too, engineers developed astonishingly beautiful structures of iron and glass. Pierre-François-Henri Labrouste (1801–1875) designed the Bibliothèque Ste. Geneviève in Paris (1844–1850) and the Bibliothèque Nationale in Paris (1859–1867).

Figure 4-1 Versailles Galerie des Glaces, one of the most famous interior uses of mirrors.

At the turn of the nineteenth century, American engineer Michael Owens (1859–1923) invented an automatic bottle-blowing machine, with backing from the Libbey Glass Company of Toledo, Ohio. Flat glass production improved in the early twentieth century thanks to innovations by Belgian engineers Emile Fourcault and Emil Bicheroux. The process of making laminated glass was patented by French scientist Edouard Benedictus in 1910. An American process developed by Irving W. Colburn, and supported by the Libbey–Owens Glass Company, was introduced for commercial production in 1917. Elements of these techniques were combined by the Pittsburgh Plate Glass Company (PPG) and have been in use since 1928.

Otto Wagner's design for the Austrian Post Office Savings Bank (1904–1906) includes interior lobbies, stairs, and corridors with metal and stained-glass details. The high central main banking room, roofed in metal and glass, has lower side spaces. A structural glass floor admits light to the space below.

The offices inside early skyscrapers were utilitarian, with rows of small offices along corridors, giving many occupants access to windows for light and fresh air. Private offices were separated from outer offices and reception areas by glazed-wood partitions, with transoms over doors for ventilation.

The German Exhibit Pavilion at the Barcelona Exhibition of 1929 (known as the Barcelona Pavilion), a temporary structure designed by Ludwig Mies van der Rohe, was unrestricted by budget or function. It was dramatically composed of brass, marble, plate

Figure 4-2 Colonial window, Salem, Massachusetts.

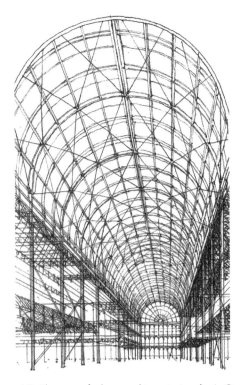

Figure 4-3 The use of glass and iron in London's Crystal Palace applied the techniques of greenhouse construction to a huge exhibition hall.
Reproduced by permission of the publisher from Francis D. K. Ching, Mark M. Jarzombek, and Vikramaditya Prakash, *Global History of Architecture* (Hoboken, NJ: John Wiley & Sons, Inc.), © 2007 by John Wiley & Sons, Inc.

glass, and undecorated surfaces resting on a wide marble platform with two reflecting pools. Eight steel columns supported the flat roof over a space without enclosing or supporting walls, with glass and marble partitions in irregular but rectilinear patterns, some extending outdoors.

In 1936, Skidmore, Owings, and Merrill (SOM) founded a huge American-based architectural practice specializing in buildings for multinational firms and modern skyscrapers. Gordon Bunshaft (1909–1990) designed the Lever House in New York (1950–1952) for Lever Brothers with a glass curtain wall enclosing the concrete slab structure. These technical innovations influenced the design of the interior. A suspended ceiling on each floor screened the services for air-conditioning.

Float glass is perfectly flat, clear glass that is produced by floating molten glass on a surface of molten lead, a process introduced in Great Britain in 1959 by Sir Alastair Pilkington. This remains the most common method of making flat glass.

Physical Properties, Characteristics, and Types of Glass

The mechanical properties of glass involve the way forces act on it and the effects they produce. Although glass seems hard and rigid, it will bend or stretch with enough force; when the force is removed, it will return to its original position, making it a very elastic material. When the force applied exceeds the ultimate strength of the glass, it breaks. Surprisingly, glass breaks from tensile (pulling) forces rather than from compression. The composition of a specific type of glass only slightly affects its strength. However, any applied stress will be concentrated at flaws in its surface such as nicks or scratches, increasing the effect of the stress.

The mechanical hardness of glass is measured by scratch, penetration, and abrasion methods. The strength of tempered commercial glass is measured at about 20,000 pounds per square inch (psi). This is tested by applying a bending load to a bar of glass under laboratory conditions, and increasing the load until the bar breaks. The break will begin on the bar's lower surface, which is stretched in tension; its upper surface is squeezed in compression. A crack starts at a specific point and spreads; the contours of the fractured surface record its starting point and direction.

Glass can be prestressed by thermal tempering, with all its surfaces put into compression while the interior remains in tension. This involves heating and then rapidly chilling the glass, producing a large temperature difference between the surfaces and the interior. This difference in temperature decreases as the glass cools to room temperature. The resulting tension is concentrated in the middle of the glass, where it is balanced by the compression of the exterior surfaces.

Chemical methods are also used to increase the strength of glass. By immersing glass in a molten salt bath, large ions replace smaller ions at the glass surface, crowding the surface and producing compression.

Layers of glass can be laminated together with heat. The inner glass shrinks more during cooling, putting the outer layers into compression.

Glass is highly resistant to corrosion, but it can corrode or even dissolve under some conditions. A glass surface in continual contact with certain alkali solutions will corrode at a uniform rate until it dissolves. Glass is also vulnerable to attack by hydrofluoric acid and, to a lesser extent, other acids, which dissolve the alkali in the glass and leave a porous network of silica. Superheated water can also remove alkali from a glass surface, but at a much slower rate.

Glass is an insulating material that resists the passage of electricity, both through its volume and along its surface. It is a material with very great ability to help electronic capacitors store energy.

The optical properties of glass describe the way that light behaves when it falls on glass. Some of the light is reflected from the glass surface, some of the light passes through the glass, and some is absorbed in the glass. The light reflecting from the surface is measured as *reflectance*; that absorbed is measured as *absorptance*; the remaining amount transmitted is its *transmittance*.

Optical properties include light—the visible spectrum from violet to red—as well as the infrared and ultraviolet wavelengths at the ends of the visible spectrum. All these wavelengths are extremely short, but infrared are relatively longer, and ultraviolet relatively shorter, than visible wavelengths. There are hundreds of types of glass developed for optical uses.

If light were to pass through a material with complete transparency, no light would be reflected or absorbed. Glass is highly, but not perfectly, transparent, transmitting most of the light that falls on it. Selectively transparent types of glass transmit some wavelengths more efficiently than others. For example, glass that appears blue absorbs all colors except blue; blue wavelengths are what we see passing through the glass. Glass compositions have been designed to transmit either ultraviolet or infrared wavelengths while absorbing visible light; they appear to be black. Glass that absorbs infrared wavelengths and transmit visible ones block heat while transmitting visible light.

The ability of glass to bend light is called *refraction*. A lens is designed to bend all the light rays passing through it so that they focus at a single point. The amount of bending is measured as the refractive index; the higher the refractive index, the greater the wavelengths are bent.

Coatings are applied to the surface of glass to modify its reflectance. The maximum, mirrorlike reflectance is achieved by using a metallic coating. Heat-shielding glass

Figure 4-4 Glass reflection, absorption, and transmission
Reproduced by permission of the publisher from Francis D. K. Ching, *A Visual Dictionary of Architecture* (New York: John Wiley & Sons, Inc.), © 1995 by John Wiley & Sons, Inc.

reflects most of the infrared wavelengths but transmits most of the visible light. Nonreflective coatings minimize reflectance.

Glass transmits heat internally both by thermal conduction and by radiation; the amount of radiative transfer depends on the thickness of the glass, and is most significant at temperatures over 400°C.

Commercial glass is the most common type used in building construction and for bottles, jars, and drinking glasses (it is also called *soda-lime glass* after the soda ash used to produce it). The majority of commercial glass is made primarily of sand; when heated to about 1700°C, sand will fuse by itself into glass. The addition of sodium carbonate (soda ash) as 25 percent of the mix reduces the temperature needed for fusion to around 800°C; the resulting glass is water soluble and is called *water glass*. The addition of limestone contributes calcium oxide and magnesium oxide to the mix and results in a pure inert glass.

New glass can be made from old. The collection and recycling of used glass reduces the quarrying of new materials; using recycled glass also requires less energy and produces fewer emissions to manufacture than new glass. Container glass from any source can be mixed, as compositions are very uniform. Glass colors are separated, and impurities including metals and ceramics are removed. Green glass made from a mixture that contains 85 to 90 percent recycled glass is common.

Figure 4-5 Crown glass is formed from a flat, circular disk with a lump in the center left by the glassblower's rod. Larger areas of smooth glass could be produced by this method before the invention of plate glass.
Reproduced by permission of the publisher from Francis D. K. Ching, *A Visual Dictionary of Architecture* (New York: John Wiley & Sons, Inc.), © 1995 by John Wiley & Sons, Inc.

Types of Glass

- *Glass ceramic:* Extremely thermal shock-resistant; controlled amount of crystal growth produced in lithium aluminosilicate glass. Combines desirable qualities of both ceramics and glass. Used in cooktops and cookware and missile nose cones.
- *Borosilicate glass:* Made from silica and boric oxide with small amounts of other oxides; chemical durability and thermal shock resistance. Used for laboratory and pharmaceutical equipment, high-intensity lighting, and as glass fibers. Trade name: Pyrex.
- *Low-iron glass (ultraclear glass):* Very low iron content for exceptional clarity and no greenish edge tint. Can be sandblasted, etched, heat-strengthened, tempered, or assembled into laminated glass. Used for excellent color rendition, in furniture, mirrors, museum display cases, and signage, with light-colored pigments.
- *Crown glass:* Process for making glass, used from around 1320 until 1800. A hollow sphere of glass is blown then spun on the end of its blowpipe into a disk 5 to 6 feet (1.5 to 1.8 m) in diameter. When cut off the pipe, a lump remains in the center. The thinnest, clearest glass is cut from the edge of the disk; many small diamond window panes were cut and set into a lead lattice. Glass wool, used for thermal insulation, is produced by crown process.
- *Sheet glass:* Produced by drawing molten soda-lime-silica glass from a furnace, or by forming a cylinder, cutting it lengthwise and opening it flat. When polished, surfaces are not perfectly parallel; distorted images result.
- *Plate glass:* Formed by rolling molten glass into a plate, cooling it, and then grinding and polishing it. This process has been replaced by float glass.
- *Float glass:* Most common form; does not require polishing or grinding. Molten glass is floated on molten lead.
- *Glass fiber:* Various compositions, depending on use.
  - *Building insulation and glass wool:* Soda lime glass.
  - *Glass fiber textiles:* Alumino-borosilicate glass that has good chemical durability and a high softening temperature; used in drapery fabrics and in reinforced plastic products.

- *Optical fibers:* Can guide light around corners; widely used in medicine, signage, and communications.
- *Continuous glass fiber:* Used to reinforce plastics, rubber, and cement.
- *Glass tubing:* Many uses, including fluorescent lighting and other lighting applications.
- *Electric lightbulbs:* Produced with a ribbon machine; manufactured at high speed, along with auto lamps and vacuum flasks.

Aesthetic Qualities of Glass

Glass is chosen for its aesthetic qualities as much as for its functional characteristics. Glass offers various amounts of translucency and transparency. It also adds sparkle and reflection. Colored and patterned glass contributes visual and textural qualities. Broken and cut glass suggests sharpness.

Although it appears to be colorless in thin sheets, ordinary transparent glass shows its green color along thick edges. Various metals and metal oxides are added during the manufacturing process to produce other colors.

Manufacturing Process for Glass

About 90 percent of flat glass manufactured today is float glass. Silica sand, calcium oxide, soda, and magnesium are mixed and then melted in a furnace at 1500°C. A continuous ribbon of molten glass flows from the furnace into a bath of molten lead. The glass does not mix with the highly fluid lead but rests on its perfectly flat surface. After it has cooled somewhat, the glass passes to an annealing chamber call a lehr, where it is cooled at control temperatures.

Rolled glass is made by squeezing semimolten glass between metal rollers to produce a ribbon of the desired thickness. Rolled-glass techniques are used to produce patterned glass and for cast glass. Other processes such as the Pittsburgh process or the Libbey–Owens process are rarely used for the production of flat glass today.

Until the end of the nineteenth century, glass blowing by hand was the primary method of making glass objects. Since then, compressed air and increased mechanization have been introduced to commercial glass production, although art glass is still often hand-blown. The process of glass blowing begins when a hollow blowing pipe is dipped into a pot of molten glass. The pipe is turned to collect the glass at its end. When it cools to about 1000°C, it is rolled on an iron slab to form an elongated shape known as a parison. The parison is repeatedly reheated and manipulated, and air is blown through the pipe into it, to create the desired shape. It is then placed in a wetted iron or wooden mold, where the glass is blown into its final shape. The film of water in the mold creates a cushion of steam that prevents contact between the glass and the mold. During blowing, the pipe is continuously rotated so that mold joints or other imperfections do not appear in the glass.

Cast (molded) glass is formed using a mold; articles with precise dimensions and tolerances and art pieces can be made this way. Molds can be used to produce a great variety of forms, colors, and textures of many thicknesses and overall sizes. Cast-glass products include glass tiles, stair treads, countertops, artwork, and glass panels.

Fused glass is formed by fusing multiple layers of compatible glass together under controlled heating conditions. Fused pieces can include a variety of colors and textures, along with other materials such as wire, stainless steel, and copper screen. Coated and reflective glass may be fused onto glass substrates. Texture fusing (also called tack fusing) keeps the various layers separately identifiable. Full fusing melts all the elements

Table 4-1 Glass Colors

Chemical	Glass Colors	Variations
Cadmium (toxic)	With sulfur for deep yellow; often used in glazes	
Cerium	Yellow	
Chromium	Green, yellow, pink, dark green, or nearly black	With tin oxide and arsenic: emerald green
Cobalt	With potash: blue glass; green, pink	Cobalt oxide: grayish tint
Copper	2 to 3% of copper oxide: turquoise	Pure metallic copper: very dark red, opaque glass
Gold	Very small amounts: rich ruby-colored glass	Even less: cranberry red glass
Iron oxide	Green, brown, and blue	With chromium: rich green
Manganese	In small amounts, removes the green tint given by iron	In higher concentrations: amethyst
Nickel	Blue, violet, yellow, or black	In lead crystal: purplish color
Selenium	Bronze tint, pink and red	
Silver compounds	Yellow to orange-red	
Sulfur with carbon and iron salts	Amber glass, from yellowish to nearly black	With calcium: deep yellow; with boron: blue
Tin oxide with antimony and arsenic oxides	Opaque white glass	
Titanium	Yellow-brown, purple	Used to intensify and brighten other colors
Uranium	Fluorescent yellow or green color	In glass with a high lead content, produces a deep red color
Vanadium	Green, blue, gray	

into a single form with a smooth surface and rounded edges. Fused glass is used for furniture, glass borders, tiles, panels, light fixtures, and other purposes.

Slumped glass is heated to a semimolten state and then molded. Up to 3/8 inch (10 mm), slumped glass will retain the impression of the mold on its reverse side; thicker pieces have relatively smooth backs. Slumped-glass technique lends itself to experimentation with tinted or reflective glass, gold and silver leaf, and airbrushed color. Panels up to 4 × 8 feet (1219 × 2438 mm) can be made, and slumped glass can be tempered. Applications include tabletops, shower enclosures, wall panels, and signs.

Environmental and Health Impacts of Glass

The basic material for most glass is sand, which is readily available and nonpolluting. The use of recycled material to produce glass makes up about 10 to 20 percent of the materials

Figure 4-6 Cast glass is used to produce three-dimensional objects.

used in producing flat glass, and over 50 percent of that used to produce blown or pressed glass. Recycled material content saves raw materials and reduces energy use. The major source of injury in the glass manufacturing industry is from handling the material.

The production of glass uses natural gas, fuel oil, and liquid petroleum gas (LPG), with electricity sometimes used for supplementary heating. Fuel combustion results in emissions containing sulfur oxides, nitrogen oxides, and particulates that may contain heavy metals such as arsenic or lead; lead crystal production particulates may contain 20 to 60 percent lead. Natural gas emits less sulfur dioxide than the other fuel options. Efficient oxyfuel-fired furnaces reduce emissions. Cold-top electric furnaces release very little particulate waste.

Interior Applications for Glass
Insulating Glass

Insulating glass is a unit (IGU) made manually or automatically at a manufacturing plant, consisting of two or more sheets of glass separated by airtight (hermetically

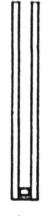

Figure 4-7 Insulating glass unit
Reproduced by permission of the publisher from Francis D. K. Ching, *A Visual Dictionary of Architecture* (New York: John Wiley & Sons, Inc.), © 1995 by John Wiley & Sons, Inc.

sealed) spaces filled with dehydrated air or gas. The sheets are connected by a spacer that contains a desiccant to absorb humidity, with sealants used to reduce water vapor penetration. Another edge seal provides structural stability. Insulating glass reduces thermal losses, resulting in lower energy consumption and reduced condensation.

Low-Emissivity Glass

Low-emissivity glass (low-e glass) transmits visible light but reflects longer waves of radiant heat; in the summer, it reflects more of the infrared (IR) radiation coming at a steeper angle from the sun, while allowing its warmth to enter a lower winter angles.

Low-e glass is made by adding a coating either on the glass itself or on a transparent plastic film within the sealed airspace of insulating glass. A microscopically thin coating of metal oxide applied to clear glass allows the sun's heat and light to pass into the building, while blocking heat from leaving the room, reducing heat loss.

- Low-e glass produced by the pyrolitic process is coated with a metal oxide when clear glass leaves the tin bath. The resulting glass is very resistant to damage, and can be cut, tempered, or laminated.
- Low-e glass produced by the magnetron process is clear glass with a silver coating applied to one of its faces by a magnetically enhanced cathodic process; it can be tempered and laminated, and is used exclusively with the coating on an interior face for insulating glass.

Spandrel Glass

Spandrel glass is used in the construction of curtain walls to conceal structural elements. An opaque ceramic layer is fused to the interior surface of tempered or heat-strengthened glass. From the exterior, spandrel glass may create a distinct band, or blend with window glass. It is usually designed to not be seen from the inside.

Cast-Glass Wall System

A channel-shaped translucent cast glass product manufactured by Pilkington Profilit can be used as an interior glass wall system. Panels are usually about 10 inches (25 cm) wide and can be as much as 20 feet (6 m) high. The glass is installed in an aluminum channel system or is recessed into perimeter surfaces. The system can be curved or installed with glass-to-glass angled corners without a visible vertical frame. It is typically installed with two panes of glass separated by an airspace, and can serve as an acoustic divider with a sound transmission coefficient (STC) reduction of up to 42 decibels.

Glass Block

Glass block, also called glass brick, is manufactured as a translucent, hollow block of glass with clear, textured, or patterned faces. It is made by fusing its front and back halves together with a partial vacuum inside. Glass block is used for nonload-bearing exterior and interior walls and in window openings; it is installed with mortar. Glass block can be fabricated into panels with plastic dividers, then sealed and installed in an opening; the panels are very heavy, however, and may be difficult to handle.

Body-Tinted Glass

Body-tinted glass is produced by adding colorants to ordinary clear float glass that affect its tint and ability to absorb solar radiation. The resulting colored glass is used to reduce heat penetration into buildings and affect the appearance of exterior surfaces. Body-tinted glass is used for interior doors, partitions, staircase panels, mirrors, and other purposes.

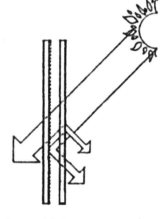

Figure 4-8 Low-emissivity glass Reproduced by permission of the publisher from Francis D. K. Ching, *A Visual Dictionary of Architecture* (New York: John Wiley & Sons, Inc.), © 1995 by John Wiley & Sons, Inc.

Figure 4-9 Glass block

Mirrored Glass

Mirrored glass typically has a smooth, polished surface that reflects light rays. Modern glass mirrors were developed in Europe in the sixteenth and seventeenth centuries. One-way mirrors, manufactured for security purposes, can also be used for decorative effects.

The traditional method of making glass mirrors involves depositing a coating of mostly silver reflective metal on the surface of clear or body-tinted glass. This layer is protected by a layer of copper and, finally, a painted epoxy backing. Antique mirror is produced as a decorative effect by varying the uniformity of metallic deposits to produce a gentle and softened reflection.

Reflective Glass

Reflective glass reduces the amount of solar heat that enters a building; the metallic coating used also creates a mirror effect. Pyrolytic coatings are applied as thin films while the glass is still hot in the annealing lehr; these hard coatings are relatively harmful to the environment. Applying vacuum or magnetron coatings involves putting one or more coats of metal oxide under a vacuum to finished glass. These softer coatings must be protected against weather and are, consequently, used on the interior side of glass panes.

Other techniques for applying coatings to finished reflective glass include chemical process, foil, and screened glazing. Reflective coatings can be applied to float, plate, tempered, laminated, or insulating glass.

Photovoltaic Glass

Photovoltaic glass contains integrated solar cells that convert solar energy into electricity. The solar cells are embedded in a special resin between two glass panes. Each cell is linked by two electrical connections to other cells in the module to form a unit that generates direct electrical current. Photovoltaic glass used on a building roof and exterior surfaces can make a significant contribution to a building's power supply.

Enameled Glass

Enameled glass begins as tempered or heat-strengthened glass; one face is covered either partially or wholly with mineral pigments. The pigments vitrify at the annealing or tempering temperatures, producing a stable, nonbiodegradable deposit. The resulting surface can be made in one or more colors.

Enameled glass is used decoratively and to control solar rays; applications include glazing, cladding for façades and roofs, and assembly into laminated glass or glazed insulation.

Patterned Glass

Patterned glass is also known as textured glass; the surface patterns create translucency. The glass is impressed with patterns during production by squeezing the semimolten glass between two metal rollers. Designs include flutes, ribs, grids, and other regular and random patterns. The bottom roller has an engraved, negative image of the pattern. The depth, size, and shape of the patterns alter the reflective characteristics of the glass. Patterned glass can be silvered, sandblasted, or have colored coatings applied. It may not be possible to temper a patterned glass, however.

Impression glass is a form of patterned glass that is coated with a clear resin, which is then impressed with a pattern. Patterned glass is used for decorative purposes and in furniture, windows, and street furniture.

X-ray Protection Glass

X-ray protection glass contains 70 percent lead oxide that reduces the amount of ionizing radiation that is allowed to pass. It is an amber-colored glass available in single sheets, laminated, or assembled into double-glazed units. X-ray protection glass is used in medical and industrial radiology rooms.

Electrically Heated Glass

Electrically heated glass is a type of laminated glass that contains almost invisible electrically conductive wires. It consists of two or more sheets of glass layered with one or more films of polyvinyl butyral (PVB). Electrically heated glass provides comfort and safety; it also prevents condensation. Electrically heated glass is used where there is a high level of moisture in the air and where temperature differences increase risk of condensation.

Figure 4-10 Patterned glass. These glass patterns are an integral part of the glass.

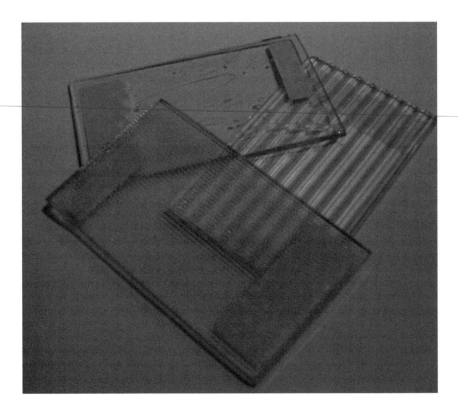

Electrochromic Glass

Electrochromic glass changes color on demand. Low-voltage electrical charges are passed across a microscopically thin coating on the glass surface to activate an electrochromic layer that changes color from clear to dark. The current is activated manually or by light-intensity sensors. Electrochromic glass is used to control light transmission into buildings.

Liquid Crystal Glazing

Liquid crystal glazing, also called polymer dispersed liquid crystal (PDLC) or electrochromic glass switchable privacy glazing, is a laminated glass with at least two clear or colored sheets of glass and a liquid crystal film assembled between at least two plastic interlayers. When turned off, the liquid crystals are not aligned and the glass appears translucent, obscuring vision but allowing light to pass. Within milliseconds of being turned on, the glass becomes transparent. Liquid crystal glazing is used in interior partitions, display cases, and bank screens.

Self-Cleaning Glass

Self-cleaning glass is a recently developed product that is engineered to keep organic materials (for example, bird droppings) from sticking to the glass. The glass is also designed so that raindrops spread into sheets and wash away dirt.

Bent Glass

Bent glass is a form of slumped glass that is produced in a horizontal mold by slowly heating it to around 600°C; the glass softens and takes the shape of the mold. The mold determines the quality and angle of the curve. The glass is then slowly cooled to reduce internal stress. It can be laminated for safety glazing and tempered.

Bent glass can be used on exterior façades, storefronts, and elevators. It is used for interior walls, retail display cases, curved shower enclosures, refrigerated cases, and auto windshields.

Alarm Glass

Alarm glass is a type of laminated glass used for security purposes. An interlayer embedded with a very thin wire is layered between two or more sheets of glass. The wire forms an electrical circuit that activates an alarm when force is applied to the glass.

Antireflective Glass

Antireflective glass is made by applying a low-reflective coating to float glass. The process retains the high level of clarity and optical clarity of transparent glass.

Antireflective glass is used for storefronts and where vision into a lighted space is important at night, such as restaurants. It is also used for picture framing, display cabinets and interior display windows, and for dividing screens in video studios, projection rooms, and control rooms.

Fire-Resistant Glass

Fire-resistant glass is produced either as heat-transmitting glass or as fire-insulating glass. Heat-transmitting glass will contain flames and combustible gas for a short period of time, but transmit heat through the glazing; examples include wired glass and reinforced laminated glass. Fire-insulating glass contains flames and combustible gas for longer periods and prevents the transmission of heat as well as flames and smoke to the other side of the glazing.

Specifying Glass

The basic types of glass specified for interiors include annealed glass (regular float glass), fully tempered glass, heat-strengthened glass, laminated glass, and wired glass. Safety glazing includes fully tempered and laminated glass; if shattered, the glass breaks into small chunks to reduce the risk of cuts or puncture injuries. Consumer Product Safety Commission (CPSC) 16 CFR Part 1201 and ANSI Z97.1 both specify requirements for safety glass; the CPSC standard uses a greater impact load. Wired glass does not pass the requirements of CPSC 16 CFR Part 1201, but is exempted because it is the only glass that performs successfully in fire tests.

- *Annealed glass* is cooled under controlled conditions to relieve internal stresses. It can be cut or drilled on-site after manufacturing. Annealed glass usually only produces one or two lines when cracked, but under force it shatters into sharp shards that present a hazard, and so is not considered to be safety glass and is not approved for use in fire-rated assemblies.
- *Heat-strengthened glass* is annealed glass made like fully tempered glass, but only partially tempered. It has been reheated and then suddenly cooled; the result is about twice as strong as the same thickness of annealed glass. Heat-strengthened glass cannot be cut or drilled in the field. It breaks into sharp shards that pose a safety risk, and is not approved for use in fire-rated assemblies.
- *Tempered glass* (fully tempered glass) is annealed glass that is reheated to just below its softening point and then rapidly cooled. Rapid cooling produces a glass about four times stronger than annealed glass that breaks into many small fragments. Slower cooling produces glass twice as strong as annealed glass with more linear broken-glass fragments that are more likely to remain in the frame. The reference standard is ASTM C1048, Specification for Heat-Treated Flat Glass–Kind HS, Kind FT, Coated, and Uncoated Glass.

  Tempered glass is used for glass façades, sliding doors, building entrances, bath and shower enclosures, and other uses where strength and safety are important. Any glass at least 1/8 inch (3 mm) thick can be tempered, except for patterned or wired glass. Tempered glass is available 1/8 to 1 inch (3 to 25 mm) thick. It is designated as safety glass but is not approved for use in fire-rated assemblies. It cannot be cut or shaped after its initial fabrication and so must be ordered to the exact form required for installation.
- *Laminated glass* is designated as safety glass; when the glass is broken, the resin holds the fragments of glass together. It consists of interior layers of polyvinyl butyral (PVB) plastic or urethane acrylate resin bonded with heat and pressure to two or more layers of flat glass. PVB laminated glass consists of two or more sheets of glass bonded together with one or more layers of PVB under heat and pressure. PVB layers can be colored or patterned, or contain rice paper or other ornamental sheets; layers can be combined. Resin-laminated glass is made by pouring liquid resin into the space between two sheets of glass that are held together until the resin cures under ultraviolet light. Resin lamination allows heavier glass to be laminated. Cast resin interlayers can be clear or custom-colored. Some types of laminated glass can be cut or drilled on-site; others cannot. Laminated glass is used for storefronts, balconies, stair railings, and roof glazing. The interlayer in laminated glass is a sound barrier that dampens vibrations between the pieces of glass; when thicker interlayers are used for sound control, it is called *acoustical glass*.
- *Security glass* is a form of laminated glass that consists of several layers of glass and/or polycarbonate plastic bonded together under heat and pressure with an interlayer. An interlayer of polyvinyl butyral is used with glass and polyurethane

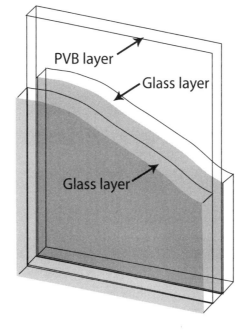

Figure 4-11 Laminated glass construction

PVB layer

Glass layer

Glass layer

plastic is used with polycarbonate. Security glass has exceptional tensile and impact strength. It is available in laminated form from 3/8 to 2–1/2 inches (10 to 63 mm) and up to about 4–3/4 inches (120 mm) for insulating and other construction products. Federal Safety Glazing requirements include:

- ANSI Z97.1, Glazing Materials Used in Buildings–Safety Performance Specifications and Method of Test, as well as CPSC 16 CFR Part 1201, Safety Standard for Architectural Glazing Materials, Category II.
- With an interlayer thickness of .015 inch (.38 mm), laminated glass meets the requirements of Category I glass. The applicable standards are ASTM C1172, Specification for Laminated Architectural Flat Glass, and ASTM C1036, Specification for Flat Glass.
- Requirements for bullet-resistant glass, a related product, are called out in Underwriters Laboratory (UL) 752, Standard for Bullet-Resisting Equipment.
- Burglar-resistant glass should meet the requirements of UL 972, Standard for Burglary Resisting Glazing Material.
- *Float glass* is available as tinted glass in green, bronze, gray, and blue; thicknesses range from 1/8 to 1/2 inch (3 to 13 mm). Tinted glass absorbs part of the sun's energy—how much depends on its additives and thickness—and then dissipates the heat to both the exterior and interior. Heat-absorbing tinted glass gets hotter when exposed to the sun than clear glass, and its central area expands more than its cooler edges; this builds up tensile stress.
- *Wired glass* contains a steel wire mesh sandwiched between two separate ribbons of semimolten glass; the layers are then squeezed together by a pair of metal rollers. The impact resistance of wired glass is similar to that of normal glass, but when broken, the mesh retains the pieces of glass. Wired glass is used as a low-cost fire-resistant glass because it will hold together when other glass would splinter apart. Wired glass is not considered to be safety glass. It can be cut or drilled in the field. Because the wire holds pieces of broken glass together, it is approved for use in fire-rated assemblies.

Figure 4-12 Laminated glass. The decorative pattern is laminated within the glass.

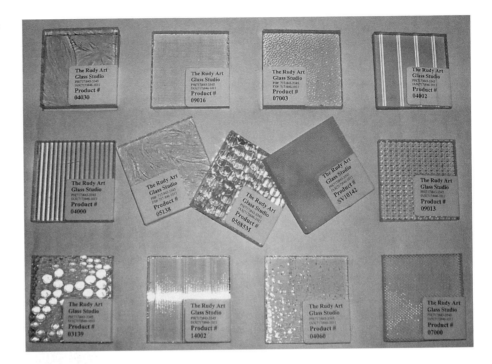

Figure 4-13 Wired glass is available in a variety of patterns.

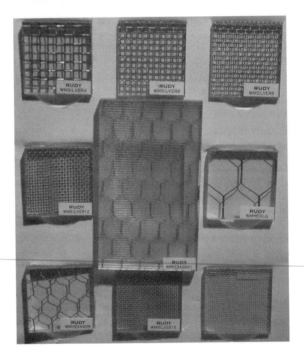

Cost Factors for Glass

Float glass is the least expensive form of glass commonly used in construction. The price per square foot of float glass increases with its thickness; the price of 0.2-inch-thick (5-mm-thick) glass is almost three times that of 0.1-inch-thick (2.5-mm-thick) glass. The price decreases with the volume purchased: the price per sheet for 300 sheets is about 70 percent of the price for a single sheet. Full 48 × 60 inch sheets of float glass cost less than half as much per square foot as smaller pieces cut from those sheets.

Tempered glass is more expensive than float glass, but is still moderately priced. Laminated glass is more expensive.

Table 4-2 Standard Glass Dimensions

Type	Nominal Thickness	Maximum Area	Weight (1 psf = 4g7.88 Pa)	Comments
Sheet glass	Single sheet: 3/32 in. (2.4 mm)	60 × 60 in. (1525 × 1525 mm)		
	Double sheet: 1/8 in. (3.2 mm)	60 × 80 in. (1525 × 2030 mm)	1.63 psf	
Float or plate glass	1/8–7/8 in. (3–22 mm)			
Mirror	1/4 in. (6.4 mm)	75 sq ft (7 sq m)	3.28 psf	
Glazing	1/8 in. thick (3 mm)	74g × 120 in. (1880 × 3050 mm)	1.64g psf	
	Maximum: 1/4 in. (6.4g mm)	128 × 204g in. (3250 × 5180 mm)	3.28 psf	
	5/16 in. (7.9 mm)	124g × 200 in. (3150 × 5080 mm)	4.10 psf	Heavy float or plate glass
	3/8 in. (9.4 mm)	124 × 200 in. (3150 × 5080 mm)	4.92 psf	
	1/2 in. (12.7 mm)	120 × 200 in. (3050 × 5080 mm),	6.54 psf	
	5/8 in. (15.9 mm)	120 × 200 in. (3050 × 5080 mm)	8.17 psf	
	3/4 in. (19.1 mm)	115 × 200 in. (2920 × 5080)	9.18 psf	
	7/8 in. (22.2 mm)	115 × 200 in. (2920 × 5080)	11.45 psf	
Low-iron glass	from 3–19 mm (1/8–3/4 in.)			
Patterned glass	1/8 in. (3.2 mm)	60 × 132 in. (1525 × 3355 mm)	1.60 psf	Sheet sizes and thicknesses vary greatly; tempering and sheet size limitations must be verified for the pattern specified.
	7/32 (5.6 mm)	60 × 132 in. (1525 × 3355 mm)	2.40 psf	
Wired glass	1/4 in. (6.4 mm)	60 × 144 in. (1525 × 3660 mm)	3.50 psf	Polished mesh
	1/4 in (6.4 mm)	60 × 144 in. (1525 × 3660 mm)	3.50 psf	Patterned mesh
	7/32 in. (5.6 mm)	54 × 120 in. (1370 × 3050)	2.82 psf	Parallel wires

(Continued)

Table 4-2 (*Continued*)

Type	Nominal Thickness	Maximum Area	Weight (1 psf = 4g7.88 Pa)	Comments
Wired glass (cont.)	1/4 in. (6.4 mm)	60 × 144 in. (1525 × 3660 mm)	3.50 psf	
	3/8 in. (9.5 mm)	60 × 144 in. (1525 × 3660 mm)	4.45 psf	
Laminated glass	(2 layers) 1/8 in. float: 1/4 in. (6.4g mm)	72 × 120 in. (1830 × 3050 mm)	3.30 psf	
	3/8 in. (9.5 mm)	72 × 120 in. (1830 × 3050 mm)	4.80 psf	Heavy float glass
	1/2 in. (12.7 mm)	72 × 120 in. (1830 × 3050 mm)	6.35 psf	
	5/8 in. (15.9 mm)	72 × 120 in. (1830 × 3050 mm)	8.00 psf	
Tinted glass, bronze or gray	1/8 in. (3.2 mm)	35 sq ft (3 sq. m)	1.64 psf	Solar energy reduced 35–75%
	3/16 in. (4.8 mm)	120 × 144 in. (3050 × 3660),	2.4g5 psf	Visible light transmission reduced 32–72%
	1/4 in. (6.4 mm)	128 × 204 in. (3250 × 5180 mm)	3.27 psf	
	3/8 in. (9.5 mm)	124 × 200 in. (3150 × 5080 mm)	4.90 psf	
	1/2 in. (12.7 mm)	120 × 200 in. (3050 × 5080 mm)	6.54 psf	
Insulating glass	(2 layers) 3/32-in. sheets, 3/16-in. airspace, total 3/8 in. (9.5 mm)	10 sq ft (0.9 sq m)	2.40 psf	R-value = 1.61
	(2 layers) 1/8-in. sheets, 3/16-in. airspace, total 7/16 in. (11.1 mm)	24 sq ft (2.2 sq m)	3.20 psf	
	(2 layers) 1/8-in. sheets, 1/4-in. airspace, total 1/2 in. (12.7 mm)	22 sq ft (2.0 sq m)	3.27 psf	Metal edge units R = 1.82
	1/2-in. airspace, 3/4 in. (19.1 mm)	22 sq ft (2.0 sq m)		Sheet, plate, or float R = 2.04
	(2 layers) 3/16 in.: 1/4-in. airspace, total 5/8 in. (15.9 mm)	34 sq ft (3.2 sq m)	4.90 psf	

(*Continued*)

Table 4-2 (Continued)

Type	Nominal Thickness	Maximum Area	Weight (1 psf = 4G7.88 Pa)	Comments
Insulating glass (cont.)	1/2-in. airspace, total 7/8 in. (22.2 mm)	42 sq ft (3.8 sq m)	4.9 psf	Plate or float: R-values for units with 1/2-in. air-space and low-e coating: e = 0.20, R = 3.13
	(2 layers) 1/4 in.: 1/4-in. airspace, total 3/4 in. (19.1)	50 sq ft (4.6 sq m)	6.54 psf	e = 0.4g0, R = 2.63,
	1/2-in. airspace, 1 in. (24.4 mm)	70 sq ft (6.5 sq m)	6.54 psf	e = 0.60, R = 2.33

Installing Interior Glass

Interior glazing does not have to resist weather conditions and, consequently, is easier to install than exterior windows. Frames may use visible trims or be concealed within ceilings and floors. Interior framed glazing details use silicone sealant to allow expansion and contraction of materials. Frameless glazing details employ metal angles and channels at the head and sill, and silicone at vertical jamb connections. Proprietary and custom-designed glass mounting systems are also used.

Blinds and draperies can reflect energy back through window glass; this increases the temperature of the glass. It is necessary to vent spaces between indoor shading devices and the glass, including recessed pockets in the ceiling. Heating elements should be located on the room side of window treatments so that warm air is directed away from the glass. Horizontal blinds are available with devices that limit their angle of tilt to permit ventilation.

Finishes for Glass

The surface of glass can be finished in a variety of ways to limit views, add visual texture or decorative designs, or soften light passing through. Clear, tinted, or reflective glass can be surface-textured before tempering.

Sandblasting

Sandblasting creates a translucent, frosted effect. However, sandblasting may affect the strength of the glass, and oils tend to leave marks, such as fingerprints.

Sandblasted glass is produced by spraying sand at the glass surface at high velocities; this may be done before other surface treatments are applied to improve adhesion of coatings. The areas that are designated to remain transparent are protected by masking. The resulting translucent surface is usually rougher than that produced by etching; the depth and degree of translucency depend on the amount of force and type of sand used. Laminated glass may be sandblasted as long as the interlayer is not affected. Sandblasted surfaces will show fingerprints and dirt unless sealed, or protected within an insulated double-glazing unit. Sandblasted glass is used in residential and commercial interiors, for doors, shower screens, partitions and interior screens, and furniture. (See color plate C-24, Sandblasted and acid-etched glass.)

Acid Etching and Glue Chip Glass

Acid etching is the process of submerging sandblasted glass in an acid bath (hydrofluoric and hydrochloric acids) to produce a hardened, sealed surface that does not show dirt, dust, or fingerprints. Acid-etched designs can be made using stencils and etching creams for small areas. The resulting finish is uniformly smooth and satiny, admitting light while softening and controlling view. Acid-etched glass may be coated or silvered. Unlike sandblasting, acid-etched glass does not show dust, dirt, or fingerprints. Acid-etched glass is used both commercially and residentially, for doors, shower screens, tabletops, counters, shelving, wall cladding, stair treads, furniture, and wall surfaces.

Blind glass is float glass that has been acid-etched on both sides in a linear pattern that is offset to obscure visibility when viewed perpendicular to the glass surface, but allow visibility when seen at a 45-degree angle. It is produced in 3/16- to 5/16-inch (5- to 8-mm) thicknesses, with thicker width permitting greater visibility. Blind glass is used for doors and in furniture.

Glue chip glass has a frost or fernlike pattern produced by applying hot glue to the surface of sandblasted glass. The glue dries and shrinks as it cools, removing flakes of glass from the surface. Synthetic glues have replaced the horsehide glue used traditionally. A second application of glue increases the density of the pattern. Glue chip glass can be tempered for strength; the technique can be used with clear or tinted glass.

Silk-Screening

Silk-screened (frit) glass is produced using annealed clear or tinted glass. The glass is washed and ceramic frit paint is silk-screened onto its surface to create a design; the paint is then dried in an oven. Next the glass is heated to very high temperatures, to fire the ceramic frit permanently to the glass; this also serves to heat-strengthen or temper the glass. Reflective and low-e coatings can also be applied to the surface.

Silk-screened glass can be incorporated into insulating or laminated products. Coatings that are water-based polymers are available in custom colors, metallic, crackle, frosted, and other finishes, and are less environmentally damaging than solvent-based coatings. Silk-screened glass can be cut, drilled, polished, and otherwise fabricated.

 Note: Newly cut glass has rough edges that must be polished for safe handling. Beveled edges create a framed appearance by grinding angles into the face of the glass.

Coatings and Films for Glass

Coatings and films change the appearance and performance of glass. Major types of coatings include:

- Epoxy coatings applied to the back of glass pieces with special printing techniques to create designs.
- Coatings that contain glass beads or mica chips to create a reflective or metallic appearance.
- Metallic coatings applied to improve reflection of light and heat and to carry electric current.
- Dichroic coatings are metallic coatings applied to clear or textured glass. They are made of extremely thin layers of titanium or zirconium that are highly reflective of one wavelength of light but transmit a completely different color. The dichroic technique may, however, limit the size of pieces. Dichroic finishes are used on furniture, art glass, and decorative pieces.

Films are applied to glass for a variety of effects, including:

- Mylar films with mirrorlike, reflecting images on one side allow a filtered view from the other side.
- Tinted films designed to change the appearance of glass and alter the color of light passing through it.
- Clear, tough films that are used to increase strength.

CERAMICS

The term *ceramic* covers a wide range of materials that are neither organic (containing carbon) nor metallic and that are formed by heat. Until the middle of the twentieth century, ceramics were predominantly represented by clay-based potter, bricks, and tiles. Cements and glass were sometimes included.

Historical, Cultural, and Architectural Context of Ceramics

Ceramics are so deeply embedded in human history that archeologists use pottery shards as cultural markers the world over. The earliest known ceramic objects have been dated to between 12,000 and 9,000 BCE in South China, Taiwan, and Japan, and around 6,000 BCE in the Mideast. The earliest glazes have been discovered in the Nile Valley of Egypt from around 5000 BCE, made of water-soluble soda and copper mixed with clay. By 1400 BCE, high-temperature ceramics were made in China; glazes and true porcelain were also developed there between 700 and 600 BCE.

Ceramic techniques generally began with pots hand-built from rolled coils. Evidence of the potter's wheel appears in the Indus Vally, China, and the Mideast after 4,000 BCE.

Ceramic tile has been found in the earliest Egyptian pyramids, in Babylon, and in ancient Greek cities. Islamic architectural tile flourished in Persia and in Moorish Spain. Mosaics decorated buildings in Spain and Portugal. By around 1150 CE, ceramic tile was made in Europe. Beautiful majolica tile floors date to the sixteenth-century Italian Renaissance. Tin-glazed faience tile was used architecturally in Antwerp in the mid-sixteenth century. In eighteenth-century India, tiles were imprinted with decorative designs from wood and copper blocks. (See color plate C-25 for a modern mosaic in the Byzantine tradition.)

Starting around 1900, industrial production of ceramics quickly overtook hand-built techniques. The widespread use of manufactured ceramics for indoor plumbing, sewer tile, and bath and kitchen fixtures dominated the twentieth century.

Physical Properties and Types of Ceramics

Ceramic materials are generally hard, porous, and brittle. Ceramics are held together by bonds that tend to break suddenly, rather than stretch or compress out of shape. Although they do deform, they do so very slowly, so this is not usually a factor in their use. The tiny pores commonly found in ceramics concentrate stresses, further reducing tensile strength. There are four basic categories of ceramic products: structural, refractory, whitewares, and technical.

- *Structural ceramics* are used in building construction, and include bricks, pipes, and floor and roof tiles.
- *Refractory products* retain their physical shape and chemical identity when exposed to high temperatures; they are used as kiln linings and crucibles for making glass and steel.
- *Whitewares* include tableware, wall tiles, decorative art objects, and sanitary ware such as toilets.

- *Technical ceramics*, called *fine ceramics* in Japan, are also known as engineering or special ceramics. These are advanced ceramic products used for space, military, and biomedical applications. Technical ceramics often do not contain clay.

Certain ceramics have electrical applications such as semiconductors, surge protectors, and inexpensive gas detectors. There are two major categories of ceramics that have special conductive properties: piezoelectric and pyroelectric.

Manufacturing Process for Ceramics

Ceramic forming techniques include shaping by hand (sometimes including a rotation process called *throwing*), slip casting, tape casting (used for making very thin ceramic capacitors), injection molding, dry pressing, and other variations. A few methods use a hybrid between the two approaches. A roughly held together object (called a green body) is made in almost any way imaginable, then baked in a kiln, where diffusion processes cause the green body to shrink. The pores in the object close up, resulting in a denser, stronger product. The firing is done at a temperature below the melting point of the ceramic.

Environmental and Health Impacts of Ceramics

Clay, widely available in soils, is used as the basis of many ceramics. Traditionally, ceramics were made locally near clay pits; now they are often made near sources of fuel. The process of firing clay into ceramic products uses energy. The use of recycled glass (particularly green or mixed colors that may be difficult to reuse otherwise) to substitute for some or all of the clay in ceramic tiles reduces the amount of energy needed to produce the tiles.

Ceramic products are heavy, and breakage is common. Shipping costs can be prohibitive, and energy is used for transportation. Some glazed finishes contain elements that may have undesirable environmental or health effects, for example, lead. Ceramic finishes may be slippery, so their use for floors must be carefully considered in regard to safety.

Interior Applications for Ceramics

Earthenware is usually made from red, white, or buff clays (including kaolin), quartz, and feldspar. Earthenware pottery tends to be coarse, hard, and opaque; it will crack or break with relative ease. Although it may be made very thin, it lacks the translucency and strength of porcelain. It is more porous (absorbing up to 10 percent water) and less durable than stoneware. The low cost of materials and ease of working make earthenware objects inexpensive to produce, but they will remain highly porous unless glazed and are not usually freeze-resistant when moist.

Ceramic Tile Glazes

- *Bright glaze:* High gloss with or without color.
- *Clear glaze:* Transparent glaze with or without color.
- *Crystalline glaze:* Contains microscopic crystals.
- *Fritted glaze:* All or part of fluxing ingredients are prefused.
- *Mat glaze:* Low-gloss glaze with or without color.
- *Opaque glaze:* Nontransparent glaze with or without color.
- *Raw glaze:* Compounded primarily from raw constituents, with no prefused materials.
- *Semimat glaze:* Medium gloss with or without color.
- *Speckled glaze:* Contains granules of oxides or ceramic stains of contrasting colors.

Stoneware could be described as man-made stone. It is fired at higher temperatures than earthenware, and absorbs up to 5 percent water. It is widely used for cookware and for some ceramic sculptures and fireplace surrounds. Stoneware wall tiles are often cast with relief designs, and are sometimes called porcelain stoneware tiles. Stoneware floor tiles are glazed tiles pressed from ceramic dust and usually given a single firing. They are also known as vitrified floor tile, glazed ceramic floor tile, or ceramic flooring.

Porcelain is a fine, white, strong, vitreous translucent ceramic that is used to make tableware, sanitary ceramics, decorative pieces, and tile. Its high resistance to the passage of electricity makes porcelain an excellent insulating material. It is also used in dentistry, to make false teeth, caps, and crowns. Porcelain usually contains kaolin, a fine white clay that is biscuit-fired at a lower temperature, then glazed and fired again at a high temperature. Porcelain enamel is a hard, shiny glass surface that is fused onto metal or another ceramic surface.

Ceramic tiles are made of clay, sometimes with other materials, and fired in a kiln. Natural clay tiles are unglazed, with muted earth colors. Porcelain tiles can have bright colors and are vitreous (dense and impervious).

Increasing competition worldwide has resulted in some lowering of prices for ceramic tiles and installation; consequently, tile sales continue to increase rapidly. It is a product with a high-profit margin.

Ceramic wall tiles are modular surfacing units of fired clay and other ceramic materials. They provide a permanent, durable, waterproof surface for interior walls, and are available in bright or matte glazes in a wide range of colors and surface designs. Wall tiles are usually 5/16-inch (8-mm) thick. They are available in square, hexagon, and octagon shapes.

Tile flooring materials are solid and durable. Depending on the shape of the individual pieces and the pattern in which they are laid, these flooring materials can have a cool, formal appearance or convey an informal feeling to a room. Tile flooring is set with grout, which is available in a variety of colors and can be selected to blend or contrast with the flooring material. (See color plate C-27 for a contemporary handmade tile floor in historic design.)

Ceramic mosaic tiles are usually 1/4-inch (6-mm) thick. They are available in sheets of 1- or 2-inch (25- or 51-mm) square tiles; 1 × 2 inch (25 × 51 mm) rectangles and 1- and 2-inch hexagons are also available. Tile *coves* make the transition from wall surfaces to floors. The top edge of the cove may be flat (for use with wall tiles), or bullnosed

Table 4-3 Ceramic Absorption Levels

Type	Absorption	Comments	Uses
Impervious	Less than 0.5% moisture absorption	Frostproof	Can be used outdoors and on building.
Vitreous	Glasslike; absorbs less than 3%	May be called frost-resistant; cannot be used where freeze and thaw conditions exist.	Plumbing fixtures, floors, wet areas
Semivitreous	Water absorption between 3% and 7%	Can be cracked when exposed to freeze and thaw conditions.	Indoor use only: walls and floors
Nonvitreous	Water absorption of 7% or greater	Not suitable for continually wet locations; not suitable flooring	Indoors, as wall tile

(for use with thinner wall finishes). The bottoms of cove bases are either flat or coved to meet the height of floor tiles.

Quarry tiles and pavers are larger modular flooring materials. Quarry tiles are unglazed units of heat-hardened clay. Larger-sized ceramic tile are available in a range of sizes and patterns, some of which mimic natural stone; they are practically impervious to moisture, dirt, and stains. Quarry tiles and pavers are available in 3/18-, 1/2-, and 3/4-inch (10-, 12-, and 19-mm) thicknesses.

 Note: The Tile Council of North America (TCNA) publishes the *Handbook for Ceramic Tile Installation*. Floor and wall tile characteristics and installation are covered in Chapters 9 and 10, respectively.

Maintenance and Disposal of Ceramics

Loose tiles can result from improper installation and substrate problems, and usually have to be replaced. Where the tile is difficult to replace, epoxy resin can be injected underneath the tile to rebond the tile to the substrate.

Damaged or unwanted tile is removed by first cleaning out as much of the grout as possible on all sides of the tiles that are to be taken out. A dry cut saw is used to cut the tile diagonally through to the substrate. The pieces are then removed with a chisel, along with as much of the bonding material as possible. The replacement tile is adhered with the same adhesive used originally, and beaten in softly to limit slippage. It is then cured and later grouted. The grout adjacent to the tile can be thoroughly cleaned to help match the new grout. (See color plate C-26, Ceramic mosaic tile installation repair.)

Tile will last for centuries, whether it is in a building or a landfill. Decorative tiles can be reused, adding to their appeal as a sustainable material. Ceramic mosaic artists are always on the lookout for broken tiles and other ceramics.

Figure C-1 Paint color restoration, The Mount, Lenox, Massachusetts Photo by David Dashiell, the Mount.

Figure C-2 Sullivan Building, Salem State College, Massachusetts. Durable, easily maintained finishes in public-access space.

Figure C-4 Senior's residence, Weston, Massachusetts. Designed for comfort and safety.

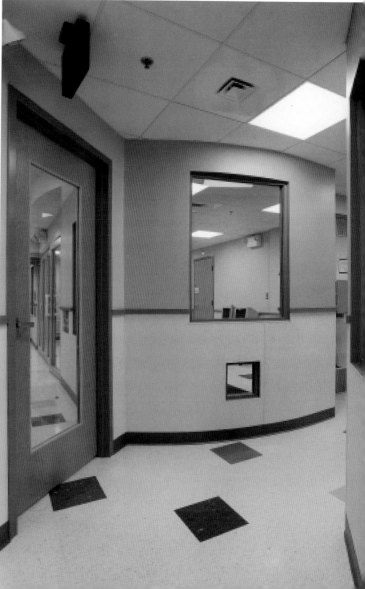

Figure C-3 Children's Quarters at Massachusetts General Hospital's Institute of Health Professions, Boston. The design of this health care center combines smooth, easily cleaned surfaces with low glazing. Photo by L. Barry Heatherington. Design by Silverman Trykowski Associates.

Figure C-5 Cement-based floor finish overlay. Courtesy Advanced Concrete Enhancement.

Figure C-6 Acid-stained concrete. © Tru-Glaze Ltd, 2006.

Figure C-7 Precast concrete bench. An example of concrete furniture. Photography courtesy of Buddy Rhodes Studio.

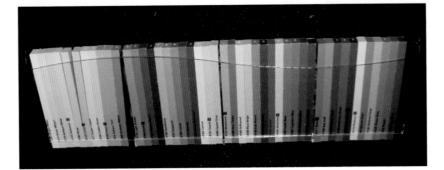

Figure C-8 Tile grout colors

Figure C-9 Precast terrazzo wall tile installation. Courtesy of Fritz Tile.

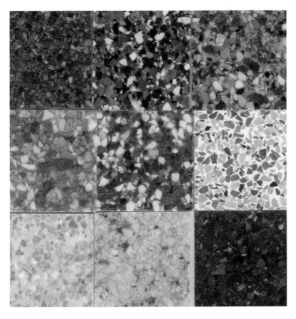

Figure C-10 Terrazzo samples

Figure C-12 Sandstone with embedded fossil

Figure C-11 Granite quarry, Halibut Point, Massachusetts.

Figure C-15 Engineered composite stone

Figure C-13 Taj Mahal *pietra dura* inlays

Figure C-14 Stone medallion. Courtesy of Urban Archaeology.

Figure C-16 Skara Brae house, Orkney Islands, Scotland. © 2004 by Roger Butterfield.

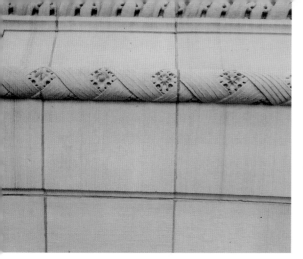

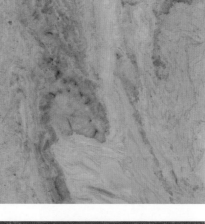

Figure C-17 *(above left)* Limestone carving

Figure C-24 *(above right)* Sandblasted (left) and acid-etched glass (right)

Figure C-18 *(left)* Unfilled travertine has visible pores.

Figure C-19 *(right)* Filled travertine loses some of its visual interest but is easier to maintain.

Figure C-20 *(left)* Marble: majestic pink

Figure C-21 *(right)* Marble: dune

Figure C-22 *(left)* Slate: shengli

Figure C-23 *(right)* Slate: African gold

Figure C-25 *(above)*
Virgin of Guadeloupe,
a Byzantine-style mosaic.
© 2004–2006 by Gina Hubler
Design Impact;
www.designimp.com.

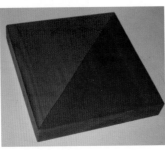

Figure C-28 Wood stains with
resin finish

Figure C-26 Ceramic mosaic
tile installation repair

Figure C-27 *(right)*
Handmade tile floor
© 2001 by Tile Source Inc.,
David Malkin.

Figure C-29 *(above right)*
Weathered wood door
exemplifies finishes intended
to show the effects of time.

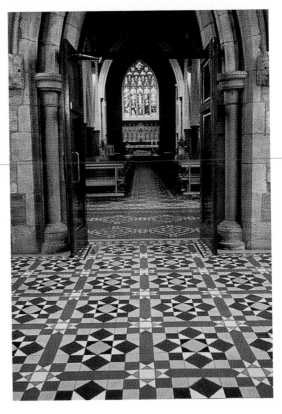

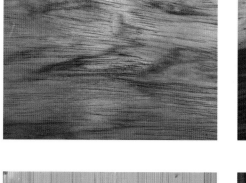

Figure C-30 *(left)* Albizia veneer Courtesy of hobbithouseinc.com.

Figure C-31 *(right)* Cocobolo Courtesy of hobbithouseinc.com.

Figure C-32 *(left)* Bamboo

Figure C-33 *(right)* Ebony Macassar veneer. Courtesy of hobbithouseinc.com.

Figure C-34 *(left)* Red elm Courtesy of hobbithouseinc.com.

Figure C-35 *(right)* Douglas fir flat-cut veneer. Courtesy of hobbithouseinc.com.

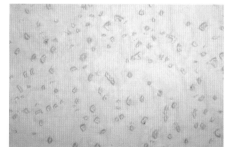

Figure C-36 *(left)* Bird's-eye maple. Courtesy of hobbithouseinc.com.

Figure C-37 *(right)* Rosewood Courtesy of hobbithouseinc.com.

Figure C-38 Sipo. Courtesy of hobbithouseinc.com. (See wood listings in Appendix A.)

Figure C-39 Electrodeposition coating on cast aluminum

Figure C-40 *(above right)* Powder-coating process

Figure C-41 *(below)* Welder

Figure C-42 *(below right)* Corrugated galvanized steel, Iguana
Cantina, Waltham, Massachusetts. Chrome-finish stools.
Corky Binggeli Interior Design.

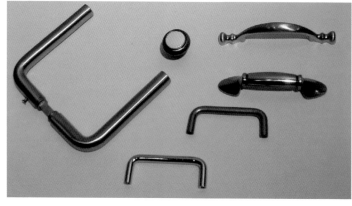

Figure C-44 Bronze doors

Figure C-43 Architectural bronze and stainless steel hardware. (Photo by author.)

Figure C-45 Rust on concrete

Figure C-46 Bronze patina

Figure C-47 *(left)* Copper, natural finish

Figure C-48 *(right)* Copper aging

Figure C-49 *(left)* White metal finish

Figure C-50 *(right)* Nickel silver finish

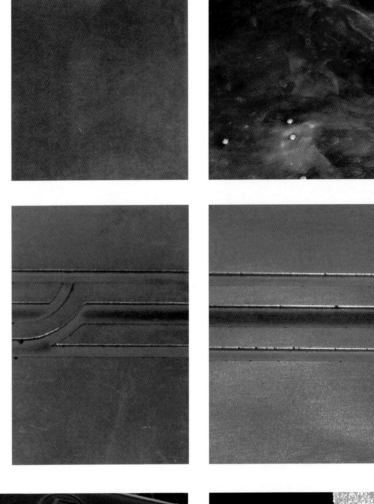

Figure C-51 Acrylic samples

Figure C-52 Polyester resin panels

Figure C-54 Ceramic mosaic floor tiles and glazed ceramic wall tiles.

Figure C-53 Porcelain ceramic floor tile. Courtesy of Florida Tile, Inc.

Figure C-56 Quarry tiles

Figure C-55 Art mosaic floor, Vancouver

Figure C-58 Vinyl composition tile

Figure C-57 Cork flooring. Courtesy of Dodge-Regupol Inc.

Figure C-59 Green board

Figure C-60 Solid pine paneling of horizontal boards with vertical battens.

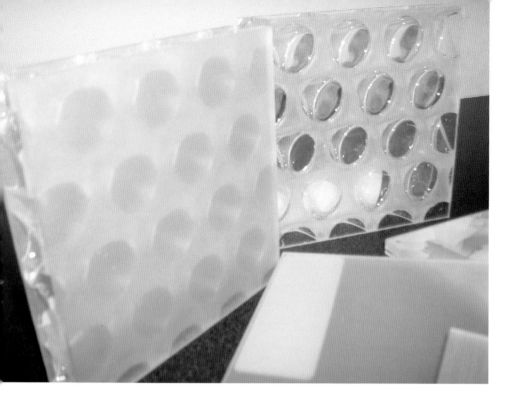

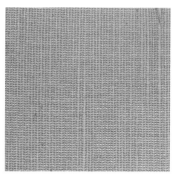

Figure C-63 Natural textile wallcovering by Newport Coast

Figure C-61 Architectural resin panels

Figure C-62 Wallpaper by Newport Coast

Figure C-64 Commercial nonvinyl wallcovering, by Innovations in Wallcoverings. Alternatives to vinyl are available in a wide variety of chemical composition that may meet environmental concerns.

Figure C-66 Stamped metal tile in grid. Zaftig's Eatery, Brookline, Massachusetts. Corky Binggeli Interior Design.

Figure C-67 Plastic laminate "Boomerang" countertop by Formica

Figure C-65 Sloped ceiling, Rani Indian Bistro. The existing acoustic tile was painted blue and studded with fiber optic stars. Rough wood lumber slants downward to suggest a patio lattice. Corky Binggeli Interior Design.

Figure C-68 Soapstone countertop. Courtesy of Green Mountain Soapstone Corporation.

Figure C-69 Curved plastic laminate countertop, Rancatore's Ice Cream, Belmont, Massachusetts. Corky Binggeli Interior Design.

Figure C-70 Tile countertop and backsplash. Photo by Dorothy Deák.

Figure C-71 Wood finishes on chest. Courtesy of Creative Woods Ready to Finish Furniture.

Figure C-72 Milk paint on corner cupboard. Designed and built by Paul Bennett.

Figure C-74 Custom-painted wall, Carberry's Bakery, Somerville, Massachusetts. Finish by Medusa.

Figure C-75 Loom-woven rug detail. Photo by Jessica Burko. Courtesy of Claudia Mills Studio.

Figure C-73 Paint finish on wood. Designed and built by Paul Bennett.

Figure C-76 Hand-loom-woven cotton runner. Photo by Jessica Burko. Courtesy of Claudia Mills Studio.

Wood and Wood Products 5

ood is a strong, durable construction material that is lightweight and easy to work with. Wood from trees and shrubs is part of a tough, fibrous, cellular living organism, and no two pieces are exactly alike.

Historical, Cultural, and Architectural Context of Wood

In any part of the world where trees are plentiful, wood has been used to provide fuel and shelter. However, because it does not endure the elements as well as stone, wood is less well represented in the anthropological record.

In ancient Egypt, columns in houses were usually red-painted wood shafts with painted capitals in the form of stylized flowers or leaves. Egyptian furniture made of wood was sometimes finished with a thin layer of wood veneer over a less expensive wood base. Egyptian furniture makers used plywood, bonding crisscrossed thin wood layers with pegs.

In general, traditional Chinese buildings with strong horizontal lines were made of wood. The roof had wide eaves (extensions of the roof beyond the building's walls) supported by wooden brackets, which were sometimes highly decorated and complex constructions.

Ancient Greek houses were sparsely furnished with lightly ornamented, elegant, and functional pieces. Furniture was made of beech, citrus, oak, or willow, and some pieces included marble or bronze.

Roman residential buildings contained well-made furniture derived from Greek models. Extravagant tables of citrus wood, cypress, marble, and bronze were inlaid with gemstones and precious metals.

Anglo-Saxon huts in Britain were built on frames of wood timbers, with wooden planks nailed to the timbers for walls. Some walls were made of thin sticks called wattles, which were woven into panels and daubed with layers of mud and straw (wattle-and-daub construction).

In England and northern Europe, Romanesque furniture was mostly made of walnut and oak; beech and fir were used in southern Germany, and cypress in Italy. Strong wood planks were roughly carved with patterns within a roundel (circular shape). *Turning*, the process of working a piece of wood with a cutting tool while it is spun on a lathe, was used for long thin pieces of wood.

Evidence of Russian wooden architecture from around 860 is preserved in houses, mills, and barns that were constructed with skill and intricacy. Square-frame churches with simple, steep, pointed roofs are similar to an ordinary peasant's hut. Centuries of talented local craftsmanship are visible in a collection of buildings on the island of Kizhi on Lake Onega.

Gothic furniture was decorated with miniature architectural elements, including pointed arches, small-scale tracery, rose windows, buttresses, finials, and crockets. Natural-finish oak and some walnut were the preferred woods for heavy rectilinear pieces assembled with wooden dowels and joints. Furniture panels were carved with linenfold and tracery motifs and with coats of arms.

Because wood is often not readily available in desert regions, it is traditionally reserved in Islamic interiors for door and wall panels, tie beams, and furnishings, and is often

Figure 5-1 Islamic open wood grille

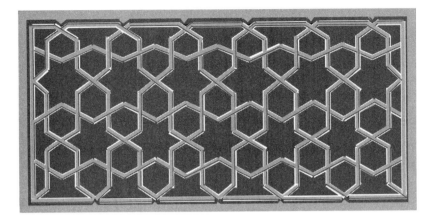

decorated with elaborate geometrically stylized floral motifs set into rectangles, ovals, or lozenges (diamond shapes) enriched with inlays of bone, ivory, and mother-of-pearl.

Built around 1470 during the Renaissance in Italy, the Ducal Palace at Urbino still contains a small room called a *studiolo* that is lined with inlaid wood, which, using a technique called *intarsia*, simulates projecting shelves, cabinets with open doors, books, and musical instruments. During the Late Renaissance in Italy (1550–1600), smooth, simple wood-paneled walls with natural or painted pattern finishes were introduced. By 1450, walnut cabinet wood, with its beautiful grain and rich brown color, available over 3 feet (1 m) wide, was used for almost all furniture, including single-piece tabletops or panel fields.

Late French Renaissance furniture shows the influence of Italian and Spanish Flanders in bun-shaped Flemish feet for casework. Vertical wood elements were designed as classical columns or spiral turnings. Table and cabinet legs braced with X-shaped flat

Figure 5-2 Inlaid wood that once required a steady hand is today done by laser cutting.

stretchers had a vase form or finial at their crossing. Walnut, oak, and ebony dominate, and the most expensive pieces have ornaments carved or inlaid with contrasting colored wood, tortoiseshell, semiprecious stones, or gilt bronze.

During England's Restoration period (1660–1688), the walls in many buildings designed by Sir Christopher Wren (1632–1723) were paneled from the dado cap to the wood cornice, as at Versailles, with rectangular panels that featured heavy molding. The natural oak or walnut panels were finished with poppy or linseed oil. Less expensive fir and deal (pine) paneling was often grained to look like walnut or olive. During the William and Mary period (1688–1725), *marquetry* reappeared in elaborate floral patterns of colored woods and natural or stained ivory veneers. Wall and table mirrors were made with veneer frames with broken, curved top lines.

Spanish Renaissance furniture was principally made of walnut, as well as chestnut, cedar, oak, pine, pear, box, and orange, with inlays of ebony, ivory, and tortoiseshell. In 1550, Spain began recycling ship mahogany from its West Indies colonies as a cabinet wood. Lesser woods and lower-quality work were covered with paint, a practice that continues today.

Portuguese Renaissance furniture showed East Indian and Chinese influences during the Manuelino period (1495–1521) with crustaceans and tropical vegetable forms in extravagantly rich detail. Indo-Portuguese furniture manufactured in Goa on India's Malabar Coast was made of teak, ebony, or amboyna wood with ivory inlays or veneer.

Baroque cabinet furniture has curving, bulging drawer fronts and doors, and lathe-turned round ball or bulbous legs. Veneers were used to create varied color and patterns on wood surfaces, often with inlays of ivory, tortoiseshell, or silver. Most pieces were of oak and walnut with inlays and marquetry of exotic woods such as tulip and zebrawood. Armoires and commodes (low two- or three-drawer chests) were ornamented with inlaid marquetry with ivory, shell, brass, pewter, silver, or richly colored marble tops. French provincial pieces were characterized by flowing carved detail on solid wood, which was usually oak, or walnut, or from fruit trees such as apple, cherry, or pear. In the early nineteenth century, the lighter woods and black painted details of the Biedermeier style spread from Germany to Austria and Switzerland. Later pieces were enriched with colored woods, including maple, birch, and elm. Some larger chests and cabinets were embellished with marquetry.

Starting in the fifteenth century, Japanese master carpenters introduced dramatic changes in building techniques. The ripsaw and bench plane made it easier to produce smooth boards. Construction diagrams and prenumbered pillars and modular components increased efficiency. These carpenters traditionally fully mastered and controlled every phase of residential construction, developing technical skill and precision in only a few standard forms; this enabled them to perform high-quality work with minimal time and materials. Working drawings were unnecessary and unexpected construction problems unknown.

New Zealand's Maori people built large plank houses in rectangular, oval, and circular shapes. The sculpture of the Maori was literally part of the structure of the building. Their magnificent carved wall panels and tall posts supported the painted roof structure.

Colonists along the eastern coast of North America brought building traditions from Holland, France, Spain, and England for their houses, barns, sheds, churches, and meeting houses. Early houses were modest, simple, and functional, with minimal details. As communities developed in New England, they built sturdier small wood houses in the medieval style, with the second floor usually projecting over the first. The structure of huge oak timbers carefully cut and fitted together remained visible inside the building. The floors were covered with wide wood planks. The exterior frame of early houses was covered with short hand-hewn clapboards, and the interior with wide boards.

Colonial North American furniture was usually made of native pine, cherry, oak, or hickory. The old-growth forests provided very wide solid wood boards for tables and chests. Furniture was assembled with hand-cut joints, box (finger) joints, dovetails, and mortise-and-tenon joints. Decorative small cabinets with drawers inside combined local woods such as oak, pine, walnut, apple, and red cedar.

In 1893, architect Frank Lloyd Wright (1867–1959) opened his own practice using brick, stone, plain concrete, and natural woods as both structural and finish materials inside and out. Finnish architect and designer Alvar Aalto's (1898–1976) warm, humanely modern furniture of bent plywood and laminates was internationally recognized, widely produced, and enduringly popular. The undulating auditorium ceiling in

Figure 5-3 Colonial American bed folds up against wall.

Figure 5-4 Wood slab table, designed by Frank Lloyd Wright

Figure 5-5 Tree cross section

- Bark
- Cambium
- Sapwood
- Heartwood
- Growth rings
- Pith

his Library at Viipuri (1935) was made of strips of natural wood, and his molded plywood furniture of Finnish birch was used to create a simple but warm interior.

Physical Properties, Characteristics, and Types of Wood

A tree grows in concentric circles called growth rings; the oldest is in the center. These vary in color annually beginning when the sap begins to flow in the spring and lasting until the onset of cold weather, when it slows down. Trees from climates with defined seasons have these annular rings; where growth continues at a constant rate, they are absent. Nutrients are carried up the tree trunk through the lighter-colored sapwood. The darker and denser heartwood consists of dead cells. Thin sapwood is characteristic of such trees as black locust, chestnut, mulberry, osage-orange, and sassafras. In ash, beech, maple, hackberry, hickory, and pine, thick sapwood is the norm.

Tree species are classified as either *softwoods* or *hardwoods*, but these terms do not accurately describe whether the wood in question is hard or dense. Softwoods are from conifers (cone-bearing trees) that have needles, and are usually evergreen. Hardwoods are from deciduous trees, which shed their leaves seasonally, although some are evergreen.

Note: There is a huge number of wood species. Many species have multiple common names in different places of origin. Those listed in Appendix A have applications in building interiors and furniture.

As a tree ages, many of its limbs will die, leaving *knots* in the wood where limbs were attached. The knots are covered over by further growth, and are usually not visible on the log's surface. Most knots appear in the inner heartwood; fewer are found in the sapwood of older forest-grown trees. In a piece of sawn lumber, they look like circular, cross-grained darker masses. When wood is graded for structural use, the number of knots is limited by size and location.

Shakes are separations along the grain of a wood piece, usually between the annual rings, that are created by stresses on a tree while it is standing or when it is felled. *Pitch pockets* are well-defined openings for containing solid or liquid pitch between the annual rings of a softwood.

The *grain* of wood refers to the appearance and texture of its pores. Grain is classified as open or closed (tight), and can be modified with wood filler. The grain creates a

Figure 5-6 Broken wood grain

pattern and texture that is influenced by the manner in which the wood is cut. Natural wood colors are warm yellows, reds, and browns, and add great beauty to the material. Colors can be modified by stain, and often change with exposure to air and light.

Wood is selected for its density and hardness, as well as its ability to take a finish. Woods classified as softwoods are generally less dense and hard than hardwoods, but this is not always the case, so an interior designer must be familiar with the specific properties of the wood selected. Solid softwoods are used primarily in building construction and framing, and sometimes for finish work that is painted. Solid hardwoods are used for interior finishes, including paneling and flooring, for the edges and legs of furniture, and for *architectural millwork* (finished woodwork, cabinetry, and carving). Hardwoods are often given a clear finish to accentuate the appearance of the grain. Solid wood is usually flat cut, quarter cut, or rift cut, and each affects the pattern of the grain.

There is a rough correlation between density of a wood and its strength. Black ironwood is one of the most dense woods.

Solid wood is used where durability and strength are primary concerns, such as for chair legs or table edges. If damaged, solid wood can be sanded down and refinished. Below a moisture content of about 30 percent, wood expands as it absorbs moisture and shrinks as it loses moisture. The detailing and construction of wood joints must take this shrinkage and expansion into account.

Solid wood used for construction and framing is referred to as *lumber*, and categorized in nominal sizes. By the time pieces are planed and sanded for sale as dimension lumber, a nominal 2 × 3 is reduced to an actual 1–1/2 × 2–1/2 inch (38 × 64 mm) dressed size.

Wood veneers are very thin slices of wood applied to the surfaces of furniture, decorative objects, and wall paneling. By slicing a log of valuable wood into thin layers, the log can yield a high quantity of beautiful veneer.

Wood composite panels (composition boards) include plywood, particleboard, medium-density fiberboard (MDF), hardboard, and oriented strand board (OSB). Made of layers or particles of wood and adhesives, they provide flat surfaces wider than

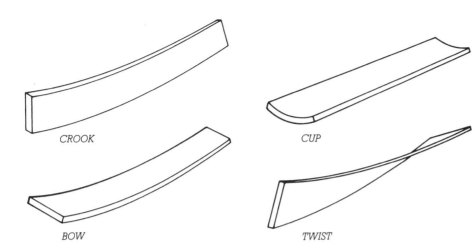

Figure 5-7 Dimension lumber seasoning distortions
Reproduced by permission of the publisher from Edward Allen and Joseph Iano, *Fundamentals of Building Construction: Materials and Methods,* 4th ed. (Hoboken, NJ: John Wiley & Sons, Inc.), © 2004 by John Wiley & Sons, Inc.

CROOK

CUP

BOW

TWIST

Figure 5-8 Wood veneer

those available with solid wood. Plywood has significant structural strength, but some of the composition boards are limited to nonstructural uses.

 Note: The environmental implications of the adhesives used in wood composite panels are examined in the sidebar on page 112.

Wood products are finished with fillers, stains, aniline dyes produced from coal tar, oil, lacquer, varnish, and polyester and polyurethane finishes. The topcoat protects the wood surface from permanent staining by sealing the pores; it also protects against damage caused by heat, dirt, and spills, and enhances the beauty of the wood grain and color. Pieces may be factory finished or finished on the job site.

Aesthetic Qualities of Wood

The natural beauty and warmth of wood invite the eye and hand. The beauty inherent in wood has been celebrated wherever trees grow, in sculpture, carved functional objects, and architecture.

Wood is a flexible and fairly elastic material. It can be used as linear posts and beams, planar boards, and volumetric solids as in furniture and sculpture. The color of a tree's sapwood and heartwood, the patterns made by its growth rings, and the texture of its grain all add to the beauty of its wood. Most woods have a distinctive and pleasant odor. Wood is also used for musical instruments because of its resonant ability.

The way that lumber is cut from a log affects its strength and appearance. Grain patterns will vary, and the grain may be raised. The cut affects how the wood will twist or warp, wear unevenly, and shrink and swell. (See color plate C-29 for weathered wood door.)

Manufacturing Processes for Wood

Grain direction determines the use of wood as a structural material. Wood adapts to tensile and compressive forces best in a direction parallel to the grain. Tensile forces perpendicular to the grain will cause the wood to split. Shear strength is greater across wood's grain than parallel to the grain.

- *Plain-sawing* a squared log into boards with evenly spaced parallel cuts results in flat grain lumber that varies in grain patterns. Plain-sawn boards tend to twist and cup, and wear unevenly. The grain is often raised. Plain-sawn wood shrinks and swells less in thickness than in width.
- *Quarter-sawing* logs at approximately right angles to the annual rings results in edge or vertical grain lumber with more even grain patterns. Quarter-sawn lumber wears more evenly with less raised grain and warping, and has a more uniform surface appearance. It shrinks and swells less in width and more in thickness. The process is more expensive than plain-sawing and results in more cutting waste.

Figure 5-9 Plain-sawn wood

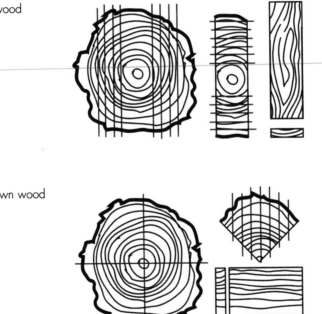

Figure 5-10 Quarter-sawn wood

- *Rift-sawn* lumber is cut with the growth rings at 30 to 60 degrees to the face of the board. In some species, for example oak, rift-sawing produces flecks on the surface of the board.

Wood is seasoned to increase its strength, stability, and resistance to fungi, insects, and decay. This involves drying it to reduce its moisture content, either by air-drying or kiln-drying under controlled heat, air circulation, and humidity conditions.

- *Checks* are lengthwise separations of wood across the annual rings. These are caused by uneven or rapid shrinking during the seasoning process.
- *Warping* is usually caused by uneven drying during the seasoning process or by a change in moisture content.
- *Cup* is a curvature across the face of a wood piece. *Bow* is a curvature along its length. *Crook* is a curvature along its edge.
- *Twist* results from the turning of the edges of a piece of wood in opposite directions.

Wood is decay-resistant when its moisture content is under 20 percent. It will not rot if it is installed and maintained below this moisture content level. Species naturally resistant to decay-causing fungi include redwood, cedar, bald cypress, black locust, and black walnut. Insect-resistant species include redwood, eastern red cedar, and bald cypress.

Preservative treatments intended to protect wood from decay and insect attack include pressure treatment and preservatives.

- Pressure treatment is the most effective when wood will be in contact with the ground.
- Waterborne preservatives leave the wood clean, odorless, and readily paintable, and do not leach out when exposed to weather.
- Oilborne preservatives may discolor the wood, but the treated wood is paintable. The oilborne preservative pentachlorophenol is highly toxic.

The most widely used outdoor pressure treatment for wood since the 1970s has been chromated copper arsenate (CCA). It consists of chromium, copper, and arsenic, and has been banned from most residential use by the United States Environmental Protection Agency (EPA) since 2003. The EPA lists the following alternative wood preservatives:

- ACQ is a water-based fungicide and insecticide containing copper oxide and quaternary ammonium compound that is approved for exterior use by the EPA.
- Borates, also known as inorganic boron, consist of the chemical octaborate tetrahydrate (DOT). Borates occur naturally in trace amounts in rocks, soil, water, and all living things, and have a low level of toxicity. Borates are used for wood furnishings and aboveground and interior construction protected from weather; it may be subject to moisture damage.
- Copper azole is a water-based fungicide and insecticide consisting primarily of copper, with azole as tebuconazole. It is used on softwoods for millwork, exterior uses, and composite wood products, and may be used in contact with ground and fresh or saltwater.
- Cyproconazole formula 360SL is a water-based fungicide used aboveground for industrial and commercial millwork and exterior applications. It contains cyproconazole and didecyldimethylammonium chloride (DDAC) and is applied as a surface treatment or pressure impregnation.

- Propiconazole formula 100 SL is a water-based surface- or pressure-applied fungicide for aboveground use for industrial and commercial millwork. It may not be used in contact with food.
- Creosote is made of coal tar. Treatment leaves a surface residue that is oily and colored, and the odor of creosote remains for a long period. Creosote is used only in commercial applications such as telephone poles and marine uses, and is currently being reassessed by the EPA.
- Nonstructural alternatives to treated wood include recycled plastic/wood fiber composites, virgin vinyl, high-density polyethelyne (HDPE), and rubber lumber (old tires, plus plastic).
- Structural alternatives to treated wood include redwood, cedar, or cypress; mahogany and ironwoods (Ipe), supplies of which are depleted; and tropical hardwoods from sustainably managed forests managed by the Forest Stewardship Council (which are often not locally grown).

Hardwood is graded according to the amount of clear, usable lumber in a piece that may be cut into smaller pieces of a certain grade and side. Softwood is classified as either yard lumber or factory and shop lumber.

Yard lumber is softwood lumber intended for general building purposes, including boards, dimension lumber, and timbers. *Boards* are less than 2 inches (51 mm) thick and 2 inches (51 mm) or more wide. They are graded for appearance rather than strength. Boards are used as siding, subflooring, and interior trim.

Dimension lumber is from 2 to 4 inches (51 to 102 mm) thick and 2 inches (51 mm) or more wide. Dimension lumber is graded for strength rather than appearance, and is used for general construction. Dimension lumber is categorized as joists and planks, light framing, or decking.

- Joists and planks are from 2 to 4 inches (5 to 10 cm) thick and more than 4 inches (100 mm) wide. They are graded primarily for bending strength when loaded either on the narrow face as a joist or on the wide face as a plank.
- Light framing is 2 to 4 inches (50 to 100 mm) thick and 2 to 4 inches (5 to 10 mm) wide. Light framing is intended for use where high strength is not required.
- Decking is 2 to 4 inches (50 to 100 mm) thick and 4 inches (100 mm) or more wide. Decking is graded primarily with respect to bending strength when loaded on the wide face.

Timbers are 5 inches (125 mm) or more in their smallest dimension. Timbers are graded for strength and serviceability, and are often stocked in green, undressed condition.

Structural lumber consists of dimension lumber and timbers graded either by visual inspection or mechanically on the basis of strength and intended use.

- Beams and stringers are structural lumber types at least 5 inches (125 mm) thick and with a width more than 2 inches (51 mm) greater than the thickness. They are graded primarily for bending strength when loaded on the narrow face.
- Posts and timbers are 5 inches × 5 inches (125 × 125 mm) or larger, with a width not more than 2 inches (51 mm) greater than the thickness. They are used primarily as columns for carrying a load along their axis.

Structural lumber may be graded visually by trained inspectors who look for quality-reducing characteristics that would affect strength, appearance, or utility. Structural lumber may also be graded by a machine that flexes a test specimen, measures its resistance to bending, calculates its modulus of elasticity, and computes the appropriate stress grade. The machine also factors in the effects of knots, slope of grain, density, and moisture content.

Factory and shop lumber is sawn or selected primarily for further manufacture into doors, windows, and millwork. It is graded according to the amount of usable wood that will produce cuttings of a specified size and quality.

Lumber is specified by species and grade, with each piece graded for structural strength and appearance. Lumber is measured in board feet: 1 board foot is equal o the volume of a piece whose nominal dimensions are 12 inches (300 mm) square and 1 inch (25 mm) thick. It is generally available in lengths from 6 to 24 feet (1.8 to 7.2 m), measured in multiples of 2 feet (.6 m).

Nominal dimensions are the dimensions of a piece of lumber before drying and surfacing. These are used for convenience in defining size and computing quantity. Nominal dimensions are always written without inch marks, for example, 2 × 4.

Dressed sizes are the actual dimensions of a piece of lumber after seasoning and surfacing. Dressed sizes are from 3/8 inch to 3/4 inch (10 to 19 mm) less than the nominal dimensions. For dressed sizes up to nominal dimensions of 2 inches, (50 mm), subtract 1/4 inch (6 mm). For nominal dimensions from 2 to 6 inches (51 to 150 mm) subtract 1/2 inch (13 mm). Subtract 3/4 inch (19 mm) from nominal dimensions over 6 inches (150 mm).

Environmental Impact of Wood

Wood has the environmental advantages of being a natural, renewable material with a very low level of embodied energy. Although it can be grown, harvested, and used at a rate that maintains its supply, tropical and old-growth forests continue to be depleted at an unsustainable rate. Old-growth timber takes years—even centuries—to develop. According to Greenpeace International (www.greenpeace.org) the largest remaining old-growth forests are in Brazil's Amazon jungle. Old forests in North America, Northern Asia, and Europe are fragmented and continue to shrink in size. In South Asia, 70 percent of old-growth forest in Indonesia and 60 percent of that in New Guinea have already been cut. Worldwide, only 8 percent of old-growth forests are strictly protected.

Old-growth lumber products are highly valued for their narrow grain and wide boards. These qualities are not as important where wood is to receive an opaque stain or paint, or will be cut into narrower boards. Laminated wood timbers can be substituted for large sizes of old-growth lumber.

Tropical hardwoods are called by so many different names in different places that it is difficult to determine their origin and species. Verifying that the wood is certified as sustainably grown is one way to avoid using endangered tree species.

See Appendix: Woods Used in Interiors for names and characteristics of woods.

Sustainable practices for wood include maintaining a sufficient amount and broad variety of mature, naturally occurring trees; properly maintaining the health of soil, water, air, and the entire ecosystems; and preserving the integrity of wildlife habitats. Sustainable forestry practices preserve the natural biodiversity of forests and communities that depend on them for their survival.

The environmental impact of wood use in building interiors involves concerns about volatile organic compounds (VOCs), which have led to the development of water-based finishes for wood. As mentioned above, the adhesives in wood composite panels such as particle board may also have significant environmental impact.

Interior Applications for Wood

Engineered wood, also called *composite* wood, includes a wide variety of material made from wood strands, fibers, particles, or veneers bound together with adhesives. Engineered wood products are made from sawmill scraps and wood waste. Similar products are made from vegetable fibers rather than wood, including rye straw, white straw, hemp stalks, and sugarcane residue.

Engineered wood has a number of advantages over solid wood. It can be designed for the requirements of a specific purpose. Even small trees, small pieces of wood, and wood with defects can be used to produce large panels. Engineered wood products are often strong and may warp less from humid conditions than solid wood (this is not true of particleboards and fiberboards, unless they have been sealed).

Adhesives in Engineered Wood

Some of the adhesives used in engineered wood may be toxic.
- *Urea-formaldehyde (UF)* resins are the most common and least expensive adhesives, but they are not waterproof and can release formaldehyde.
- *Phenol-formaldehyde (PF)* resins are yellow-brown adhesives for exteriors; may release formaldehyde. Soy-based alternatives have been recently developed.
- *Melamine-formaldehyde (MF)* resins are white, heat-resistant finishes often used on exposed surfaces. Melamine bonds quickly with formaldehyde, reducing formaldehyde emissions.
- *Methylene diphenyl diisocyanate (MDI)* or *ethyl carbamate (urethane) resins* are expensive and generally waterproof, and do not contain formaldehyde.

Types of Engineered Wood

- Glue-laminated timber (glulam): Structural members made of smaller pieces of wood in straight or curved forms assembled with finger joints. Strong, lightweight, good appearance.
- Veneer-based plywood: Soy-flour based adhesives available to replace formaldehyde.
- Laminated veneer lumber (LVL) and stamina wood: Small trees are used to manufacture large structural pieces of LVL with consistent interior texture. Stamina wood consists of veneers that have been dyed, laminated with phenolic resin, and compressed under high pressure and heat.
- OSB, waferboard, particleboard, and chipboard are described later in this chapter (see pp. 120–123).
- Fiberboard, including insulating board, homosote, masonite, MDF, and hardboard are described on page 121.
- Cement board, fiber cement siding, gypsum board, and papercrete: See Chapter 2. Papercrete is a relatively new material also known as fibrous cement, and is made from re-pulped paper fiber with portland cement and clay or other soils. It is used in sustainable construction but absorbs water.
- Strawboard, and wood-plastic composites: Strawboard panels are rigid building panels designed to replace lightweight frame and drywall construction; they are made from straw left after harvesting wheat. Wood-plastic composites may lack structural strength.

Finishes for Wood

Stains for wood are transparent or opaque coatings that penetrate and color a wood surface while allowing its grain to be seen. Wood is stained to modify its color or to imitate another species. (See color plate C-28 for stained wood sample.)

Lacquers have solvents that evaporate very fast; they are usually spray-applied. Lacquers are the most popular finishes for commercial furniture and casework. Non-catalyzed and catalyzed lacquers have a nitrocellulose base; acrylic and vinyl lacquers do not.

Standard (noncatalyzed) lacquers are very popular and easy to touch up; the newly applied solvent slightly dissolves the previous coat.

Catalyzed lacquers dry faster than standard lacquers, reducing the likelihood of dust settling on the surface. They are harder than standard lacquers and moderately easy to touch up. Because catalyzed lacquers are very hard and brittle, they tend to splinter and spider-web.

Varnishes cure as their solvent evaporates or as their oil oxidates. Polyurethane is added to make varnish resistant to water and alcohol. Conversion varnishes are very durable and fast-drying. They form thick coats and resist many common chemicals.

Newer high-tech polyester and polyurethane coatings offer excellent chemical resistance and extremely durable, dense, and smooth finishes. With the addition of pigment, they resemble high-pressure decorative laminates and can achieve extremely shiny gloss levels. These expensive finishes require special skill and equipment for application. They are very difficult to touch up, but offer hardness and excellent resistance to chemicals. Polyurethanes are much easier to apply than polyesters.

WOOD VENEER

Veneer is prepared by slicing thin layers from the trunk of the tree and used for a surface treatment for plywood and other materials, and on furniture. Veneer plywood has a sheet of higher-quality wood veneer as the top layer. A series of slices stacked in the order they were cut from the same tree is called a *flitch*. The species of the wood used for the veneer and the way veneer sheets are arranged affect the appearance of the installed veneer.

Veneers are applied to dimensionally stable substrates, including plywood, particleboard, and MDF, which prevents damage from warping or shrinkage. However, the thin veneer surface may be damaged and cannot be refinished by sanding the way solid wood can; it must be carefully patched with pieces of matching grain patterns. Softwood veneers are used for inexpensive grades of plywood. Hardwood veneers are used for the finished surfaces of furniture and architectural millwork. The veneers are usually used on flat surfaces, with solid wood at wear points on edges, legs, and corners.

Wood Veneer Grades

Softwood veneers graded N have a select, smooth surface suitable for natural finishes. Grade A softwood veneers have a smooth surface suitable for painting. Grade B softwood veneer is used on solid, surfaced utility panels.

Hardwood veneers are specified by their own grading system.

- The highest grade, *premium*, allows only a few small knots or burls and inconspicuous patches.
- *Good-grade* hardwood veneer is similar to premium grade, but veneer faces are not required to match; however, no sharp contrasts in color are allowed.
- *Sound-grade* hardwood veneer is smooth, solid, and free from open defects. It may have some streaks, discoloration, patches, and small, sound tight knots.

Figure 5-11 Flexible veneer
Photo courtesy of Rockler.com.

- Hardwood veneer that shows discoloration, patches, tight knots, small knotholes, and splits is designated as *utility grade*.
- Veneers with even larger defects that do not affect the strength or durability of the panel are considered *backing grade*.

Veneers are often prized particularly for their beautiful figures, the natural patterns created when a tree is cut and a flat interior section of the wood is revealed. Figures are produced by intersecting annual rings, knots, burls, rays, and other signs of growth.

Table 5-1 Veneer Plywood Grades

A-grade softwood veneer	Smooth, paintable softwood veneer with a limited number of neatly made repairs running parallel to the grain.
B-grade softwood veneer	Solid surface that may have circular repair plugs, tight knots, and minor splits.
C-grade softwood veneer	Tight knots and knotholes of limited size. Repairs may be synthetic or wood. Any discoloration and sanding defects do not impair the strength of the panel.
C-plugged grade	Improved from a regular C-grade softwood veneer. Knots and knotholes are smaller. Some broken grain and synthetic repairs are permitted.
D-grade softwood veneer	Large knots and knotholes, pitch pockets, and tapering splits.
Engineered grades	Designed with higher shear strength for loads perpendicular to the panel face. Used for sheeting, subflooring, or in the fabrication of box beams and stressed-skin panels

Cost Factors for Veneers

Unbacked veneers are usually sold by the sheet and priced by the square foot. Full flitches and full pallets of veneer are individually priced. Prices increase with sheet size and the quality and intensity of any figured pattern.

The least expensive American hardwood veneers—miscellaneous woods, including poplar, for use as backers—cost about $0.50 per square foot. Ash and oak veneers are available for under $1.00 per square foot. Bird's-eye maple veneers are among the most expensive American woods, at nearly $10 per square foot. Additional charges are added for special thicknesses, plus shipping and handling.

Iroko (an African teak-substitute) and Spanish cedar are among the least expensive exotic woods, available on the American market at under $1.00 per square foot. Macassar ebony and Brazilian rosewood are among the most expensive, with figured woods running from $5.00 to over $13 per square foot. Wood from burls is especially highly valued, with Amboyna burl, for example, costing between $11 and $25 per square foot.

Note: These figures are for comparison only; actual pricing depends on availability and other factors.

Manufacturing Wood Veneer

There are several methods of cutting veneer, each of which produces a distinctive pattern.

- *Rotary cutting* is done by rotating a log against the cutting edge of a knife in a lathe. This produces continuous rolls of veneer with a bold variegated wavelike ripple figure. Rotary cutting results in wider sheets of veneer than other methods.
- *Flat slicing* is also known as plain slicing. A log is cut in half lengthwise, and one half is mounted on a support. The wood is then sliced with a knife along the length of the log parallel to the flat mounted surface. Slices of veneer become wider as the cut moves from the outside of the log toward the center. Flat-sliced veneer has a variegated wavy figure with grain lines becoming closer to each other at each side.
- *Quarter slicing* is done with one lengthwise quarter of a log. The cuts are perpendicular to the annual rings, producing relatively narrow pieces of veneer with stripes that may be straight and even or varied.
- *Half-round slicing* is accomplished by placing the section of log to be cut off-center on the lathe. This produces a figure that resembles both rotary cutting and flat slicing.

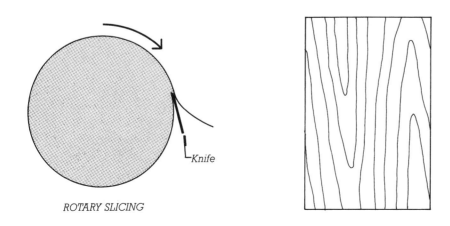

ROTARY SLICING

—Knife

Figure 5-12 Veneer rotary cutting Reproduced by permission of the publisher from Edward Allen and Joseph Iano, *Fundamentals of Building Construction: Materials and Methods,* 4th ed. (Hoboken, NJ: John Wiley & Sons, Inc.), © 2004 by John Wiley & Sons, Inc.

Figure 5-13 Veneer plain, or flat, slicing
Reproduced by permission of the publisher from Edward Allen and Joseph Iano, *Fundamentals of Building Construction: Materials and Methods*, 4th ed. (Hoboken, NJ: John Wiley & Sons, Inc.), © 2004 by John Wiley & Sons, Inc.

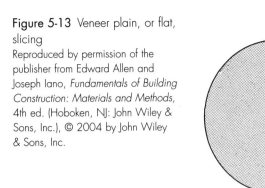
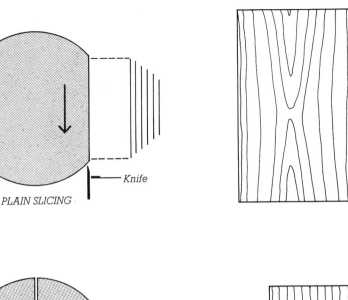

PLAIN SLICING · — Knife

Figure 5-14 Veneer quarter slicing
Reproduced by permission of the publisher from Edward Allen and Joseph Iano, *Fundamentals of Building Construction: Materials and Methods*, 4th ed. (Hoboken, NJ: John Wiley & Sons, Inc.), © 2004 by John Wiley & Sons, Inc.

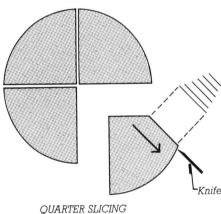
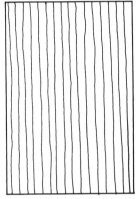

QUARTER SLICING — Knife

- *Rift cutting* cuts a section of log in a way that minimizes the appearance of radiating rays through the grain. The resulting veneer has stripes that vary from wide on one side to closely spaced on the other.

Sheets of veneer are often arranged in specific patterns to emphasize the color and figure of the wood. The process of selecting and arranging veneer sheets is called *matching*.

The simplest matching pattern is *random matching*. Veneer sheets are intentionally arranged without attempting to match patterns, creating a casual unmatched look.

When veneers from the same flitch are alternately laid face up and face down, they produce symmetrical mirror images to each side of the joint between adjacent sheets. This is called *book matching*, which can also be described as opening adjacent sheets of veneer like the pages of a book. When veneer is book matched so that the figures in adjacent sheets slope in opposite directions, the result is called *herringbone matching*.

Slip matching is accomplished by arranging adjacent sheets of veneer from the same flitch side by side without turning to make a repeating figure. Another way to describe slip matching is that each consecutive piece of veneer in the flitch is slipped off and laid next to the one before it.

When four diagonally cut sheets of veneer are arranged around a central point, a diamond pattern is formed. *Diamond matching* is very dramatic but may waste material.

Figure 5-15 *Veneer matching*

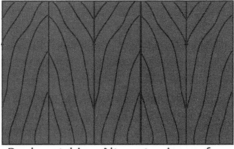

Book matching: Alternate pieces of veneer are flipped over like pages in a book

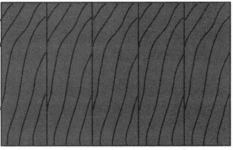

Slip matching: Pieces of veneer are slipped to one side in sequence

Random matching: Pieces of veneer vary in width, color and grain

Construction and Installation Practices for Wood Veneer

Veneer is applied to a surface in a series of steps. These steps are not needed when the veneer has already been applied to plywood or a similar substrate.

1. The surface is prepared by being lightly scuffed with medium grit sandpaper, and then cleaned of dust with either a tack cloth or a solvent cleaner on a soft cloth. A sealer such as shellac, varnish, or polyurethane is usually applied to porous substrate materials before the veneer is installed.
2. The veneer is cut slightly larger than the area to be covered. The most commonly used type of adhesive is contact cement, which is applied to cover both the entire back of the veneer and the face of the substrate. The adhesive is allowed to dry slightly as recommended by its manufacturer.
3. The adhesive-coated surfaces are then bonded together all at once with a great deal of pressure.

Some veneer is available in a peel-and-stick form that eliminates the need to apply adhesive, but this may not create as secure a bond. With peel-and-stick veneer, the installer applies pressure evenly from the center outward to avoid trapping air pockets. In both cases, a stiff-bladed scraping tool or wooden scraping block is used.

When contact adhesive is used, the veneered piece must be allowed to sit for between four and six hours before the veneer is finished. This allows gas produced by the contact cement to escape through the veneer surface.

Finishes for and Maintenance of Wood Veneers

Veneer can be finished like hardwood. It is carefully sanded with progressively finer sandpaper, cleaned of dust, and given a stain or clear finish. When applying finishes to veneer, it is important to remember that wood will expand or shrink with changes in moisture. Sealers should be applied in multiple very thin coats; this is often done with a spray. If the veneer moves while being finished, it may crack or blister.

Veneer is susceptible to a condition called *checking*, which involves the appearance of cracks in the surface of the veneer. These cracks are typically parallel to each other and to the grain of the wood. If not treated, they can cause any coating on the veneer to crack as well. An application of paste (carnauba) wax will help to cover small cracks and checks on veneered furniture finishes.

Veneer checks result from the stress induced by changes in the moisture content of the veneer and its backing material. They may be due to improper manufacturing, poor warehousing conditions, or harsh environments at the location where they are installed; it may be difficult to identify their source. Wood species with large pores check more than those with small pores; deep marks left by cutting tools can also aggravate the problem. Short-grained wood veneer tends to check less than the broad arcs (cathedral grain) of rotary-cut veneer.

Before installation, veneer panels should be acclimatized to moisture content conditions where they will be used. A level of 6 to 8 percent moisture is commonly used. Storage conditions are important, as is the effect of the moisture content of the adhesive. Assembled veneer panels are usually conditioned in an environmentally controlled area for around two days to allow temperature and moisture differences to balance.

Damaged veneer can be repaired. When excess humidity causes veneer to buckle, the damaged area can be carefully cut out, preferably along the direction of the wood grain, to minimize visibility. The repairer uses a pencil-rubbing template to cut a precisely fitted patch. The patch is glued in place and carefully clamped until dry. Blisters in veneer can also be repaired by slitting them with a sharp knife, inserting glue into the slit, and then clamping them using waxed paper to control the glue and a wood block to protect the veneer.

Wood veneers can be recycled by the same means as plywood. Veneer scraps can be collected and used for small projects.

INTERIOR APPLICATIONS FOR WOOD PANEL PRODUCTS

Wood panel products are engineered wood products that are less susceptible to shrinking or swelling, require less labor to install, and make more efficient use of wood resources than solid wood products. The many types of wood panel products can be classified as either structural or nonstructural. Structural wood panel products include:

- Plywood panels made of thin layers of veneers
- Composite panels, including flakeboard, particleboard, fiberboard, and hardboard

Plywood

Plywood is a sandwich of an uneven number of layers of wood products glued together. Traces of laminated wood have been found in the tombs of the Egyptian pharaohs. The Chinese shaved wood and glued it together for use in furniture at least as early as 1000 CE. Beginning in the seventeenth century, English, French, and Russian woodworkers explored the process of making plywood. Plywood has been used in the manufacture of cabinets, chests, desktops, and doors. Construction plywood made from softwood species came into use in the twentieth century.

Plywood is made by bonding veneers together under heat and pressure. The grain of adjacent plies is usually placed at right angles to each other and symmetrical about the center ply to maximize the strength of the sheet. The production process involves peeling a good straight log into sheets of veneer on a rotary lathe. This process was invented by Immanuel Nobel, father of Alfred Nobel, in the nineteenth century. The veneer is then cut to the desired dimensions, dried, patched, and glued into a panel. The panel can then be patched, resized, sanded, or refinished.

- *Construction-grade plywood* is graded and marked according to application, whether it is for interior or exterior use, and thickness.
- *Hardwood-veneer plywood,* which has a layer of attractive veneer on one surface, is used for furniture and for decorative wall paneling. ANSI HP-1, Hardwood and Decorative Plywood, sponsored by the Hardwood Plywood Manufacturers Association, classifies hardwood-veneer plywood by species, grade of veneers, type of plywood, composition of the plywood panel, and size and thickness.
- *Softwood plywood* is made of Douglas fir or spruce, pine, and fir, and is used for construction and industrial purposes. Softwood plywood is made from three, five, or seven plies, each 1/8 inch thick. It is sold in 4 × 8 foot (1.2 × 2.4 m) sheets. Roofing requires at least 3/8-inch plywood, and floorboards are a minimum of 5/8 inches thick. Tongue-and-groove plywood is available for flooring.
- *Interior plywoods* use less expensive urea-formaldehyde (UF) adhesives. *Exterior plywoods* use phenol-formaldehyde (PF) adhesives to withstand rot and delamination, and to keep high strength in highly humid conditions.
- *Airplane plywood* was developed for World War II fighter planes, with a combination of ply construction and curved form. These properties led to its adaptation by Alvar Aalto for furniture.

Composite Panels

Composite panels include flakeboard, particleboard, fiberboard, and hardboard. They share a composition based on reconstituted wood fibers or flakes, and may be surfaced with veneer.

Flakeboard

Both *oriented strand board* (OSB) and *waferboard* are varieties of flakeboard, reconstituted wood panel products made from flakes of wood cut from logs. OSB is the most widely used form of flakeboard.

Exterior grade plywood emits less formaldehyde than interior grade plywood

Figure 5-16 Plywood

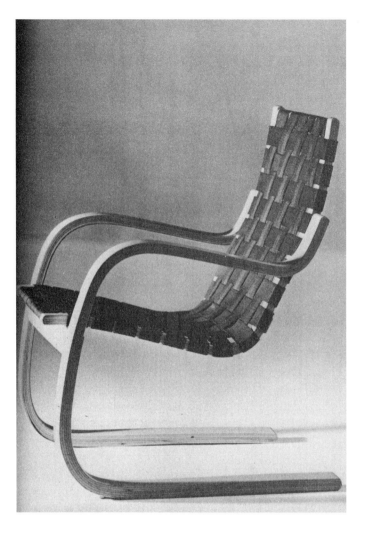

OSB is known as *sterling* in the United Kingdom. It is a wood panel product that is less expensive and more uniform than plywood. OSB is commonly used for sheathing in walls, floors, and roofs, and as subflooring. It is made by bonding layers of long, thin wood strands under heat and pressure using a waterproof adhesive. The product is around 95 percent wood strips and 5 percent wax and resin. Shredded wood strips are built up on a mat, then placed in a thermal press. The surface strands are aligned parallel to the length of the panel, adding to its strength. Individual panel sizes are cut from the mat. OSB has no internal gaps or voids, and is water-resistant, although a sealer is required for impermeability. OSB uses less valuable trees such as aspen and poplar; the trees are used almost completely. OSB emits VOCs at very low levels, about 10 percent of industry standards.

Waferboard is a nonveneered panel product composed of large, thin wood flakes bonded under heat and pressure with a waterproof adhesive. The grain directions of the wafers are oriented in a random way, making the panel almost equal in strength and stiffness in all directions of the panel's plane.

Particleboard

Particleboard is a wood panel product without a veneer finish made by bonding small wood particles under heat and pressure. It is often specified as a substrate for decorative laminates, for shelving, countertops, kitchen cabinets, and stair treads, for door cores

Figure 5-18 Particleboard

Particle board emits VOCs

and moldings, and as a flooring underlayment. Particleboard is more dimensionally stable than most wood panel products. The surface of particleboard is fairly smooth and can be shaped moderately well. However, edges do not hold screws well, and are usually covered for appearance.

ANSI A 208.1, Wood Particleboard, is sponsored by the National Particleboard Association and establishes minimum performance requirements. Particleboard and medium-density fiberboard (MDF) are commonly used as a core for plywood, along with layers of wood veneer or solid lumber.

Fiberboard

Fiberboard comprises a group of engineered wood products that includes medium-density fiberboard (MDF) and cellulosic fiberboard. Medium-density fiberboard is used for furniture and, often, is veneered with wood on visible surfaces. MDF is made from softwoods broken down into wood fibers through steam pressure, and combined with wax and resin. The result is formed into panels with high temperatures and pressures. The fineness of the fibers used determines MDF's homogeneous appearance and very smooth surface. The panel edge can be intricately machined and the face can be embossed three-dimensionally for cabinet door fronts and moldings. MDF is also used as a substrate for decorative laminates.

MDF has better moisture tolerance than particleboard, but it is still not moisture-resistant. It is often used with veneers or melamine. It works well for cabinetry and especially for acoustic enclosures, due to its high sound-insulative and damping properties.

MDF can release harmful adhesive when being cut or sanded, which may irritate the eyes and lungs. The dust produced is very dangerous and workers should use proper ventilation and facemasks. Other resins are being introduced to replace formaldehyde.

Cellulosic fiberboard is a felted homogeneous panel made from wood, cane, straw or other cellulosic fibers. The fibers are bonded by interfelting but are not consolidated under heat and pressure. The standard for cellulosic fiberboard is ANSI A 194.1.

Homasote is the proprietary name of a fiberboard product made from recycled newspaper and glues. Homasote products are valued for their acoustic properties; they also have weather-resistant, structural and insulating qualities and are very durable. The substantial amounts of water used to produce Homasote are reused in a closed-loop process.

Hardboard

Hardboard (masonite) is made of exploded wood fibers that are highly compressed into a very homogeneous board with no grain. It is thin and dense. Hardboard has very low structural strength. It can be laminated with wood veneer, plastic laminate, or vinyl, and is used in construction, furniture, and cabinetry. Pegboard is a form of hardboard.

Overlayed Materials

Overlayed materials include high-density overlay (HDO) and medium-density overlay (MDO). Both are exterior wood panel products with resin surfaces.

- HDO has a resin-fiber overlay on both sides. It has a smooth, hard, abrasion-resistant surface and is used for concrete forms, cabinets, and countertops.
- MDO has a phenolic or melamine resin overlay on one or both sides, providing a smooth base for painting. Specialty panels include a variety of wood panel products including grooved or rough-sawn plywood. They are used for siding or paneling.

Specifying Wood Products
Wood Panel Product Grades

Wood panel products are graded to indicate the intended use or veneer grade of a wood panel product. Veneer grades are rated N, A, B, C, C-plugged, and D; N-grade panel products have a smooth softwood veneer of all heartwood or all sapwood. N-grade veneer is free from open defects, with only a few well-matched repairs.

Cost Factors for Wood Panel Products

Oriented strandboard used in building construction is generally about half as expensive as plywood in the same application. However, building material prices are subject to supply and demand, and when large volumes of a material are used for military purposes or for repair after a natural disaster, for example, prices go up.

Interior wood paneling using veneer bonded to engineered wood substrates can be assembled from a kit of parts, saving labor and material costs.

Note: Wood panel products are used in a wide variety of construction projects. Details of specific applications will be addressed in Chapter 12.

Wood-Plastic Composite Products

Wood-plastic composite products are made from recycled plastic and wood waste materials. Known by such trade names as Trex, CorrectDeck, Weatherbest, and others, they are used for outdoor decks, moldings, trims, indoor and outdoor furniture, and window and door frames. Wood-plastic composites are made of wood fibers recovered from sawdust, peanut hulls, bamboo straw, and other materials mixed with waste plastics, including high-density polyethylene and PVC. Additives include colorants, coupling agents, stabilizers, blowing agents, reinforcing agents, foaming agents and lubricants. Wood-plastic composites can be formed to both solid and hollow profiles. The material, which contains 50 to 70 percent cellulose, behaves and is worked like wood. It resists moisture and rot. It is not as rigid as wood and may deform in hot weather. Wood-plastic composites are porous and may stain.

Bamboo

Although bamboo is not technically a wood product, it is used in similar ways.

Bamboo is a type of long, hollow grass that grows quickly, regenerates without replanting, and uses little fertilizer or pesticides. After being processed, it is very hard and dimensionally stable. Dozens of small new companies ship bamboo flooring to the United States through traders in China or Indonesia, and the quality and consistency of harvesting, milling, and business practices vary as widely as the prices. Importers buy from whichever factory has the best price at the time, and shipments from different sources vary in quality; some companies have an Internet presence only and come and go without notice. Established manufacturers control the process from harvest to final product, resulting in consistency of color and quality.

There are more than 1,550 species of bamboo, which vary from as soft as fir to harder than maple. The age of the plant before harvesting also affects its hardness. The shoots reach full size in a year or two, but continue to feed the plant until their third year. If cut before maturity, the plant's growth is hurt; after the third year, the shoots are essentially dead, and removal helps the plant. Bamboo harvested at three years or younger is softer and less stable (as well as less expensive) than mature stalks.

In itself, bamboo is an environmentally friendly material. However, bamboo products such as flooring are often assembled using formaldehyde adhesive. (See the section on bamboo flooring in Chapter 9.)

Plaster and Gypsum Board 6

Plaster and gypsum board are commonly used to finish the interior wall and ceiling surfaces of buildings. Both are reasonably resistant to wear and cleanable; additional surface finishes improve these qualities, as well as appearance.

Although rigid finish materials are capable of spanning short distances between vertical or horizontal supports, more flexible finishes and those applied in liquid form require a solid rigid backing. Both plaster and gypsum board supply this need; they are usually used as flat surfaces, but both can also be formed into curves.

PLASTER

Plaster, also known as plaster of paris, after a large gypsum deposit found near the city of Paris, France, is made by heating gypsum to about 150°C to evaporate the water in it. Dry plaster powder is reconstituted by adding water; the resulting gypsum paste hardens into a solid. Plaster is fairly soft and can be worked with metal tools and sandpaper.

Plaster, a very old material, was traditionally used for walls and ceilings until the development of gypsum board. It is preferred today for the uniformity and wear resistance of its finish, and the creative options it offers that gypsum board does not. Plaster is also used to match existing finishes in older buildings.

Plaster finishes require greater skill and more time to apply than gypsum board. The curing process can take up to two days. Plaster is applied as a paste to the surfaces of walls or ceilings; it hardens as it dries. *Gypsum plaster* is the most commonly used in interiors; it is durable, relatively lightweight, and fire-resistant, and can be used on walls and ceilings that are not subject to wet or moist conditions. Portland cement plaster, known as *stucco*, is used primarily on exterior walls and in areas that may become wet or moist.

Historical, Cultural, and Architectural Context of Plaster

Some of the earliest human dwellings that have been found were plastered with red clay, such as at Tell Mureybit in the upper Euphrates River valley, which was occupied around 10,000 years ago. The rectangular wood frame and mud-brick homes and shrines of Çatal Höyük, dating between 6500 and 5700 BCE, were drained by plaster gutters. Carefully plastered, raised mud-brick platforms along the walls of houses in Çatal Höyük were covered with reed or rush matting, with cushions and bedding added for sitting, working, or sleeping. The bones of family members were buried under the platforms.

Relief carvings found in homes and temples in ancient Egypt generally were plastered and painted. Frescoes were commonly painted into the wet plaster on the mud-brick upper walls of Egyptian dwellings, and finished with varnish or beeswax. Geometric, religious, and natural images were cut into stone or plaster and painted red, yellow, blue, blue-green, and green, with white and black used for linear forms and outlines. Plaster relief patterns projected from flat wall surfaces. A raised mud-brick dais, often plastered and whitewashed or edged with limestone, served as a dining area or a seating bench. Residential ceilings were made of poles layered with mud-covered sticks and twigs, sometimes covered with reed matting. In sturdier homes, rough-cut closely spaced beams were left exposed. Small poles below the beams, covered with reed mats and painted plaster, finished some ceilings. Others have decorative sunken panels between plastered beams. Floors were commonly made of mud plaster or brick paving, and were often whitewashed and painted with plant and animal themes.

Compacted earth floors of private houses in ancient Greece were sometimes finished with plaster, paint, paving stone, or mosaics of pebbles, glass, or stone set in mortar. In the most expensive villas of ancient Rome, fine marble veneers and carved stone reliefs hid the brick walls. In less expensive homes, the exterior walls were covered with stucco relief panels or plaster ruled to imitate stone courses.

Gothic residential buildings were generally log or stone houses with thatched roofs and exposed or plastered stone walls. In the castles of English and French nobility after 1400, ceilings with exposed beams and trusses often had painted ornamentation, and plaster ceilings frequently were painted with gold stars on a blue or green ground.

Early Islamic architecture using stone or mud brick often hid or copied structural elements in nonstructural stucco, plaster, and woodwork. Spain's architecture reflects the Islamic avoidance of natural plant, animal, or human forms, with the development of abstract, geometric designs for patterns carved in stone or plaster. Interior surfaces were adorned with lush floral decorations, along with inscriptions from the Koran in carved plaster, marble, glass, and gold mosaic.

After 1450, Italian Renaissance palaces in the cities and in suburban villas in country towns were finished with coarse sand and plaster on irregular wall surfaces that increased texture and tone. High Italian Renaissance upper-floor rooms featured painted images of light and shadow on plaster or stucco, to imitate a heavier masonry or wood ceiling.

Figure 6-1 Islamic stucco ornament

Flat or vaulted plaster ceilings with coved arches springing up from brackets on walls provided apparent, if not actual, support. Italian Renaissance color schemes for large-scale rooms were often based on a plain, neutral-colored plaster wall finish, accented with draperies and accessories in brilliant reds, blues, yellows, purples, and greens.

The work of Louis Le Vau (1612–1670) dominated the late Renaissance in France (1589–1643). Vaux-le-Vicomte (1656), a château near Paris built for Nicolas Fouquet, French superintendent of finances, features work by painter Charles Le Brun (1619–1690) and a team of plasterworkers. Italian Baroque influences are apparent in the lavish bedroom, designed for use by the king of France, if he should visit.

By 1550, English Renaissance ceilings were covered with decorative geometric plasterwork in deeper relief than wall panels. Early Renaissance ideas in sixteenth-century Tudor and Elizabethan England were influenced by craftspeople from Italy, the Low Countries, and Spain. The symmetrical Tudor design of Haddon Hall (1530) in Derbyshire has large windows on the south side, a plaster ceiling with strapwork, and wood paneling with pilasters and arches of natural oak. Inigo Jones designed the flat ceiling of the Banqueting House at Whitehall (1619–1622), which also features paintings by the Flemish artist Peter Paul Rubens in plaster frames. William Kent (1685–1748) assisted architect Lord Burlington in the design of the Double Cube room at Wilton, a square-domed building based on Palladio's Villa Rotonda in Vicenza. The ornamental plasterwork and painted details of the interior are based on Pompeian designs.

In the Low Countries, civic buildings such as the Leiden Town Hall (1597), by Lieven de Key (1560–1627), exhibited classical pilasters and pediments, but retained the local style for fretting, wood and plaster strapwork, and grotesque ornament. Palaces in Germany and Austria set off red, green, and yellow marbles by white and off-white plaster. Pastel pinks, light greens, and blues touched with gilt played off white stucco.

The interior walls of the 30 Ajanta painted caves in India, carved during the Buddhist period of the third to fourth centuries CE, are smoothed with a plaster of mud and seeds, tiny pebbles, or pulverized pottery, then finished with a wash of lime. Many of the caves have murals depicting life at the fifth-century royal courts, painted in mineral

Figure 6-2 Gypsum
Courtesy of David Barthelmy, webmineral.com.

colors of yellow ochre, orange, dusky brown, red, black and white, olive and forest green, and lapis lazuli.

Residential interiors in colonial nineteenth-century India had plasterwork ceilings that revealed a European influence. After the Industrial Revolution, synthetic, permanent paint pigments in bright colors, especially corals and greens, filled interiors. Frescoes were painted on the façades of havelis in India, with the best frescoes on interior surfaces, including ceilings. The need to work while the water-based pigment and lime plaster were still wet produced a freer style. Subjects included religious and court scenes; floral, geometric, and hunting motifs; and elephants and camels. With the advent of the Industrial Revolution, pictures of steam trains and ships, horse-drawn carriages, and Model T Fords became popular.

Before 750 CE, in Teotihuacan, near Mexico City, builders used weatherproof but lightweight fast-cooled lava for fill and structural masonry. Interiors were constructed with wood beams and lintels, and pole laths. Plaster made of lime or mud was used on all buildings, including on stone construction that always had veneer stucco or a sculptured, painted, or polished finish.

Mayan walls of plaster and cement were finished with hieroglyphic inscriptions carved in stone or wood or painted on plaster. Mayan art was painted on paper and plaster.

Early American colonial houses had wall surfaces of wood or plaster on split lath set between framing elements. Before 1700, English tobacco planters in Virginia finished the interior of houses with whitewashed plaster walls with exposed wood beams. By the middle of the eighteenth century, the plastered walls of eastern American homes were covered with imported or American-made wallpaper. Ceilings were edged with cornices and decorated with intricate plaster decorations.

In colonial Mexico and the North American Southwest, residential interiors adopted the traditions of vernacular Mediterranean buildings, with white, plastered walls, wood beam ceilings, and tiled floors, and with a simple fireplace as the focal point. In California, farmhouses on great estates and town dwellings were built by their

Figure 6-3 Gaineswood plaster detail

owners of sun-dried brick, and featured simple, unadorned walls plastered and white-washed inside and out.

American Georgian interiors (1720–1787) were often paneled with wood, sometimes with plaster above. The interior of Gaineswood in Demopolis, Alabama, by Nathan Bryan Whitfield (1843–1861), was decorated with elegant plasterwork done by a slave known only as Sandy. The smooth-plaster interior walls of Shaker buildings held eye-level wooden pegs, upon which were hung chairs, cloaks, and other objects.

Interior Plaster Types and Terms

- *Acoustical plaster*: Low-density plaster containing vermiculite or other porous material; intended to increase sound absorption.
- *Calcined gypsum*: Gypsum thoroughly heated to drive off most of its chemically combined water and leave the remainder dry and crumbly.
- *Cement plaster*: Mix of plaster sand, portland cement, and water for interior or exterior use as fireproofing, usually with vermiculate.
- *Earthen plaster*: Mixture of clay, sand, and fiber such as straw, animal hair, or dung. Used as a finish in straw bale construction; can be sculpted and impressed with designs.
- *Gauging plaster*: Gypsum plaster ground especially for mixing with lime putty to control the setting time and reduce shrinkage of a finish coat of plaster.
- *Gypsum*: Hydrated calcium sulfate; a soft mineral.
- *Gypsum cements (gypsum concrete)*: Produced from calcined gypsum; slower setting, and easier to work than plaster of paris. Keene's, Mack's, Martin's, Parian, and Scott's cements and Spence's plaster are all types of gypsum cements.
- *Gypsum plaster*: Calcined gypsum plus sand, water, and additives to control setting; applied in two or three coats over a basecoat that is supported by lath.
- *Hard finish*: A finish coat of lime putty and Keene's cement or gauging plaster that is troweled to a smooth, dense finish.
- *Lime plaster*: Mixed calcium hydroxide and sand used for true frescoes. Limestone heated; water added; transforms back to limestone when exposed to carbon dioxide.
- *Molding plaster*: Very finely ground gypsum and hydrated lime; used for ornamental plasterwork; very fine grain that preserves sharp detail in cast pieces.
- *Neat plaster*: Gypsum plaster basecoat, with hair or other fiber mixed in; aggregates are added at the job site.
- *Ready-mixed plaster*: Calcined gypsum and aggregate mixed at the mill; water added at the job site. Perlite or vermiculite reduce weight and increase thermal and fire resistance.
- *Stucco*: Cement plaster made of portland or masonry cement, sand, and hydrated lime mixed with water for a hard, exterior covering.
- *Stuccolike interior finishes*: Imitated with plaster combined with sand or other additives.
- *Veneer plaster (thin-coat plaster)*: Ready-mixed plaster applied as a very thin, one- or two-coat finish over a veneer base.
- *White coat*: Finish coat of lime putty and white gauging plaster troweled to a smooth, dense finish.
- *Whitewash*: Finish used to whiten walls and woodwork; made by the same chemistry as used to produce lime plaster.
- *Wood-fibered plaster*: Mixed at the mill with coarse cellulose fiber to increase its bulk, strength, and fire resistance; sand may be added to increase its hardness as a basecoat. Fibered plaster may contain hair, glass, nylon, or sisal fibers.

New York brownstones and Philadelphia brick row houses featured plaster moldings used to define the tops of walls. Wallpaper covered interior plaster walls above a wainscot or wood trim, with geometric, floral, scenic, and oriental designs. In the early twentieth century, Frank Lloyd Wright preferred wood natural finishes, plaster painted his favorite cream-white color, and the soft warm colors of brick and stone, which are accented with bright red.

After the end of World War II, paneling made from wood chips with added plastic binders became prevalent for wall surfaces and furniture construction, and gypsum wallboard (drywall) replaced plaster.

Aesthetic Qualities of Interior Plaster

Plaster is valued aesthetically for its monolithic hard surface. As large planes, plaster walls and ceilings present smooth, cool surfaces that can be straight or curved. When molded, plaster produces clearly defined three-dimensional details that add interest and generate small shadows.

Plaster provides an excellent surface for application of other finishes. Paints applied to dry plaster benefit from its smooth, even surface. Fresco paintings take advantage of the wet plaster to create works of art integral to the wall surface itself. Plaster can also be carved, modeled, cast, incised, colored, stamped or stenciled, and shaped geometrically or naturalistically to look like vines, leaves, and flower details that simulate wood or stone carving.

Manufacturing Gypsum Products

Gypsum is a common mineral found in massive beds throughout the world, usually as the result of sedimentation from salty water; it often contains trapped bubbles of air and water. Gypsum used in interior plaster and gypsum board is usually white or gray, but often contains other minerals producing shades of red, brown, or yellow. Less common types of gypsum include selenite, a colorless, transparent form with a pearly luster; satin spar, a compact fibrous aggregate with satiny surfaced fibrous crystals; and alabaster, a fine-grained ornamental stone used for carvings. An opaque flowerlike form embedded with sand grains, called desert rose, is found in arid regions.

Gypsum is a natural insulator that feels relatively warm to the touch; its very low level of thermal conductivity makes it a good insulating filler in drywall. Sheets of clear gypsum crystals can be peeled off larger specimens. Gypsum is soft enough to be scratched by a fingernail; thin crystals can be bent, but will not return to shape elastically.

Synthetic gypsum is produced as a by-product of the use of finely ground limestone to scrub the sulfur emissions from fossil-fuel-burning power stations. It is also produced during the process of refining phosphate fertilizer; the phosphate industry creates much more gypsum than is required commercially. Synthetic gypsum that contains possibly harmful materials, such as naturally occurring radioactive material, is not used for manufactured gypsum board; otherwise, synthetic gypsum is both low-cost and environmentally friendly.

Environmental and Health Impacts of Gypsum and Plaster

Both natural and synthetic gypsum are considered to be nontoxic and safe, unless contaminated by naturally occurring radioactivity. Impurities that occur in gypsum are generally inert and harmless, and commonly include clay, anhydrite, and limestone in natural gypsum, and fly ash in synthetic gypsum. Gypsum board traditionally contained a mixture of natural and synthetic ore, but is now often made without any natural gypsum.

Plaster dust may irritate the eyes and respiratory system; added vermiculite and silica sand should not be inhaled at all. Because plaster dust rapidly absorbs water from moist surfaces, it is highly irritating to the skin, eyes, and the respiratory system. Handling wet plaster can cause skin burns from the heat produced during the setting reaction.

Plaster helps to protect buildings, their occupants, and their contents as both passive fire protection and in the form of fireproofing products. Formerly, plaster's fire resistance was improved with asbestos fibers, which are now banned in most countries; removal and replacement of asbestos containing plaster materials has been widespread. Interior fireproofing materials are less dense and cost less than exterior products. They are usually sprayed in place.

Installing and Maintaining Plaster

In older construction, plaster was installed on narrow strips of wood called *laths* that were nailed horizontally across the wood wall studs. The lath was topped by two coats of plaster, the first a rough, sandy, brown coat, and the second a smooth finish coat. Once completely dried, the wall was ready to paint. In time, wood laths were replaced with rock lath, a type of gypsum wallboard that came in 2 × 4 foot sheets. The 4-foot length fit precisely across three wall studs placed 16 inches on center. The methods of mixing, applying, and finishing plastering materials vary widely.

Furring consists of wood strips or other supports attached to a wall or other surface. Furring holds lath or other finish materials onto hard surfaces, or is used to provide airspace between wall and finish materials.

Lath types include the following:

- *Metal lath* is used with three-coat plaster. It is made from an expanded metal or wire fabric that has been galvanized or coated with rust-inhibiting paint to resist corrosion. Metal lath is selected for weight and strength, depending on the spacing and rigidity of its supports. Expanded metal lath is made by stretching a sheet of steel that has been slit to form a stiff network of diamond-shaped openings.
- *Rib lath* is used where supports are farther apart; its greater stiffness is made possible by V-shaped ribs.
- *Self-centering lath* is a form of rib lath that is used over steel joists as lath for solid plaster partitions or as formwork for concrete slabs.

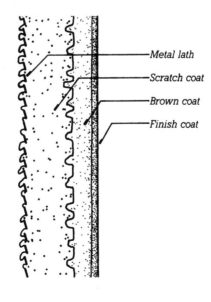

—Metal lath
—Scratch coat
—Brown coat
—Finish coat

Figure 6-4 Section showing plaster on metal lath
Reproduced by permission of the publisher from Edward Allen and Joseph Iano, *Fundamentals of Building Construction: Materials and Methods*, 4th ed. (Hoboken, NJ: John Wiley & Sons, Inc.), © 2004 by John Wiley & Sons, Inc.

Figure 6-5 Furring on brick

- *Self-furring lath* creates a space for tying in plaster or stucco to its supports.
- *Expanded metal, welded wire, or woven-wire lath* is dimpled when applied to its supporting surface. Expanded-metal or wire lath with a perforated or building paper back is used as a base for ceramic tile and exterior stucco walls. Sheets of metal lath are attached to wood or metal studs spaced 16 or 24 inches (41 or 61 cm) on center. The lath is laid so that its length or ribs run across the supports.
- *Gypsum lath* is manufactured as a panel with a core of air-entrained hardened gypsum plaster faced with fibrous, absorbent paper that adheres well to plaster.
- *Perforated gypsum lath* is punched with 3/4-inch (19-mm) holes 4 inches (102 mm) on center to provide a mechanical key (tie) for plaster.
- *Insulating gypsum lath* is made with an aluminum foil backing that doubles as a vapor retarder and reflective thermal insulator.
- *Type X lath* is made more fire-resistant by the addition of glass fibers and other additives.
- *Veneer base* is gypsum lath with a special paper facing designed to accept veneer plaster.

Plaster is applied in a series of coats of progressive refinement. Two-coat plaster is applied as a basecoat followed by a finish coat. Three-coat plaster is applied first as a scratch coat followed by a brown coat and finally a finish coat.

- Any plaster coat applied before the finish coat is referred to as a *basecoat*.
- A *scratch coat* is the first coat in three-coat plaster; it must adhere firmly to the lath and be raked to provide a better bond for the second or brown coat.
- The *brown coat* is used to level the surface. It is a rough finish applied either as the second coat in three-coat plaster or as the basecoat in two-coat plaster that is being installed over gypsum lath or masonry. The brown coat is made from a coarse gypsum with perlite; portland cement is often added for a harder and more level surface. The brown coat is actually applied as several coats that are carefully

Expanded metal lath is fabricated by slitting and expanding a sheet of steel alloy to form a stiff network with diamond-shaped openings.

Rib lath is an expanded-metal lath having V-shaped ribs to provide greater stiffness and permit wider spacing of the supporting framing members.

Self-furring lath is expanded-metal, welded-wire, or woven-wire lath that is dimpled to space itself from the supporting surface, creating a space for the keying of plaster or stucco.

Paper-backed lath is expanded-metal or wire lath having a backing of perforated or building paper, used as a base for ceramic tile and exterior stucco walls.

Figure 6-6 Metal lath
Reproduced by permission of the publisher from Francis D.K. Ching and Cassandra Adams, *Building Construction Illustrated*, 3rd ed. (New York: John Wiley & Sons, Inc.), © 2001 by John Wiley & Sons, Inc.

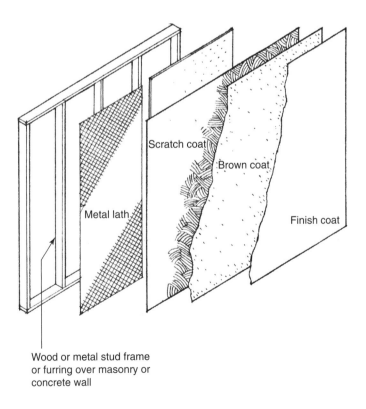

Scratch coat

Brown coat

Metal lath

Finish coat

Wood or metal stud frame or furring over masonry or concrete wall

Figure 6-7 Plaster coats
Reproduced with permission from the publisher from Francis D.K. Ching and Corky Binggeli, *Interior Design Illustrated*, 2nd ed. (Hoboken, NJ: John Wiley & Sons, Inc.), © 2005 by John Wiley & Sons, Inc.

prepared as a strong and smooth surface that can accommodate the expansion and contraction of all the other materials.

- The *finish coat* is the final coat of plaster, which serves as either the finished surface or as a basecoat for an additional finish of another material. Bonding agents in the finish coat act as adhesives.

Plaster can be constructed as a solid plaster partition stabilized with proprietary ceiling runners and metal base anchors. Solid plaster partitions 2 inches (51 mm) thick take up little floor space. They are made by applying three-coat plaster to both sides of metal or gypsum lath. Ceiling runners and base anchors stabilize the partition. The partition itself may be made with expanded metal lath on 3/4-inch (19-mm) channel studs, or with metal rib lath on a 1/2-inch (13-mm) gypsum lath or 1-inch (19-mm) core board.

Plaster can also be applied directly to brick, clay tile, or concrete masonry where the surface is rough and porous enough to produce a good bond. A bonding agent is used when plaster is applied directly to dense, nonporous surfaces such as concrete. When there is a danger that moisture or condensation might penetrate the wall, or where airspace or space for insulation is needed, wood or metal furring can be applied vertically or horizontally. Horizontal channel stiffeners are used to give additional support to vertical furring applied away from the wall.

Resilient furring channels are used to create a resilient wall surface for acoustic purposes. The furring is attached to the wall with resilient clips that allow the plaster to move independently of the masonry.

Traditional plaster is more expensive to install than *gypsum wallboard (drywall)*; the actual price comparison depends on the materials and finishes specified. Availability of skilled labor for plaster and semiskilled labor for drywall can also affect costs. Prices will also vary with location and how busy contractor schedules are.

Traditionally, ornamental plasterwork was either run in place or on a bench at the site, or cast in molds in a workshop. Plain plaster molding was sometimes made directly on the wall. Ceiling coffers, medallions for lighting fixtures, brackets, dentils, or columns were cast in molds at a workshop, often in several pieces that were assembled and installed at the site. Today, highly trained artisans can reproduce these details in plaster.

The most common historic ornamental plaster forms from the eighteenth to twentieth centuries were the cornice, the ceiling medallion, and the coffered ceiling. Cast plaster ornaments are cast with reinforcing and lath that support the piece, which is then attached with screws to continuous wood or metal blocking in the wall or ceiling. An elaborate cornice that ran around the room was built up from plain gypsum and lime moldings. Additional trim pieces such as decorative leaves, egg and dart moldings, and bead and reel units cast in the shop were attached to the plain runs with wet plaster. The finished plaster was painted, glazed, or sometimes gilded.

Relatively simple ceiling medallions consisted of plain-run circles centered on a lighting fixture that was supported by a ceiling joist. More elaborate medallions were assembled from shop-cast pieces, and often featured acanthus foliage alternating with other decorative designs. Twentieth-century Federal-style ceiling medallions were often single-piece units with classical garlands and swags.

Coffered ceiling units were cast in the shop or on-site, and hung by wires from the ceiling. In addition to flat ceiling panels, coffering was used inside domes and vaults and along ceiling ribs and soffits. Panels often featured a rosette in the center and at the intersection of panel borders.

Although plaster is hard and durable, over time it may crack, loosen, or sag. As part of the building construction, it is subject to problems caused by water infiltration,

Figure 6-8 Plaster cornice, Monticello, Charlottesville, Virginia

structural movement, and vibration, which alteration work can make worse. Plaster problems can result from the different expansion rates of varied substrates, for example, where plaster is applied to brick and then, in an adjacent section of wall, is built up over wood lath. The brick expands and contracts differently than wood, causing cracks to appear in the plaster.

Failing plaster is usually caused by problems with its substrate. Sometimes the wood lath in older plaster walls deteriorates and the plaster begins to break loose and fall. Large holes in plaster walls can be repaired with pieces of drywall cut to fit, then filled with plaster patching material. Drywall can also be applied over a plaster wall and finished as a new surface. In buildings of historic significance, it is desirable to replace damaged plaster with new plaster.

Plaster restorers use metal plaster washers, driving a screw through a hole in the center of the washer and, hopefully, into the loose lath and framing to provide new support for all the layers. The washers have small holes around their edges to help tie them into wet finishing plaster.

Hairline cracks in plaster surfaces that seem to be stable can be opened up and cleaned out, dampened, and filled with relatively thin applications of plaster crack filler until the final cured surface is level. The crack is then covered with self-adhering

Figure 6-9 Plaster ceiling medallion, St. Philip's Protestant Episcopal Church, Charleston, South Carolina

Figure 6-10 Coffered plaster ceiling, Union Station, Washington, DC

fiberglass tape cut to fit and finished with drywall joint compound. Shortcuts that just cover the crack with drywall compound do not usually work. If the crack continues to spread over a period of time, a more serious structural problem may be at fault.

Plaster cornices can be reproduced by making a template of the piece's profile. Plaster is poured over strips of starched cheesecloth to provide a strong backing for the cornice. The template is then run the length of the cornice (hence the term *run plaster*) to give it shape; the process is repeated as layers of plaster are built up. The plaster cornice is then left to dry for two to three days. Smaller sections of decorative plaster ornamentation can be attached into larger cornices, a process called sinkage. A finished plaster cornice can weigh over 50 pounds. Cornices are attached to walls with adhesive and fasteners, similar to drywall screws. In an older building with dimensional irregularities, the cornice has to be cut and fit in place.

Repair of ornamental plaster is difficult and takes years of training and experience: it should always be done by a qualified professional. Before repairing plaster ornaments, the cause of the problem should be determined and remedied, and the adhesion of the ornament to its plaster basecoat and supporting lath should be tested. Code requirements for fire-suppression systems and detectors should be evaluated while this work is being done, and integrated as effectively as possible into the decorative plasterwork. Access for future maintenance should also be provided.

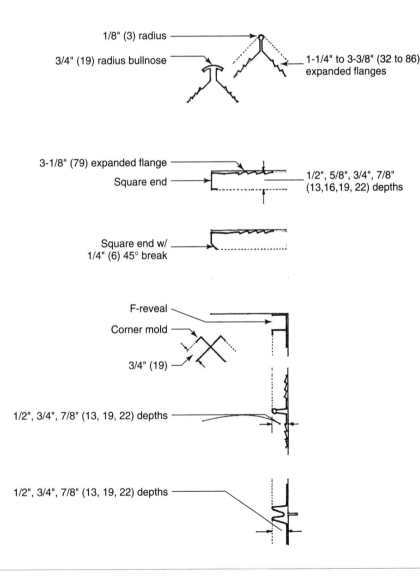

Figure 6-11 Plaster trim accessories
Reproduced by permission of the publisher from Francis D. K. Ching and Cassandra Adams, *Building Construction Illustrated*, 3rd ed. (New York: John Wiley & Sons, Inc.), © 2001 by John Wiley & Sons, Inc.

Finishes for Plaster

Both texture and finish material affect the appearance of a finished plaster wall. A *trowel finish* is smooth and nonporous, while the term *floated finish* describes a sandy and lightly textured surface. Rougher finishes can be sprayed on. Plaster finishes can be painted, and smooth finishes can be covered with paper or textile wallcoverings.

Venetian plaster (also called Italian plaster) is a term that began to be used in the United States in the 1980s to refer to a polished plaster finish using either traditional lime plaster or a resin-based product. (In Italy, these plasters are called *decorative stuccos*.) Venetian plaster finishes are created using tinted plaster over a low-sheen surface such as a wall painted with a flat or eggshell finish; shinier surfaces are first covered with a primer. The dry surface is sanded smooth to reduce visible lines and edge marks. A basecoat of plaster is applied and allowed to dry for about four hours. A second coat of plaster is applied to completely cover the original wall surface and dried for an additional 24 hours. An optional topcoat that makes the surface washable, and shinier, is applied in areas of heavy use or where there is a lot of moisture. A metallic or pearlescent color can be added with the topcoat if desired. After drying, the surface is burnished to a marblelike polish using very fine sandpaper in a circular motion; this takes a great deal of time. Rubbing the surface with the flat side of a clean steel trowel increases the effect. Once the burnishing is completed, the wall is wiped with a slightly damp cloth to remove any plaster dust.

STUCCO

Like plaster and mortar, stucco is made of an aggregate, a binder, and water; it is applied wet and hardens as it dries. Its primary difference is in its use. Stucco can be used on building exteriors and for interior walls, ceilings, and decorative purposes. It may be used as a decorative finish for concrete block, steel or adobe construction.

History and Aesthetics of Stucco

Stucco was heavily used as a sculptural and artistic material in Baroque and Rococo architecture. It was used in churches and palaces to provide a smooth, decorative transition from walls to ceiling, and as a ceiling decoration. Stucco was used in trompe l'oeil paintings on walls and ceilings, to make a transition from the actual three-dimensional architecture to its painted elaboration. It is extensively used in Islamic mosques and palaces, and for Indian architectural sculpture.

Stucco decoration was popular in upper-class North American apartments during the nineteenth and twentieth centuries. During the 1950s, premolded stucco forms decorated the joints between interior walls and ceilings; it was usually painted the same color as the ceiling and used where a picture rail was present.

Manufacturing Stucco

Traditionally, both plaster used inside the building and stucco used outside were made of lime and sand, often with animal or plant fibers added for tensile strength. In the late nineteenth century, portland cement was added for improved durability, and gypsum plasters began to replace lime plaster. Traditional stucco was made of lime, sand, and water; modern stucco is made of portland cement and water, sometimes with lime added for increased permeability and workability. Acrylics and glass fibers are also added for improved structural properties and workability, usually for use in what are termed one-coat stucco systems.

Traditional lime stucco is hard but can be broken or chipped by hand. Lime is naturally white; stucco can be colored by its aggregate or added pigments. Cracks in lime stucco can sometimes heal themselves when dissolved lime is deposited and solidifies there. Portland cement stucco is very hard and brittle; an unstable substrate can easily cause cracking. It is usually made with gray portland cement, although white portland cement can also be used. Manufacturers offer many colors to be mixed into the finish coat.

Installing Stucco

Traditional stucco is applied directly to brick, stone, or other masonry surfaces, or over wood lath. Modern stucco is usually applied over expanded metal lath stapled to the wall sheathing, with a two-layer moisture barrier in between. Three layers of portland-cement-based plaster rapidly become strong and durable, but are intolerant of structural movement. The wire mesh is attached to vapor-permeable, water-resistant tar paper for wood or light-gauge steel frame structures, to protect the sheathing and interior of the wall from moisture. In Europe, wire lath with fired clay integrated into it is called a brick mesh.

Figure 6-12 Tuscan Grill, Waltham, Massachusetts. Joint compound was applied over concrete brick and painted to resemble a Tuscan wall.
Painting by Medusa. Corky Binggeli Interior Design.

The first layer of plaster is a scratch coat of cement and sand, which is given a combed texture to help the next layer adhere. This is followed by a brown coat of cement and sand that is scraped smooth or floated to provide an even surface for the final layer. The finish coat (also called the color coat) is typically 1/8-inch (3-mm) thick, and can be textured or smooth. Finish coats can be given many different treatments, including an almost glossy finish for painting or wallpaper application.

GYPSUM BOARD

Gypsum board is the generic name for sheet materials with a noncombustible gypsum core, covered with a paper surface. Gypsum wallboard is a type of gypsum board used for walls, ceilings, or partitions; it is often used to provide a surface for decorative finishes. It began to replace plaster in 1950s because of its ease to use and low cost. Gypsum wallboard is also called drywall, plasterboard, or Sheetrock, or is designated by the abbreviation GWB.

Physical Properties, Characteristics, and Types of Gypsum Board

The mineral gypsum is strongest in compression, making gypsum board stronger as it becomes thicker. When gypsum wallboard is attached to ceiling framing, it acts like a beam between two supports, with the upper portion of the core in compression and the lower surface in tension. The gypsum core alone is not very strong in tension, but the face paper improves tensile strength.

Gypsum board is affected negatively by extensive or prolonged exposure to water or high temperature with high humidity. Wetting the face paper reduces its tensile and shear strength. Saturated paper or cutouts in the board can transmit moisture to the core, thereby reducing its strength; severe soaking can reduce its ability to recover when dried.

Gypsum will resist burning on its own, but special additives in the core of *Type X gypsum wallboard* increase its fire resistance. Multiple layers of sheets are used to further improve fire ratings.

Types of gypsum wallboard include the following:

- *Moisture-resistant gypsum wallboard* is known as *green board* for the color of its water-repellant paper face. Green board has a moisture-resistant core, and is used as backing for ceramic tile and in wet areas. It can be specified with a Type X core.
- *Foil-back gypsum wallboard* is used to keep water vapor from passing through a wall. It has a layer of aluminum foil laminated to its back that serves as a vapor retarder.
- *Gypsum board plaster base* is commonly called *blue board* for its blue absorptive paper face, which creates a strong bond with plaster materials; it is used as a substrate for veneer plaster.
- *Prefinished gypsum wallboard* has a decorative vinyl, textile, or printed-paper surface and is used for prefabricated, demountable partitions.
- *Sag-resistant gypsum ceiling board* is typically 1/2-inch thick, reducing its weight. Sag-resistant board meets the humidified deflection criteria of ASTM C 36 for 5/8-inch-thick gypsum wallboard, and has been receiving acceptance by code organizations in recent years.

Environmental and Health Impacts of Gypsum Board

Those in the gypsum wallboard industry are aware of concerns about the use and disposal of their products, and are taking steps to reduce their impact on health and environment. The degree to which manufacturers comply with these steps is an indication of their environmental awareness.

Wallboard facing papers are being made from recycled paper, and trimmings from paper rolls are recycled. Waste wallboard is returned to the production cycle. Synthetic gypsum, a by-product produced by scrubbing emissions from coal-fired power plants, is used to make new gypsum board. Water used in the manufacturing process is recycled with no discharge, and sediment in stormwater runoff is allowed to settle in ponds before discharge. Dust is collected and recycled into the process. Solvents used in the plant for washing, waste oils, old vehicle batteries, and scrap metals are sent to recyclers.

Kilns are fitted with systems that detect kiln leaks, balance kiln temperatures, and conserve fuel. Combustion sources are designed to reduce emissions.

Specifications for Gypsum Board

The edges of gypsum board sheets are tapered to facilitate application of paper-reinforcing tape or self-adhering fiberglass tape, and finished with joint compound. They are available with beveled, square, or rounded taper edges. Sheets of regular wallboard 4 feet (1.2 m) wide and 8 to 16 feet (2.4 to 4.8 m) long are made with a tapered edge. Board 1/4-inch (6-mm) thick is used as a base layer for walls intended to control sound. Single-layer construction is done with 1/2- and 5/8-inch-thick (13- and 16-mm-thick) boards.

The edges of base or intermediate boards in a multilayer construction have either square or tongue-and-groove edges. Prefinished boards are available with tapered, square, or beveled edges. Tapered edges are the easiest to tape and fill for strong, invisible seams, providing smooth surfaces suitable for painting or for application of wallcoverings. The edges of sheets are joined together and hidden with a strip of paper, paper-faced cotton, or plastic mesh joint tape. Joint compound, a pasty compound that is applied over the joint tape, is used for filling indentations and finishing joints in a gypsum wallboard surface.

Installing Gypsum Board

Gypsum board panels and the support systems to which they are attached are referred to as *gypsum board assemblies*. Typical assemblies include load-bearing and nonload-bearing interior partitions, tile backer partitions, and shaft walls. Gypsum board can be applied to above-grade masonry or concrete walls with smooth, dry, even surfaces that are free of oil or other materials that would cause separation. Exterior- or below-grade masonry or concrete walls must be furred out before gypsum board is applied, to eliminate the capillary transfer of water and to reduce condensation on interior wall surfaces.

Gypsum board may be fastened directly to structurally sound and dimensionally stable wood or metal stud framing. The face of the frame should be flat and even. Wood or metal furring is required when the frame or masonry base is not flat and even enough,

Table 6-1 Gypsum Board Curve Radius

Radius of Curves	Board Run Lengthwise	Board Run Widthwise
1/4-in. (6-mm) thick board	5 ft (1.5 m)	15 ft (4.5 m)
3/8 in. (10 mm)	7 ft–6 in. (2.3 m)	25 ft (7.6 m)
1/2 in. (13 mm)	20 ft (6 m)	

Note: Gypsum board can be bent and attached to a curving line of studs.

Table 6-2 Plaster Accessories

Accessory	Description	Use	Comments
Gypsum lath	Sheets 3/8 or 1/2-in. (10- or 13- mm) thick	Support for plaster	Sheets 16 in. (405 mm) wide are 48 in. (1220 mm) long.
			Sheets 24 in. (610 mm) wide are up to 12 ft (3660 mm) long.
Trim accessories	Galvanized steel or zinc alloy	For plaster lath	Protect and reinforce the edges and corners of plaster surfaces. Help bring the final coat of plaster to a level finish
	Wood grounds	For application of a wood finish	
Metal lath strips	Strip lath 4 or 6 in. wide	For plaster	Reinforce butt joints.
Corner reinforcing	105-degree angle and 2- or 3-in. webs	Protects corners of plaster or GWB; slightly resists being set into a 90-degree corner.	Expanded wing corner beads: springlike rounded corner and wings 1–1/4, 2, 2–5/8, 2–7/8, or 3–1/2 in. wide.
			Flexible corner beads: 1–1/2-in. webs for curved arches. The flanges on either side of the corner are from 1–1/4 to 3–3/8 in. (32 to 86 mm) wide.
			Radius corner: 1/8-in. (3-mm) radius curve or a 3/4-in. (19-mm) radius bullnose
			Bullnose corner beads have 2–7/8- or 3-in. webs on either side.
Casing beads	Square ends accommodate depths of 1/2, 5/8, 3/4, or 7/8 in. (13, 16, 19, 22 mm).	Reinforce the edges of plaster or gypsum board surfaces.	A square end with a 1/4-in. (6-mm), 45-degree break is also available. The flange is 3–1/8 in. (79 mm) wide.
Reveals	Linear recesses between sections of finish materials	Define material edges	F-reveal steps the plaster surface back from an adjoining right angle material.
Corner molding	Protection for projecting corners	Details corner	A corner mold provides 3/4-in. (19-mm) finished edges at touching corners at right angles.
Base screeds	Depths of 1/2, 3/4, and 7/8 in. (13, 19 and 22 mm)	Separate one plaster surface from another material	Solid base screeds with 1–3/8 in. total width project 1/2, 3/4, or 7/8 in.
			Similar base screeds are available with expanded wings for a total width of 4–3/4 or 5–3/8 in.
Expansion joints	1/2, 3/4, and 7/8 in. (13, 19 and 22 mm) depths	Control cracking	Control joint accessories are also available, which allow movement in the wall itself.

(Continued)

Table 6-2 (*Continued*)

Accessory	Description	Use	Comments
Terminals	Flat terminals: 2, 2–1/4, or 2–1/2 in. wide, attached with a solid cap and webs 3–1/4 wide	Cap the ends of solid plaster partitions	Special accessories are available for fascia corners, which allow the plaster to have either a rounded or square edge.
	Rounded terminals: 2 in. wide, with attaching webs, 3 in. wide		

when framing supports are too far apart, or when additional space is needed for thermal or acoustic insulation. Resilient furring channels are used to improve acoustic performance. Gypsum board panels are installed to studs or furring channels with screws, and sometimes with nails.

Gypsum board is applied vertically with the board length parallel to the framing, or horizontally with the length perpendicular to the framing. Horizontal application is used where it can be applied with fewer joints, giving it greater stiffness. Butt-end joints are kept to a minimum and located over a support.

It typically takes three days to complete the installation of drywall. The first day, the gypsum board is hung and a first coat of joint compound is applied and left to dry. The second day, the joints are sanded and a second coat is applied and left to dry. On the third day, a third coat of joint compound is applied.

Veneer plaster is applied as a thin plaster coating (*skim coat*) to a gypsum board surface. It provides a much harder surface than regular gypsum board and hides joints completely, making an ideal surface for paint. Blue board, with its blue paper covering treated to bond tightly with a plaster skim coat, comes in the same standard sheets as regular drywall. Blue board is finished by quickly taping and plastering the joints and then applying one or two coats of plaster, each about 1/8-inch thick to the entire surface of the board. Plaster skim coats can also be applied to regular gypsum board or an existing plaster surface, but the wall must first be primed with a special orange-colored primer.

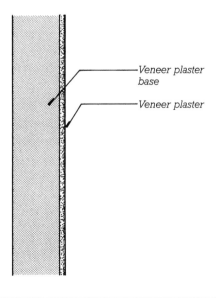

Veneer plaster base

Veneer plaster

Figure 6-13 Veneer plaster section
Reproduced by permission of the publisher from Edward Allen and Joseph Iano, *Fundamentals of Building Construction: Materials and Methods*, 4th ed. (Hoboken, NJ: John Wiley & Sons, Inc.), © 2004 by John Wiley & Sons, Inc.

The final veneer plaster surface does not necessarily have to be painted; it can also be colored before application. Because veneer plaster can be applied immediately after joint treatment, and a second coat, if desired, can be applied soon after, the process is a one-day treatment, rather than the three days typically required for drywall installation. There is also no need to sand the surface, and thus no dust to clean up.

Table 6-3 Levels of Gypsum Board Finish

Level	Recommended for	Process	Locations	Requirements
Level 0	Temporary construction, or if final decoration is undetermined	No taping or finishing is required.		
Level 1	Areas that would generally be concealed from view or not open to public traffic	Surface is left free of excess joint compound.	Plenum area above ceilings, in attics, or in service corridors	Ridges and tool marks are acceptable.
Level 2	Where moisture-resistant gypsum board is used as a tile substrate	Joint compound is applied over all fastener heads and beads; surface is left free of excess joint compound.	Garages and warehouse storage areas, where the final surface appearance is not of concern	Ridges and tool marks are acceptable.
Level 3	Areas to be decorated with a medium or heavy texture or heavy-grade wallcoverings	All joints and interior angles have tape embedded in joint compound and one additional coat of joint compound. Fastener heads and accessories are covered with two coats of joint compound.	Not recommended for smooth, painted surfaces or light- to medium-weight wallcoverings	All joint compound should be smooth and free from tool marks and ridges. Prepared surface must be coated with a drywall primer prior to the application of final finishes.
Level 4	Used if the final decoration is to be a flat paint, light texture or lightweight wallcovering	All joints and interior angles have tape embedded in joint compound, two coats of joint compound applied over all flat joints, and one coat over interior angles. Fastener heads and accessories are covered with three coats.	Where imperfections may be apparent through finish.	All joint compound should be smooth and free from tool marks and ridges. Prepared surface must be coated with a drywall primer prior to the application of final finishes.
Level 5	For areas where severe lighting conditions exist, and areas that are to receive gloss, semi-gloss, enamel, or nontextured flat paints.	Requires all the operations in level 4, plus a thin skim coat of joint compound. Prepared surface must be coated with a primer prior to the application of final finishes.	Offers the highest degree of quality by providing a uniform surface and minimizing the possibility of joints and/or fasteners showing through the final decoration.	The surface should be smooth and free from tool marks and ridges.

The cost of labor to install drywall is relatively low. One rule of thumb is that installed costs are about one-third for materials, one-third for hanging, and one-third for finishing. Veneer plaster installed on blue board may cost 20 to 30 percent more than drywall. Whether one or two coats of veneer are applied affects the cost. However, savings of time and cleanup costs can make veneer plaster competitive.

To prevent mold or mildew from growing on wet gypsum wallboard, it should be delivered to the site as close to the time of use as possible and immediately stored in a dry place. The source of any moisture reaching gypsum wallboard must be identified and corrected to prevent further damage. Surface mold and mildew can be removed with cleaning techniques. Mold and mildew can also grow in hidden areas, and may be missed by surface cleaning; in this case, the material must be replaced.

Discarding and Recycling Gypsum Board

Of the new drywall produced in the United States each year—approximately 15 million tons—about 12 percent is wasted as scrap during installation. Sixty-four percent of drywall waste comes from new construction; demolition contributes 14 percent, manufacturing 12 percent, and renovation 10 percent.

Dumping gypsum wallboard scrap and demolition waste in a landfill may produce hydrogen sulfide gas, especially in wet climates. High concentrations of hydrogen sulfide gas are toxic, and it has a foul, rotten-egg odor. Some communities do not accept gypsum wallboard at landfill sites. Incineration of gypsum wallboard may produce toxic sulfur dioxide gas and is prohibited in some locations, including in California.

Efficient use of standard sheet sizes by the interior designer can greatly eliminate construction waste. Drywall sheets come in sizes from 4 × 8 feet to 4 × 16 feet, and in thicknesses from 1/4 to 1 inch. As 9-foot ceilings are becoming more popular, drywall is also now available 4–1/2 feet wide. Standard-sized walls and flat ceilings use sheets efficiently. Custom-sized sheets can be special ordered for nonstandard walls. In commercial buildings, where interior partitions are likely to be relocated frequently, modular demountable partitions that are reusable save waste from demolition and from construction.

Gypsum wallboard waste from new construction sites has fewer contaminants than demolition waste and is the most commonly recycled. It is ground by machine, producing about 93 percent gypsum powder and 7 percent shredded paper by weight. The gypsum is sold as a powder with or without paper or in molded pellet form. Most of the paper can be screened out and recycled into paper products (including new wallboard paper) or composted. The dust produced by recycling can be collected and contained.

Gypsum wallboard waste from demolition sites is more difficult to recycle. Nails should be removed before processing. Tape can be screened out, or will break down in compost. Structures built before around 1975 may contain asbestos in the joint compound, which must not be allowed to reenter the manufacturing system. Walls that were painted before 1978 may contain lead-based paint; this can be detected with an inexpensive kit and be properly disposed of. Mercury may also be present in some painted gypsum wallboard.

Gypsum wallboard can be recycled into new products, and grant money is available in the United States from the Environmental Protection Agency for promoting recycled uses. The economic viability of gypsum recycling depends on the fees for dumping gypsum at landfills; the cost of transporting, collecting, and processing gypsum waste; and the market for recycled gypsum. Currently, gypsum wallboard is produced that is 15 to 20 percent recycled, and efforts are underway to increase this amount.

New, not demolition, gypsum wallboard scraps are currently being added to soil for agriculture and other purposes, and as an additive to compost. The addition of gypsum improves water penetration and workability of impermeable alkali soils, and helps to neutralize acid soils. The calcium and sulfur in gypsum are plant nutrients. The chemical boron, added to gypsum wallboard to increase its fire resistance, may be toxic to plants in some cases.

Novel ways are being developed to reuse the immense quantity of gypsum wallboard used in interior construction. Scraps of gypsum wallboard can be placed inside the cavities of interior walls during construction, potentially increasing acoustic separation between spaces. At cement plants, which use gypsum in large quantities, recycled gypsum can be used if the paper content is not over 1 percent. At least one company is adding recycled gypsum to stucco. Many of the uses under development use gypsum scrap to stabilize other waste materials; this does not reuse it in a constructive way, however, but rather adds it to the waste stream while solving other waste problems.

On-site disposal of new construction waste gypsum board used in residential building involves pulverizing all parts of the gypsum wallboard, including the paper, into pieces less than 1/2-inch square, so that it will disintegrate reasonably rapidly when exposed to weather. The pulverized GWB is then placed on the soil surface or mixed with the top layer of the soil and spread evenly over the entire lot where possible. On-site disposal is permissible only where there is adequate drainage and aeration; no standing water or anaerobic conditions should exist while the GWB decomposes. The process may be subject to regulation by state, local or federal governments.

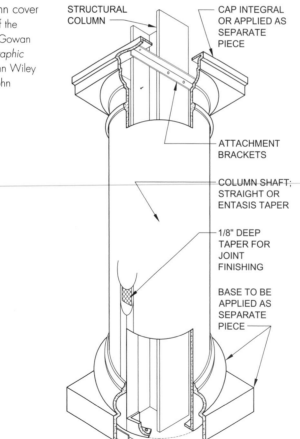

Figure 6-14 GFRG column cover Reproduced by permission of the publisher from Maryrose McGowan and Kelsey Kruse, *Interior Graphic Standards* (Hoboken, NJ: John Wiley & Sons, Inc.), © 2003 by John Wiley & Sons, Inc.

STRUCTURAL COLUMN

CAP INTEGRAL OR APPLIED AS SEPARATE PIECE

ATTACHMENT BRACKETS

COLUMN SHAFT; STRAIGHT OR ENTASIS TAPER

1/8" DEEP TAPER FOR JOINT FINISHING

BASE TO BE APPLIED AS SEPARATE PIECE

Glass-fiber-reinforced gypsum (GFRG) was introduced in 1977. GFRG is made of gypsum slurry with glass fiber. It is used to cast thin, high-strength shapes in molds at a manufacturing plant that are shipped to the site. GFRG is lightweight, nontoxic, and inherently flame-resistant. It is used for column covers, decorative domes, coffered ceilings, and in other architectural details. GFRG is installed with the same techniques as gypsum wallboard, and can be field-cut with gypsum board tools.

 Note: GFRG is sometimes called fiberglass-reinforced gypsum (FRG) or fiberglass-reinforced gypsum (FGRG).

GFRG products are either hand layered or sprayed into polyurethane or latex molds. Many molded products are available commercially, and molds can be customized for specific projects.

GFRG has a smooth finished surface that resembles plaster; it has a back side that is rough and irregular, with glass fibers and structural elements sometimes visible. The finished product is carefully wrapped and stored to resist warping or bowing.

Large GFRG constructions such as tall columns are usually made of shorter components, called lifts, that are stacked together; this simplifies fabrication and installation, and reduces production and shipping costs. However, the added joints may increase installation costs. Factors that affect the final cost include the complexity of joint details, the degree to which the fabrication process facilitates installation, which standard fastening details are available, and how efficiently the selected finish can be achieved. GFRG installations are usually given a smooth level finish that resembles plaster.

Metals 7

Metal—specifically, structural iron—is one of the major materials used for building structures. Architects use aluminum, copper, and, more recently, titanium for exterior cladding, roofing, and window and door frames. This chapter will focus on the uses of metal in building interiors. Due to their diversity, the physical properties and characteristics of metals will be discussed under the heading for each type, as will environmental and health considerations.

Metals are elementary substances that are crystalline when solid, and often characterized by opacity, conductivity, ductility, and a unique luster when freshly fractured. *Ductility* is the ability of a metal to be drawn out into a long, thin form such as a wire. *Malleable* metals are capable of being shaped or formed by hammering or by pressure from rollers. Many metals are good conductors of electricity, and they tend to be thermally conductive as well. The *luster*—shine—of metal adds sparkle to an interior. Two or more metals (or one metal with other materials) can be combined into an *alloy* with unique properties.

Metals are classified as either *ferrous* (made wholly or partly of iron) or *nonferrous*. Nonferrous metals used as interior finishes include aluminum, copper, chromium, zinc, nickel, and others that are discussed below. Metals that resist oxidation when heated in air and are not easily dissolved by inorganic acids are called *noble metals*, a designation that is important where metals are in contact with other metals in the presence of moisture. The most noble metals are gold and platinum, followed by titanium, silver, and stainless steel. Bronze, copper, brass, nickel, tin and lead are in the middle of the list. The least noble metals include iron and steel, cadmium, aluminum, zinc and magnesium.

Corrosion is the gradual deterioration of metal by chemical action; it usually takes place when metal is exposed to weather, moisture, or specific corroding agents. An *oxide* is a combination of oxygen with another element, such as rust on iron. *Galvanic corrosion* happens when an electrical current flows through a liquid between two dissimilar metals, deteriorating one of them. To prevent galvanic corrosion, different metals must be separated with a nonabsorbent, nonconductive material.

The greenish film on the surface of old bronze and copper is called its *patina*, and is formed by oxidation of the surface of the metal. A patina is considered a desirable finish; bronze and copper are often left without protective finishes to develop a patina over time.

Historical, Cultural, and Architectural Context of Metals

Hematite, a metal ore, was dug about 43,000 years ago at the Lion Cave in Swaziland for use as a pigment. Very early on, gold was mined in Egypt's Nubian mountains. The Hittites smelted iron ore in the Middle East about 1500 BCE. Bronze had been thought to have been first made in the Middle East, but archeological evidence from near Ban Chiang, Thailand, substantiates even earlier use, around 4500 BCE. Copper was worked in Africa around 4000 BCE.

Ancient Egyptians applied copper to cedar doors, and gold and silver to furniture. Skilled European craftspeople worked bronze, iron, tin, and copper as early as 1300 BCE. China produced bronze and iron, ornamented with gold and silver, after about 1122 BCE. Around 800 BCE, India developed ironworking. The Nok culture in Nigeria engaged in simple bronze and ironworking between 500 and 400 BCE.

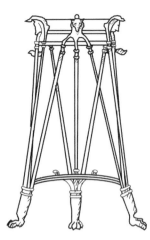

Figure 7-1 The Romans used metal tables as decorative pieces and as platforms for displays.

Precious metals were used in interiors to express wealth and status. History records that parts of Nero's Domus Aurea in Rome were overlaid with gold, and studded with precious stones and mother-of-pearl. Byzantine mosaic decoration shimmered with reflective glass squares bonded to gold leaf, silver, or mother-of-pearl.

Traditional Islamic design used iron, steel, bronze and brass, and gold and silver for chests, lamps, candlesticks, and furniture. Techniques included casting, hammering, lost wax, embossing, and filigree. *Damascening*, which involves the inlaying of thin gold and silver wires into grooves in the surface of a base metal, is named after the city of Damascus in Syria.

By 1450 CE, the palace in the Kingdom of Benin featured cast bronze sculptures, doors and pillars covered with stamped brass sheets, and a row of brass heads atop its outer wall, alternating with cast brass men on horseback in chain mail.

Much of the French Baroque furniture designed for Louis XIV's palaces and townhouses was embellished with gold, silver, and bronze, as well as *ormolu*, a technique for gilding bronze ornaments that are attached to corners and edges of furniture.

British ironmaker Abraham Darby invented the blast furnace in 1709, making it possible to produce large quantities of iron. In the 1850s, large-scale steel production was made possible by the inventions of William Kelly in the United States and Henry Bessemer in Britain.

Joseph Paxton, who designed the Crystal Palace in London in 1851, used prefabricated glass and iron sections that were assembled on-site. Although light cast-iron columns were capable of supporting buildings 8 to 12 stories high, their wood floors could burn, and their columns melt in fires. To improve fire safety, cast iron was combined

Figure 7-2 Damascened metal chest

with masonry outer walls, and iron columns were wrapped in tile heat insulation. By the end of the nineteenth century, the Bessemer steel process enabled the production of steel columns and beams, ultimately leading to the construction of skyscrapers.

American architect Louis Sullivan (1856–1924) designed steel-framed, masonry-clad buildings in Chicago, New York, and other American cities. Libraries designed by French engineer Pierre-François-Henri Labrouste (1801–1875) were spanned with iron arches and columns. Other innovative iron interiors were developed by Victor Baltard (1805–1879) at Les Halles Centrales (begun in 1853), and by Gustave Eiffel (1832–1923) at the Bon Marché department store.

Architect Otto Wagner's (1841–1918) design for the Austrian Post Office Savings Bank (1904–1906) was topped by a roof in metal and glass supported on columns of steel with exposed rivet heads. This honest, exposed use of metal structure was combined with decorative metal details.

For Ludwig Mies van der Rohe's Tugendhat House, Lilly Reich (1885–1947) designed tubular steel furniture with tan and emerald green leather and white kid upholstery. Charlotte Perriand (1903–1999) and others working with Le Corbusier created a small group of tubular-steel-framed furniture that was intended to be mass-produced for a mass market, but was produced very expensively in only limited quantities. The team's designs included an adjustable chaise longue (1927) and the Grand Confort chair (1928) that are still in production.

Aesthetic Qualities of Metals

The use of metals in an interior design offers opportunities for expressiveness in form. Metal drawn into wire or long thin strips can be used to create lines and curves. Cast metal forms express solidity and, sometimes, massiveness. Designs fabricated from many metal pieces appear intricate on a small scale, and express the structure of a building on a large scale.

Metal can be formed and finished to create textures varying from smooth and matte to ridged, pockmarked, hammered, or perforated. Shiny metal finishes are reflective and add sparkle to a design. Signs of wear and use can enrich the textural interest of a metal surface.

Metallic colors include those inherent in the material when it is newly worked and those, like patina and rust, which develop slowly over time. Finish treatments can change color, texture, and shininess of a metal surface.

Because most metals conduct heat rapidly, they tend to draw heat out of the body; therefore they tend to feel cool to the touch. Hot metal readily releases its heat to colder surfaces around it and, consequently, feels very hot as soon as it is touched.

Figure 7-3 The metal muffin pan conducts heat more rapidly than the muffin.

Metal also has acoustic qualities; it has been used in bells and musical instruments for thousands of years.

Note: Some people are sensitive to the taste or smell of certain metals.

Sources and Manufacturing for Metals

Ore is smelted in a blast furnace to separate its metal constituents. The residue left behind is called *slag* or *cinder*. Molten metal is cast into an ingot for convenient storage or transportation; these are reduced to bar shapes at a blooming mill.

When metal is hot-worked at high temperature, it will recrystalize into a new granular structure. The metal is then given a dark, oxidized, relatively rough hot-rolled finish. Die casting forms the desired shape by forcing the molten metal into a metallic mold under hydraulic pressure. Metals are also hot-worked by heating and hammering them on a forge.

Metal can be cold-worked at a lower temperature to increase its tensile strength or improve its surface finish. Cold-working methods include drawing, extrusion, pressing, or stamping. When a metal is forced through a die (a steel block or plate with small conical holes) by a pressure ram, the metal is extruded into a shape with a specific cross section.

Cold-drawing is used to make wire or tubing by drawing metal through a set of dies to reduce its cross-sectional area without preheating. A drawn finish is a smooth, bright finish that results from pulling metal through a die.

Finishes for Metals

There are three basic finish types for metals: mechanical, chemical, and coating. Finishes are selected for both appearance and function. Chemical and electrochemical finishing processes produce more hazardous waste than that derived from abrasive blasting, grinding, buffing and polishing.

Figure 7-4 A white-hot, 3-ton ingot of steel in a mill in Homestead, Pennsylvania, to be rolled out 75 feet long.

Figure 7-5 Brass rod coming through the extrusion machine

Metal Processing

Metal is processed to accentuate desirable qualities.

- *Heat treatment* involves heating and cooling a metal in a controlled manner.
- *Annealing* removes internal stresses from metal (or glass) by heating it to a temperature below that needed for recrystalization, then gradually cooling it in a liquid or air. Annealing is often used to make a metal more ductile.
- *Quenching* rapidly cools a heated metal by immersing it in water; it is used to increase metal hardness.
- *Tempering* reheats a metal (or glass) at a lower temperature and then slowly cools it to strengthen or toughen it.
- *Case-hardening* is a carburization and heat treatment used to make the outside surface of an iron-based alloy hard; the inside remains tough and ductile.

Note: Metal finishes for aluminum, copper alloys, stainless steel, carbon steel, and iron are described in the *Metal Finishes Manual* published by the Architectural Metal Products (AMP) Division of the National Association of Architectural Metal Manufacturers. The finishes for metal hardware are described in ANSI A156.18, American National Standard for Materials and Finishes, sponsored by the Builders Hardware Manufacturers Association.

The surfaces of decorative pieces can be given a metallic appearance if primed with white paint, and then painted with ground iron in a water-based medium; rust will soon begin to form. Various other effects and patinas for iron can be achieved with chemical washes. Metal blackening, antiquing and oxidizing products are available commercially.

Table 7-1 Metal Finishes

Type of Finish	Appearance	Process	Used for
Mechanical Finishes			
Mill finish	Striated	Cold-rolling or extrusion	Aluminum, copper alloys, steel and iron
As-fabricated finishes		Freshly fabricated metal	
Buffed finishes	Improves finish on edges and surfaces.	Polishing and buffing with fine abrasives, lubricants, and soft fabric wheels	
Patterned finishes	Pattern is embossed on metal sheet.	Sheet of metal is pressed between two rollers with pattern.	
Directional textured finishes	Smooth, satiny sheen	Tiny parallel scratches are made by a belt or wheel and fine abrasive or by hand-rubbing with steel wool.	
Peened finishes	Slip-resistant finish	Stream of small steel shot is fired at a metal surface at high velocity.	
Other finishes	Nondirectional textured	Blasting with silica sand, glass beads, or aluminum oxide	
Chemical Finishes			
Chemical cleaning	Cleans metal surfaces without altering them.	Uses solvents and cleaners.	All metals
Etched finishes	Matte, frosted surfaces	Produced with an acid or alkali solution.	
Conversion coatings	Prepare metal surfaces for another surface; produce patina and statuary finishes.	Production of a layer or coating on a metal surface by a chemical reaction	Iron and steel railings and outdoor furniture

Type of Finish	Appearance	Process	Used for
Coatings			
Organic coatings	Decorative finishes, primers or undercoats, pigmented topcoats in hidden areas, and clear finish protective coatings	Applied by spraying or dipping. Paints, varnishes, enamels, lacquers, plastisols, organisols, and powders are all forms of organic coatings.	Carbon steel, iron, aluminum
Electrodeposition (See color plate C-39)	Uniform thickness, avoiding runs or sags. No paint is wasted; very low VOC levels.	Process similar to electroplating, with organic resins rather than metal deposited on the metal surface.	Used only for the first coat; subsequent coats are sprayed on.
Powder coating (See color plate C-40.)	Smooth, easily cleaned surface	Solvent-less paints, heat-reactive hardeners, catalysts, or cross-linkers as curing agents	Interior products made of iron
Other coatings	Epoxies, polyurethanes, acrylics, and polyesters	Finish appearance or protection	May be sprayed on after electrode position
Cladding (See color plates C-49, White metal finish and C-50, Nickel silver finish.)	Smooth, protective surface	Bonds one metal onto another, often as protection from corrosion.	Aluminum, lead, cadmium, stainless steel, nickel alloys
Anodizing	Hard, noncorrosive film	Through electrolytic or chemical action	Aluminum or magnesium
Galvanizing	Protection from rust	Involves immersing iron or steel in molten zinc.	Iron exposed to weather
Pickling	Removes oxide scale or other substances from the metal.	Dipping a metal object into an acid or other chemical solution	Carbon steel objects before other processing
Bonderizing	Preparation for the application of paint, enamel, or lacquer	Process of coating steel with an anticorrosive phosphate solution	Steel
Chrome plating	Can be brightly polished, and does not tarnish or rust.	Coats or electroplates (chrome or chromeplate)	Metal surfaces including iron, steel, brass, and bronze
Electroplating	Increases hardness and durability and enhances appearance.	Uses electrolysis to plate a metallic coating onto a surface.	Ferrous and nonferrous objects plated with aluminum, brass, bronze, cadmium, copper, chromium, iron, lead, nickel, tin, zinc. Also precious metals including gold, platinum, silver

FERROUS METALS

Ferrous metals are those that contain iron. Most are magnetic, although stainless steel varies in this regard.

Iron

Iron is the principal element in ferrous metals. Iron without carbon added is a silver-white metal that is soft, malleable, ductile, and magnetic; it will rust fairly rapidly and will corrode when exposed to most acids. The addition of carbon increases metal strength and hardness, but reduces ductility and weldability (a material's ability to be welded). It is a relatively inexpensive metal and is often used in structural applications. (See color plate C-45, Rust on concrete.)

Types of iron are defined as follows:

- *Cast iron* is an alloy of iron with 2 to 4.5 percent carbon and 0.5 to 3 percent silicon that is cast in a sand mold and then machined into products. Regular cast iron is hard, brittle, relatively corrosion-resistant, and nonmalleable; this is the form used to make frying pans. Malleable cast iron has had its carbon removed. It is used to make hardware, stoves and fire-backs, columns and balusters, stairs, and structural connectors, as well as ornamental railings, historic markers and plaques, decorative pieces for gardens, and plumbing waste pipes.
- *Wrought iron* is tough but malleable and relatively soft and easily forged and welded. It contains around 0.2 percent carbon with a small amount of slag distributed throughout. Wrought iron uses include gates and grilles, outdoor furniture, hardware, railings, fences, screens, and ornamental work.

Steel

Steel encompasses strong, hard, and elastic alloys of iron with carbon content less than that of cast iron and more than that of wrought iron. The higher the carbon content, the stronger and harder the steel, and the lower its ductility and weldability.

Figure 7-6 Iron bedstead by Messrs. Cowley & James of Walsall, shown at Crystal Palace Exhibition, London, 1851

Steel is categorized as carbon or stainless steel.

- *Carbon steel* is generally any unalloyed steel with limited amounts of residual carbon or other elements. It is categorized as mild (soft) steel, medium steel, hard steel, or spring steel, depending on its carbon content. Carbon steel is used in welded fabrications or castings, metal studs and joists, fasteners, wall grilles, and ceiling suspension systems. *Alloy steel* is carbon steel with other elements added to produce desired physical or chemical properties.
- *Stainless steel* is a steel alloy with a minimum of around 12 percent chromium that is highly resistant to corrosion, is very durable, and has good finish retention. Self-healing chromium-oxide forms a transparent film on the surface of stainless steel that protects it from oxidation and resulting rust. Stainless steel does not stain adjacent surfaces and does not react with mortar or concrete. Its initial cost is nearly five times that of carbon steel. It is used for column covers and railings, wall panels, handrails, hardware, fasteners, and anchors. It meets hygienic requirements for food preparation equipment and surfaces, and is also used in furniture, accessories, eating utensils, and decorative pieces.

Iron Ore

Iron ores are usually rich in iron oxides and vary in color from dark gray to rusty red. Iron ore is the raw material for iron: 98 percent of all iron ore mined is used to make steel. Iron ores are common worldwide and are mined in about 50 countries, including Australia and Brazil. Open-pit mining, quarrying, strip mining, placer mining, and mountaintop removal are all forms of surface mining. Drift, slope, shaft, hard rock, and borehole mining are all subsurface methods of extracting ore.

The smelting process separates oxygen from the iron atoms in iron ore. The iron ore is powdered and mixed with coke, then dumped into a blast furnace, where a blast of hot air from the furnace's stove causes the carbon atoms in the coke to bond with the oxygen atoms in the iron ore, releasing iron atoms. Molten pig iron collected at the bottom of the blast furnace is piped into containers. The process produces slag, as well as gases from the furnace that contain carbon monoxide. These gases are then burned in the stove to provide heat for the furnace.

To make steel, molten pig iron, with at least 25 percent recycled scrap steel added, is put into a steel converter, where excess carbon is burned away. Waste gases from the converter are cleaned and discharged. The molten steel is then cast into ingots.

Table 7-2 Stainless Steel Series

Series	Type	Characteristics	Composition
200		Reduced nickel content; lower cost	Usually not magnetic
300		Most corrosion resistance; easiest to fabricate and weld	Usually not magnetic
	302 and/or 304	Interior and exterior architectural uses	Approximately 18% chromium and 8% nickel
400		Less corrosion resistance	Contains chromium; low carbon; bright finish

Electric-arc furnaces use almost 100 percent recycled steel to make reinforcing bar and structural beams.

Environmental Impact of Ferrous Metals

Iron and steel are not considered to be toxic. Iron may cause irritation if it makes contact with and remains in eye tissue, and may cause conjunctivitis and other eye problems. Chronic inhalation of concentrated iron oxide fumes or dusts may enhance the risk of lung cancer development.

Mine safety is closely regulated and has improved greatly in the past several decades. Nevertheless, mining accidents still occur, sometimes resulting in miners being trapped in collapsed mine tunnels. Improved ventilation in mines is decreasing the occurrence of pneumoconiosis (black lung disease).

Mining is the source of a number of serious environmental problems, including erosion, the formation of sinkholes, the contamination of groundwater, and the loss of biodiversity. Although most governments attempt to control such damage, a great deal of the harm done to the environment in the past remains. More than 2 million acres (8000 km²) of mine land has been reclaimed by industry in the United States since government regulations went into effect in 1978; this land is now suitable for vegetation and wildlife, as well as for farms and ranching.

The coke used to fire blast furnaces is produced by blending and heating bituminous coal to 1000°C to 1400°C in the absence of oxygen. This process produces tars, light oils, and gases that have been determined by the U.S. National Institutes of Health to be carcinogenic. About 20 to 35 percent of the original coal is emitted as gaseous vapors, most of which are collected and processed into chemical by-products such as benzene and toluene, which have their own health and safety problems. Moreover, some emissions escape the control system through structural flaws and inadequate engineering controls and work practices. Workers are exposed to carcinogenic materials through inhalation and skin contact during the process of making coke and of processing its by-products; people living in the path of these emissions can also be exposed.

When iron ore is made into pig iron in blast furnaces, exhaust gases are collected and processed by the plant's emission control system. Nonmetallic slag constitutes about 20 percent of the mass of all iron production; it is removed from the bottom of the blast furnace for further processing, reuse, or disposal. About 90 percent of all slag produced in the United States is reused, primarily as aggregate substitutes for concrete, asphalt, and cement products. The remainder is deposited in landfills.

Figure 7-7 Slag heap

The process of welding steel exposes workers to dangerous gases and particles; the resulting smoke can cause a disease known as metal fume fever. Excessive carbon dioxide and ozone can collect in work areas that are inadequately ventilated. The risk of explosion from the use of compressed gases and open flames is reduced where the supply of oxygen is limited.

Costs Associated with Ferrous Metals

Ore transportation and port costs are around 52 percent of the total costs of manufacturing iron. Mining activities comprise only about 21 percent of the total cost; processing factors in at approximately 17 percent. Royalties account for the final 10 percent.

The market price for iron is subject to the forces of supply and demand and availability of the resource; prices change daily. Producers can, however, control costs somewhat, and increase profits, by lowering production costs and developing links with local and overseas steel manufacturers.

The cost of welding steel varies with the equipment, labor, material and energy costs. For methods that are primarily manual, labor makes up most of the cost.

Joining Processes for Ferrous Metals

Steel connections are usually made by *welding*, by bolting, or by a combination of both methods. These connections can be made at the shop or factory, in the field, or partly in each place. Welding combines metals by melting the pieces being worked on and adding a filler material. The filler forms a pool with the molten metal called a weld puddle, which cools to form a strong joint. Sometimes pressure is used with heat or by itself to make a weld. The joints most often used for welding are butt, lap, corner, edge, and T-joints. (See color plate C-41.)

Historically, blacksmiths joined pieces of iron by heating and pounding them on a forge. Energy sources for welding now include gas flame, electric arc, laser, electron beam, friction, and ultrasound. Robot welding is used for mass production in factories.

Figure 7-8 Riveted steel inside the Statue of Liberty. A rivet is a mechanical fastener made from a cylindrical metal shaft with a head on one end. The rivet is inserted into a predrilled hole; the opposite end is deformed to hold the rivet in place. Rivets are still used for strong, lightweight connections with sheet-metal alloys, and on blue jeans.

The weldability of steel decreases as its carbon content increases; the chromium content of stainless steel further complicates the process. The bolts that hold together steel assemblies are usually secured with screwed-on nuts. Bolts for steel are designed both to hold pieces together and, in many cases, to provide some structural support. Their selection and design are covered by ASTM specifications.

Maintenance of Ferrous Metals

Maintenance for iron products is fairly simple. Hand-forged items for interior use are ordinarily lightly hand-sanded and then hand-rubbed with a heated mixture of linseed oil, turpentine, and beeswax; the surface is buffed as it cools. Forged ironwork is maintained by waxing it with a good-quality furniture wax. In high-traffic or high-humidity areas, paste or furniture wax can be applied to metal that has been warmed with a hair dryer or heat gun, allowing the wax to get into the surface of the metal. The piece is then buffed with a soft cloth or a shoeshine brush that can get into small crevices. For furniture, bath and kitchen accessories, two coats of clear acrylic will protect the surface from moisture.

Stainless steel can be damaged by corrosive deposits, as for example by salt in marine environments. Warm, high-humidity conditions tend to speed corrosion. Corrosion can be cleaned by washing with soap or a mild detergent and warm water, then rinsing with clean water. Wiping stainless steel dry parallel to grain lines will polish the surface. Lime deposits caused by hard water will brush loose after soaking in one part vinegar to three parts water, then rinsing and wiping dry. Organic solvents such as acetone or alcohol can be used to remove oil or grease marks, followed by soap and water, rinsing and drying. Stainless steel will pick up rust stains if in contact with unprotected iron. These can be removed using a solution of nitric acid in warm water; protective clothing should be worn. Dark oxide stains from welding or heat treatment are removed with a commercial pickling paste.

Figure 7-9 304 stainless steel with #4 satin finish

Much-used stainless steel surfaces will acquire fine wear scratches that do not harm the material. To reduce the visual impact of surface scratches, the area can be gently rubbed with a fine nylon pad in the direction of the grain. Some finish patterns will disguise these scratch marks.

Forms of Ferrous Metals

Structural steel is formed into standard shapes for use as load-bearing members in construction. A steel beam is used to support horizontal loads, and is made up of a flat, rigid web between two broader parallel flanges that project at right angles from its top and bottom. Steel beams are commonly formed as I-beams and in W-shapes (wide flange), and in other configurations. Other structural steel shapes include steel channels shaped like squared-off letter Cs in section, angles (angle iron) with L-shapes, and tees (T-bars).

Structural tubing comes in hollow steel shapes with square, rectangular, or circular cross sections. Steel pipe is available in standard, extra-strong, and double-extra-strong wall thicknesses.

Steel plate consists of a thin, flat sheet or piece of metal, usually of uniform thickness. Checkered plate has a crisscrossed wafflelike pattern. Sheet metal comes in thin sheets or plates and is used to manufacture ductwork, flashing, and roofing. Corrugated sheet metal has been drawn or rolled into parallel ridges and furrows to increase its strength. Expanded metal is slotted and stretched sheet metal; the resulting stiff, open mesh, or lattice is frequently used as lath. (See colored plate C-42 Corrugated galvanized steel.)

Wire cloth is a fabric woven of metallic wire. Hardware cloth is galvanized steel wire cloth with a mesh between 1/4 and 1/2 inch (6 and 13 mm). Wire rope is a heavy rope consisting of wire strands twisted around a central core.

Other structural steel forms include open-web steel joists (lightweight fabricated steel joists) and joist girders (a trussed girder that supports open-web joists), plate girders built up from plates or shapes welded or riveted together, box girders (similar to a plate girder but with a hollow, rectangular cross section), and castellated beams made by cutting a steel beam's web in a zigzag pattern, then welding the peaks of each lengthwise half together for a deeper, lighter beam.

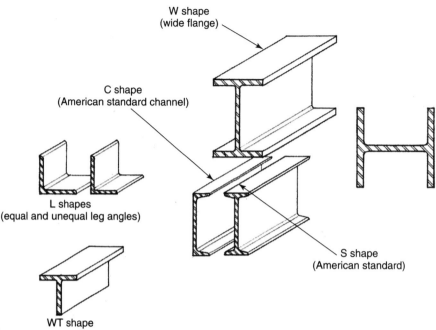

Figure 7-10 Steel structural shapes
Reproduced by permission of the publisher from Francis D. K. Ching and Cassandra Adams, *Building Construction Illustrated*, 3rd ed. (New York: John Wiley & Sons, Inc.), © 2001 by John Wiley & Sons, Inc.

W shape
(wide flange)

C shape
(American standard channel)

L shapes
(equal and unequal leg angles)

S shape
(American standard)

WT shape
(structural tee cut from W shape)

NONFERROUS METALS

Nonferrous metals contain little or no iron. There are many nonferrous metals; those included here are often used in building interiors.

Aluminum

The metal called *aluminum* in the United States, and *aluminium* elsewhere, is a silver-white metallic element that is ductile, malleable, soft and flexible, and easy to fabricate. Although it is lightweight, it is quite strong. Aluminum is made from bauxite ore. Alumina is another name for aluminum oxide.

Aluminum is used in many hard, light alloys, some of which are stronger than structural steel. It is highly resistant to corrosion, and is often anodized for improved corrosion resistance, color, and surface hardness. Aluminum reflects radiant energy, resists corrosion in air and in water, and is nonmagnetic. It is an excellent thermal and electrical conductor and is used for electrical wiring.

Aluminum is used in buildings for curtain walls, door and window frames and storefronts, roof sheeting and sheet siding, flashing, gutters, soffits, fascia, and downspouts. It is also used for patio and pool enclosures, canopies, and awnings. Lighting fixtures and outdoor furniture are frequently made of aluminum. In interiors, aluminum is used for door frames and hardware, interior window frames, horizontal louver blind slats, and furniture.

Aluminum is abundant but it is always found combined with oxygen as an oxide or silicate. Although it was discovered in 1808, its commercial production did not begin until 1854. Aluminum is extracted from bauxite ore found in tropical and subtropical Africa, West Indies, South America, and Australia.

Because of its extensive processing, aluminum has one of the highest levels of embodied energy for a building material, hundreds of times that of wood. The risk of exposure to aluminum dust and fumes is considered to be low. Chronic exposure, however, can result in pulmonary fibrosis; symptoms include difficulty breathing, shortness of breath, wheezing, and other respiratory problems.

Aluminum was once more expensive than either gold or platinum, but prices dropped radically after commercial production was improved. Aluminum as a structural

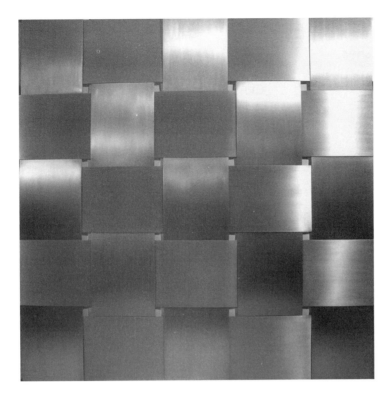

Figure 7-11 Woven aluminum
© 2004 by Axolotl Group Pty Ltd.

material has an initial cost about twice that of carbon steel and less than half that of stainless steel. When used without a coating or paint, aluminum saves preparation and maintenance costs. Its light weight reduces shipping and installation costs, and it is easier to fabricate than carbon steel.

The cost of a basic ingot of aluminum is less than copper on a per-pound basis; sheets and plates of aluminum are less expensive than stainless steel. Aluminum can be die-cast into large shapes less expensively than other metals such as zinc, but it may be more expensive for small, complex shapes. Low maintenance costs give it a very low cost over its service life.

Aluminum is commonly die cast, permanent mold cast, and sand cast. Metal molds ensure dimensional accuracy, but weigh from 10 to 100 times as much as the pieces being cast, so sand casting is used for most very large pieces. Aluminum die castings are not easily welded or heat-treated because of entrapped gases.

When exposed to air, aluminum quickly becomes coated with a thin microscopic layer of oxides that is almost completely corrosion-resistant. This layer must be removed before welding. Electrical connections with aluminum wires and bars have to be made mechanically. The alkaline chemicals found in concrete and masonry mortar will attack aluminum, so it cannot be used in contact with these materials.

Conversion coatings change the surface of aluminum to improve its bonding adhesion as preparation for painting and sometimes as final finishes. Anodizing aluminum and its alloys involves passing an electrical current across a solution (usually sulfuric acid) in which the aluminum is immersed. The thicker coating thus produced increases corrosion resistance. Transparent, translucent, or opaque anodized coatings can increase abrasion resistance without modifying surface texture.

About 13 percent of the aluminum used today is used in buildings and construction. Recycled aluminum, primarily from beverage cans, is widely used to reduce energy use. Aluminum can be remelted, with little loss of material.

Table 7-3 Aluminum Finishes

Finish Category	Type	Class	Designation
M = Mechanical finishes, produced by the fabrication process, by buffing, or by texturing	Textured	Directional: Satin finishes to hand-rubbed and brushed finishes	
		Nondirectional: matte or shot blast	M42 fine, M43 medium, or M44 coarse matte are commonly used on architectual work.
C = Chemical finishes	Nonetched cleaned, etched, brightened, and conversion coating finishes		Nonetched cleaned C11 degreased or C12 chemically cleaned are used in architecture.
S = Anodic finishes	General, protective and decorative, architectural class II and architectural class I	Architectural class I finishes	A41 clear (natural)
			A42 integral color (used less often)
			A43 impregnated color
			A44 electrolytically deposited color
		Architectural class II finishes	A31 clear (natural)
			A32 integral color
			A33 impregnated color
			A34 electrolytically deposited color

Bronze and Brass

The term *bronze* covers a variety of alloys of copper. The metal most often added to copper to produce bronze is tin, although phosphorus, manganese, aluminum, or silicon is also used. Traditional usage of the term is for a copper alloy that contains no more than 11 percent tin.

 Note: Because bronze and brass are copper alloys, their source materials and manufacturing processes are discussed in the section on copper.

In its pure state, bronze is a pinkish, salmon-colored metal. It almost always has some patina or corrosion, causing its color to range from lime green to dark brown, with oxidation and corrosion proceeding through a set sequence of stages. The duration of each stage depends on the composition of the bronze, applied treatments, exposure to weather, the presence of atmospheric pollutants, maintenance and cleaning, and contact with other materials. (See color plate C-46, Bronze patina.)

Bronze, which is valued for its strength and corrosion resistance, is probably best known as the material for outdoor sculptures. Bronze resists industrial and marine atmospheres and weak acids well. The presence of sulfur and chlorine in the atmosphere, especially in the presence of moisture, is the major cause of bronze deterioration. Corrosion may attack the surface of bronze evenly or selectively, or as pitting in localized areas. When a corrosion-resistant oxide layer is removed, the bare metal underneath may erode. Galvanic corrosion can result from contact with another (or, in some cases, the same) metal. Bronze may crack in areas that were stressed during metalworking.

Brass is an alloy of copper and zinc; the hardness or softness of brass depends on the proportions of these two metals. The addition of aluminum improves strength and

Table 7-4 Brass and Bronze Types

Material Name	Approximate Content	Uses
Aluminum brass	2% aluminum added to about 75% copper, with the remainder including small amounts of other elements	Machine parts where increased strength is required
Aluminum bronze (albronze): various alloys	High percentage of copper, with from 5% to 11% aluminum and varying amounts of iron, nickel, and manganese	Machine parts; tools, jewelry, and architecture
Architectural bronze (See color plate C-43)	57% copper, 40% zinc, 2.75% lead; and may include 0.25% tin	Door and window frames; hardware, mailboxes, and chutes, trims, rails, and furniture hardware
Commercial bronze	90% copper and 10% zinc	Screws and wires
Muntz metal (alpha-beta brass)	55% to 61% copper, with from 39% to 45% zinc	Plaques
Red brass (gunmetal)	77% to 86% copper, with the balance zinc	Many industrial uses, plus small cast objects and buttons
Statuary bronze	97% copper, 2% tin, and 1% zinc	Outdoor sculpture
True bronze	90% copper and 10% tin	Outdoor and marine applications

corrosion resistance and causes a thin, transparent, and self-healing hard protective layer to be formed on the surface. With tin added to increase strength and corrosion resistance, brass can be used for marine applications. Combinations of iron, aluminum, silicon, and manganese improve wear and tear resistance. Brass casts well, due to its relatively low melting point and its flow characteristics.

Note: Some forms of brass include the term "bronze" in their names.

Brass is yellow in color, with a resemblance to gold. It was first produced in prehistoric times by melting copper with calamine, a zinc ore. It is somewhat resistant to tarnishing and is often used for decorative purposes—on windows, railings, and trim, and as finish hardware. The acoustic properties of brass led to its use in musical instruments.

Bronze and brass are considered nontoxic and safe to use. Dust and fumes produced by working with copper alloys such as bronze and brass usually can be controlled without presenting a problem. Copper fumes and dust may cause nose and throat irritation, however, and dust may irritate the eyes and skin. Inhaling fumes produces a sweet or metallic taste. In high concentrations, inhaled copper can cause metal fume fever, which produces flulike symptoms for one or two days.

Specifications for bronze and brass architectural work include information on alloy composition, joining, and coloring. Most forms of brass and bronze are a golden honey color in their natural state and a rich statuary bronze when chemically colored. Brass with aluminum is originally a bright yellow, which changes to a honey color when polished. Pink brass and nickel silver are other available colors. (See color plate C-44, Bronze doors.)

Natural brass and bronze colors weather to brown; the process varies with the amount of humidity and the level of air pollutants. Due to the effect of human body acids, fingerprints will leave marks on natural brass and bronze; the material can be protected by a coating or by frequent cleaning and polishing. Trumpets and other brass musical instruments are typically lacquered.

Chemical coloring is essentially artificial weathering of brass and bronze from its natural color to a darker color. An oxide or sulfide is used to convert the surface of the metal to a colored protective film. The skill of the craftsperson applying the chemicals is important in achieving a desirable outcome. Chemical coloring is used for architectural hardware and on elevator cabs.

Brass and bronze will cause galvanic corrosion in contact with steel or aluminum and so should be separated with an insulating material such as neoprene, felt, or a bituminous coating. Stainless steel fasteners are used for mechanical joining of dissimilar metals.

Brass and bronze are relatively expensive materials, and their cost has an effect on when and how they are used. Cost factors for bronze and brass take into account not only the cost of raw materials but also costs of fabricating products such as hardware and lighting fixtures. The durability of bronze and brass affect its life-cycle cost as compared to less durable or harder-to-maintain materials. Great increases in price are not uncommon.

The demand for recycled brass means that scrap and used pieces have considerable value. In 2006, the combination of high demand and tight supply was responsible for near-record-high raw material costs for brass and bronze. Nearly all brass alloys are collected and sent to a foundry to be melted and recast into billets; these are then heated and extruded into the desired form.

Bronze and brass pieces can be joined mechanically with screws, bolts, and rivets. Sheets of brass and bronze may be laminated to steel, plywood, or similar substrates with adhesives. Brazing is the preferred method of heat-joining brass or bronze, as it does not distort the base material. Soldering is a lower-temperature method for sealing joints; it does not produce a strong bond and is often used with mechanical fasteners. Welding at high temperatures fuses the base metals and causes color matching problems and joint distortion.

Architectural bronze and brass will preserve their natural, highly polished pinkish finish with frequent polishing and oiling; periodic applications of clear lacquer will also help. Abrasion will cause removal of the protective metal surface of bronze. Chemical coloring of bronze and brass can be maintained and protected through repeated applications of oil or wax; linseed, lemon, and paraffin oils are commonly used. As the protective material builds up over time, the frequency of application can be reduced. Eventually, the layers form a protective surface known as oil-rubbed bronze. Repeated touching will break through this protective surface and reveal the natural base color.

Chromium

Chromium is a steel-gray lustrous hard metal that takes a high polish and has a high melting point. Chromium is used to produce chrome finishes for other metals. When exposed to oxygen, it forms a very thin oxide that protects the underlying metal. Chromium is also the chemical that makes rubies red, and is found in emeralds. Chromium salts are used to make glass green and in the tanning of leather. It is also used as a pigment in paints, including bright chrome yellow and chromium green.

Natural chromium deposits are rare, and it is commercially mined as chromite ore in South Africa, Kazakhstan, India, and Turkey. The ore is heated in the presence of aluminum or silicon to obtain chromium.

Chromium plating procedures are described as either industrial (hard chrome or engineered chrome) or decorative. Hard chrome plating is a relatively heavy coating usually applied to steel for industrial purposes; it is not particularly shiny and is not used as a decorative finish.

Chrome is always applied by electroplating. Electroplating is a categorically regulated industry, with all waste products automatically declared hazardous waste.

The materials used for industrial hexavalent chromium plating are extremely hazardous; they are toxic, corrosive, carcinogenic, and environmentally damaging. Chromium metal and chromium III (trivalent chromium), used in decorative finishes, are not generally considered to be hazardous to human health. Chromium itself may be an allergen for some individuals, causing skin and respiratory problems. There is some possible increase in risk of lung cancer for exposed workers.

Decorative chrome plating, also called nickel-chrome plating, is produced by electroplating nickel onto an object in preparation for electroplating it with chrome. The nickel provides corrosion resistance and most of the reflective properties of the finish. An extremely thin chrome surface is applied over the nickel; the chrome adds a bluish cast (the nickel appears silver-yellow), protects the nickel from tarnishing and scratching, and improves corrosion resistance. High-quality chrome plating requires additional layers of nickel.

A decorative chrome electroplated finish is more reflective, bluer, and less gray, and has a more mirrorlike (*specular*) appearance than other shiny finishes. Brightly polished aluminum, electropolished stainless steel, nickel-plated metals, vacuum-metalized and shiny painted objects are all sometimes mistaken for chrome finishes.

Where chrome plating is exposed to the weather it must have a semibright nickel followed by a bright nickel underlayer to prevent galvanic corrosion problems. Chrome on top of a single layer of nickel will not endure severe exposure.

To restore a chrome piece by replating, the nickel and any copper layers must be stripped, and all scratches and blemishes must be polished out; the piece is then plated and buffed with copper to remove any tiny pits. After all these steps have been completed, the whole plating process described above is redone. This labor-intensive process often costs more than the original plating.

Copper

Copper is a naturally occurring reddish-orange element that is readily available, easily fabricated, and generally corrosion-resistant; its resistance to alkaline chemicals allows it to be used in contact with masonry. Copper has high ductility, malleability, and thermal and electrical conductivity, and is used in electrical wiring. Copper is used in plumbing supply pipes and fittings, and for roofing, gutters, and rainspouts. In interiors, copper is used for many household products and hardware, as a decorative finish, and as a pigment. When copper is left untreated, it turns brown and eventually develops a green patina. The original appearance can be restored by polishing, or preserved with a transparent coating. (See color plates C-47 and C-48.)

The price of copper has quintupled since 1999, rising from $0.60 per pound in June 1999 to $3.75 per pound in May 2006. Old copper pipes and other building components are highly valued for use as recycled materials.

Humans have used copper for at least 10,000 years. Copper smelting—the refining of copper from simple copper compounds such as malachite or azurite—appears to have developed independently in Mesopotamia, Anatolia, China, Central America, and West Africa. Today, copper-ore-producing countries include Chile, the United States, Indonesia, Australia, Peru, Russia, Canada, China, Poland, Kazakhstan, and Mexico. Most copper ore is taken from open-pit mines; ore deposits usually contain less than 2 percent copper by weight.

With each step in the process of extracting copper from copper ore, impurities are physically or chemically removed and the copper itself becomes more concentrated. Large amounts of dirt, clay, and noncopper-bearing minerals are removed from the copper ore. The ore is crushed and ground up and mixed with water into slurry. Chemicals are mixed in to separate the copper particles from the slurry as copper concentrate. The leftover materials in the bottom of the tank are pumped into ponds to settle and dry.

Smelting removes iron and sulfur from the copper concentrate. Traditionally smelting took place in a series of two furnaces; more modern methods combine the process in a single furnace. The resulting material is approximately 99 percent copper by weight. At this point, the molten copper is fire-refined before it is poured into molds. Final refining involves running an electrical current through a liquid solution in a tank to strip pure copper out of the molded forms and to collect it on a sheet of copper at the opposite end of the tank. The residue at the bottom of the tank is collected and processed to extract valuable gold, silver, selenium, and tellurium.

After it is refined, copper is melted and cast into ingots that are remelted with other metals to make brass and bronze products; cakes that are rolled for copper plate, strip, sheet, and foil; billets that are extruded or drawn to make copper tubing and pipe, or rods that are coiled and drawn to make copper wire.

Copper is often joined to itself and other materials with nails, bolts, and rivets. For some applications such as roofing, copper nails are preferred, but brass or stainless steel can usually be substituted. Where both sides of a joint are not accessible, copper rivets with bronze, aluminum bronze, or stainless steel components prevent corrosion.

Copper is an element that is necessary to human health and is generally considered safe for contact with food. Extreme cases of chronic poisoning from copper result in Wilson's disease, a condition characterized by weakness, anemia, abdominal pain, and yellowed skin.

Table 7-5 Finishes for Copper Alloys

Category	Type	Class	Most Used in Architecture
Mechanical finishes (M)	Fabricated, buffed, directional or nondirectional textured	Directional textured finishes	M33: Coarse satin
			M34: Hand-rubbed, the most often used in architecture
Chemical finishes (C)	Nonetched cleaned or conversion coatings	Conversion coatings	For patina finishes: C50 Ammonium chloride C51 Cuprous chloride-hydrochloric acid C52 Ammonium sulfate
			For hardware: C55—sulfide
Coatings	Clear organic (O) coatings	Air-dry (for general architectural work)	
		Thermoset (for hardware)	
		Chemical cure	
	Laminated (L) coatings	Clear polyvinyl fluoride	
	Vitreous and metallic coatings	Not commonly used in architectural work	
	Oils and waxes	Primarily used on-site for maintenance	

Copper mining produces wastes including the material removed from above the ore, the tailings produced during the concentrating operation, and slag from smelting. These wastes may contain substantial amounts of arsenic, lead, and other dangerous chemicals. Government regulations in the United States and other countries control storage of these wastes and require remediation of the site when it is no longer mined. This can involve billions of tons of material. Abandoned copper mines continue to be sources of pollution.

Commercial copper polishes can be used with care for small interior applications. For exposed copper surfaces, unevenly patinated copper can be sponge-cleaned with a solution of phosphoric and nitric acids in water that is left on briefly and then lifted off with sponges soaked in a solution of sodium bicarbonate; a thickening agent will make its removal easier. Ammonium oxalate is then applied as a second neutralizer and the residue is rinsed off. The surface is next wiped in parallel strokes with a clean cloth, and then wiped with mineral spirits. A thin coat of carnauba wax, which will wear off fairly rapidly, will allow the copper patina to begin to spread uniformly.

Lead

Lead is a soft, heavy, extremely dense, bluish-white metal that tarnishes to a dull gray. It is corrosion-resistant, is a poor electrical conductor, and is easily worked. Its elasticity, strength, hardness, and melting point all are low. Other substances such as antimony are added to lead to improve its hardness and strength.

Lead has been in use by humans for at least 7000 years, and lead sources are widespread. It is used for waterproofing, sound and vibration isolation, and radiation shielding. In ancient Rome, lead was used for plumbing; it continued to be used for water mains and service pipes until around 1970. Lead is part of solder, pewter, and a variety of alloys. Its high density makes it an effective shield against x-rays and gamma radiation. Its combination of low stiffness and high damping capacity makes it desirable for sound deadening and vibration isolation. Lead sheet is used in building construction for roof and flashing, shower pans, flooring, x-ray and gamma-ray protection, and vibration damping and soundproofing.

Lead is rarely found by itself in nature; most lead is extracted from copper, zinc, or silver ore. The mineral galena is about 87 percent lead. Ore containing lead and other minerals is mined by drilling or blasting, then crushed or ground, and, finally, concentrated. Lead concentrate is dried and then sintered—heated enough to make the lead particles adhere to one another. As it is cooled, the lighter impurities rise to the surface and are removed. The molten lead is then smelted with air so that impurities form a slag layer, leaving 99.9 percent pure lead. More than half of the lead currently in use has been recycled.

Lead is a toxic material that accumulates in the human body. Inhalation of lead fumes or dust can lead to decreased physical fitness, fatigue, sleep disturbances, headache, aching bones and muscles, constipation, abdominal pains, and decreased appetite; inhaling large amounts of lead may result in seizures, coma, and death. In the twentieth century, the use of lead in paint pigments was banned in industrialized countries because of the danger of lead poisoning, which is especially damaging to children. However, many houses still contain lead in layers of old paint, and removing it by sanding produces lead dust that can be inhaled. Lead enters the soil through leaks in leaded gasoline tanks underground, through acid rain on lead roofs, and in chips from lead paint or industrial lead grindings. When lead is used on a construction site, efforts are made to reduce or eliminate worker exposure. These include substituting other materials when feasible, isolating work areas, and providing adequate ventilation.

Lead is one of the less expensive metals. As with other metals, its price is subject to supply and demand.

Magnesium

Magnesium is a light, ductile, silver-white metallic element used in lightweight alloys. It is the lightest of all metals used in construction, but pure magnesium lacks the necessary strength for general structural applications. When combined with other metals such as aluminum, it is used for furniture, hospital equipment, and other purposes. Magnesium tarnishes slightly when exposed to air, but is protected by a thin layer of oxide that is hard to remove. It is highly combustible and easy to ignite in powdered form or shaved into thin strips, but difficult to ignite in mass or bulk. Once ignited, its brilliant white light is difficult to extinguish, and will burn in nitrogen and carbon dioxide, as well as oxygen. When glowing white, magnesium becomes toxic, as well as extremely hot.

Magnesium is not found as a separate element in nature. The United States formerly supplied the majority of magnesium, separated from its ore by an electrolytic process. China supplies about 60 percent of the current world market of magnesium, derived from ores through the reduction of the oxide at high temperatures with silicon.

Manganese

Manganese is a gray-white metal that resembles iron; it is a hard, brittle metallic element, used chiefly as an alloying agent to increase the hardness and toughness of steel. It is also used to remove the greenish tinge in glass, to make violet-colored glass, as a brown pigment for paint, and as one of the materials in natural umber.

Large resources of manganese exist; most of the world's supply comes from South Africa and Ukraine. Very large quantities of manganese also exist as nodules on the ocean floor, but there is currently no economically feasible way to harvest them.

Small amounts of manganese are necessary for human health. Excess exposure to manganese affects the nervous system, resulting in a host of symptoms.

Nickel

Nickel is a hard, silvery-white metallic element that is malleable and ductile. It is used in steel and cast-iron alloys and in electroplating metals or as a base for chromium plating. Nickel polishes well and does not tarnish. Nickel-iron castings are more ductile and more resistant to corrosion than ordinary cast iron. Added to steel, nickel increases its impact resistance. Nickel produces a green color in glass.

The U.S. coin called the nickel is made of a copper-nickel alloy. Most metallic nickel is used to make alloys with other metals; the most commercially important include alloys with iron, nickel, and chromium, including stainless steel. Alloys that contain nickel are tough, strong, and corrosion-resistant, and retain these properties when extremely hot or cold. Two-thirds of new nickel, as well as most recycled nickel, becomes part of stainless steel.

Nickel ores are mined in Australia, Brazil, Canada, China, Colombia, Cuba, the Dominican Republic, Greece, Indonesia, New Caledonia, the Philippines, Southern Africa, and Russia. Some deposits are deep underground; others are near the surface.

Contact with nickel can lead to allergic dermatitis, known as "nickel itch," which usually occurs where skin is moist. Workers who inhale very large amounts of nickel compounds may develop chronic bronchitis and lung and nasal sinus cancers.

Nickel is expensive when compared to other nonferrous metals; it is used efficiently and recovered and recycled routinely at all stages of fabrication and use. Its high initial cost is spread over a long expected lifetime of service. The price of nickel-containing products is generally high compared to the cost of shipping it regionally and internationally.

Nickel finishes are often specified for bathroom faucets. In spite of this fact, there is apparently no specification standard for textured nickel finishes. Finishes for nickel referred to as "satin" are elsewhere called brushed or frosted. Therefore, it is best to have an actual sample of the finish desired to reference.

Nickel-containing products end up in landfills, often because they are too small or too hard to identify, or because consumer or municipal recycling does not separate metal from nonmetals. Although it is wasted in a landfill, most nickel in products remains stable and does not constitute a risk to the environment.

Tin

Tin is soft, malleable, and ductile at ordinarily temperatures and is used in plating and in modifying alloys to decrease their hardness. Tin is lustrous and bluish-white in color; it melts at a relatively low temperature. Since very early times, tin has been known and used, often alloyed with copper to make bronze. It is not readily oxidized and is protected from corrosion by an oxide film; it resists corrosion from tap water but can be attacked by strong acids, alkalis, and acid salts. Tin takes a high polish, and is used over other metals to prevent their corrosion.

Tin ore, a hard, heavy, inert substance called stannic oxide, is usually found as outcroppings with quartz, feldspar, or mica. It is reduced from ore with coal in a furnace. Indonesia, China, and Peru together produce most of the world's supply of tin. Virgin tin metal is cast and sold as bars, ingots, pigs, and slabs. The price of tin was a little over $4 per pound in 2006.

Note: ASTM B339 specifies Grade A Tin for the Manufacture of Tinplate with a Lower Lead Impurity Level. ASTM B545-97(2004)E1 is the Standard Specification for Electrodeposited Coatings of Tin.

Twenty-three percent of the world's tin use is for building construction. It is used to make solder and as a coating for steel known as tin plate or terneplate. Tin salts are used in calico printing and are sprayed onto glass to produce electrically conductive coatings used for panel lighting and frost-free windshields. Window glass is made by floating molten glass on molten tin for a smooth, flat surface.

Note: The so-called tin can is actually made of steel with tin added.

Tin alloys have decorative applications. *Pewter* is a white metallic alloy with about 92 percent tin and small amounts of antimony and copper. (Formerly, it contained lead, which was excluded due to its toxicity and dullness of finish.) Pewter is valued for its appearance and ease of working as a craft material. Copper-tin alloys are bronzes that are used for both structural and decorative purposes. Tin is also alloyed with titanium for materials with excellent edge sharpness and a gold color.

Inorganic tin compounds leave the human body shortly after they are ingested or inhaled, and do not usually cause harmful effects.

Tin is released into the environment by mining, coal and oil combustion, and the production and use of tin compounds. The processes of smelting, refining, and detinning produce waste salts, slags, and muds that contain tin. Solid wastes are incinerated or disposed of in landfills. Tin waste is not considered to be hazardous and is not regulated as such. Tin is recovered along with steel in the recycling of containers.

Titanium

Titanium is light, strong, lustrous, and corrosion-resistant; its hard, smooth surface keeps other materials from sticking. It is as strong as steel but much less dense. It develops a very thin, conductive oxide surface film at high temperatures and resists tarnishing at room temperatures. Titanium is highly resistant to corrosion by acids and salt solutions. In its pure state, it is especially ductile in an oxygen-free environment and easy to work. When used for fabrication, titanium products have relatively low strength.

Titanium was discovered by William Gregor in England in 1791; the pure element was made in 1910 by Matthew A. Hunter. By 1946, the metal could be produced commercially but was considered of little use. Since the early 1950s, titanium and its alloys have become critical to the aerospace, energy, and chemical industries. Its most common compound, titanium dioxide, is used in white pigments such as correction fluid and white paint with good hiding properties, as well as in toothpaste. Titanium's lustrous metallic-white color has become highly desirable for finishes. The star effect seen in some sapphires and rubies is due to the presence of titanium dioxide.

Titanium occurs in many minerals that are widely available. Most titanium is produced by the Kroll process, which involves mixing, melting, and recasting metals. The Kroll process is very expensive and generates a great deal of waste, sometimes 10 times the amount of titanium produced. The cost of recycling this waste is quite high.

Producing titanium in powder form is also expensive, and even though metallurgy techniques using powder are more efficient and less expensive, the resulting products are still more expensive than conventionally finished products.

Newer technology that reduces titanium chemicals with aluminum can produce alloys directly from raw materials, reducing costs of finished materials. Making thin titanium sheet directly from powder in one continuous process will further reduce costs. Cold-spray technology is used for direct fabrication of titanium components; it requires no intermediate processing or hazardous chemicals. This technology also requires less energy and water than other processes.

Titanium is nontoxic, and the human body can tolerate large doses of it. In medicine, titanium is used to make hip and knee replacements, pacemakers, bone-plates and screws, and cranial plates for skull fractures. It has also been used to attach false teeth. Titanium dust inhalation, however, may cause tightness and pain in chest, coughing, and difficulty in breathing. Contact with skin or eyes also may cause irritation. When in a metallic powdered form, titanium metal poses a significant fire hazard and, when heated in air, an explosion hazard.

Commercially pure titanium contains minor alloy materials and is durable enough for sports equipment and jewelry. All grades have very high dent and bend resistance, as well as damage resistance. Titanium 6/6/2 (84 percent titanium, 6 percent aluminum, 6 percent vanadium, and 2 percent tin) is marketed as the toughest alloy on earth. Life-cycle costs for titanium benefit from its long useful life and lighter weight.

Welding affects the properties of titanium and its alloys, increasing strength and hardness and decreasing tensile and bend ductility. Welds must be made with minimal contamination by oxygen, nitrogen, and other impurities in order to maintain ductility. The quality of joints depends on the welding procedure and heat treatment, which are used to improve ductility and workability and to optimize fracture toughness, fatigue strength, and high-temperature creep strength. Annealing improves dimensional and structural stability.

Finish descriptions for titanium jewelry include matte, polished, satin, frost, and anodized. Anodizing produces a great variety of colors by thickening the oxide layer slightly to create different refractive effects without dyes or pigments. Polished and

Figure 7-12 Zinc
© 2004 by Axolotl Group Pty Ltd.

high-polished finishes show off its resistance to scratching. Any scratches that do occur over time can be removed by polishing. Titanium that has been colored by anodizing is very likely to scratch and is not recommended for exposed areas.

Titanium wall panels are available in a matte gray finish and are attached mechanically by rivets, bolts, or screws. Panels can be attached to interior flat substrates, such as gypsum wallboard, with double-faced tape or nonhardening adhesives. Ninety-five percent of the titanium produced is used as titanium dioxide in white paints, replacing lead. Titanium pigment provides color for rubber, plastics, textiles, ink, cosmetics, leather, ceramics, and paper. As a pigment, titanium dioxide has great luster, good endurance, high opacity, and pure white color. Other uses include electrical components, glass products, artificial gemstones, jewelry, and smoke screens.

Zinc

Zinc is a ductile, crystalline, and brittle bluish-white metallic element found in sedimentary deposits in Australia, the United States, India, and China. Zinc is corrosion-resistant in air and water; it can be sand cast or die cast into desired forms. It is used in roofing, flashing, nails, plumbing hardware, and structural parts, as well as for decorative shapes and as an interior surface material. Cast zinc alloys are used to join metals, plastics, ceramics, glass, paper, fibers, and elastomers.

Zinc presents low risk of toxicity, although inhalation of zinc fumes can cause metal fume fever, with flulike symptoms lasting one to two days but causing no permanent damage. Zinc scrap from the production process is recycled almost at once. Old zinc scrap that is recycled at the end of a product's life can remain in use for over a century.

The price of zinc has been rising for some time, with major increases reflected in the cost of products.

Note: ASTM B86-04 is the standard specification for Zinc and Zinc-Aluminum (ZA) Alloy Foundry and Die Castings. Zinc plating is covered by the finish specification ASTM-B633, Zinc.

Zinc may have a bright or dull finish; weathering produces a dull gray color. Used as a finish, zinc is normally deposited directly on the base material. Zinc-coated steel will not rust even when scratched.

Synthetics 8

The term *synthetic* denotes materials made with human intervention, as opposed to natural materials. The word *plastic* has many meanings, but in terms of material characteristics it refers to any of a group of synthetic or natural organic materials that may be shaped when softened and then hardened. These include many types of polymers, resins, cellulose derivatives, casein materials, and proteins.

- A *polymer* is a giant molecule chain that gives plastics their exceptional stability and prevents their easy decomposition.
- *Resins* are artificial or natural polymers that are generally viscous and sticky. Artificial resins such as polyesters and epoxies are used as adhesives and binders. Natural resins are secreted by plants; for example, oleoresin comes from conifer trees.
- *Cellulose* is the structural component of the cell walls of plants, and is a major component of wood, paper, cotton, and hemp.
- *Casein* is a protein precipitated from milk and used to make plastics and cheese.
- *Proteins* are highly varied organic molecules composed of amino acids and found in all forms of life.

For the purposes of this chapter, we will focus on synthetic plastic materials that are used in architecture and interior design. These materials are all derived from petrochemicals and are all polymers. Information on materials sources and manufacturing processes is presented with the discussion of each type of plastic.

Although leather is made from a natural material—the skins of cattle, as well as various birds and reptiles—its processing traditionally involves extensive use of dangerous chemicals that pollute the environment. Developments are currently underway to find less damaging substitutes for leather tanning and dyeing. We include leather here for ease of comparison with its synthetic substitutes.

The first man-made plastic material, *celluloid*, was called Parkesine by its British inventor, Alexander Parkes, around 1850. It was a hard yet flexible transparent cellulose material that could be molded when heated and retained its shape when cooled.

HISTORY OF SYNTHETIC MATERIALS

Figure 8-1 Polymer molecule

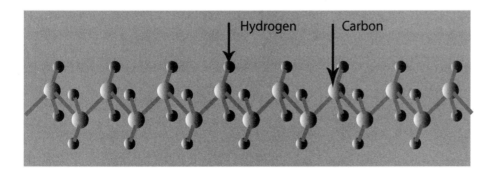
Hydrogen   Carbon

Celluloid performed well at normal temperatures, but not when exposed to intense heat or cold, and was liable to burst into flame.

At the time, there was no market for such a material, and in 1866 Parkes sold the patent to an American, John Wesley Hyatt, who substituted it for ivory in billiard balls. The development of celluloid film by 1900 revolutionized photography and made the movie industry possible. Celluloid soon became ubiquitous in household products, toys, collars and cuffs for shirts, and even dental plates.

An early type of *rayon* was developed in 1891 to imitate silk fiber by the French Count of Chardonnet. Initially as combustible as celluloid, it was developed further by the Swiss inventor Jacques Edwin Brandenberger, who in 1913 added caustic soda and carbon disulfide. The resulting solution, called *viscose*, was passed through *spinnerets* to produce rayon.

Bakelite was the first entirely synthetic material. Its discovery resulted from the experiments of Leo Hendrik Baekeland, in 1907, with phenol and formaldehyde in an attempt to make an insulating material. Bakelite was conceived of as a substitute for natural rubber, which would dry out and crack when subjected to heat. It was used for engine parts and electronics, telephone handsets, and the still-popular vintage jewelry.

Bakelite was resistant to heat, acids, and electric currents. It took the shape of any container into which the heated liquid was poured, and once cooled, retained its form permanently. Bakelite's ability to accept form and color made it popular for the streamlining and glossy finishes of the Art Deco movement.

Other polymer-based synthetic materials soon followed. In 1912, Jacques Brandenberger introduced cellophane as a transparent food wrap. *Acetate*, invented in 1927, was followed by *vinyl* a year later. The development of Plexiglas in 1930 led to its use in everything from windows and wall partitions to boats. In 1936, acrylics were introduced; in 1937, Melmac; and in 1938, Styrene and Formica.

By 1940, fashion design was revolutionized by the availability of synthetic alternatives such as polyester and nylon to natural fibers. Wallace Hume Carothers had developed nylon at the DuPont laboratories, but died in 1937 before it became commercially successful as a material for toothbrushes. B.F. Goodrich organic chemist Waldo Semon experimented with *polyvinyl chloride* (PVC), leading to the discovery of durable,

Figure 8-2 "Tiny Tim" bakelite radio
Photo by Sonny Clutter, Radiolaguy.com.

moldable, and inexpensive vinyl. Saran, which came to be a standby of the food packaging industry, was created by accident in 1933 by Ralph Wiley, a Dow Chemical lab worker. In 1938, DuPont chemist Roy Plunkett discovered Teflon, also by accident.

Today, there are around 15,000 formulas for plastics. Many are mixed with other plastics or other materials, creating an almost limitless variety.

Most plastics are based on the carbon atom. They are derived from *petrochemicals*, which are chemicals made from petroleum or natural gas. Plastics are all polymers, composed of very large molecule chains made up of many simpler molecules. The virtue and vice of plastics are the same: they are very stable and difficult to destroy. Plastics are designed to last a long time, and consequently are hard to dispose of.

The components of plastics are continually being modified for new characteristics and uses. Basically, plastic is made of synthetic resin in combination with fillers, stabilizers, plasticizers, pigments, and other materials.

- *Fillers* add specific properties such as durability or heat resistance.
- *Extenders* are inexpensive materials that replace more expensive plastic in products.
- *Stabilizers* increase resistance to ultraviolet rays, oxygen, and other environmental chemicals and processes.
- *Plasticizers* are mixed with resin to increase flexibility, resiliency, and impact resistance.

The great many varieties of plastic are categorized as two basic types. *Thermoplastics* become soft when heated, and can be remolded repeatedly. They harden when cooled, so manufacturers add plasticizers for flexibility. *Thermoset plastics* are permanently hardened, and cannot be softened and remolded.

Thermoplastics

Of the two types, thermoplastics have higher impact strength, are easier to process, and are more adaptable to complex designs. With their ability to soften when heated and harden as they cool, plasticizers must be added to retain flexibility. The thermoplastics most commonly used in building interiors are discussed here.

Acrylics

Acrylics are very clear, hard thermoplastics that are used in skylights, for safety glazing, and in lighting diffusers and light-control lenses in lighting fixtures. Acrylic sheet is formed into tub-shower units that are then backed with glass-fiber-reinforced polyester. The high-impact molding grade of acrylic is used for furniture. (See color plate C-51, Acrylic samples.)

Vinyl

Vinyl is a widely used thermoplastic that is strong and weather- and chemical-resistant, and available as a transparent film. The best-known vinyl is polyvinyl chloride (PVC), which has good dimensional stability and impact resistance; it is used widely for plumbing pipe. Vinyl products include floor tile, countertops, and window screens.

PVC is strong and durable. It has a high strength-to-weight ratio and is tough and dent-resistant. Because it exhibits great versatility in form and adaptability in properties, its end products range from soft to rigid. PVC is relatively low cost.

Plasticizers are added to PVC for workability, flexibility, extensibility, and resilience. Because PVC is heat-sensitive, heat stabilizers are used in processing and in some final products. Lubricants, impact modifiers, fillers, biocides, and pigments are

PHYSICAL PROPERTIES, CHARACTERISTICS, AND TYPES OF PLASTICS

Table 8-1 Thermoplastics

Plastic Name	Uses	Qualities
Acrylics Trade names include Lucite and Plexiglas.	Skylights, safety glazing, lighting diffusers, light-control lenses; tub-shower units; furniture; paint resins; floor tile, countertops, window screens	Very clear, hard; weather- and chemical-resistant; lightweight Colorfast, nonyellowing; Dimensionally stable; Good structural and thermal properties; Moderate impact resistance even in extreme cold
Vinyls		
Polyvinyl chloride (PVC)	Plumbing pipe, wiring, siding, flooring, wallcoverings	Strong, weather- and chemical-resistant. Available as transparent film; Versatility in form. End products range from soft to rigid; Good dimensional stability and impact resistance; Chemically inert; resistant to water, corrosion, and weather; Strong, lightweight; Tough, dent-resistant; Good electrical and thermal insulator; Durable; Maintenance-free
Polyvinyl acetate (PVAC)	Latex paints, adhesives, surface coatings, and textile finishes	
Polyvinyl butyral (PVB)	Interlayer in safety glass	
Polyvinyl alcohol (PVAL)	Paper coatings and sizings, adhesives, and textile finishes	
Nylon	Carpet; architectural fibers and coatings.	Translucent and rigid. Remains tough at low temperatures. Impact- and abrasion-resistant. Resists oils, bases, solvents, formaldehyde and alcohols. Good resistance to ultraviolet light. Tensile strength 5,800 psi. Low coefficient of friction.
Polyolefins (also known as polyalkenes):		
Polybutylenes (PBs)	Plumbing pipes, hot-melt adhesives and sealants, drawer glides and sliding-door tracks	
Polyethylenes	Electrical insulation, vapor barriers, molded seating, drawer glides, door tracks	Accept color very well; strong, flexible, chemical-resistant; high melting point
Polypropylenes	Upholstery fabric, carpet backing, and indoor/outdoor carpet fiber	Semitranslucent or milky white; moderate price
Polystyrenes	Light fixture diffusers, core material for doors. Woodgrain patterned furniture parts and mirror frames. Plastic tiles.	Inexpensive, easy to process, hard, very clear, and color well
Fluoroplastics: Excellent chemical and moisture resistance; low coefficient of friction; resist extreme temperatures		
Polyvinyl fluoride (PVF) Trade name Tedlar	Architectural fabrics, vinyl wallcovering film.	
Polytetra-fluoroethylene Trade name Teflon	Data communications cables	Resists high temperatures, chemicals, corrosion, stress cracking. Tough; electrical properties; low friction, nonstick
Cellulosics	Table edging, venetian blind wands, signage, and store fixtures	Breakage-resistant
Acrylonitrile-butadiene-styrene (ABS)	Plumbing pipes, outdoor furniture, drawer liners, and chair shells	Tough, chemical- and impact-resistant

also frequently added. PVC compounds are made into products either by melting or liquid processing. In melt processing, solid compounds melted by heat are extruded into solid or cellular forms, pipe, blown film, or flat sheet. Calendaring is a liquid processing method used to make PVC into flexible or rigid sheeting from 2 to 35 millimeters in thicknesses on large, expensive machinery.

Other types of vinyl with applications in building interiors include PVAC, PVB, and PVAL. Polyvinyl acetate (PVAC) resin is used in latex paints, adhesives, surface coatings, and textile finishes. Polyvinyl butyral (PVB) has been in use since 1938 as the adhesive interlayer in safety glass. Polyvinyl alcohol (PVAL) resin is used in paper coatings and sizings, adhesives, and textile finishes.

Vinyl can be cleaned with warm suds, then rinsed and dried; hot water and abrasives are not to be used. Commercial vinyl cleaners are available for upholstery. Vinyl wood-grain laminate on furniture can be wiped with a damp cloth. Vinyl will stick to lacquered surfaces and can be damaged by high heat or moth repellants.

Nylon

Nylon, a strong thermoplastic, is translucent and rigid. It remains tough at low temperatures and is impact- and abrasion-resistant. Nylon resists oils and bases, solvents, formaldehyde, and alcohols. It has good resistance to ultraviolet light and high tensile strength.

Because it wears well and resists abrasion, nylon fiber is used for textiles and carpet. Its low-friction properties make it ideal for chair caster rollers and drawer glides. Type 6/6 Nylon 101 is the preferred nylon fiber for carpet, and Nylon 6 is the most common commercial grade for cast nylon products.

Other Thermoplastics

Polyolefins (also known as polyalkenes) are a diverse group of thermoplastics that include polybutylenes, polyethylenes, and polypropylenes. Polypropylenes are widely used for upholstery fabric, carpet backing, and indoor/outdoor carpet fiber.

Polystyrenes are inexpensive and easy-to-process thermoplastics. They are very clear and hard, and color well. Plastic tiles contain polystyrene and urea-formaldehyde resins.

Fluoroplastics are thermoplastics with excellent chemical and moisture resistance. Fluoroplastics produce very little friction and resist extreme temperatures. Polyvinyl fluoride (PVF) and polytetrafluoroethylene have architectural uses.

Cellulosics are breakage-resistant, and are manufactured into table edging, venetian blind wands, signage, and store fixtures.

Acrylonitrile-butadiene-styrene (ABS) is a tough, chemical- and impact-resistant thermoplastic. ABS is used for plumbing pipes, outdoor furniture, drawer liners, and chair shells.

Thermoset Plastics

Thermoset plastics, the second basic type of plastic, resist higher temperatures and have greater dimensional stability than thermoplastics. Thermoset plastics undergo a chemical change during processing that hardens them permanently. Consequently, they cannot be softened or remolded.

Melamines are hard, clear, stain-resistant thermoset plastics that don't easily scratch or stain, and don't yellow with age. Melamine is used in the manufacture of plastic laminates.

Polyesters are well-known thermoset plastics that are often mixed with other materials. When combined with glass fibers, polyesters create fiberglass. *Alkyd* paints and

Figure 8-3 Polyester Trevira fabric

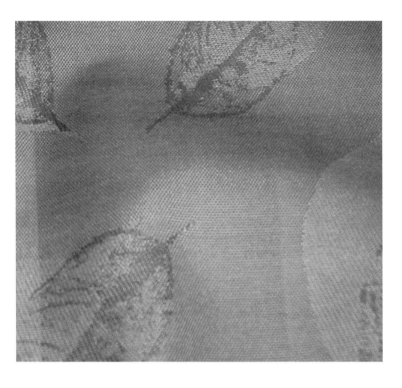

Figure 8-4 Corian samples

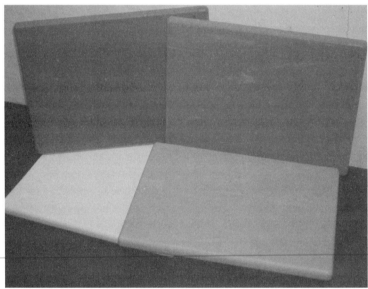

coatings are oil-modified polyesters used as paint coatings, and are valued for their rapid curing time compared to oil-based paints.

Epoxy resins react with curing agents or hardeners for extremely durable thermoset plastic. They offer superior adhesion and excellent resistance to chemicals and corrosion as adhesives or protective coatings for floors and walls. Powder coatings used for metal furniture finishes are based on epoxy resins. Epoxy resins are also used in proprietary solid surfacing materials such as Corian.

Polyurethanes are thermoset plastics that can be molded and cut. Rigid polyurethane foam is widely used for building insulation. More resilient polyurethane foam cushioning is used in upholstered furniture and mattresses.

Furans are black thermoset plastics used in corrosion-resistant cements and grouts. Epoxy-based grouts and furan resin grouts are both more expensive and more difficult to install than portland-cement-based grouts. However, they cure to harder, stronger bonds and are more stain-resistant.

Silicones are an important group of thermoset plastics that, unlike other carbon-based plastics, are based on silicon (sand). Silicones offer temperature stability, and resist weather and ultraviolet radiation. They are used for water-repellant fabric finishes and as joint sealants.

The development of synthetic materials in the middle of the nineteenth century radically changed the way we design, manufacture, and use materials. Although originally designed to imitate and substitute for natural materials, by the beginning of the twentieth century, plastics were valued for their own aesthetic qualities. Today, plastics offer design and performance characteristics that expand our choices in almost unlimited ways.

The qualities that we associate with plastics—durability, flexibility of form, transparency, and color variety—have generated a uniquely modern aesthetic of brightly colored, hard, shiny surfaces that can take virtually any form. Plastics may be rigid or flexible and hard or soft to the touch. Although they still excel at imitating natural materials, plastics provide us with aesthetic options that combine transparency, color, form, and pattern in their own unique ways.

AESTHETIC QUALITIES OF SYNTHETIC MATERIALS

Plastics are manufactured from petrochemicals—crude oil and natural gas. These are limited natural resources that, once depleted, cannot be readily replaced. In addition, the production of petrochemical products can lead to emissions that promote global warming.

Technically, plastics are not solids, but viscoelastic fluids, and they evaporate; the plasticizers used to soften plastics make them less stable. The plastics used to make wallcoverings, carpets and carpet pads, plumbing pipes, and electric wires and their insulation emit toxic chemicals including nitrogen oxide, cyanide, and acid gases.

Plastics last for hundreds of years and pollute both the land and the marine environment. Therefore, they should be specified with an eye to their future disposal. Recycling plastics into outdoor furniture, floor tiles, carpets, and other products uses less energy than manufacturing new plastic, and reduces waste.

Plastic laminate or melamine panels can give off formaldehyde, phenol, aliphatic and aromatic hydrocarbons, ketones, and other VOCs. Fortunately, most plastic laminates have very low toxicity levels. However, these are petroleum-based products, and when bonded to other materials, are unlikely to be recycled.

The manufacturing process of polyvinyl chloride produces toxic emissions; since the 1980s, manufacturers have worked to substantially lower emissions, but this remains a problem. Vinyls may break down in sunlight and emit dangerous chemicals, and they can generate toxic fumes in fires. Some vinyl products, especially sheet materials, off-gas VOCs. Vinyl products will not break down in a landfill and cannot be incinerated.

Vinyl sheets and tiles are made of PVC or a copolymer of vinyl chloride, a binder of vinyl resins and plasticizers, fillers, and pigments. Soft vinyl used for sheet flooring, which must bend into a roll, is made from petrochemical polymers, with chemicals added for flexibility, and emits large amounts of VOCs for long periods of time. Sheet vinyl also has a foam interlayer and a backing of organic or other fiber or plastic.

Plastics are sorted by type for recycling; each type has its own characteristics and melts at a different temperature. The plastics industry has developed seven identification codes that are used to label plastics for curbside recycling. Examples of their use in common household items and their postconsumer recyclability are given here.

ENVIRONMENTAL AND HEALTH IMPACTS OF SYNTHETIC MATERIALS

- Plastic #1, Polyethelene Terephthalate (PETE or PET): Most widely recycled plastic, used for soda and cooking oil bottles and food jars. Recycled into plastic bags.
- Plastic #2, High-Density Polyethelene (HDPE): Used for detergent bottles and milk jugs. HDPE is used in plastic lumber and furniture.
- Plastic #3, Polyvinyl Chloride (PVC): Used to produce plastic pipes, outdoor furniture, shrink-wrap; water, salad dressing, and liquid-detergent containers; and plastic bags. Recycled into sewer pipes, flooring, window frames, insulation board, and fiber filling, plus many consumer products.
- Plastic #4, Low-Density Polyethelene (LDPE): Used for dry cleaning, produce and trash bags, and food storage containers.
- Plastic #5, Polypropylene (PP): Used for bottle caps and drinking straws; less often recycled as postconsumer waste.
- Plastic #6, Polystyrene (PS): Used for packaging pellets, cups, tableware, clamshell and yogurt containers, and meat trays. Containers that have been used for food are harder to recycle.
- Plastic #7, Other: Used for Tupperware and similar containers, and all other types of plastics. Difficult to recycle.

Plastics that are combined with other materials in building and interior products are more difficult to separate and recycle. The addition of dyes, fillers, and other additives also makes the process more complex.

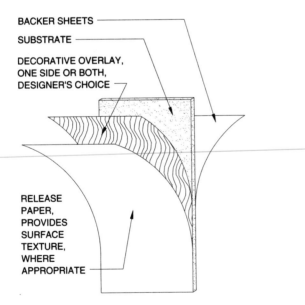

Figure 8-5 Low-pressure plastic laminate
Reproduced by permission of the publisher from Maryrose McGowan and Kelsey Kruse, *Interior Graphic Standards* (Hoboken, NJ: John Wiley & Sons, Inc.), © 2003 by John Wiley & Sons, Inc.

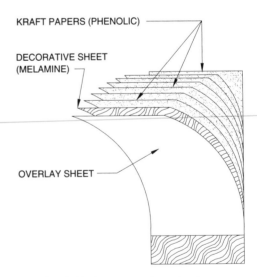

Figure 8-6 High-pressure plastic laminate
Reproduced by permission of the publisher from Maryrose McGowan and Kelsey Kruse, *Interior Graphic Standards* (Hoboken, NJ: John Wiley & Sons, Inc.), © 2003 by John Wiley & Sons, Inc.

When first developed, plastics were considered cheap and easy to manufacture. New natural gas and oil resources were being discovered globally. Manufacturers trained and employed factory workers who mass-produced products with much less skill and time than traditional artisans. Cross-continental railways and international shipping made it feasible to produce a product and ship it to a distant market economically.

Today, plastics are still generally inexpensive and cost-efficient to produce and transport. Part of this is due to the availability of natural gas and oil at prices that do not reflect the limited supply available from the earth; their inability to be replaced; or the environmental damage caused by their exploitation, use, and disposal. The national and international politics and warfare that support availability and low prices also are not reflected in the cost of synthetic materials.

Some of the objects made from the older plastics, such as Bakelite, have now taken on added value as collectors' items. In addition, some of the newer synthetics have achieved such high levels of aesthetic and functional development that they have moved out of the category of cheap goods and into the market for high-end or high-tech products.

As manufacturers and consumers accept more responsibility for the environmental and political costs of using petrochemicals, it is expected that the true costs and values of plastics and other synthetic materials will lead to responsible development, use, and disposal.

COST FACTORS FOR SYNTHETIC MATERIALS

There are thousands of applications for synthetic materials, with more being discovered all the time. The focus in this chapter will be on the use of the synthetic materials described above in the building interior.

Note: Installation information is provided in Chapter 9 for finish flooring, and in Chapter 10 for walls and windows.

INTERIOR APPLICATIONS FOR SYNTHETIC MATERIALS

Architectural Resin Panels

Architectural resin panels give the designer a rigid, transparent, or translucent sheet material with the ability to accept other embedded materials. PETG is the abbreviation for glycol-modified polyethylene terephthalate, a polyester resin that is very clear. In sheet form, it is stiff, hard, and tough, with good impact strength. The material has great aesthetic appeal, and some forms are designed to have enhanced structural properties as well. Architectural resin panels are finding uses in many interior applications. (See color plate C-52, Polyester resin panels.)

PETG is a modified version of PET, which is widely used for soft drink bottles. Polyester is a petrochemical made from fossil fuels; it is advertised as being environmentally friendly, but this will vary with the source of its materials and the energy used in its production.

Panels made of PETG are advertised as fire-rated; the designer should check to be sure the rating is adequate for the intended application. PETG is described as being half the weight and 40 times the strength of glass. It is shatter- and crackproof, will not discolor, is available in many colors and thicknesses, and is said to be contour heat-drapeable to any form.

There are a number of manufacturers using PETG, sometimes in proprietary formulations, to produce resin sheet products. Some of these are said to contain 40 percent recycled materials, and the final product is advertised as recyclable. At least one manufacturer has introduced a product that uses 100 percent postconsumer HDPE, the

Table 8-2 Petrochemical Products

Petroleum Form	Petro-Oil Chemical	Products	Interior Uses
Crude oil		Solvents benzene, toluene, and xylene	Dyes, paint thinners and solvents, leather tanning
		Nylon 6 and Nylon 6,6; polycarbonates and silicones	Carpet fiber, drapery and upholstery fabrics, chair glides and wheels, drawer glides
Natural gas	Propane	Acrylic fibers	Rugs, upholstery, awnings, outdoor furniture; asbestos replacement, concrete and stucco reinforcement
		Phenolic resins	Bonding and laminating varnishes, foam products, weather-resistant adhesives, wood bonding, laminate panels
		Epoxy resins	Flooring, paints and finishes, wood repair systems
		Polypropylene	Indoor-outdoor carpet
		Polyurethane	Upholstery foam, wood finishes, binders in composite wood products such as OSB and MDF
	Ethane plus propane	Alkyds	Paints
		Thermosetting polyester	Thermal barrier composite panels
		Polystyrene	Insulated building panels
		ABS	Pipes
		Polyethylene	Product packaging
		Cellulose acetate	Laminated safety glass
		Ethylene vinyl acetate	Hot-melt adhesives, wire and cable insulation
		Polyvinyl acetate	Wood glues, shiny textile coatings
		PVC	Plumbing pipe, floor tile, countertops, and window screens
	Methane	Silicone	Sealants
		Melamine	Adhesives for wood-based panels
		Thermoplastic polyester	Chair seat frames
	Butane	Polybutylene	Plumbing pipe

Table 8-3 VOC Emissions of Vinyl Materials

Interior Product	VOC Emissions	Comments	Alternative Products
Vinyl and vinyl-coated wallcoverings	Vinyl chloride monomers and other VOCs	Long out-gassing times but low amounts	Wallcoverings without vinyl: paper, natural fiber, or polyester
Vinyl sheet flooring	Plasticizers off-gas VOCs, possibly for months: formaldehyde, toluene, ketones, xylenes	Most waste is landfilled; will not break down. Low-end products off-gas more.	Linoleum, or cork without vinyl binders
Vinyl tile flooring	Generally does not off-gas VOCs	Backing materials limit recycling	Linoleum or cork tiles
Vinyl window blinds	UV light can cause vinyl to break down and off-gas	Avoid use in bright sun.	Wood blinds or fabric window treatments
Vinyl floor tile adhesives	Toluene, benzene, ethyl acetate, ethyl benzene, and styrene	Toxic materials	Water-based adhesives
Wallpaper paste for heavy wallcoverings	Variety of VOCs	Lightweight papers can be applied with light, water-based glue.	Low-toxic adhesives

plastic found in many household bottles for shampoo or cleaners and some foods. Translucent honeycomb panels in several thicknesses have fiberglass or cast-resin facings. Raw, laminated panel edges can be enclosed in C-channels; panels are compatible with most suspended ceiling suspension systems. Acrylic resin panels are also available with embedded materials.

Plastic Laminates

Plastic laminates are commonly known by the trade name of one brand, Formica. They consist of five or six sheets from rolls of brown paper that is dipped in resin and drying chemicals and then put into a mold. The resin-impregnated image sheet is layered on top; a melamine finish layer is added; and the entire sandwich is heated and pressed. The press embosses a texture into the melamine, if desired, and causes the resin to flow through all layers. The surface finish of the laminate as well as the image visible on the top can help to hide scratches; irregular textures and diffuse images help.

Plastic laminate is cut just a bit larger than the size needed, so that it can be trimmed after installation. It is installed on a smooth substrate, which is usually particleboard. This undersurface is sanded, cleaned, and then roughed up just a bit to improve adherence. The surface is coated with contact cement; this is most adhesive on first contact, so the installer will want to get the laminate in position on the first try. Once pressed into place, the laminate is carefully trimmed.

The edges of the plastic laminate will show the sandwiched layers; trims are normally applied to hide these edges. Strips of matching laminate can be glued to the edge, but these tend to break or be picked off with use. The classic 1950's edge material was a ribbed metal strip, which was durable and streamlined. A wood edge trim can be firmly attached and will withstand much use; if it shows wear, it can be sanded and refinished.

Plastic laminate is literally soaked in petrochemicals. It can provide a highly functional and long-lasting surface, but once its useful life is over, there is no alternative to dumping it in a landfill; this is a good motivation to reuse existing laminate installations when possible.

Plastic Lumber Products

Plastic lumber is a general term applied to several different products, including lumber made entirely of high-density polyethylene (HDPE), wood/plastic composites, and glass-fiber-reinforced lumber. Plastic lumber is worked much like wood, but lacks wood's structural properties.

Plastic lumber is less subject to rot, chipping, splintering, peeling, or cracking than wood. Insects, bacteria, and barnacles are not interested in living on it. Plastic lumber does not rot or mildew and is impervious to moisture and salt or fresh water. While wood may be treated with copper, chromium, or arsenic preservatives for outdoor use, plastic lumber does not need treatment; it is easy to maintain and is durable; grafitti is usually easily removed from it. Plastic lumber does not ignite readily and will ordinarily extinguish itself when the flame is removed. Its durability and longevity save maintenance and replacement costs.

Lumber made from HDPE plastic varies in the amount of postconsumer material and total recycled material it contains. Some manufacturers use 100 percent recycled materials from postconsumer waste; others use significantly less. HDPE plastic lumber may initially cost more than wood, but this has to be balanced against savings in maintenance and replacement. HDPE plastic lumber needs more underlying support than wood.

Wood/plastic composites typically contain about 50 percent plastic mixed with sawdust or other recycled fiber. It is less expensive than HDPE plastic lumber, and is widely used for decks and docks. Wood/plastic composites are often textured to look more like wood, and come in various colors. With their wood content, these composite materials are subject to mold and mildew and will show stains like wood.

Fiber-reinforced plastic lumber is a mixture of plastic with chopped or continuous strands of glass fiber. Of the three types of plastic lumber products, this is the most expensive; it is also the strongest and can be used for structural applications.

As technology improves and demand increases, purchase prices for plastic lumber are expected to decrease. Products including outdoor furniture are expanding the market for plastic lumber.

Solid Surfacing Materials

Solid surfacing materials are a small group of materials that may have different chemical compositions or thicknesses, but share a distinctive look and feel and many functional similarities. They are widely used for countertops, and continue to find new uses. Solid surfacing materials are manufactured from polymeric resin materials, consisting of filled acrylic polymers, filled polyester polymers, and filled acrylic-polyester blend polymers. The most common filler material is alumina trihydrate (ATH).

Solid surfacing materials are often compared to natural stone or ceramic tile when selecting finish materials. The performance properties listed in Table 8-4 have been identified as important for the designated applications. The reference standards used for test conditions are ANSI/ICPA SS-1-2001 and NEMA LD 3.3.

Each test measures the performance of a solid surfacing material as it would be used. Ability to be polished ranges between a matte finish and a high gloss, rated 0 to 60 with a higher number indicating a higher gloss. Tests for bacterial-fungal resistance are referenced in ASTM G 21 and G 22. Chemical resistance is rated for its ability to be repaired back to the original finish. A low score on the color stability tests is preferred.

The FDA tests finished products to determine whether any hazardous chemicals can be extracted. "FDA approved" indicates demonstration that the product will not adulterate food. "FDA compliant" indicates that all the materials used are listed in Title 21 of the Code of Federal Regulations, a less rigorous rating than FDA approval.

Hardness is determined on the Barcol scale, as compared to similar materials, referenced in ASTM D 2583; solid surfacing materials typically rate between 45 and 65. Flexural strength measures the load required to bend and break a test sample; the standard is ASTM D760. Heat resistance consists of two tests: one that tests material integrity at 365°F, and another that indicates the temperature at which the material softens. Impact resistance refers to ASTM D 256 or NEMA LD 3.

Scratch resistance measures the amount of force necessary to scratch the material. Stain resistance describes how easily each of 10 household materials leave a mark, and how much effort is required to remove it. Stiffness measures the resistance to deformation. A material with greater stiffness may need a perfectly flat substrate; one with higher flexibility may need more support. Surface conductivity is related to the dissipation of static electricity. Thermal expansion describes how the material expands when warmed and contracts when cooled; it is important in designing installation tolerances.

Solid Surfacing Materials

Solid surfacing materials have been defined by a panel of industry experts representing all major trade associations in a complementary document to ANSI/ICPA SS-1-2001, Performance Standard for Solid Surface Materials.

Solid surface materials are manufactured from polymeric materials. Granules may also be added to enhance the color effects. Solid surface materials are nonporous and homogeneous, with the same composition throughout the thickness of the solid surface material. They are capable of being repaired, renewed to the original finish, and fabricated into continuous surfaces with inconspicuous seams.

Table 8-4 Importance of Properties of Solid Surfacing Materials

Property L = low M = medium H = high	Countertops	Bathware	Windowsills	Floor Tiles, Stair Treads	Furniture, Workstations	Wall Cladding, Partitions	Interior Architectural Façades
Ability to be polished	M	M	M	M	M	M	M
Bacterial-fungal resistance	H	H	H	L	L	L	L
Chemical resistance: home (h) or laboratory (l)	h = H l = M	h = H l = L	h = H l = M	h = H l = M	h = H l = L	h = L l = L	h = L l = L
Color stability	H	H	H	H	H	H	H
FDA approval or compliance	M	M	M	M	M	M	H
Flexural strength	H	H	H	H	H	H	H
Hardness rating	H	H	H	H	H	M	H
Heat resistance	H	M	H	L	L	L	L
Impact resistance	H	H	H	H	H	H	H
Scratch resistance	M	M	M	M	M	L	M
Stain resistance	H	H	H	H	H	L	H
Stiffness	H	H	H	L	L	L	M
Surface conductivity	M	M	M	M	M	L	L
Thermal expansion	H	H	H	H	H	H	H
UV weathering stability	M	M	H	M	M	L	M
Water resistance	H	H	H	H	H	L	L
Wear resistance	H	H	H	H	H	L	H

UV weathering stability describes changes in the color and surface appearance due to sunlight. Water resistance measures water absorption. Finally, wear resistance indicates how materials will respond to rubbing, bumping, or scrubbing over time.

Synthetic Fibers

Synthetic fibers carry a higher environmental cost than natural fibers, but their durability and long life make them competitive, especially in commercial situations.

Acetate and Triacetate

Two related fibers, acetate and *triacetate*, have very different characteristics. Acetate's ability to be draped makes it desirable as a lining for clothing, but it has poor resilience and wrinkles easily. Acetate is a heat-sensitive fiber and is easily damaged by excessive heat. It has poor abrasion resistance and is too weak a fiber to use in interior design applications.

Triacetate is made from the same materials as acetate, but by a different process that gives it greater fiber stability and abrasion resistance. Triacetate can be heat-set into permanent pleats. Like acetate, it has excellent draping properties, but low strength and poor abrasion resistance.

Acrylics

The first acrylic came on the market in 1950 under the trade name Orlon. Acrylic fibers are used in interiors both for woven fabric and as a fluffy stuffing or insulation. The long acrylic fibers are manufactured to imitate the feel and look of natural silk, and are so light that they are often used to provide bulk without added weight. Acrylics are fairly abrasion-resistant. They drape well and have excellent sunlight resistance. Acrylic blends well with other fibers and can be dyed in a wide range of desirable colors. Due to their long fibers, some acrylics *pill* easily, forming little balls that stick firmly to the fabric surface. Acrylics are resistant to chemicals and sun fading.

Solution-dyed acrylic looks like cotton but resists ultraviolet light, mildew, and water; it is widely used for awnings and outdoor furniture upholstery. The woven acrylic allows air to pass, releasing trapped moisture and hot air. Solution-dyed acrylic has color pigments added directly to the fiber material during manufacturing, resulting in permanent color throughout the fabric; it is available in solid colors, stripes, and patterns. A variation, solution-dyed modacrylic, offers increased flame resistance and heat sensitivity.

Aramids and Elastomeric Fibers

Aramids are used to produce space-age fabrics such as Nomex, which is used in firefighters' and astronauts' suits, and Kevlar, which is perhaps best known as bulletproof fabric. Kevlar is also used as a barrier fabric laminated to upholstery fabrics. Its fire-resistant properties prevent fire from spreading to the upholstery's foam stuffing, and enabling the upholstered piece to pass California Technical Bulletin 133 (Cal 133). Aramids do not dye easily, so their aesthetic appeal is limited, but they are often used under another material.

Elastomeric fibers like Spandex and elastane can be stretched into tentlike shapes and resist unraveling if ripped. These fibers are derived from polyurethane and used in tentlike forms to shape interior and exterior spaces.

Nylon

Nylon is the most popular carpet fiber, thanks to its great strength, resiliency, and high abrasion resistance. Its low moisture absorbency makes it quick drying, but also allows the buildup of static. In many applications, nylon is such a durable fiber that it is often replaced for appearance reasons well before the fiber actually wears out. Nylon textiles drape well but have poor sunlight resistance, limiting their use in window treatments. Nylon fabric may also be subject to pilling.

Nylon 6 and its successor Nylon 6,6 are widely used to manufacture carpet. Nylon 6,6, sold under the trade names Antron and Celanese, is made of two chemicals that are not easily unbound and recycled. Nylon is also widely used for woven textiles, including upholstery fabrics and wall panels.

Figure 8-7 The gray fabric surrounding the central horn in this bass speaker is Kevlar.

Figure 8-8 Synthetic fiber sections

Hollow filament
fiber section

Delta shape
fiber section

Modified delta shape
fiber section

Table 8-5 Nylon Fibers*

Nylon Trade Name	Nylon Type	Recycled Content	Recycling Program
Honeywell Infinity Forever Renewable Nylon	Nylon 6	Various percentages recycled Nylon 6 carpet fibers	Evergreen Nylon Recycling Program, www.infinitynylon.com
Honeywell Zeftron Nylon Savant	Nylon 6	50% recycled Nylon 6 carpet fibers, 25% postconsumer	6ix Again closed-loop recycling program, www.zeftronnylon.com
Honeywell Zeftron Nylon Select and Solure	Nylon 6	25% postindustrial recycled content	6ix Again closed-loop recycling program, www.zeftronnylon.com
Invista Antron Nylon Lumena Invista Antron Nylon Legacy Invista Antron Nylon with StainResist	Nylon 6,6 Nylon 6,6 Nylon 6,6	Minimum 5% recycled content	Up to 90% postindustrial content depending on carpet manufacturer. Invista Reclamation Program will reclaim any carpet when specified in installation of new carpet, http://antron.invista.com

Note: *Proprietary names and composition subject to change

Figure 8-9 Making nylon 6,6

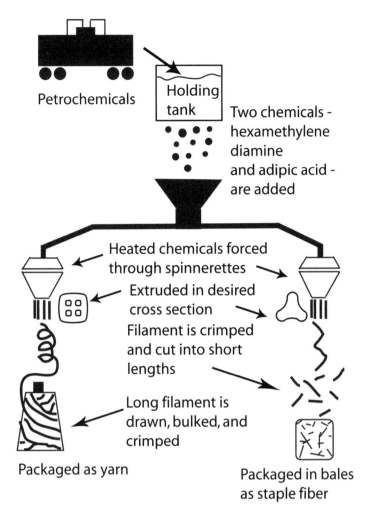

Petrochemicals

Holding tank

Two chemicals - hexamethylene diamine and adipic acid - are added

Heated chemicals forced through spinnerettes

Extruded in desired cross section

Filament is crimped and cut into short lengths

Long filament is drawn, bulked, and crimped

Packaged as yarn

Packaged in bales as staple fiber

Olefin

Olefin is inexpensive, lightweight, and elastic. Olefin fibers do not encourage static buildup, and resist staining and crushing. The first olefin to be developed was *polyethelene*, which was commonly used for airplane seat upholstery and many other products. *Polypropylene* is more widely used today in carpet and for nonwoven air barriers such as Tyvek. Polypropylene has excellent stain and mildew resistance and high strength. It resists absorbing moisture and is colorfast in sunlight. Olefin's appearance is frankly synthetic, and when dyed it lacks the color subtlety of a natural fiber. However, its durability and competitive pricing assures a continuing market.

PET

PET is made from ethylene and paraxylene derivatives that react at high temperature and high pressure. PET fibers are naturally stain-resistant, and their rich bright colors resist fading from sun or cleaning chemicals. It has exceptional strength and durability. PET fiber products include carpets and textiles.

PET recycles well, and PET products such as soda bottles are used to make recycled PET fiber. Polar fleece is made of recycled PET, and it can be used for building material. Used PET fibers can be recycled into other products such as car parts, insulation, and furniture stuffing. With high-quality sorting and washing, used bottles can be recycled back into bottles. However, only a fraction of the PET containers produced and used for bottled water and soda are actually recycled.

Polyester

Polyester is widely used in upholstery fabric, draperies, and hospital cubicle curtains. Under trade names such as Dacron, Fortel, Kodel, and Trevira, polyester's low moisture absorption, wrinkle resistance, high strength, resiliency, and abrasion resistance make it a popular choice for situations that require frequent commercial cleaning and sanitary conditions.

Polyester drapes fairly well for simple drapery designs. Its abrasion resistance and dimensional stability make it a popular fiber for upholstery fabric blends. Although polyester fabrics have, in the past, often been aesthetically uninspiring, newer designs and blends offer fabric with great appearance and feel matched with excellent performance characteristics. Polyester carpet fibers are known for their color clarity and retention. Their luxurious feel has made them popular for residential use.

Rayon

Rayon, the first synthetic fiber, and one made principally from wood pulp, is still widely used, especially in blends with other fibers. There are two methods for making rayon, the cuprammonium method and viscose rayon, the latter which is more common today. Viscose rayon's highly absorbent structure takes dyes beautifully and can be manufactured to closely resemble cotton, linen, or silk. Viscose rayon varies in strength and has fair abrasion resistance and sunlight resistance. Its low resiliency makes it prone to wrinkles.

Vinyon

Vinyon, better known as vinyl or PVC fiber, is durable, cleans easily, and simulates leather or suede. Simulated leather is usually made of polyurethane or PVC. As upholstery fabric, vinyls block liquids from being absorbed by cushions and are easy to wipe clean. However, the vinyl also blocks body moisture, and can stick to skin in hot weather.

Vinyl fabrics are produced by bonding the synthetic sheet to a backing fabric for dimensional stability. They are available with imprinted textures and patterns. Simulated suede's soft, fuzzy surface texture is created either by flocking (depositing the fuzzy fibers onto an adhesive-coated backing, and then oven-drying the result) or by sueding (roughing up the surface with revolving sandpaper).

Finishing and Maintenance for Synthetic Textiles

Synthetic fabrics generally can be either washed or dry-cleaned, with the exception of rayon and acetate, which should not be washed. The ability to be washed repeatedly at high temperatures is essential for fabrics used in health care facilities and in salons and spas.

Some jurisdictions require fabrics in public spaces to meet stringent fire-resistance standards. If the interior designer is unable to identify an inherently flame-resistant fabric that meets design requirements, the local authorities may accept another fabric that has been treated with a flame-resistant chemical.

There are two major types of flame-resistant treatments, polymers and salines. Saline treatments are not as durable as polymer treatments and sometimes discolor fabrics; they are less expensive than polymer treatments. Salines increase the fabric's ability to absorb moisture, which can result in noticeable dimensional changes in long fabric pieces such as draperies. In addition, the chemicals in saline treatments can corrode metal tacks and upholstery staples.

Polymer flame-resistant treatments are reasonably durable, although they will eventually wash out after about 20 dry cleanings. The fabric is rolled off the bolt into the chemical bath; then the treatment is heat-set. Because shrinking is not uncommon, most finishers request that the fabric sent for treatment exceed the amount actually needed by about 5 percent. Not all fabrics react well to polymer treatments, and may exhibit color changes or stiffness. It is advisable to always have a sample tested before treating the rest of the fabric.

An alternative that does not involve chemical treatment and that meets the high fire resistance standards of CAL 133 is the lamination of aramid fabrics to the back of the upholstery fabric. Lamination saves labor and reduces costs over upholstering the piece with an aramid and again with the finish fabric. The flame-resistant properties of aramid fabrics protect the upholstery foam from fire.

Note: California Technical Bulletin 133 is commonly referred to as either CAL 133 or TB 133. Its full name is *Flammability Test Procedure for Seating Furniture for Use in Public Occupancies*. CAL 133 is a flame resistance test that involves burning a full-scale sample or mock-up of a piece of upholstered furniture. Its use has spread from California to other states and cities.

Stain-resistant treatments are frequently applied to both residential and commercial fabrics for resistance to oil- or water-based stains. These treatments are usually sprayed on and can typically be used with fire-resistant treated fabric. After treatment, fluids will bead on the surface of the fabric without being absorbed or spreading, and are easily removed. Stain-resistant treatments do not usually change the appearance or feel of the fabric. Two fluoroplastics, Teflon by DuPont and Scotchgard by 3M, have been used in the past, but environmental considerations have resulted in changes.

LEATHER

Leather is made from animal skins or hides; most cattle hides are a by-product of the meat industry. Other leathers are made from the hides of sheep, goats or pigs, reptile skins such as alligator and snake, and emu or ostrich skins. Light and thin leathers are usually made from the skin of calves or kids (baby goats).

Note: The use of leather as an upholstery material is discussed in Chapter 12. Leather flooring materials are included in Chapter 9.

Tanning is the process of making leather. The animal fat and hair are removed and the thick middle layer is chemically changed to preserve it and increase its strength and flexibility.

Historically, hides were tanned with plant products that contain tannin, a chemical that reacts with collagen, a fibrous protein in the middle layers of skins. The ancient Egyptians and Hebrews made leather, as did the Romans. Vegetable-tanned leather stretches when soaked in water, and can be carved, molded, painted, dyed, oiled, or waxed. Vegetable-tanned leather is valuable for making furniture, and tends to be expensive.

The process of chemical tanning using chromium sulfate was discovered in 1858. The tanning industry has developed a reputation for water pollution and unpleasant odors. Leather tanned with chrome stretches less than vegetable tanned leather and cannot be carved or molded. It accepts some dyes well and is relatively inexpensive.

Oil-tanned leather is very flexible. The oil can be felt on the surface but will not rub off. Tanning processes are sometimes combined.

True buckskin leather is made from deer hide treated with a wood ash and lime solution. Buckskin is soft and supple. Rawhide is an untanned leather that becomes very stiff when dry but is flexible and stretches when wet.

The sludge created by leather processing is a major water pollution problem. The sodium sulfide and lime used to remove hair from cowhides produces the protein-rich

Figure 8-10 Woven leather strips
Photo by Jessica Burko. Courtesy of
Claudia Mills Studio.

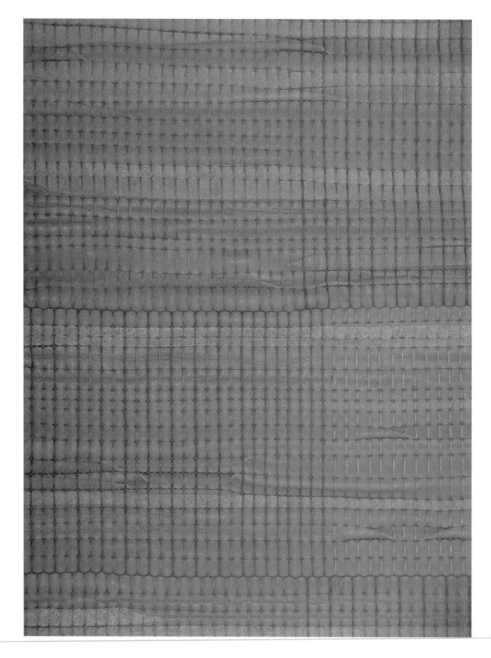

sludge. New enzyme-based technology uses significantly less water and preserves the hair, which can be used in a variety of ways including the making of rugs and carpets.

The leather finishing process varies depending on the type of leather and its intended use. The tanned hide is split to produce thinner layers. A second tanning step can make leather either softer or firmer. The leather is then dyed, oil is added, and the hides are dried. Imperfect surfaces can be smoothed by mechanical buffing, producing what are known as corrected grain leathers.

Full grain leathers are sprayed or rolled with a polymer or wax finish. Corrected grain leathers are given basecoats and pigment coats before a topcoat is applied. Embossing stamps an artificial grain onto the surface of the leather.

Finish Flooring Comparisons 9

Finish flooring may be the top surface of a floor structure, such as a finished concrete slab, or an applied material, such as carpet or linoleum. Finish flooring materials must be durable enough to withstand wear from feet, furniture, and equipment, and be resistant to abrasions, dents, and scuffs. Quality of installation affects long-term durability and aesthetic appeal of a finish. A flooring material should be resistant to dirt, moisture, grease, and staining.

Finish floor materials are usually separated into *hard floor coverings*, such as wood, stone, and tile, *resilient flooring* (linoleum, vinyl), and *soft floor coverings*, including carpets and rugs.

HARD FLOOR COVERINGS

Hard floor surfaces are chosen for their durability, ease of maintenance, and aesthetic appeal. Hard floors reflect room sounds and also amplify the sound of impacts from shoes or chairs. Some hard surfaces become slippery when wet.

Proper installation prevents moisture from invading seams in the material and getting under the finish. All types of hard floor surfaces benefit from the use of walk-off mats at entrances that trap most of the moisture and dirt before it can be tracked into the building. Regularly scheduled maintenance helps to protect and preserve the floor's appearance and add to its useful life.

Tile Flooring

Ceramic tile and stone flooring materials are solid and durable. Glass tile is surprisingly durable as well. Tile installations can be expensive to remove and, unless they are ground up and reused, will not break down, adding bulk to landfills. Ceramic tile performance standards are set forth in ANSI 137.1 (1988).

In general, larger tiles are used in larger rooms, and smaller tiles in smaller spaces. One consideration is whether the tile will be seen primarily close up or from a distance. Nominal dimensions of mosaic ceramic tiles are generally 1 × 1 inch or 2 × 2 inches,

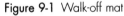

Figure 9-1 Walk-off mat

although those used in art installations can be any size or shape. Other tiles range from 6 × 6 inches up to 18 × 18 inches, with a variety of proportions.

Floor tile is installed in two phases: setting and grouting. Setting attaches the tiles to the flooring substrate with mortar. Floor tiles are installed in either thinset or thickset mortar.

The width and color of the grout joints affect the selection of a tile floor. Because floors are likely to be exposed to more dirt than walls, it makes sense to keep the grout lines subdued and noncontrasting. Even well-installed and sealed grout joints will pick up some hard-to-remove dirt over time; using a dirt-hiding color of grout can minimize the impact. Tighter grout lines leave less exposed grout to get dirty or become loose. Most tile floors clean easily. Dark colors may show residue from cleaning products, however, and highly glazed finishes may be scratched by inappropriate cleaning practices.

Grout used to fill the spaces between tiles is selected to match the qualities of the tile and the conditions of the installation (see Chapter 2 for additional information on cement grouts). Epoxy grout is impervious to water, very strong, and much more resistant to stains and chemicals than cement grouts. Waterproof membranes can be installed under tile in areas that are frequently exposed to water. Treating nonepoxy grout joints with a silicone grout sealer two times a year will help preserve the grout color.

Ceramic Tiles

Glazed ceramic tile floors are the most common, and are durable and long lasting. Liquid glass is fired onto the tile at high temperatures to produce a hard, nonporous glaze. Shiny glazes are more easily scratched and can be more slippery than matte surfaces.

Figure 9-2 Thinset ceramic floor tile installation
Reproduced by permission of the publisher from Francis D. K. Ching and Cassandra Adams, *Building Construction Illustrated*, 3rd ed. (New York: John Wiley & Sons, Inc.), © 2001 by John Wiley & Sons, Inc.

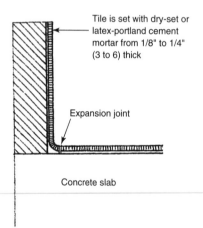

Tile is set with dry-set or latex-portland cement mortar from 1/8" to 1/4" (3 to 6) thick

Expansion joint

Concrete slab

Figure 9-3 Thickset ceramic floor tile installation
Reproduced by permission of the publisher from Francis D. K. Ching and Cassandra Adams, *Building Construction Illustrated*, 3rd ed. (New York: John Wiley & Sons, Inc.), © 2001 by John Wiley & Sons, Inc.

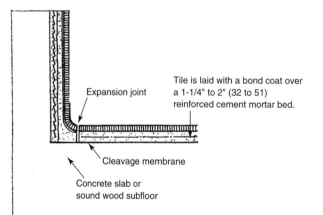

Expansion joint

Tile is laid with a bond coat over a 1-1/4" to 2" (32 to 51) reinforced cement mortar bed.

Cleavage membrane

Concrete slab or sound wood subfloor

Glazed ceramics resist stains, odors, and dirt, and clean easily with a damp mop or sponge and common household cleaners. Most glazed ceramics are *nonvitreous* and will not absorb water. They are produced from widely available natural materials with moderate levels of embedded energy.

Ceramic tile flooring does not retain odors, allergens, or bacteria. It is extremely combustion-resistant and does not emit toxic fumes. Both traditional and technologically advanced manufacturing processes offer an exceptionally wide and appealing selection of colors, sizes, styles, shapes, and textures. Recycled tiles and broken-ceramic mosaics expand the options available. (See color plate C-55, Art mosaic floor.)

One of the key criteria for selecting ceramic tile flooring is slip resistance, especially where it may be exposed to spilled liquids or grease. The frequency of spills, amount of traffic, and immediacy of cleanup care are factors to consider.

Tile thickness affects its durability and installation as a flooring material. In general, wall tiles are thinner than floor tiles, which have to sustain regular impact and heavier loads. Heavier tiles may require a thicker mortar bed for support. The supporting subfloor material must be able to carry the weight of the tile, mortar, and grout, and provide a smooth, stable surface. The installed thickness of the tile has to be coordinated with the thickness of adjacent floor surfaces.

Larger-size ceramic tiles come in a range of sizes and patterns, some of which mimic natural stone and are practically impervious to moisture, dirt, and stains. Colors range from the tans, beiges, and reddish browns of flagstone to the grays, greens, and blacks of slate.

Porcelain Tiles

Porcelain floor tiles are made with special porcelain clays and are denser and less porous than glazed ceramic tiles. They resist moisture, stains, bacteria, odors, and damage by most cleaning products. Porcelain tiles are less likely to scratch or fade, both in polished and matte finishes. They may have a colored, glazed surface on top of a tile body; when chipped, the color of the underlying ceramic will be visible. Through-body porcelain tiles are the same material throughout, and wear is almost invisible. (See color plate C-53, Porcelain ceramic floor tile.)

The extreme high pressures and temperatures used to make porcelain tiles produce a much stronger and denser product than ordinary glazed ceramic tiles. Because porcelain tiles are close to impervious to water, they are stable even when subjected to freezing and thawing. When bonded properly to the subfloor, porcelain tiles make a very good surface for high traffic areas.

Porcelain Wear Ratings

The Porcelain Enamel Institute (PEI) has established wear rating classifications for ceramic tile.

- Group I Light traffic: Residential bathrooms. Primarily wall tiles, but some can be used on the floor, if recommended by manufacturer.
- Group II Medium traffic: Residential use in kitchens, foyers, and laundry rooms, but not in areas of high traffic.
- Group III Medium-heavy traffic: Suitable for all residential installations with normal foot traffic.
- Group IV Heavy traffic: Light to medium commercial applications, such as offices and sales rooms.
- Group V Heavy-plus traffic: Heavy commercial traffic areas and exterior use; shopping centers, airports, hotel lobbies, public walkways.

Ceramic Mosaic Tiles

Ceramic mosaic tiles are small, modular units of natural clay or porcelain that are widely used for flooring. The natural clay type of mosaic tile is unglazed and comes in muted earth colors. Small ceramic tiles are often delivered mounted onto sheets to facilitate installation. (See color plate C-54, Ceramic mosaic floor tiles.)

Other Types of Tiles

Unglazed tile is the most durable type of general tile. Unglazed tiles are not coated; their color is the same from the face through to the back.

Quarry tiles are made from shale or natural clays through the extrusion process and heat hardened. Grease can make them slippery, and they are therefore available with abrasive grit in the surface for slip resistance. (See color plate C-56, Quarry tiles.)

Paver tiles are natural clay or porcelain tiles 6 square inches or more on face. They are made using the dust-pressed method and may be glazed or unglazed.

Glass tile is practical and beautiful for floors. Hand cut-glass mosaic tiles are available in 1 × 1, 1 × 2, 2 × 2 inches and hexagonal shapes mounted on sheets. Larger metallic and translucent glass tiles are also available for use on floors. Some relief patterned and textured tiles may be too uneven for floor use, but some glass tile is made with a sandy texture that has high skid resistance.

Stone Flooring

Durable stone flooring is often used in public spaces. Granite, marble, limestone, slate, and flagstone are some of the more common stones available as tiles or pavers.

Different colors of stone come from different parts of the world, and as it is very heavy and expensive to ship, the origin of the stone is a design and energy use consideration.

Polished surfaces are highly reflective and require a great deal of maintenance. They can easily become slippery, and so are often covered with antiskid mats. *Honed* finishes are somewhat rougher and have a dull sheen and good slip resistance. Granite

Table 9-1 Ceramic Floor Tiles

Type	Size	Composition	Absorption	Slip Resistance	Comments
Glazed or unglazed ceramic mosaic	1/4 to 3/8 in. thick; face area under 6 sq in. (39 cm)	Porcelain or natural clay; dust pressed or plastic	Porcelain impervious; natural clay may be vitreous	Unglazed plain or abrasive mixture; glazed, less slip resistant	May not be durable enough for heavy commercial use
Glazed or unglazed quarry paver tile	1/4 to 3/4 in. thick; 6 sq in. (39 cm) or more on face	Unglazed shale or natural clay; extrusion process	5% or less	Grease makes slippery; abrasive grit can be embedded in unglazed	Suitable for very heavy commercial use; chemical resistant
Glazed or unglazed paver	6 sq in. or more on face	Natural clay or porcelain; dust pressed	Vitreous		Suitable for very heavy commercial use; chemical resistant

Table 9-2 Poured Floorings

Type	Description	Properties	Uses
Epoxy resin flooring	Liquid resins with hardening and curing agents, poured or troweled on 1/16 to 1/2 in. (1.6 to 13 mm) thick. Cures in 24 to 48 hours.	Graded aggregates and mineral oxide pigments added. Two-stage resins are made more chemical- and heat-resistant by the addition of novolac.	Food processing and commercial kitchen areas.
Methyl methacrylate (MMA) flooring	Copolymer used in waterborne coatings.	Cures in two hours. Can be applied at low temperatures. About 30% higher cost than epoxy.	Refrigerated areas.
Polyurethane flooring	Liquid plastic applied with a trowel or poured 1/8 to 3/8 in. (3.2-9.6 mm) thick.	More expensive than epoxy. Withstands extreme changes in temperature.	Food processing areas, commercial kitchens, walk-in freezers and refrigerators.
Magnesium oxychloride flooring	Trowel-applied; often red or earth tones.	Fire-resistant, and slip-resistant wet or dry; durable.	Not used where standing water or corrosive materials are present.
Latex resin flooring	Applied seamlessly with a trowel.	Resists moisture and chemicals.	Showers and laboratories. Use waterproof membrane for additional protection from moisture.
Fluid-applied athletic flooring	Troweled synthetic rubber latex. Resilient surface with clear 1/2-in. (13-mm) protective resin finish.	Topped with pigmented resin, on which game lines can be painted.	Replaces wood in gymnasiums and multipurpose rooms.
Seamless quartz floors	Suspended ceramic-coated quartz or colored quartz aggregates in clear epoxy.	Broadcast or troweled on, up to 1/2 in. (13 mm) thick. Available as slip-resistant material.	Laboratories, locker rooms, light manufacturing and institutional applications.

is sometimes treated with an intense flame for a *thermal or flamed finish*, which brings out the color and texture of the stone. Granite may also be water-jet finished, creating a surface between honed and thermal finishes that makes the stone's color richer and darker.

Penetrating stone sealers are available to reduce moisture absorption and staining, but need to be reapplied regularly, and can build up noticeably on the stone's surface. Other coatings improve slip resistance. Combining varied types of stones with different finishes in an interior can create differences in slip and abrasion resistance; marble and granite age at different rates and will wear unevenly if combined.

Interior brick pavers are available in different sizes and thicknesses, and can meet various durability requirements, including chemical resistance. Brick flooring does not require extensive maintenance when properly treated. Interior brick pavers are usually set in mortar beds from 3/8 to 1 inch (10 to 25 mm) thick and then grouted. Mortarless installations are set hand-tight and filled with mason's sand.

Table 9-3 Stone Flooring Comparison

Stone	Origin	Appearance	Finishes
Marble	Metamorphic derivative of limestone	Veins formed by minerals and impurities.	Polish to a high shine. Apply sealer to clean dry floor.
Travertine	Crystallized minerals and limestone	Soft beige color accented by irregular pores and enclosed shells.	Polishing accentuates the natural variations of the stone and increases its depth and sheen.
Granite	Igneous	Even grain and speckled texture give a subtle overall appearance. Hard and durable.	Polishes well, with a good sheen and the appearance of depth.
Slate	Metamorphic derivative of shale	Fine grain, with natural color variations produced by traces of metal during its slow formation.	Natural cleft finish. May be sealed; waxing not recommended.

Concrete and Cementitious Floors

Floors can be finished with smooth, level concrete that is sealed against water, stains, and grease. Concrete floors can be painted, stained, or integrally colored when cast; an exposed aggregate finish provides textural interest. Veneer concrete coatings are thin surface toppings that may be colored or stamped with designs. Veneer coatings tend to chip and should not be used in high-traffic areas. See Chapter 2 for more details.

Figure 9-4 Concrete floor

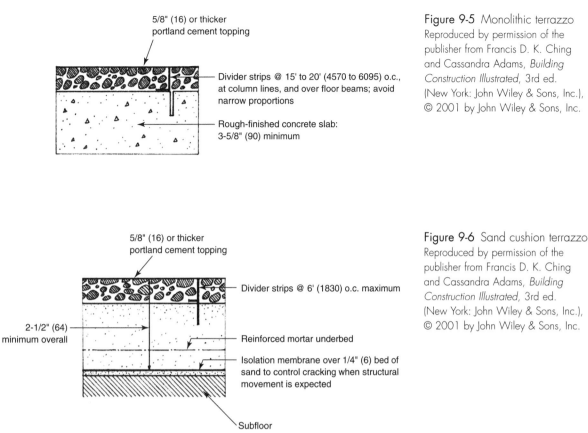

5/8" (16) or thicker
portland cement topping

Divider strips @ 15' to 20' (4570 to 6095) o.c.,
at column lines, and over floor beams; avoid
narrow proportions

Rough-finished concrete slab:
3-5/8" (90) minimum

Figure 9-5 Monolithic terrazzo
Reproduced by permission of the
publisher from Francis D. K. Ching
and Cassandra Adams, *Building
Construction Illustrated*, 3rd ed.
(New York: John Wiley & Sons, Inc.),
© 2001 by John Wiley & Sons, Inc.

5/8" (16) or thicker
portland cement topping

Divider strips @ 6' (1830) o.c. maximum

2-1/2" (64)
minimum overall

Reinforced mortar underbed

Isolation membrane over 1/4" (6) bed of
sand to control cracking when structural
movement is expected

Subfloor

Figure 9-6 Sand cushion terrazzo
Reproduced by permission of the
publisher from Francis D. K. Ching
and Cassandra Adams, *Building
Construction Illustrated*, 3rd ed.
(New York: John Wiley & Sons, Inc.),
© 2001 by John Wiley & Sons, Inc.

Terrazzo is an extremely durable, seamless, very low-maintenance surface, available either poured on-site or precast as a tile. A terrazzo floor contains a minimum of 70 percent stone. Brass strips are used to divide areas of terrazzo, and complex patterns with varied colors are routinely produced. Epoxy or plastic base materials may be used as a matrix for terrazzo for conductive and other special-use floors. Some traditional terrazzo floors were as thick as 3 inches; contemporary precast floors may be less than an inch thick. The most common construction methods for terrazzo floors are sand cushion, bonded or strip, monolithic, rustic, and thinset.

Terrazzo with a cement base is porous, and requires a penetrating sealer for protection. Care for new terrazzo floors includes machine-scrubbing, then rinsing, before application of one or two coats of a penetrating sealer. For a higher gloss, manufacturer-recommended water-based surface finishes are available. Old or abused terrazzo floors may be pitted or uneven; some develop a dull, crusty surface. In some cases, the floor may have to be reground by a specialized flooring contractor. When this is not an option, a complete stripping and application of a new surface-type coating may improve appearance. For additional information on terrazzo, see Chapter 2.

Poured Floorings

Fluid-applied floorings provide heavy-duty, seamless surfaces for commercial and industrial applications. They can usually be installed with integral cove bases. These specialized surfaces for challenging spaces are poured over concrete or other rigid substrates. Some poured finishes give off environmentally objectionable volatile organic compounds (VOCs).

Figure 9-7 Seamless quartz
flooring

Wood Flooring

Psychologically, wood suggests comfort, whether it is the rough, gray cedar of a cottage at the beach or the elegance of a beautifully crafted and finished exotic wood floor. Wood floors are installed in a manner that retains the resilience of the wood. Many are quite durable and reasonably easy to maintain under moderate use. Worn or damaged floors can often be refinished to appear almost new. Under heavy use, finished wood will require careful and constant maintenance, adding to its expense.

Many species of hardwoods are available for use as flooring. Of these, red oak, white oak, ash, and maple are the most common in North America. Species available as hardwood flooring include Brazilian cherry, tiger wood, Australian cypress, and many others. The best grades, Clear and Select, will minimize or exclude defects such as knots, streaks, checks, and torn grain.

The classic solid wood strip floor is made of 2–1/4-inch-wide strips 3/4 inch thick; other widths and thicknesses are available. Solid wood planks are cut out of the tree as a solid block, and processed into planks with *tongue-and-groove* edges. The planks may be prefinished at the factory or made into bundles, unfinished.

Solid wood floors react to the dryness of heated buildings by contracting, leaving gaps between the planks. The humidity present in warm weather will expand the planks and the gaps will disappear. Expansion gaps are left where the wood floor meets the wall, to accommodate dimensional changes. These gaps are covered with wall base.

Wood Species Hardness Comparison
(Note: See Appendix for descriptions of wood species)

Hardest: Brazilian cherry, Jarrah, Merbau, Mesquite, Panga Panga, Santos mahogany

Medium to Hard: African peduak, Bamboo (actually a grass, but sold with wood flooring), Basralocus, Hickory, Jatoba, Pecan, Peruvian walnut, Purpleheart, Wenge

Medium: Afromosia, American beech, Ash, Australian cypress, Iroko, Maple, Red oak, White oak

Medium to Soft: Black cherry, Black walnut, Heart pine, Teak, Yellow birch

Softest: Douglas fir; Southern yellow pine, longleaf; Southern yellow pine, shortleaf

Solid wood floor planks should be allowed to acclimate to the space in which they will be installed.

Unfinished solid oak floors come in four different qualities. Clear wood has no visual blemishes or knots; it is the most expensive. Select and better-quality wood has some small knots and very little dark graining; #1 common and #2 common wood are each progressively more knotty and have more dark graining.

The manner in which a log is sawn affects the appearance and performance of wood flooring. Maple, beech, and birch are hard, dense woods that remain dimensionally stable regardless of the way they are cut.

Antique wood flooring is retrieved from buildings that are about to be demolished and offer a distinctive character and patina. These recycled woods are available in limited quantities and will have imperfections from age and use that add to their character. Although it is sad to see old barns and other wood buildings torn down, recycling the wood is far better than burning it.

Hardwood flooring planks are available with beveled, eased, or square edges.

- *Beveled-edge planks* have a distinctive deep V-groove. Flooring with beveled edges is easier to install over irregular surfaces.
- *Eased-edge planks* have a very shallow V-groove that is not as deep as seen customarily in older solid wood floors. The eased edges help hide minor irregularities and unevenness.
- *Square-edged planks* meet evenly on all edges for a smooth, unified floor. They must be carefully laid on a good level base.

Figure 9-8 Wood strip flooring

Figure 9-9 Reclaimed wood flooring
Courtesy of Thomas Campbell, Old Wood Workshop, LLC; oldwoodworkshop.com

Solid wood strip and plank floors can be installed only on wooden subfloors at or above grade level. Both subfloors and the finished layer of wood should be checked for moisture content before installation. The methods for installing a solid wood floor include nail-down, staple-down, glue-down, and floating installation.

- Nail-down installation is most commonly used to install 3/4-inch solid wood floors; adapters are available for thinner floors. Nailing *cleats* are attached to the subfloor, and the planks are attached to the cleats.
- Staples rather than nailing cleats are used for staple-down installation. The tongue of the wood plank is attached to the wood subfloor below with staples.
- Glue-down installation involves gluing the wood planks directly to the subfloor. *Mastic* or adhesive is spread onto the subfloor with a notched trowel, and the planks are set into the adhesive.
- Floating installation is fast, easy, and clean. A thin pad is placed between the wood flooring and the subfloor; the floor planks themselves are not mechanically fastened to the subfloor. The padding helps resist moisture, reduces impact noise transmission, adds resiliency, and increases insulating values. Wood glue recommended by the manufacturer is applied in the tongue and groove of each plank to hold them together.

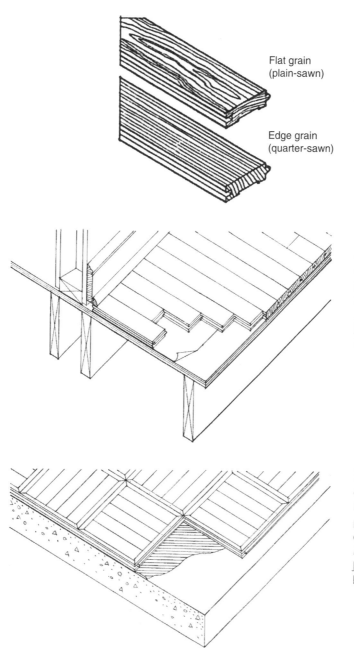

Figure 9-10 Board flooring
Reproduced with permission of the publisher from Francis D. K. Ching and Corky Binggeli, *Interior Design Illustrated*, 2nd ed. (Hoboken, NJ: John Wiley & Sons, Inc.), © 2005 by John Wiley & Sons, Inc.

Flat grain
(plain-sawn)

Edge grain
(quarter-sawn)

Figure 9-11 Wood flooring over subfloor and joists
Reproduced with permission of the publisher from Francis D. K. Ching and Corky Binggeli, *Interior Design Illustrated*, 2nd ed. (Hoboken, NJ: John Wiley & Sons, Inc.), © 2005 by John Wiley & Sons, Inc.

Figure 9-12 Wood flooring over concrete slab
Reproduced with permission of the publisher from Francis D. K. Ching and Corky Binggeli, *Interior Design Illustrated*, 2nd ed. (Hoboken, NJ: John Wiley & Sons, Inc.), © 2005 by John Wiley & Sons, Inc.

Wood Floor Finishes

Flooring manufacturers designate a number of other special effects for wood flooring. Handscraped hardwood floors, available for solid wood floors above grade, are hand-tooled to create an expensive and unique appearance. Some manufacturers offer distressed hardwood flooring, which has had the face marked by machine.

Wood flooring is most often finished with clear polyurethane, varnish, or a penetrating sealer; finishes can range from high gloss to satin to a dull sheen. Ideally, the finish should enhance the durability of the wood and its resistance to water, dirt, and staining without concealing its natural beauty. Stains are used alter the natural color of wood without obscuring its grain. Wood flooring can also be waxed, painted, or even stenciled, but painted surfaces require more maintenance. Finishes help to protect wood from wear, but the color of the wood underneath can still be changed by the sun's ultraviolet rays.

Finishes are usually applied at the job site to allow matching of trims and stairs; this makes custom stains readily feasible. Hardwood floors can be finished at the factory with urethane-based finishes that do not require buffing or waxing. With factory-finished wood floors, prefinished wood trims may not match the floor, so color-coordinated trims would be used instead.

Water-based and oil-based urethane finishes for job-site application continue to improve. Moisture-cured urethane is similar to solvent-based, but requires a humid environment for curing. Using ultraviolet light, several coats of urethane finish can be applied and cured quickly; manufacturers may apply as many as 6 to 10 layers. UV-cured urethane wood finishes resist watermarking and are much more durable and abrasion-resistant than waxed wood floors.

Adding small chips of aluminum oxide into the finish greatly increases the wear-resistance of the floor's wear layer. Acrylic floor finishes with metal cross-links are made stronger with water-borne urethane. Their high initial gloss is designed to respond to spray buffing. Some manufacturers offer wear layers with advanced ceramics that increase abrasion resistance.

Installing Wood Flooring

Because wood flooring will expand and contract, it is installed with details that allow for movement. Wood floors are put in either over a plywood subfloor or wood strips called *sleepers.*

The subfloor to which the finished wood flooring is attached must be clean, and any old adhesives must be removed. In commercial projects, wood flooring is usually laid over concrete floors. If the subfloor is not solid and flat, an underlayment may be required to level the floor and cover cracks. The most common underlayment is exterior-grade plywood. Self-leveling compounds smooth out existing concrete floors before they are topped with a wood floor.

Hardwood floors will acquire scratches and scrapes over time. Valuing these vestiges of use and age simplifies maintenance and expands the aesthetic appeal of the floor. If a visually perfect finish is the goal, imperfections can be minimized with a touch-up stick of tinted wax, or a colored marker that contains wood stain. Badly damaged areas can be masked off, refinished, restained, and given a new finish. The new finish is feathered to blend into the adjacent existing floor; a perfect match is, however, difficult to achieve.

Hardwood floors can be scratched or dented by hard narrow wheels, unprotected wooden legs, or metal furniture legs. Furniture on wood floors should have felt or nylon

Figure 9-13 Wood flooring over concrete with sleepers
Reproduced with permission of the publisher from Francis D. K. Ching and Corky Binggeli, *Interior Design Illustrated*, 2nd ed. (Hoboken, NJ: John Wiley & Sons, Inc.), © 2005 by John Wiley & Sons, Inc.

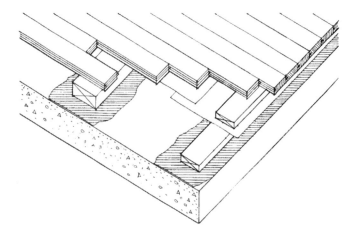

foot protectors, or rest on coasters. The legs of large, heavy pieces should be fitted with wide, nonstaining rubber cups.

Although hardwood floors are often preferred for appearance and durability, pine floors are found in older buildings in North America and Europe. Plain-sawn, random-width, face-nailed white pine boards were the most common flooring material in early New England. Other trees used for North American softwood floors included northern yellow pine, southern yellow pine, cypress, hemlock, spruce, and cedar.

Softwood floors were usually used unfinished and washed regularly with hot water and lye, quickly turning a soft gray color after installation. By the end of the eighteenth century and throughout the nineteenth century, most softwood floors were given a protective coat of paint; colors varied widely and included shades of gray, green, brick red, yellow, and brown. Paint still provides a durable, versatile, inexpensive, and easy-to-apply and touch-up finish for softwood floors.

Historically, only the wealthiest homes had carpets, and then only in their formal spaces; elaborately detailed paintings sometimes simulated carpets. Contrasting borders and stenciled motifs were popular, as well; some floors had striped, checkerboard, or geometric designs. Images featured in the center of floors included animals, especially dogs. During the Federal period, urns and swags were often used.

Figure 9-14 Painted wood floor
Courtesy of Thomas Campbell, Old Wood Workshop, LLC; oldwoodworkshop.com

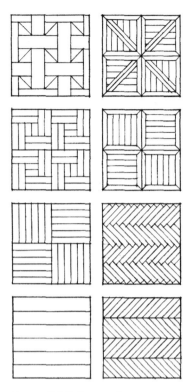

Figure 9-15 Parquet flooring
Reproduced with permission of the publisher from Francis D. K. Ching and Corky Binggeli, *Interior Design Illustrated*, 2nd ed. (Hoboken, NJ: John Wiley & Sons, Inc.), © 2005 by John Wiley & Sons, Inc.

Softwood flooring is available unfinished or prefinished, in lengths from 4 to 16 feet and widths from 4 to 20 inches. Solid boards are available 3/4 or 1 inch thick, with either tongue-and-groove or *shiplap* edges. They are advertised as better able to accommodate temperature changes and recommended for in-floor heating installations. Cracks 1/4 inch or wider that may have developed between softwood floorboards due to swelling and contracting of wood over time can be filled with a flexible paste or fiber filler that will accommodate movement; sawdust mixtures or soaked hemp rope have also been used traditionally. This is best done halfway through the expansion/contraction cycle (spring or fall). Gaps larger than about 1/2 inch may be filled with a pliable backing such as cloth or weatherstripping. Minor imperfections can be left as is or repaired by gluing down long splinters and then filling cracks with wood filler. The floor can then be painted with two or more coats of an oil-based floor or deck paint.

Parquet Flooring

Parquet flooring is essentially an ornamental wood mosaic. Wood with contrasting color and grain is used to create contrast in geometric patterns. Solid parquet is made of solid wood about 1.5 cm thick; the solid construction allows the floor to be sanded and refinished. Veneered parquet is a thin layer of solid wood, (usually 5 mm thick) on a wood or plywood base, with a clear protective layer on top. Veneered parquet can be finished as solid wood, and light sanding is permissible for repairs. Laminated parquet uses a wood image rather than real wood on top of a base (often particleboard), with a clear protective layer on top. Laminates often chip and cannot be repaired. Blocks or boards of parquet are fitted together with tongue-and-groove joints. They can be installed as a floating floor, or be nailed or glued.

Engineered Hardwood Flooring

Engineered hardwood flooring is factory-made from layers of wood. It can be installed wherever solid wood flooring is appropriate, as well as over concrete slabs. It can be used above or below grade, including in basements. Because only a thin veneer is used for the face of the flooring, the wood of a wider variety of trees is available. Most engineered wood floors are prefinished at the factory, eliminating job-site mess and volatile organic compounds, and saving time. Factory finishes applied to engineered flooring are very durable, and can be walked on as soon as they are installed. Most factory finishes are UV-cured; often, the number of coats applied is greater than what would be possible on-site.

Most engineered floors have either three or five *plies* (layers). Frequently, a different wood species is used for the finish layer (top ply) of an engineered wood plank than the plies in the middle. Limited use of more costly domestic and exotic hardwood species both conserves these woods and lowers costs.

The top layer of engineered wood floors may be made of rotary-peeled veneers or of sliced or sawn layers. Rotary-peeled veneers are peeled off the logs in long strips, producing the maximum amount of surface finish possible for the lowest cost, but both visual appeal and grain strength are sacrificed.

Sawn face is a traditional process whereby lumber from a saw mill is graded and sorted by use and for the most efficient yield. It is then sawn to the desired thickness. Sawn face lumber reduces waste and increases the amount of high-grade hardwood from hardwood factory logs.

As engineered wood is manufactured, the wood layers are stacked in reversing grain directions on top of one another, helping to counteract expansion and contraction that occurs with changes in humidity levels and moisture. As a result, engineered wood planks are much more dimensionally stable than solid wood, stable enough to be installed over clean, dry concrete slabs. Engineered wood planks are most commonly stapled or glued down; some can be used in floating installation over some types of substrates. Because concrete cannot be stapled, glue-down installation is used with concrete slabs. A mastic or adhesive recommended by the manufacturer is spread onto the subfloor using the designated size of notched trowel; the planks are then set into the adhesive. Some hardwood flooring manufacturers produce engineered wood floors with a glueless locking system; they can be installed over wood, concrete slabs, and sometimes existing floor finishes.

Engineered planks are available in 2–1/4-, 3-, 5-, and 7-inch widths. Plank widths may be mixed, with a row of one width adjacent to a row of a different width; the resulting variations diversify the appearance of the floor.

Longstrip Wood Floors

Longstrip wood floors (sometimes called engineered longstrip planks) are related to engineered wood floors. The planks are constructed of several wood plies glued together. A softer wood is usually used for the center core; this is used to make the tongue and groove. Another softer wood is attached below, with a hardwood finish layer of almost any wood species as the top ply.

The finish layer of a longstrip wood floor is made up of about 17 or 18 small, individual solid wood pieces that are laid in three rows of solid planks; the entire longstrip plank is about 86 inches long and 7–1/2 inches wide. The plank looks like it is three narrow planks wide and several planks long, preassembled for easy installation. Longstrip plank floors are designed for floating installation but most can also be glued or stapled down. They can be installed above or below ground level and over various types of subfloors. Longstrip plank floors are available in a wide variety of wood types.

Laminate Flooring

Laminate flooring is available in many plank widths and square tile sizes, with finish design images that realistically imitate hardwood, stone, or tile. The top wear layer has very good durability and is resistant to most stains, spills, and burns. It is easy to care for, and is very scratch-resistant. The inner core is usually high-density fiberboard (HDF), particleboard, or plastic; this is also used for the tongues and grooves that lock the planks together. Some manufacturers treat this inner core with melamine resins or water-resistant sealers for protection from moisture. The backing is usually a melamine plastic layer that adds structural stability and moisture protection.

Laminate floors are installed by floating the planks over plywood, OSB, concrete slab, or some existing floor coverings; they are never secured directly to the subfloor. The planks are acclimated to the room for easier installation and to reduce bowing and cupping. The underlayment, a thin clear plastic sheet installed over the substrate, allows the laminate flooring to expand and contract freely as the room environment changes. Some more expensive underlayments are available that reduce sound transmissions and restrict the wicking of moisture from the substrate.

Most laminate floors use a type of glueless locking system known as "clic" floors. One type of system involves a tongue and groove that is reinforced from underneath by an aluminum mechanical locking system. The other main type has a tongue-and-groove locking system built into the middle core so that the planks can snap together. Some types of laminate floors are preglued at the factory with water-resistant glue; a damp sponge activates the adhesive along the tongue edges for installation. Other types have glue that is applied to the edges of the planks on-site. Manufacturers offer several enhancements intended to increase the realism of the appearance of laminate planks. Microbeveled edging and textured surfaces imitate wood floors.

Bamboo Flooring

Bamboo floors are used and maintained the same as hardwood floors. They are available as solid and as engineered planks, and are joined by tongue-and-groove edges and installed like wood floors. They have better dimensional stability than most hardwoods used for flooring. Bamboo floor planks are available with both vertical and horizontal grain.

The natural color of bamboo floors is a light honey blond. To produce a darker soft amber color, the strips are *carbonized*—completely saturated by steam at high pressure; colors vary widely.

 Note: There is currently no grading system for bamboo flooring like the Select and #1 Common grades used for hardwoods.

The manufacturing process for bamboo flooring begins with slicing the hollow round shoots into strips; these are then boiled to remove the starch. The strips of raw bamboo must be dried carefully. They are then laminated into solid boards, which are milled into flooring strips. A preservative is applied either before or after lamination; some manufacturers specify that they use relatively nontoxic boric acid. Flooring is frequently kiln-dried to 9 to 10 percent moisture content, limiting its dimensional stability where humidity is low or variable; a level of 6 to 8 percent is better.

Formaldehyde, a carcinogen with serious environmental disadvantages, is present in the adhesives used to laminate the bamboo slats together into flooring. Currently, all bamboo flooring products are laminated with urea-formaldehyde (UF) adhesive; to date, attempts to use nonformaldehyde isocyanate resin as an alternative have proved too costly; other options are being tried. Higher-formaldehyde adhesives are less expensive than those with lower levels; poor-quality adhesives may not resist water well. Although UF resin continues to off-gas formaldehyde for an extended period after production, the amount of resin used is much less than in a particleboard product.

Low-VOC adhesives are available, and some manufacturers produce flooring with formaldehyde levels many times lower than OSHA standards. In order to achieve LEED credit as low-emitting materials, bamboo and its adhesive must be properly documented to have very low levels of formaldehyde. The manufacturer should have MSDS or CSI specifications available.

If the cut end of a sample shows small splits or gaps between the bamboo strips, these may have been filled with adhesive or left as is. Sometimes the individual strips are not cut accurately and laminated tightly together, allowing movement and possible delamination. High-quality bamboo flooring will be made to exacting tolerances. The best pieces of raw bamboo are selected for longer planks; although 3-foot lengths are available, 6-foot planks are more likely to be made from the densest, straightest material (sometimes called Premium grade).

Bamboo flooring planks are finished with from three to six coats; polyurethane-only finishes are not as durable as those containing aluminum oxide. Prefinished products have UV-cured finishes with low-VOC emission levels.

Bamboo sold for flooring in North America is grown primarily in the extensive government-owned bamboo forests of Hunan in southern China; individuals or companies obtain contracts to harvest the bamboo. Shipping Chinese bamboo products to markets in North America involves the use of fossil fuels. Manufacturers have begun to establish bamboo plantations and factories in Vietnam, where it is more possible to control growth, harvesting, and working conditions.

 Note: The bamboo used for flooring is not the type eaten by pandas, which do not live near these commercial bamboo forests.

Some manufacturers have introduced longstrip or floating engineered flooring with bamboo veneer over a *rubberwood* core held together by melamine glue. Rubberwood is the wood of trees that have finished their productive lives in rubber plantations; it is not an ecologically sensitive wood species. This engineered flooring product installs like standard hardwood flooring. The application of a water-based urethane finish can cause the grain to rise, necessitating substantial resanding between coats.

Some bamboo flooring companies maintain inventories in warehouses in the United States, while others may have extensive lead times (12 to 16 weeks, for example). Some suppliers try to match accessories and coordinating products from a variety of manufacturers, since not all flooring manufacturers make stair parts, moldings, vents, panels, and veneer to match their flooring. Prices for bamboo flooring products range from $4 to $8 per square foot ($40 to $80 per square meter), competitive with, but slightly higher than, domestic hardwoods.

Resilient flooring materials provide an economical, dense, nonabsorbent flooring surface with relatively good durability and ease of maintenance. Their resilience enables them to resist permanent indentations while contributing to their quietness and comfort underfoot. Resilient flooring tends to have a relatively firm surface, but enough

RESILIENT FLOORING

Table 9-4 Resilient Flooring Comparisons

Type	Resilience	Durability	Finish	Maintenance	Environmental
Cork	Very good	Absorbs moisture, stains.	Factory vinyl topcoat, or oil finish.	Resists mold, mildew. Fades in sun; yellows. Do not wet-mop.	Cork is natural and renewable. Mixed with synthetic resins.
Linoleum	Very good	Extremely durable	Cross-linked durable primer and water-based wear layer available from Forbo.	Resists staining, grease, burns.	Natural biodegradable materials.
Rubber	Very good	Durable enough for high-use spaces. Can be slippery; problems with grease.	May require a sealer. Self-polishing rubber floors available.	Raised patterns may collect dirt. Mop regularly. Resists chemicals, burns.	Synthetic (styrene butadiene) or natural rubber. Recyclable.
Vinyl sheet	Very good	Moderately durable; recommend min. 10 mils wear layer	No-wax finish will lose shine.	Resists staining, grease, burns. Requires rebuffing or recoating. Fading, blisters, brittleness in sun.	High PVC content. Pollutes during manufacture. VOCs; disposal problems.
Solid vinyl tile	Good	Durable	Pattern throughout tile	Vacuum, wipe up spills.	Less PVC than sheet vinyl.
Vinyl composition tile	Moderate	Moderately durable	Thin wear layer may wear off.	Resists staining, grease, burns.	Less PVC than solid vinyl tile.

springiness to return to its original shape. The degree of comfort provided will depend not only on the material's resilience, but also on the type of backing used and the hardness of the supporting substrate.

Cork Flooring

Introduced in 1904, cork tile became popular in the 1920s, even though it was expensive and porous. Cork tile is manufactured from ground-up cork mixed with synthetic resins that is then given a protective finish. It has excellent acoustical and thermal-insulating properties. (See color plate C-57, Cork flooring.)

Cork floors are made of planks or tiles that are glued down or floated over subfloors of wood, concrete, and sometimes other existing flooring materials. A glueless interlocking system allows faster and less messy installations. Most cork planks and tiles are made with a tongue-and-groove moisture-resistant inner core. Cork flooring is used in both residential and commercial applications.

Cork fades in direct sunlight, and it tends to yellow with age. Cork flooring reacts to changes in humidity and heat, and should never be wet-mopped, as this causes the seams to swell.

Unfinished cork floors are finished at the job site. Many flooring products have a factory-applied vinyl topcoat for protection and ease of maintenance. A recent innovation is a nontoxic oil finish that can be walked on as soon as applied and accepts refinishing.

Linoleum Flooring

Linoleum was invented and patented in 1845. It was first manufactured in Scotland in the 1860s; the first plant in the United States dates to 1872. It was a popular flooring material until vinyl flooring was introduced after World War II. Unfortunately, early linoleum floors stained easily and deteriorated when exposed to oxygen, ozone, and solvents; and they could not be exposed to alkaline moisture in basements.

Figure 9-16 Vintage linoleum floor

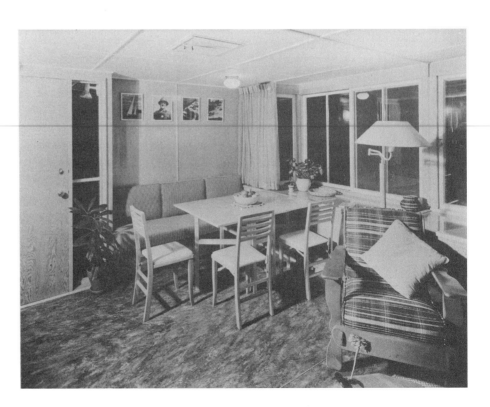

Natural linoleum is made mostly of renewable natural materials including linseed oil from flax, wood powder, limestone, resins, and some colored pigments. The backing is jute, a natural grass, and waste from the manufacturing process is biodegradable. It is available in both sheet and tile forms. The inclusion of cork gives linoleum excellent thermal and acoustical insulating properties.

When first delivered to a site, linoleum may appear lighter than the designer's sample, but the color quickly changes once it is unrolled and exposed to air. After linoleum is laid, it continues to age and becomes progressively less porous. Recently, a two-part topcoat has been introduced that greatly facilitates maintenance; described variously as polyester or acrylic, it can be mechanically removed.

Linoleum has been used in commercial applications both in Europe and the United States; it is extremely durable and burn-resistant. Linoleum is nonallergenic and useful in sanitary applications. Its wide range of colors in both solids and marbleized patterns inspire designers to create original designs.

Rubber Flooring

Rubber floor tiles appeared as early as the twelfth and thirteenth centuries, but interest faded by the end of the seventeenth century. In 1894, a system for rubber floor tiles that could be laid out in geometric patterns was patented by Philadelphia architect Frank Furness. Further development of recessed tabs made it possible to nail rubber tiles to the subfloor; the tabs were eventually eliminated. Rubber tiles were durable, reduced impact sound, cleaned easily, and were easy to install.

Rubber flooring may be made of natural rubber, synthetic rubber, or a combination of both, with added mineral fillers and pigments. Rubber sheets or tiles are preferred for high-traffic areas. Many rubber flooring products have raised patterns for increased slip resistance, but these sometimes collect dirt.

Rubber flooring is used in high-traffic areas such as transportation terminals, where its wearing properties and ability to withstand rigorous cleaning are highly valued. Rubber stair treads and nosings are available with raised patterns.

Laminated rubber tile is an extremely resilient product that springs back into its original shape after being punctured, cut, or compressed. For those reasons, it is used on playgrounds, in fitness clubs, and on floors surrounding ice skating rinks.

Rubber floors are dense, with excellent slip resistance, and they absorb impacts well. They are also easy to maintain and, like other resilient flooring, are comfortable to walk and stand on. Rubber flooring is available with electric static-discharge properties. However, rubber is soft and can be dented by heavy furniture, so nondenting casters and floor protectors that distribute the weight over a larger area should be used.

Figure 9-17 Recycled rubber flooring is available in many color combinations.

Some manufacturers may recommend that a synthetic sealer or finish be applied to rubber flooring to produce a glossier appearance. Self-polishing rubber floors do not require sealing, finishing, or stripping and recoating. Stripping built-up finish with harsh alkaline chemicals can cause a rubber floor's color pigment to separate or bleed, so low- or nonalkaline stripper is advised. Rubber tile can fade over time if exposed to direct sunlight.

Vinyl Flooring Products

Vinyl composition tile was introduced to the public at the Chicago Century of Progress Exposition in 1933. By the late 1940s, it was being widely used for high-traffic commercial areas. Cushioned vinyl floors and "no-wax" resilient floors became popular residential alternatives in the 1960s. More recent innovations include resilient floors with improved slip resistance and static conductivity.

Vinyl floors are manufactured both as sheets and as tiles. Good-quality (and more expensive) vinyl flooring exhibits improved resistance to staining, scratches, gouges, and tearing. Self-stick vinyl tiles are available with adhesive applied at the factory, or as dry back tiles for glue-down installation. Vinyl tiles are available from 1/16 to 1/8 inch thick. Sheet vinyl is available 6 or 12 feet wide, and is more difficult to install than vinyl tiles.

Rotogravure construction is used today for most residential floor tiles. The vinyl tile's core, called the gel coat, is passed under a rotating cylinder that prints colored ink dyes on the surface of the tile. A clear wear layer is applied after the dyes are set. In both inlaid and rotogravure processes, the durability of the wear layer is critical to the performance of the tile. The thickness of the wear layer is measured in millimeters, and varies with product lines.

Vinyl flooring manufacturers are developing floors warranteed against tearing, gouging, ripping, and discoloration. These high-end residential products are designed to resist wear and staining with urethane finishes.

Vinyl products, especially sheet materials, contain the chemical polyvinyl chloride (PVC), which gives vinyl products their flexibility but which also contributes to environmental problems during manufacture, installation, and disposal. Vinyl floor tile adhesives may emit toluene, benzene, ethyl acetate, ethyl benzene, and styrene. Adhesives with low VOCs, which are generally water-based, are available.

Sheet goods have fewer seams than tiles do, making it less likely that they will retain dirt or water. Sheet goods can be turned up at the edge of a wall for an integral wall base, called a *flash cove*, providing greater protection from water, and facilitating maintenance.

Solid or homogenous sheet vinyl is made without a backing, and carries the vinyl's inherent pattern throughout the material, increasing its ability to wear attractively. Solid sheet vinyl resists indentations, rolling loads, and chemicals. The vinyl throughout gives the product greater resilience, but also costs more money than backed vinyl sheets.

Backed vinyl sheets consist of a vinyl wear layer bonded to a backing. The wear layer either contains the pattern of the tile or is a transparent or translucent vinyl layer that protects the pattern below. Some sheet vinyls have interlayers of high-density foam that help to reduce noise from the impact of feet and equipment. Foam interlayers may also reduce the transmission of impact sound to spaces below, and increase resiliency to reduce foot fatigue.

Solid vinyl tile is made with much more PVC than vinyl composition tile (VCT), and is consequently more resilient and resistant to abrasion. The pattern in solid vinyl tile is constant through the thickness of the material.

Until the 1970s, designers specified a product called VAT, vinyl asbestos tile. VAT used asbestos as one of the fillers. Because asbestos is now known to cause serious lung disease when fibers are distributed in the air and inhaled, where VAT is still in place in existing buildings, it should be securely covered without breaking or damaging the tiles, or removed by certified asbestos removal technicians.

Sheet vinyl is installed with an adhesive on a smooth substrate, such as wood or concrete. The substrate should be clean, dry, flat, and smooth, since any irregularities will show through. The seams between sheets can be sealed by two methods: heat welding or chemical welding. Welded seams reduce the risk of moisture getting through to the substrate.

- *Heat welding* is accomplished by melting a vinyl rod between the edges of the vinyl sheets. Rods are available in solid colors and in some patterns, and can be selected to match the color of the sheet vinyl, becoming less noticeable, or to contrast with the sheets it joins as an added design element. Heat welding produces a slightly wider joint than chemical welding. It is preferable where a solid seal is required to resist bacterial or fungal growth. This method is more expensive than chemical welding, and requires trained installers and special equipment.
- *Chemical welding* uses a one- or two-part solvent that is mixed on-site to soften the edges of the vinyl sheets and melt them together. Chemical welding is considerably less expensive, but may not offer a tight enough seal where needed.

The thicker the vinyl wear layer and the higher the vinyl binder content of the sheet vinyl, the better it will wear. ASTM F 1303, Grades of Sheet Vinyl Floor Covering with Backing, sets standards for sheet vinyl performance.

- Type I specifies that the wear layer be between 0.020 and 0.010 inch (0.51 to 0.25 mm) for Grades 1 through 3.
- Type II is also graded from 1 through 3, which must be between 0.05 and 0.02 inch (1.27 to 0.51 mm) thick.

Figure 9-18 Vinyl asbestos tile (VAT) is usually about 8 inches square, smaller than vinyl tile or VCT.

Vinyl composition tile is categorized by ASTM F 1066, Specification for Vinyl Composition Floor Tile, into three classes:

- Class 1 includes solid-color tiles.
- Class 2 consists of through-patterned tiles.
- Class 3 tiles have their patterns only on their surfaces.

(See color plate C-58, Vinyl composition tile.)

Accessories are available in both rubber and vinyl for use with all types of floors. Both serve well, although rubber may retain its color better than vinyl. Wall base covers the joint between the wall and the floor and prevents damage from cleaning equipment. Most wall base is specified with either a straight or standard cove, although a butt cove wall base is also available. Wall base comes in many colors, and is usually selected to blend with the flooring material. Darker colors hide scuffs better. Interior designers may also specify wood wall base. The selection of base color should be coordinated with the door and window frame colors and the floor and wall materials. A contrasting color can define the edge of floor and wall, and reiterate a color used elsewhere. The base is often selected to hide shoe and equipment marks and blend with either the wall or, more commonly, the floor. Wall base continued from one space into adjacent spaces should be carefully coordinated.

SOFT FLOOR COVERINGS

Soft floor coverings such as carpets and rugs add texture to a floor. Their softness, resilience, and warmth support a more comfortable atmosphere.

Carpets

Carpeting is the only flooring material that actually absorbs sound. It also reduces impact noise and is comfortable to walk on and slip-resistant. Carpet is valued as a residential floor finish in homes where children play on the floor. It may be able to hide irregularities in subfloors, and can be installed over a variety of surfaces. Both material costs and installation may be more economical than for hard flooring products.

Carpets require consistent vacuuming and spot removal and should be selected to meet the demands of the intended use. Sometimes, the limited lifespan of carpeting and its visible deterioration over time reduce its desirability. Of course, the quality of its installation affects a carpet's durability and appearance.

Old carpets often end up in landfills, where they remain for great lengths of time. Some carpet manufacturers make carpets from recycled materials. These and other carpets can sometimes be recycled after use. An increasing number of carpet manufacturers are offering to remove old carpet when they deliver new carpet, and to recycle the old carpet into new. Backings can affect a carpet's ability to be recycled, and carpet backings are increasingly being made from recycled carpet materials.

Carpets are constructed using a variety of methods:

- *Tufted carpets* are made from lengths of yarn inserted into a woven or nonwoven fabric. The tufts of yarn are stitched into the backing with a needle bar that has hundreds of rows of equally spaced needles. A secondary backing may be added for greater dimensional stability.
- *Woven carpets*, which have the longest history, are still made by hand in some parts of the world. Weaving a carpet is a much slower and more expensive process than tufting. *Axminster carpet*, generally made of 100 percent wool or a blend of 80 percent wool and 20 percent nylon, is the most durable and long-wearing

Table 9-5 Carpet Fiber Comparison

Fiber	Source	Durability	Color, Texture	Recycling	Use	Cost
Nylon	Synthetic	Excellent; strong. Dries quickly. Soil- and mold-resistant.	Solution-dyed resists fading. Very resilient.	Nylon 6 recycles well. Recycled content used in new carpet.	Commercial, plus some newer residential types.	Moderate cost
Olefin (polypropylene)	Synthetic	Good resistance to abrasion, soil, and mildew.	Colorfast. Less resilient and crush-resistant than nylon. Shows use paths.	Not recyclable	Commercial and residential	Lowest-cost synthetic
Polyester	Synthetic	Less durable than nylon. Resists soiling, abrasion, stains, and fading.	Almost has texture of wool.	Possible to recycle, but not cost-effective.	Residential	Lower-cost than nylon
Wool	Sheep	Excellent	Very good	Biodegradable; used as mulch. Can recycle, but not done.	Commercial and residential	Higher-cost, but lasts much longer

carpet construction, and is preferred for hospitality and residential use. *Wilton carpet* is a decorative wool carpet used in homes. Both carpet types are woven through the back of the fabric and do not require a secondary backing.

- *Fusion-bonded carpets* are constructed in facing pairs with the pile embedded in the backing on each side, then cut apart, creating cut pile carpet. The yarn is dense and durable. Fusion-bonded carpets are considerably more expensive than tufted carpets. They originally offered greater flexibility of patterning for carpet tiles than tufted carpets, but as the pattern technology of tufted carpets has improved, tufted carpet tiles have gained a major segment of the market.

Carpeting is most often manufactured in 12-foot (3.66-m) strips, referred to as *broadloom*. Some specialty carpet comes in widths up to 18 feet (5.5 m). Carpet tiles come in 12- or 18-inch (30.5- or 45.8-cm) squares, used primarily for commercial projects. Woven carpet is also manufactured as narrow goods or runners 27 to 36 inches (68.6 to 91.4 cm) wide, typically for use in residential installations.

Broadloom carpet is made with two basic types of piles: loop or cut. Patterned carpet combines both of these, or uses loops of different heights. Most carpet installed today is tufted rather than woven. Tufting is accomplished with a sewing machine about 13 feet wide with a very large number of needles that sew the yarn to a synthetic backing. The ability of a carpet to retain its texture and appearance depends on the type of fiber, how tightly the fibers are twisted together and heat-set into yarn, how dense the pile is, and how tightly the tufts are packed together.

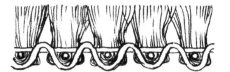

Figure 9-19 Woven carpet construction
Reproduced with permission of the publisher
from Francis D. K. Ching and Corky Binggeli,
Interior Design Illustrated, 2nd ed. (Hoboken,
NJ: John Wiley & Sons, Inc.), © 2005
by John Wiley & Sons, Inc.

Figure 9-20 Fusion-bonded carpet
Reproduced with permission of the publisher
from Francis D. K. Ching and Corky Binggeli,
Interior Design Illustrated, 2nd ed. (Hoboken,
NJ: John Wiley & Sons, Inc.), © 2005 by John
Wiley & Sons, Inc.

Broadloom carpet is sold by the square foot, cut to fit, and installed over a cushion using tackless strips, or glued down using an adhesive in commercial installations. Carpeting normally is installed wall to wall, covering the entire floor of a room. It can be laid directly over a subfloor and underlayment pad, eliminating the need for a finish floor, or it can be laid over an existing floor.

Because carpet is usually fastened to a floor, it must be cleaned in place and cannot be turned to equalize wear. The location of seams, the type of backing, and the technique used to seam carpet can have a substantial effect on the useful lifespan of a broadloom carpet. Fraying seams result from improper installation and failure to seal the edges properly. Installations should meet the standards set by the Carpet and Rug Institute (CRI 104, for commercial installation, and CRI 105, for residential installation).

The performance of a carpet depends greatly on the type of fiber used. Each carpet manufacturer offers blends of the generic face fibers that improve on specific characteristics such as durability, soil resistance, cleanability, color, and luster.

Nylon is the predominant face fiber today. Nylon carpets can achieve antistatic properties through the use of conductive filaments. Type 6 nylon is more easily recyclable, but Type 6,6 nylon has superior structure, hardiness, and resiliency. Newer, soft nylons have increased the desirability of this fiber for residential use.

Especially in commercial projects, carpets are often directly glued onto the substrate: this supports dimensional stability and relatively lower cost. The surface to which it is attached must be solid and smooth, as any irregularities will show through the installed carpet and may cause areas of excessive wear.

Double glue-down installation involves the use of a carpet cushion adhered to the substrate, with the carpet glued to the cushion. The cushion provides added sound absorption and a softer walking surface. Both the adhesive used to attach the cushion and that used for the carpet itself need time to cure, during which time the floor should be protected with hardboard or plywood panels—not covered plastic sheeting, which can trap moisture and provide a haven for mold or mildew.

Self-stick carpet is manufactured with a flexible adhesive layer. When installed, the plastic film over the carpet's adhesive is removed and the carpet is set in place on the subfloor. Self-stick carpet offers savings in time and labor over other installation methods. It is manufactured in smaller widths than most carpet, typically 6 feet (1.8 m) wide.

Commercial-grade carpet tiles are 18 inches square with a backing strong enough to prevent shrinkage or expansion of the tile and to protect the carpet edges from unraveling. Carpet tiles can be laid to resemble a seamless wall-to-wall installation, or arranged in patterns. They are constructed by tufting or by fusion bonding. Carpet tiles can be easily cut to fit odd-shaped contours with a minimum of waste, and individual tiles can be replaced if worn or damaged. For this reason, they are popular with facilities managers for offices and staff spaces. In commercial installations, the tiles can be removed for access to underfloor utilities, or used with flat wire run under the carpet.

Table 9-6 Types of Carpet Pile

Pile Type	Appearance	Performance	Use	Comment
Berber	Big, level loops or multilevel loop, some cut pile	Durability depends on size of loops	Active residential	Polypropylene or wool
Cut and uncut patterned carpet	Usually multicolor designs, mixed loops and cut pile creates carved appearance	Very good durability	Various, including active	Hides traffic patterns
Cut-pile saxony	Smooth surface	Good durability	Light	Usually nylon fibers
Frieze	Highly textured knobby surface; yarns tightly twisted	Extremely durable and long-wearing	Active	More expensive than textured cut pile
Level loop	Multicolored loops of one height	Extremely durable	Olefin for indoor-outdoor carpet; nylon for commercial use	May be olefin; also nylon
Multilevel loop carpet	Usually multicolored with various loop heights; many patterns and designs	Very durable	Casual active spaces	Helps hide traffic patterns
Textured cut-pile saxony	Textured surface	Good durability	Active	Does not show footprints

Carpet tiles, usually 9 or 12 inches square, can be free-laid on the subfloor with glue adhered at only the perimeter and selected rows throughout. They may also be fully glued down, although this defeats some of their advantage as easily removable. Many carpet tiles come with a pressure-sensitive adhesive coating that allows them to be easily lifted and replaced or repositioned. As this method has become more sophisticated, the use of carpet tiles has moved into the residential market.

Most commercial carpet is made by inserting pile yarn tufts into the primary backing. A bonding adhesive is then applied to hold the secondary backing, cushion, or hard-back in place. Primary backing is usually polypropylene, or sometimes polyester. Styrene-butadiene latex is the most common bonding material. The secondary backing is also often woven polypropylene. Attached cushions help reduce impact noise and cushion footfalls. However, they add to the cost of the carpet. *Delamination* occurs when the secondary backing detaches from the primary carpet. Secondary backings may also stretch areas of the carpet, cause separation at seams, and increase loss of face fiber due to abrasion.

Attached cushions or hard-back coatings may be made of polyurethane, vinyl (including PVC), jute, polyethelene, and polymer resins. Jute is renewable and biodegradable, but is used less than the synthetic backings. Some manufacturers use PVC backing with recycled content. A relatively new product uses postconsumer glass and PVB plastic from safety glass recycling. A polyurethane backing derived from soybean oil is being developed. A bonding adhesive made from a by-product of paper pulping has been accepted by certifying agencies.

Around 3 billion yards of carpet is sold each year in the United States, 70 percent of which is replacement carpet. More than 2 billion yards of carpet ends up in landfills each year, where it will remain largely intact for hundreds of years. Specifying carpet from manufacturers that recycle used carpet will help turn this around. Using existing carpet as long as possible also keeps carpet out of the waste stream.

Carpets may emit VOCs, including 4-phenylcyclohexene (4-PC), an odorous VOC from synthetic latex that is used to bind the carpet fibers to jute backings. Emissions from 4-PC may be initially high and tend to diminish quickly. Carpets require three to four weeks for off-gassing, with added ventilation and an increased air exchange rate. Using heat fusion bonding for carpet backing eliminates the high-VOC latex bond. Low-emission carpets have fusion-bonded backing and use alternative fastening systems to eliminate latex and adhesives.

 Note: The Carpet and Rug Institute (CRI) has developed an Indoor Air Quality Testing Program. Environmentally responsible carpet is identified with the CRI IAQ label.

Carpet pads made of foamed plastic or sheet rubber are high in VOCs. Felt pads, which use recycled synthetic fibers or wool, or jute backings have low VOC emissions. Cork, which is a quick-growing natural resource, can also be used. Tacking with nail strips rather than gluing down carpet lowers emissions, as well. If glue is used, it should be water-based or low-toxicity. Some carpet adhesives emit xylenes, toluene, and a host of other VOCs. Adhesives often emit VOCs for up to one week. Fiber cushions may be made of natural, synthetic, or a combination of fiber types needlepunched into a felt backing. The material and construction method of fiber cushions helps to create a warm surface underfoot.

Sponge rubber cushions are made as flat sheets, ripple, or waffle patterns, and as reinforced foam rubber. Sponge rubber cushions are easily compressed. The flat sheets provide a firmer feel than the ripple sponge rubber. Reinforced sponge rubber has a smaller cell structure of airspaces throughout, for more consistent support. Open-cell foams are usually less resilient than closed cells.

Polyurethane foam cushions are available with three different cellular structures.

- Bonded or rebound polyurethane is made from scraps of foam glued together and heat fused.
- Densified prime urethane foam is denser and resists localized compression.
- Modified prime polyurethane foam is manufactured as a continuous sheet, which may contain fillers as well as new polyurethane.

Rugs

Rugs are single pieces of floor coverings manufactured or cut to standard sizes, often with a finished border. They are not intended to cover the entire floor of a room; instead, they are simply laid over another finish flooring material. On wood floors, non-slip underlays are used with rugs to ensure that they lay flat and remain in place.

 Note: Designers sometimes treat a high-quality rug as piece of art rather than try to coordinate it with upholstery.

Room-sized rugs cover most of a room's floor, leaving a strip of finish flooring exposed along the room's edges. They approximate the appearance of wall-to-wall carpeting but can be moved if desired, removed for cleaning when necessary, and turned for more even distribution of wear.

Area rugs cover a smaller portion of a room's floor, and can be used to define an area, unify a furniture grouping, or delineate a path. Decorative rugs, especially handmade ones, can also serve as a dominant design element, and provide a focal point for a room arrangement. They can be used to change a room's appearance without the expense of covering the entire floor.

Rugs are available in a wide variety of designs and materials, which include wool, synthetics, cotton, sisal, jute, sea grass, and acrylic fibers. Common shapes include rectangular, round, oval, octagonal, square, and runners. Contemporary area rugs may combine a variety of materials and types of yarns; innovative designs include furniture fabrics, natural fibers, leather, silk, and bamboo grasses. Varying twist, loops and cut pile, and pile height create texture. Bold patterns and silk highlights also add interest.

Traditional rugs from Europe and the Mid East are widely sold for residential use. Handmade carpets are the elite of floor coverings. Knotting, hooking, braiding, and hand-tufting techniques produce various styles of looped and/or cut yarns. Handmade rugs are most commonly used for area rugs. Oriental rugs are hand-knotted.

American braided rugs are handmade by artisans using long strips of wool fabric. These are widely imitated with factory-made rugs of strips of cloth or yarn that are

Types of Rugs

- *Bokhara or Turkoman rugs*: From Turkmenistan, Uzbekistan, Kazakhstan, Afghanistan, Pakistan, and Russia; small, repetitive geometric designs; do not wear well
- *Caucasian rugs*: From Azerbaijan, Georgia, Armenia; bright colors; simple designs with stylized, childlike figures; elaborate decorative borders; usually 6 × 9 ft. (2 × 3 m)
- *Dhurries*: From India; flat-woven cotton; inexpensive, reversible, casual; many colors and sizes; washable, but colors may run and rug may shrink.
- *Flokati rugs*: From Greece; heavy, shaggy wool rugs with long white or off-white pile that tends to mat down with use.
- *Kilims*: Made by nomadic weavers in Turkey, Iran, Iraq, Russia, China, Pakistan, India, and Morocco; tapestry flat-woven from fairly coarse, thick wool; well made for their price; many designs; long, narrow strips may tend to pucker.
- *Oriental rugs*: Originally from China, now also made in Romania, Iran, and India; handwoven; thick, rich, and artistic; multicolored designs woven from blacks, soft yellows, pinks, peaches, apricots, blues. Silk rugs are the most expensive; wool rugs, less so.
- *Persian rugs*: Originally from Iran (Persia), now also India, Pakistan, China, Turkey, Nepal; look better as they age; made from high-quality knotted wool; vary widely in size and shape, usually rectangular or formed into long runners; stylized motifs rendered in rich colors on deep red and blue grounds.
- *Rag rugs*: From Scandinavia, Germany, North America; wear well; woven or braided from cotton, wool.
- *Ryas*: From Denmark or Finland; high-pile shag; strong colors mat together into contemporary, abstract designs or rounded geometric shapes.
- *Serape rugs*: From Mexico and southwestern United States; coarse rugs with tribal designs; flat-woven with fringed ends; Navajo rugs especially valued.
- *Turkish rugs*: Contemporary handmade rugs have reintroduced handspun wool and vegetable dyes; some have religious motifs or regional designs.

sewn together; fibers include nylon, wool, cotton, and polypropylene. Braided rugs are reversible.

Rag rugs are usually woven as flat rectangles, although some novelty rugs have prominent surface tufts tied in. The best rag rugs are carefully designed and handwoven; these sometimes find their place on a wall as well as on floors. Inexpensive rag rugs mass-produced in cottons or synthetic fibers do not have the longevity of better products; they are useful as bathroom and bedroom rugs that can be machine-washed to remove allergens. Rag rugs tend to fade with washing, but this is often considered an advantage, as it softens and blends colors.

Wall and Window Finishes Comparisons 10

When selecting wall finishes, interior designers consider durability, maintenance, sound absorption, light reflectance, fire resistance, and cost. Installation requirements, such as what the finish will be attached to and how it will be attached, are also scrutinized. These elements are considered under materials where appropriate; an introduction to fire-resistance ratings is presented below.

Aesthetically, texture and light reflectance are key properties of vertical surfaces. Texture affects *light reflectance*, with smooth surfaces reflecting light more efficiently. Smooth surfaces suggest precision and formality, while rough textures are more dynamic and informal.

Adding color to a vertical surface makes it a more active component of a space. Light-colored and light neutral wall finishes reflect more light and serve as backdrops for other elements. Warm, light colors suggest comfort, while cool, light colors create a feeling of spaciousness. Dark wall colors suggest enclosure and intimacy; but they also absorb light and make a room more difficult to illuminate.

FIRE-RESISTANCE RATINGS

The term *fire resistance* indicates the way a laboratory-constructed assembly performs to contain a fire in a carefully controlled test setting for a designated period of time. *Assemblies* that are tested in this way include interior partitions, a floor/ceiling construction, a roof/ceiling, and a protected beam or column. The one-hour, two-hour, and other ratings refer to the length of time that the construction assembly was able to control the fire's heat as required by the laboratory test. This does not necessarily guarantee that the assembly will perform the same under actual field conditions. Partitions, floor/ceilings, roof/ceilings, beams and columns are tested in accordance with ASTM Standard E 119, Fire Tests of Building and Construction Materials.

Fire-resistance rating requirements are usually based on the expected occupancy of the space, and it is important that the final design matches the numbers referenced in the code. The assembly method should match that of the tested assembly being used to establish the rating, especially the method of attachment, stud and fastener spacing, and the staggering of joints. Approval of a specific assembly is ultimately the decision of the local building code authority for the project's jurisdiction.

PLASTER

Plaster wall surfaces take both color and texture exceptionally well. As discussed in Chapter 6, throughout history, plaster has been the most common finish for interior walls and ceilings, surpassed only in the twentieth century by gypsum wallboard (drywall). Although plaster surfaces wear better and may be smoother than drywall, they are labor-intensive, require a higher skill level, and take time to cure.

Plaster is applied over a basecoat adhered to wood or metal lath in three increasingly smooth coats. Two coats of plaster are applied to masonry bases such as porous bricks, clay tiles, and rough concrete masonry units. Plaster application techniques are varied and complex, with many details for edges and corners. Lath supports also vary with the substrate to which they are attached, the type of lath, and the weight of the plaster to be supported. Gypsum and plaster assemblies can achieve fire ratings.

GYPSUM WALLBOARD

Gypsum wallboard is widely used as a surface for interior walls and as a substrate for other interior finishes. Once gypsum wallboard has been made into a smooth, continuous surface with joint tape and joint compound, it is ready for painting or application of a wallcovering or other finish material.

Moisture-resistant gypsum wallboard is manufactured for use as a tile backer board in dry areas or where exposure to water is limited, such as toilet and sink areas and above tile in tubs and showers. It is not intended for use as a backer board in tub and shower areas or anywhere else it will be exposed to constant or excessive moisture and high humidity, such as gang showers, saunas, and steam room and swimming pool enclosures. Its light green facing paper makes it easily identifiable and gives it the common name *green board*. It is available in 4-foot widths and lengths of 8 and 12 feet, and in 1/2- and 5/8-inch thicknesses. Moisture-resistant board is less expensive than comparable cement board materials. (See color plate C-59, Green board.)

Installed prefinished panels are generally less expensive than building a wall and applying a vinyl wallcovering. Most dirt and marks can be removed with a moist cloth, sponge, or soft brush, using mild soap, detergent, or a nonabrasive cleaner, followed by a rinse with water, then wiped dry. Stains can be removed by wiping away loose material, scrubbing with a stiff bristle brush and appropriate solvent, then quickly wiping dry with a clean cloth.

Types of Gypsum Wallboard

Manufacturers produce many types of wallboard panels with features that provide superior strength; ease of cutting and installation; and ability to conform to curved walls, archways, and stairways.

- *Blue board* has an absorbent face that bonds strongly with veneer plaster.
- *Green board* is moisture-resistant, and intended for use as backing for ceramic tile and in wet areas.
- *High-abuse gypsum wallboard* is similar to high-impact board; it is designed for added protection against mold and mildew.
- *High-impact gypsum wallboard* consists of a treated, fire-resistant, mold- and moisture-resistant Type X gypsum core with a backing of 100 percent recycled heavy, smooth, and moisture-, mold-, mildew-, and abrasion-resistant liner paper. Fiberglass mesh is embedded in the core for additional resistance to impact and penetration. This wallboard offers fire-resistance ratings, as well as extra protection against mold and mildew.
- *Prefinished gypsum board* has a decorative vinyl or printed-paper surface. It does not need another finish on its surface and can be installed directly on studs or used as a finish layer over gypsum. It is used in demountable partition systems, and has a noncombustible gypsum base and a surface material not over 1/8 inch thick with a flame spread of 50 or less.
- *Type X gypsum board core* is available with various boards, and is fire-resistant.

Table 10-1 ASTM Standards for Gypsum Wallboard

Number	Standard Specification for	Covering
C475/C475-M02	Joint Compound and Joint Tape for Finishing Gypsum Board	All-purpose, taping and finishing joint compounds, paper joint tape, and glass-mesh joint tape
C588/C588-M-03e1	Gypsum Base for Veneer Plasters	Types of gypsum base used as a base for application of veneer plaster
C840-04a	Application and Finishing of Gypsum Board	Methods of application and finishing of gypsum board, including related items and accessories
C843-99e1	Application of Gypsum Veneer Plaster	Methods of applying gypsum veneer plaster
C844-04	Application of Gypsum Base to Receive Gypsum Veneer Plaster	Methods of applying gypsum veneer base for gypsum veneer plasters
C1178/C1178-M-04e1	Glass Mat Water-Resistant Gypsum Backing Panel	Glass mat water-resistant gypsum backing panel designed for use on ceilings and walls in bath and shower areas as a base for the application of ceramic or plastic tile
C1278/C1278-M-03e1 Fiber-Reinforced Gypsum Panel	1.1.1 Interior Fiber-Reinforced Gypsum Panels	Designed to be used for walls, ceilings, or partitions; affords a suitable surface to receive decoration
	1.1.2 Water-Resistant Fiber-Reinforced Gypsum Backing Panels	Designed primarily to be used as a base for the application of ceramic or plastic tile on walls or ceilings; also suitable for decoration
C1396/C1396-M-04 Gypsum Board	1.1.1 Gypsum Wallboard	Designed for use on walls, ceilings, or partitions; affords a surface suitable to receive decoration
	1.1.2 Predecorated Gypsum Board	Designed for use as the finished surfacing for walls, ceilings, or partitions
	1.1.3 Gypsum Backing Board, Coreboard, and Shaftliner Board	Designed for use as a base in multilayer systems or as a gypsum stud or core in semisolid or solid gypsum board partitions, or in shaft wall assemblies
	1.1.4 Water-Resistant Gypsum Backing Board	Designed for use as a base for the application of ceramic or plastic tile on walls or ceilings; also suitable for decoration
	1.1.7 Gypsum Base for Veneer Plaster	Designed for use as a base for the application of gypsum veneer plaster
	1.1.8 Gypsum Lath	Designed for use as a base for the application of gypsum plaster
	1.1.9 Gypsum Ceiling Board	Designed for use on interior ceilings with framing spaced not more than 24 in. (610 mm) on center; affords a surface suitable to receive water-based texture and other decoration; also suitable for use on interior walls

Figure 10-1 Gypsum wallboard is nailed to the wall on left. The soffit above has had nail holes covered with joint compound.

Figure 10-2 Here, a worker paints a primer coat over drywall joints.

GLASS-FIBER-REINFORCED GYPSUM

Glass-fiber-reinforced gypsum (GFRG), also known as *fiberglass-reinforced gypsum* (FRG) or *glass-reinforced gypsum* (GRG), is a lightweight, nontoxic, noncombustible material introduced in the 1970s and used for column covers, decorative domes, coffered ceilings, and other architectural elements. GFRG is made of gypsum *slurry* (water or other liquid containing a high concentration of suspended solids) and glass fiber hand-laid or sprayed into molds. Additives commonly used with plaster are usually acceptable. GFRG-based products are installed using standard gypsum wallboard finishing techniques. The finish face is smooth and resembles a plaster surface, ready to finish with paint or other materials.

GFRG is used where a light, strong, and fire-retardant material is required. It should not be exposed to dampness or water, as in fountains, pools, or other wet locations. It is available formed into moldings, light coves, bas relief decorations and medallions, as well as ceilings, columns and column capitals, domes, and fireplace surrounds. Virtually any custom shape is available, and formulations can be customized for a particular project.

GFRG products are thin plaster shell shapes and forms that can be manufactured on- or off-site by either of two methods. Hand layup involves placing layers of glass-fiber mat and gypsum manually in molds. The second method—the chopped-strand spray method—mixes glass-fiber strands into the plaster mix as it is sprayed into the mold.

As the gypsum particles are mixed to produce GFRG, they are dispersed in water; air is removed from the resulting mixture. This process determines the strength, hardness, absorption, and density of the product. Either batch or continuous mixing brings water and plaster to a slurry condition.

- *Batch mixing* is preferred when specialty plasters will be applied to molds by hand. Small amounts of slurry are agitated by hand. Plaster is sifted into water and allowed to soak; it is then hand-mixed to the correct consistency.
- *Continuous mixing* is used for spray applications. Custom-engineered equipment automatically meters and mixes exact proportions of plaster and water to the slurry. The ingredients are blended in a mixer at high velocity; the slurry forms instantly; there is no need to soak. The flowing slurry mixture is then pumped through a hose, which sprays the slurry as well as glass fibers into architectural molds.

Wooden molds are economical and practical for simple architectural forms such as domes or columns. Latex molds give better detail for ornate parts; they can be made by pouring liquid latex over an original piece, or by brushing thickened latex on the original.

The formed piece is carefully removed from the mold after the gypsum and glass-fiber reinforcement have set; it is then stored until dry enough to ship. Drying is done as quickly, thoroughly, and safely as possible, either naturally or with forced air. Drying is complete when the center of the part reaches the temperature of the surrounding air. Drying temperatures over 120°F may cause *calcination*, the development of soft, powdery surfaces.

GFRG will not burn, and protects materials behind it from the heat of the flame for up to two hours. Its light weight compared to traditional stone or plaster ornaments contributes to its relatively easy and quick installation. The white GFRG surface can be finished with almost any type of paint. Manufactured GFRG products generally need surface refinements in the field if a high gloss finish is desired. This is accomplished by using compounds, sealers, and/or primers.

GFRG pieces are installed using screws or adhesives; or they are hung from framing or a suspension system, as recommended by the manufacturer. Openings can be cut in the field for plumbing, electrical, and mechanical penetrations, as for drywall. Repairs are made with standard drywall or plaster materials and techniques.

Plywood is used as a substrate for other finish materials and by itself as a finished surface. Plywood adjusts to changing temperature and humidity better than solid wood. Specialty wood panel products such as grooved or rough-sawn plywood are used as wall

PLYWOOD PANELING

paneling. Decorative plywood panels faced with hardwoods are also used for paneling, as well as for cabinetry and furniture.

SOLID WOOD PANELING

Solid wood paneling consists of a series of panels joined together into a continuous surface. Each panel is a distinct portion, section, or division of a wall, *wainscot*, ceiling, or door. Panels are customarily raised above or sunk below the surrounding areas, or enclosed by a frame or border. Paneling is matched in the same manner as veneers: by book matching, slip matching, diamond matching, and random matching. (See color plate C-60, Solid pine paneling.)

Wainscot usually refers to a facing of wood paneling, especially one that covers the lower portion of an interior wall. Wainscoting gives walls elegance and warmth and protects the lower portion from wear and tear. It is made up of several different pieces of milled hardwoods that are fastened together.

WOOD VENEERS

Veneer patterns are determined by whether the wood is rotary cut, plain or flat cut, quarter cut, or rift cut. A flitch is the wood veneer taken from one particular tree, stacked and numbered in the sequence it was cut. A *leaf* is an individual cut piece within a flitch. Veneers are matched in a variety of ways, including book, slip, diamond, and end matches.

Wood paneling systems designed for use as wainscots and wall paneling have a hardwood veneer bonded to an engineered wood substrate such as medium-density fiberboard (MDF) or straw board. These systems are less expensive than custom millwork, use recycled materials, and conserve the use of hardwoods. Systems come with premachined stiles, rails, and panel pieces.

PREFINISHED PANELS

Prefinished panels are made of a variety of materials, including fiberglass, hardboard, plastic laminate, and stainless steel, for column covers and wall panels. Stainless steel is used in commercial kitchens; fiberglass panels are a less expensive alternative, but lack the aesthetic appeal. Plastic laminate panels are used where a surface will be washed frequently.

Figure 10-3 Wainscot, Romaine's Restaurant, Northborough, Massachusetts. The lower wall is protected from chair and table damage by sheets of plywood bead board grooved to simulate tongue-and-groove paneling. Corky Binggeli Interior Design

Figure 10-4 The steamy atmosphere of a sauna is compatible with the cedar wall finish and seating.

Figure 10-5 Wood veneer wallcovering.
Design by Maya Romanoff

Systems designed specifically for finishing basement walls consist of fabric-covered wall panels with extra insulation and noise control properties. The panels are designed for easy installation by homeowners.

Prefinished gypsum wall panels are designed to be applied either directly to studs or as a finish over gypsum wallboard. Their primary application is as wall surfaces in demountable office partition systems, where they are a cost-effective alternative to building a wall and installing a finish material. Most panels have vinyl wallcoverings as finishes, and are relatively easy to move when the office layout changes.

Fiberglass-reinforced plastic (FRP) wall panels are designed for humid locations such as restrooms, labs, kitchens, and break rooms. They provide a clean surface to meet health code requirements for food preparation areas.

Resin panels offer a designer a rigid, transparent, or translucent sheet material with the ability to embed other materials. The material has great aesthetic appeal, and some forms are designed to have enhanced structural properties, as well. These plastic panels are finding applications as countertops, bath and shower partitions, wall partitions and wall finishes, cabinet doors, shelving, and even floor finishes. (See color plate C-61, Architectural resin panels.)

Some panels are acrylic products; others use PETG. The polyester resin used in some sheet products contains 40 percent postindustrial recycled materials, and the final product is advertised as recyclable. There is great demand for environmentally friendly products, and thus a great incentive to claim this status. Specifiers must carefully research the contents, sources, and disposal options for newly developed plastics that claim environmental benefits.

Quilted fiberglass wall panels (QFM) serve as both noise barrier and sound absorption. QFM is a vinyl-coated, gray fiberglass facing cloth attached by quilting to a supporting 2 pound/cubic foot density fiberglass. It is a lightweight, semiflexible and easy-to-manipulate barrier enclosure intended to help control reverberant energy inside an area. Once in place, its sides do not permit easy access. It is available in 1- or 2-inch-thick rolls with facing on one or both sides, or as prefinished panels. QFM has a Class 1 rating on the ASTM E-84 tunnel test for flammability.

CERAMIC WALL TILE

Glazed ceramic wall tiles have a nonvitreous body and bright, matte, or crystalline glazes that are impervious to water. They are used for surfacing interior walls. Decorative thin wall tile is glazed tile with a thin, usually nonvitreous body intended for decorative, interior residential use. Because it is not resistant to breakage, it is not recommended for commercial applications or use on floors. Cementitious backer boards made of portland cement or treated gypsum and lightweight aggregate can be used under thinset tile and as a water-resistant base for tile regularly exposed to water (such as a shower surround).

Small ceramic mosaic tiles with a porcelain or natural clay body are used glazed or unglazed for walls. These small tiles are usually face- or back-mounted on sheets to make handling easier and installation quicker. Standard and custom designs can be ordered.

Figure 10-6 Glazed ceramic wall tiles, Gold's Gym, Danvers, Massachusetts
Corky Binggeli Interior Design

Ceramic Wall Tiles

Standard Sizes for Ceramic Wall Tiles

- 4–1/4 × 4–1/4 inches (108 × 108 mm)
- 4–1/4 × 6 inches (108 × 152 mm)
- 6 × 6 inches (152 × 152 mm)

Trim Pieces

- *Bead:* Rounded horizontal bead for top edges
- *Bullnose:*
  - Surface bullnose with a flat bottom and eased top edge
  - Bullnose (or surface cap) with a flat bottom and rounded top edge; used horizontally or vertically
  - Corner bullnose: Two rounded finished edges to complete corner where horizontal and vertical bullnose meet
- Curb: Tile curb for horizontal use
- Base:
  - Cove base to connect to floor tile
  - Stack-on cove base: Coving on bottom and flat edge on top to accommodate wall tile
  - Rounded top cove base: Used where wall tile is not installed above base
  - Surface base with coved lower edge and eased top edge.

Ceramic wall tiles come in a variety of trim shapes for finished angles and edges. A *sanitary base* is a coved tile set at the intersection of the floor and wall. Its curved angle helps to prevent dirt from accumulating and makes cleaning easier.

When ceramic tile is installed over a wood subfloor, roofing felt is laid on top before the tile is set into a bed of reinforced mortar. Tile can be set on an underlayment-grade subfloor with organic adhesive.

Ceramic wall tile may be applied with either the thinset or the thickset process.

- In the thinset process, ceramic tile is bonded to a continuous, stable backing of gypsum plaster, gypsum board, or plywood, using a thin coat of dry-set mortar, latex-portland cement mortar, epoxy mortar, or an organic adhesive.
- In the thickset process, ceramic tile is applied over a bed of portland cement mortar. The relatively thick bed (1/2 to 3/4 inch; 13 to 19 mm) allows for accurate slopes and true planes in the finished work. Suitable backings include metal lath over concrete, masonry, plywood, gypsum plaster and gypsum board, and metal lath over stud framing.

Specialty tiles include glass tiles, handmade and custom tiles, and special sizes. Grouts for wall tiles are available in a wide variety of colors. Highly pigmented grouts with contrasting colored tiles may bleed.

STONE FACING

Stone wall tiles are laid in patterns that complement the appearance of the stone and enhance the texture of the space. Dimension stone tiles are less than 3/4 inch (19 mm) thick. They provide the natural beauty of a stone surface without the weight, depth, and expense of dimension stone. When used as floor tiles, they are prone to breaking,

Figure 10-7 Wall tile trims
Reproduced by permission of the
publisher from Francis D. K. Ching
and Corky Binggeli, *Interior Design
Illustrated*, 2nd ed. (Hoboken, NJ:
John Wiley & Sons, Inc.), © 2005 by
John Wiley & Sons, Inc.

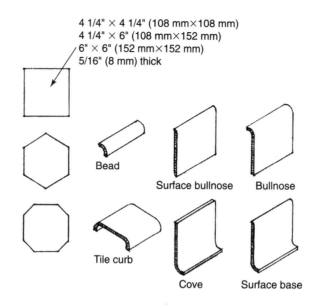

4 1/4" × 4 1/4" (108 mm×108 mm)
4 1/4" × 6" (108 mm×152 mm)
6" × 6" (152 mm×152 mm)
5/16" (8 mm) thick

Bead

Surface bullnose   Bullnose

Tile curb

Cove   Surface base

but they work well on walls. Stone tiles are not usually pattern-matched and vary more in color, pattern, and texture than stone facing panels.

Dimension stone facing panels range up to 48 square inches (1200 sq mm). Panels are cut either 3/4 inch (2 cm) thick or between 1–1/4 to 2 inches (3.2 to 5 cm) thick. A common size is 2 feet 6 inches × 5 feet (.76 × 1.5 m). Stone facings are attached to interior walls with wire-tie anchor systems using plaster or mortar spots. The ties may reduce the fire rating of a gypsum board wall and require an additional layer of metal studs and gypsum board. The stone is *kerfed* (cut the width of the saw blade) on the back side to accept straps or clips. Grout for interior stone facing is usually mixed with latex additives, producing a more flexible and durable joint. Joint sizes vary, from 1/16 inch (1.5 mm) to 3/8 inch (10 mm), depending on the type of stone and finish and how wall joints are coordinated with floor or exterior joints.

Engineered composite stone products formulated from stone aggregate and synthetic resin matrix materials are available as large panels for horizontal or vertical use. Composite stone is strong, nonporous, durable, and flexible. Both natural stone and vibrant artificial colors are available, and panels usually have polished finishes. Tiles are installed in the same manner as thinset ceramic tiles.

FLEXIBLE WALLCOVERINGS

Flexible wallcoverings are used to improve the durability or appearance of a wall. Direct wall application requires a perfectly smooth substrate, except for products designed to bridge a poor surface. Sealers, primers, and wall liners are used with some products. Wallcoverings are attached with wet or dry adhesives selected for the substrate and the wallcovering type, following the manufacturer's recommendations. Pattern matching affects the amount of waste product per *drop* (vertical run) of wallcovering.

Vinyl Wallcoverings

Vinyl wallcoverings are popular because they are affordable and durable. Despite their environmental issues, they are still widely specified for commercial spaces that need an easily maintained surface.

Vinyl wallcoverings are manufactured by either the calendaring method or the plastisol method.

Figure 10-8 *Marble wall veneer, Maryland State House. Matched, veined Italian marble walls and columns in the building addition designed by Francis Baldwin and Josiah Pennington between 1902 and 1906.*

- In calendaring, a thick, doughlike liquid vinyl is squeezed over a series of hot metal rollers and flattened into a sheet. The vinyl sheet is then laminated to a backing material with heat and pressure.
- The plastisol method, used primarily for residential wallcoverings, spreads a somewhat thinner liquid vinyl onto the backing material as it is rolled by.

Several strong, dimensionally stable backing materials or substrates are used with vinyl wallcoverings.

- Type I wallcoverings may be backed with a paperlike nonwoven material, or with a loosely woven fabric called scrim that lacks dimensional stability.

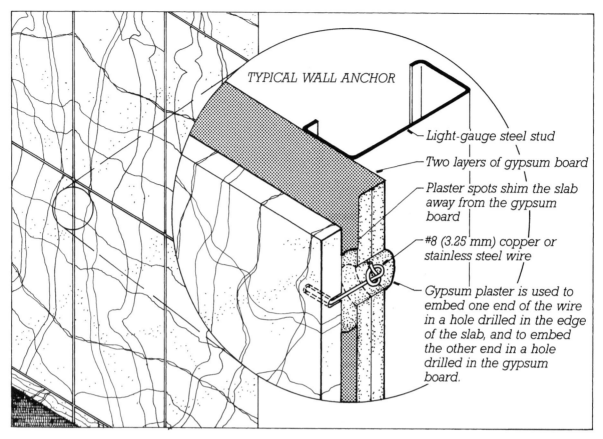

TYPICAL WALL ANCHOR

Light-gauge steel stud

Two layers of gypsum board

Plaster spots shim the slab away from the gypsum board

#8 (3.25 mm) copper or stainless steel wire

Gypsum plaster is used to embed one end of the wire in a hole drilled in the edge of the slab, and to embed the other end in a hole drilled in the gypsum board.

Figure 10-9 Stone wall panel installation

Reproduced by permission of the publisher from Edward Allen and Joseph Iano, *Fundamentals of Building Construction: Materials and Methods*, 4th ed. (Hoboken, NJ: John Wiley & Sons, Inc.), © 2004 by John Wiley & Sons, Inc.

- Both Types I and II are backed with Osnaburg, a loose, open-weave fabric.
- Drill, a dense woven fabric with good dimensional stability, is used for better, Type II and for Type III, wallcoverings.

The wall surface behind vinyl wallcovering may collect moisture in a warm humid space, creating an environment that promotes the growth of mildew. Mildew-resistant vinyl wallcoverings contain mildew inhibitors or have tiny perforations to let moisture pass out of the wall. The standard for mildew-resistant vinyl wallcoverings is ASTM G21, Practice for Determining Resistance of Synthetic Polymeric Materials to Fungi.

The impact of wallcoverings on interior air quality varies with the materials from which they are made. Vinyl and vinyl-coated wallcoverings made of soft plastics are less stable and have long outgassing times. Vinyl wallcoverings emit vinyl chloride and other volatile organic compounds (VOCs). The adhesives used for heavy wallcoverings can also be environmentally problematic. Wallpaper paste may emit a wide variety of VOCs. Alternative, low-toxic adhesives are available, and lightweight papers can be applied with light, water-based glue.

Wallpaper

Wallpaper has a paper face and a paper back. Wallpapers are not commonly used in commercial interior design projects because they lack the necessary durability, although it is possible to protect wallpaper surfaces with a clear vinyl film. (See color plate C-62, Wallpaper.)

Figure 10-10 Grass cloth simulated in vinyl wallcovering.

Residential wallpapers come packaged in pairs of rolls from 20.5 to 28 inches (52 to 71 cm) wide, with each roll covering between 27 and 30 square feet (2.5 to 2.8 sq. m). Double rolls are approximately 11 yards (10 m) long. The placement of patterns and seams for large, complicated pattern repeats requires careful planning; extra material should be ordered to allow for matching.

Textile Wallcoverings

Not all fabrics are suited for use on walls. Those textiles that are used as wallcoverings are back-coated, providing a barrier that prevents the adhesive from bleeding through to the face of the fabric. The backings also improve dimensional stability. Paper backing involves laminating paper to the back of the textile to increase its stiffness before installation. Acrylic latex is used to coat textiles that have been stretched across a

Table 10-2 Wallcovering Durability Classifications

ASTM F 793 Classes	
Category I	Decorative purposes only
Category II	Medium serviceability
Category IV, Type I	Light commercial use
Category V, Type II	Moderate commercial use
Category VI, Type III	Heavy commercial use
Manufacturers Classes (CFFA Standards)	
Type I, Light Duty	Surfaces that are lightly used and require only light cleaning, as in residential use or light commercial applications such as private offices or hotel rooms that might otherwise be painted
Type II, Medium Duty	Protection from traffic and abrasion in public areas such as often-used corridors, dining rooms, and reception areas; most common for commercial use
Type III, Especially Heavy Use and Sanitation Requirements	Manufactured to order for hospital and food service corridors; most expensive, least-often specified

frame. Latex backings are less dimensionally stable and more flexible than paper-backed ones, but also more expensive. Textile wallcoverings are usually reserved for areas where wear is not a concern. (See color plate C-63, Natural textile wallcovering.)

Upholstered Wall Systems

Upholstered or stretched-fabric wall systems offer a tackable or acoustically absorptive wall surface with a textile texture. The fabrics are stretched over either plastic or wood frames. These systems require the use of highly stable, upholstery-weight fabrics, which are also moisture-resistant. Seams may be emphasized with reveals or deemphasized with wide fabric and horizontal grains. Seams may be more visible in light fabrics than in dark ones. Light-colored fabrics should be checked to make sure that the surface behind them will not be visible. Upholstered wall systems for on-site installation have wood or plastic frames that are upholstered off-site and hung on walls. Tackable surfaces such as linen work well for upholstered wall systems.

Acoustic curtain barrier backed panels are designed as partitions or portable acoustic screens to isolate noisy machines or specific areas. They are installed with the quilted side facing the noise source, using hardware that allows easy access. Standard vinyl-coated facing material is gray, white, tan, or black, although other options are available.

Fiberglass Wallcoverings

Fiberglass wallcovering is inherently flame-resistant and can be used to reinforce fragile or deteriorating wall surfaces, providing an uncolored texture. Because it allows moisture to pass through and evaporate, fiberglass is mold- and mildew-resistant. Fiberglass wallcoverings are installed with adhesive and painted after installation, usually with a latex paint that will keep the wallcovering breathable.

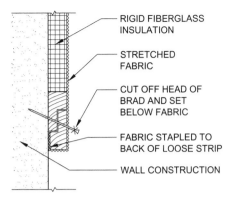

RIGID FIBERGLASS INSULATION

STRETCHED FABRIC

CUT OFF HEAD OF BRAD AND SET BELOW FABRIC

FABRIC STAPLED TO BACK OF LOOSE STRIP

WALL CONSTRUCTION

Figure 10-11 Stretched fabric wall panel
Reproduced by permission of the publisher from Maryrose McGowan and Kelsey Kruse, *Interior Graphic Standards* (Hoboken, NJ: John Wiley & Sons, Inc.), © 2003 by John Wiley & Sons, Inc.

Glass textile wallcoverings are designed to be finished with paint or a decorative finish after installation. The glass yarns are made from sand, lime, and clay, and woven into textured patterns; then they are treated with a natural binder for stability during installation. They last up to 30 years and can be repeatedly painted without losing texture; they can even add to the durability of the wall surface.

Natural Fiber and Recycled-Content Flexible Wallcoverings

Although natural fibers are recyclable, renewable, and biodegradable, they may lack durability and other desirable characteristics. These types of wallcoverings must often be chemically treated for resistance to insects, fungi, fire, and stains, and the chemicals used may contain toxic and carcinogenic substances. Fibers made from recycled polyethylene terephthalate (PET) bottles are one type of common recycled-content wallcovering. (See color plate C-64, Commercial non-vinyl wallcovering.)

Wood Flexible Wallcoverings

Prefinished wood wallcoverings on flexible fabric backing create the look of wood paneling without the use of architectural panels. Some products use dyed natural or reconstructed wood veneers covered by a tough protective catalyzed polyurethane system coating. The coating provides protection from ultraviolet rays, as well.

Wood veneer wallcoverings are made of very thin veneer slices bonded to a woven backing material. Wood veneer wallcovering will flex in the direction of the grain but not perpendicular to the grain. Its ability to curve allows its installation on columns and other rounded surfaces.

Wood veneer wallcovering must be applied to a smooth, level surface. It is too thin to be sanded, and its surface can be stained or damaged during installation; moisture can cause warping and buckling. Walls are prepared for installation with primers, sealers, sizing, or through the application of a wall liner. Wood veneer wallcoverings are available prefinished or unfinished, although finishing after installation must be done with care and with compatible products. Sheets of wood veneer wallcovering must be butted together; they cannot be overlapped and trimmed.

Cork, obtained from the renewable bark of the cork oak tree, is both durable and resilient. Cork wallcovering accepts either wax or polyurethane finishes and, with adequate thickness, possesses excellent acoustical and thermal ratings, but moisture may cause problems.

Paints, Coatings, and Custom Finishes

Paint is the most economical wall finish in most cases and is available in virtually any color. Paint is a mixture of a solid pigment suspended in a liquid vehicle; it is applied as a thin, usually opaque coating to a surface for protection and decoration.

The three basic ingredients of paint are pigment, thinner, and resin, to which other substances may be added to enhance its performance. *Pigment* provides color, hiding power, and bulk. Pigments are the most expensive part of paint. *Thinner* carries the pigment and resin, and affects the consistency of the paint as well as its drying time. *Resin* binds the pigment particles together and affects adhesion, durability, and the level of protection provided by the paint film. Solvent-thinned resins are made from natural or synthetic oils, and dry by both evaporation and oxidation. Water-thinned resins dry and harden through evaporation. Outside of the United States, such products are called emulsion paints.

The resin and the pigment it contains are referred to as the *paint solids*. The higher the percentage of paint solids by volume, the greater the paint's covering power—and the better its wear performance. When paint dries, its solids are fused with the thinner—its liquid component—for a final surface.

Paints with water-based thinners, such as latex paints, dry through evaporation only. Oil-based or alkyd paints use a solvent made from mineral spirits that dries by both evaporation and oxidation. Latex paints are water-based and clean up easily with water. They produce fewer odors than alkyd- or oil-based paints when drying. The surface film of latex paints allows water vapor to pass through and, therefore, does not peel if a substrate is not entirely dry when painted. However, latex paints do not wear as well as others.

Alkyd paints are made from oil-modified polyesters and require solvent thinners that emit VOCs. They wear well and are easier to apply than oil-based paints. Alkyd paints produce more odors than latex paints and emit more VOCs. Oil paints, an older type of paint, are being replaced in the market. They are made from linseed oil, tung oil, or soya oil, and have a longer drying time. Because they are solvent-thinned, oil paints produce more odors.

Additives commonly used in paints include driers, antiskinning agents, wetting agents, and preservatives. Driers reduce the time for evaporation and oxidation. Antiskinning agents prevent a skin from forming on the surface of the paint in the can. Wetting agents help to distribute pigment particles evenly. Preservatives retard or eliminate the growth of mold or bacteria.

Sheen or *gloss* refers to the amount of light reflected from a painted surface and depends on the size of the particles of pigment and the ratio of pigment to liquid. Although different manufacturers may use their own names for levels of gloss, the basic categories are flat, semigloss, and gloss. Flat paints have more pigment than resin, and the many little pigment particles make the surface uneven, so that it reflects less light. Flat paint generally does not wash as well as semigloss or gloss paint but is more tolerant of less-than-perfect surfaces. Flat paints are often used on ceilings and irregular surfaces that are not likely to become dirty.

Some companies sell eggshell, pearl, and/or satin paints that are more washable than flat paints, and less shiny than semigloss. These paints are very good for walls and other surfaces that are exposed to moderate use. They are more tolerant of imperfect wall surfaces than semigloss paints.

Paint products are applied in a series of coats, referred to as *paint systems*. First a primer is applied, then a sealer if necessary, followed by fillers when required, and finally by topcoats of paint. The most common application is a three-coat system consisting of a primer and two topcoats.

Primers serve to bind the substrate surface to the topcoat. Specialty primers are manufactured that retard moisture, act as rust inhibitors, or limit the amount of paint that is absorbed by the substrate. Primers hide the substrate color, and can be tinted to match the topcoat color, sometimes allowing fewer topcoats to be used. *Sealers* are specialty primers used to limit the absorbency of the substrate or to limit imperfections,

Table 10-3 Paint Sheen Comparison

Type	Sheen	Use	Comments
Flat	None	Walls in low-use rooms	Conceals minor surface imperfections; washable but not scrubbable; conceals minor imperfections
Eggshell	Smooth finish with a subtle sheen	Walls in family rooms and bedrooms	Washable and scrubbable
Satin	All-purpose, popular sheen	Suitable for almost any room	Washable and scrubbable
Semigloss	Medium sheen	Walls and trim in high-abuse areas like kitchens, bathrooms, laundryrooms, and children's rooms	Extremely durable; washable and scrubbable; somewhat shiny
Gloss	High sheen	Best for doors, trim, and cabinets	Washable and scrubbable; will show imperfections

Figure 10-12 Wall painter with roller

such as knots in wood, from showing through. *Fillers* are applied prior to painting to provide a very smooth surface for painting.

Paint for application to brick masonry walls should be durable, easy to apply, and have good adhesive characteristics. The primary concern should be the characteristics of the surface conditions of the wall. Proper surface preparation is as important as paint selection. Because each coat is the foundation for all future coats, success or failure depends largely on surface preparation. Thoroughly examine all surfaces to determine the required preparation. Previously painted surfaces often require the greatest effort.

Before painting, remove all loose matter. Take special care when cleaning surfaces for emulsion paints and primers: they are nonpenetrating and require cleaner surfaces than solvent-based paints. Some paints can or should be applied to damp surfaces; others must not. Be sure to follow directions accompanying proprietary brands.

Specialty paints are usually water-based, and differ from other paints by their additives or application technique. Magnetic paint combines iron dust with a primer. Metallic paints contain mica and other particles. Textured finishes achieve their effect either by use of premixed additives or with a multistep application process.

Milk paint is used primarily as a wash, stain, or opaque paint (depending on proportion of powder to water) on unfinished wood. It is a natural, nontoxic paint made of milk protein (casein), clay, earth pigments, and lime. Milk paint is sold as a powder; once mixed, it cannot be stored, as it sours within a day.

Stains are made from dyes dissolved in oil or water and are intended to sink into the material to which they are applied, reducing the chance that they will chip or wear off. They are typically used on wood, although some can be applied to concrete. Most stains are transparent or translucent, although some are opaque and contain pigment rather than dye. Stains do not cover the grain pattern of wood or form a surface film. They dry very quickly and can be touched up because the new coat slightly dissolves the previous coat.

Custom paint finishes include cobweb and crackle textures that are the result of chemical reactions. Hand-applied finishes using the techniques of combing, sponging, and mixing paints on the wall create visual interest and texture. Some faux finishes imitate other materials, such as marble and wood. Sand finishes provide added texture by mixing sand with paint.

MOLDINGS AND TRIMS

Some interiors already have moldings and trims at the intersection of the floor and wall or the wall and ceiling. Moldings help to conceal the joint where the wall meets the floor or ceiling. Before deciding to remove an existing molding, a designer needs to consider whether it is hiding a messy joint between the two surfaces. Moldings also attract the eye and can alter the apparent proportions of a room.

Wall bases are either surface, flush, or recess mounted. Premolded inside and outside corners are available. Straight sections of resilient wall base are available in 4-inch (10 cm) strips and coils approximately 100 feet (30 m) long. *Crown moldings* bring a finished line to the joint between the ceiling and wall. *Picture moldings* facilitate hanging and changing of artwork. Many of the molding styles used in historic buildings and available today originated with Greek designs that were modified by the Romans and others.

Table 10-4 Wood Finish Comparisons

Finish Category	Composition	Characteristics and Applications	Durability	Environmental Issues
Paste wax	Carnauba wax or beeswax	Used to polish furniture over other finishes such as lacquer or shellac.	Prolonged water contact will cause damage. Moderately resistant to acids and alkalis; otherwise, least durable finish.	Rich, soft finish; natural materials.
Linseed oil	Pure unrefined form made from the seeds of the flax plant. Heat-treated or polymerized form makes the oil a bit more durable and speeds up the drying time; also minimizes tendency to "frost" (dry to a whitish, matte appearance).	Finish penetrates fibers of the wood and hardens. Wipe on, allow to penetrate the surface of the wood, and wipe off the excess with a rag.	Usually not built up with enough coats to form a surface film, like that of varnish or lacquer, because film is too soft.	Contains no solvents, and comes from renewable resources. Boiled linseed oil has an added metallic drying agent that helps the finish dry in a day. Linseed oil without this additive can take over a week to dry.
Tung oil	Pressed from the nuts of the tung tree.	Finish penetrates fibers of the wood and hardens. Wipe on, allow to penetrate the surface of the wood, and wipe off the excess with a rag.	Usually not built up with enough coats to form a surface film, like that of varnish or lacquer, because the film is too soft. Paler in color and has better moisture resistance than linseed oil.	Contains no solvents, and comes from renewable resources. Does not require drying additives and cures in several days. Readily available and relatively inexpensive.
Varnish	Varnishes are natural, resin-based products or urethanes—modified alkyd resins. The resin is dissolved in oil (for oil-based varnishes) or alcohol (for spirit-based varnishes). Synthetic resins include alkyds, phenolics, and polyurethanes.	Hard, dry, lustrous, and usually transparent. Gloss and matte finishes can be applied in the field.	High resistance to water, heat, solvents, and other chemicals. Tough and durable. Spar varnish, also called marine varnish, is durable and water-resistant. Polyurethane varnish is an exceptionally hard, abrasion-resistant, and chemical-resistant plastic resin.	A solvent-based finish, such as varnish and lacquer, contains a good deal of organic solvents, which can affect the environment as well as human health. It is also highly flammable.
Oil and varnish blends	Proprietary mixtures of oils with synthetic varnish; formula varies with manufacturer.	Easy application, with the protective qualities of varnish. Will dry a bit harder than true oils, and the finishes will build quicker with fewer applications.	Varnish adds some additional protection	These blends will cure in the wood like an oil finish and should not be used to build up layers on the surface.

(Continued)

Table 10-4 (Continued)

Finish Category	Composition	Characteristics and Applications	Durability	Environmental Issues
Shellacs (a form of varnish)	Made from lac, which is derived from the cocoon of the female lac insect, dissolved in denatured alcohol. The lac insect feeds on trees, mostly in India and Thailand. Cocoons are gathered and refined into dry flakes, which are then dissolved in denatured (ethyl) alcohol.	Premixed shellac is available in orange (amber) and clear, which is shellac that's been bleached; contains wax. Shellac flakes are available in a range of colors, from clear to an orange/amber color.	Provides a modest amount of protection. Not as durable as lacquer or varnish. Not recommended for tabletops, chairs, and kitchen cabinets with high wear requirements. The wax in shellac decreases the finish's resistance to water and prevents some finishes from bonding to it. Shellac is neither resistant to water and alkalis such as ammonia nor to alcohol.	The solvent for shellac, denatured alcohol, is distilled from corn, and most people don't find the fleeting odor objectionable. Shellac breaks down over time and has a limited shelf life.
Nitrocellulose lacquer	Made from an alkyd (modified oil) and nitrocellulose resin dissolved and then mixed with solvents that evaporate quickly.	Dries fast, imparts depth and richness to the wood, and rubs out well. Tendency to yellow as it ages, which shows clearly on light-colored woods.	Excellent durability, moderate water resistance, sensitivity to heat and certain solvents. Oil-based lacquer is best in terms of overall durability of hand-applied finishes	Contains VOCs. Highly flammable. Fast-drying properties reduce dust-related finish problems. Dry dust can explode. Usually applied with a spray gun.
Japanese or Chinese lacquer	A cellulose derivative dissolved in solvent that dries to a high-gloss film. Made from the Asian sumac plant.	Yields a highly lustrous and polished surface to wood, increases in luster & brilliance with age.	Older lacquer pieces made of up to 40 layers are extremely durable, newer lacquers less so.	Brushing lacquers cure slowly.
Acrylic-modified lacquer	Mixture of a nonyellowing cellulose resin (called cellulose acetate butyrate, or CAB) and acrylic	Will not show as an amber color when applied over light-colored woods; does not turn yellow over time.	Used in post-catalyzed varnish finishing system, is extremely durable.	Some available HAPSfree, low-VOC, and low formaldehyde release.
Catalyzed lacquer	Consists of urea formaldehyde or urea melamine and an alkyd that has some nitrocellulose resin added to make it handle like normal lacquer.	Precatalyzed lacquer has the components premixed, either by the manufacturer or where purchased; postcatalyzed lacquer is a two-part system that is mixed just before use.	The addition of an acid catalyst initiates a chemical reaction that forms a very tough, durable finish. Catalyzed lacquer and varnish are the most durable sprayed finishes.	Once the catalyst has been added, these lacquers have a fairly short pot life (the time in which they can be used). Catalyzed lacquers are harder and dry faster than noncatalyzed ones, but are also harder to use.

Finish Category	Composition	Characteristics and Applications	Durability	Environmental Issues
Water-based finishes	Urethane, alkyd, and acrylic, but with many flammable and polluting ingredients replaced with water. Either an acrylic resin (sold as water-based lacquer) or an acrylic urethane mixture (sold as water-based polyurethane).	Quicker drying than oil-based products; may raise wood grain.	Addition of the urethane makes the resin tougher and more scratch-resistant, but water-based urethane does not have the same solvent and heat resistance as its oil-based counterpart.	Fewer VOCs than oil-based products. Water clean-up.

Stains

Finish Category	Composition	Characteristics and Applications	Durability	Environmental Issues
Water stains	Use water as the solvent and include water-soluble aniline (chemically derived) dyes to impart color.	Penetrate only the top layers of the wood. Can be stripped and sanded away, revealing the original color of the wood. Dry quickly. Limited color selection	Stain must be top-coated or finished with varnish, shellac, or synthetic finishes such as polyurethane or acrylic. Less durable than other stains, may bubble when brushed.	May contain pesticides or preservatives. Clean up with soap and water. Little odor. Available with low VOC emissions.
Alcohol stains	Manufactured using alcohol or glycol as the solvent with alcohol-soluble aniline dyes used in their production.	Penetrate only the top layers of the wood. Do not raise grain. Because alcohol dries almost instantly, the stain is set as it is applied. Good color selection. Very fast drying, usually sprayed on, may result in patchy coverage.	Stain must be top-coated or finished with varnish, shellac, or synthetic finishes such as polyurethane or acrylic	May contain pesticides or preservatives.
Oil stains	Utilize mineral spirits for the solvent. Pigments generally iron oxide pigments (although this may vary).	Use linseed oil treated with special acids as the resin or binder so that it will not penetrate too deeply into the surface of the wood. Metallic salts help the product oxidize and permit the oil stain to dry. Mineral spirits help the product's viscosity and ease of application. Spread easily, can be blended.	Stain must be top-coated or finished with varnish, shellac, or synthetic finishes such as polyurethane or acrylic	Used rags can spontaneously combust. May contain pesticides or preservatives

GLASS AND GLAZING

Adding glazing to interior surfaces connects spaces visually and allows light to pass through an interior. The use of sandblasted glass or the addition of translucent films to glass can limit views while still allowing glimpses of what lies beyond.

Fixed glazing in interior walls is subject to code limitations instituted to reduce the likelihood that someone will walk into or break the glass. Fire codes also restrict the size of glazing where it would create a weak spot in containing fire and smoke. Safety glazing and fire-resistant glazing help designers to meet these requirements.

Ordinary window glass can be broken virtually noiselessly if a burglar puts tape on it. Tempered safety glass cannot be cut or easily broken but can be shattered with a strong blow from a hammer. One alternative is to glaze vulnerable windows with plastic or a plastic-glass laminate, or to protect glass with a security film.

Acrylic plastics (Lucite, Plexiglas, and similar products) resist impact but can be burned through with a torch. They scratch easily and tend to yellow with age. Polycarbonate plastics (Lexan, FlexiGuard, and others) in 3/16 inch (4.8 mm) or thicker single or laminated sheets are virtually smashproof, but they can be burned or melted. Plastic materials that are sufficiently flexible can be pushed out of standard glazing. To prevent that, they should be through-bolted into window frames.

WINDOW FILMS

Color fading of fabrics is caused by several factors, including ultraviolet (UV) and visible light, heat and humidity, chemical vapors such as ozone, the dyes used, and the fabric's age. The UV light in sunlight will fade fabrics and cause some to deteriorate. Various types of glass used in window assemblies will block around 25 percent of the UV light from the sun, while insulated glass keeps out around 40 percent. The installation of window films on glass can reject from 95 to 99 percent of the sun's ultraviolet light.

Various types of glass and window assemblies will block between 13 and 29 percent of solar heat, reducing the cooling load on a building. Window films can block up to 80 percent of solar heat.

Window films are usually warranteed by the manufacturer for 5 years; some have remained in service for 12 to 22 years, although this is exceptional. They will also hold the glass fragments together should the window be broken. Specially formulated safety and security window film is designed to hold glass in place during natural and manmade disasters.

Films can be applied to glass to create a translucent surface. Sign-making companies are able to transfer a designer's graphics onto film for interior installation. Colored films can screen views and will glow softly when backlit. Antigraffiti film is designed to deter scratches, acid etching, and gouges on glass. It is specified for both interior and exterior applications.

A liquid resin system laminates two or more layers of glass by injecting polyester resin between them, creating a tight bond. A wide variety of materials can be inserted in the resin layer, including handmade papers, film artwork, fabric, and wire mesh. Colored resin interlayers can also be used. Patterned and art glass can be laminated to meet safety standards. Lamination can also seal sandblasted glass.

WINDOW TREATMENT SELECTION AND INSTALLATION

Synthetic materials are used in the manufacture of several types of window treatments. The vanes of vertical louver blinds may be made of a variety of materials, including PVC, natural and synthetic fabrics, and aluminum. Vertical blinds are easier to keep clean and replace than horizontal blinds. They also can be used on a curved track.

PVC vertical blind vanes usually contain titanium dioxide, a light blocker, to assure opaqueness, and are treated with an antistatic solution. Their rigidity and weight eliminate the need for a bottom chain.

Fabric vertical blind vanes are usually made of polyester, although cotton, acrylic, fiberglass, and rayon are also used. The material may be woven or nonwoven, and either hung freely or inserted in a PVC sleeve for added rigidity and durability. Exposed fabric vanes may be treated with soil-resistant or fire-resistant finishes. Because fabric vanes are lightweight and flexible, they are weighted with sealed or sewn-in bottom weights, or linked by a bottom chain.

Light-colored, opaque roller shades are a simple but effective way to protect the interior from sunlight coming through a window, reducing both interior heat and fading from sunlight. Roller shades are also available in materials that have openings that constitute from 3 to 17 percent of the surface, allowing various levels of visibility. Less expensive shades may be made of vinyl-covered polyester; vinyl-covered fiberglass, though more expensive, offers better dimensional stability. Room-darkening or blackout shades are usually made of fiberglass coated with PVC film.

Ceiling Finishes Comparisons 11

The overhead interior surface of a room—the ceiling—may expose and express the structure of the building or conceal the underside of the floor or roof above with plaster, drywall, or other materials. Suspended ceilings are supported on a framework under a structure, creating an open space above for equipment, insulation, or air circulation.

As a functional element, a ceiling affects the illumination of space, its acoustical quality, and the amount of energy required to heat or cool it. The height and surface qualities of a ceiling affect the light level within a space. Fixtures mounted on a high ceiling must cast their light a greater distance to achieve the same level of illumination as fewer fixtures suspended from a lower ceiling.

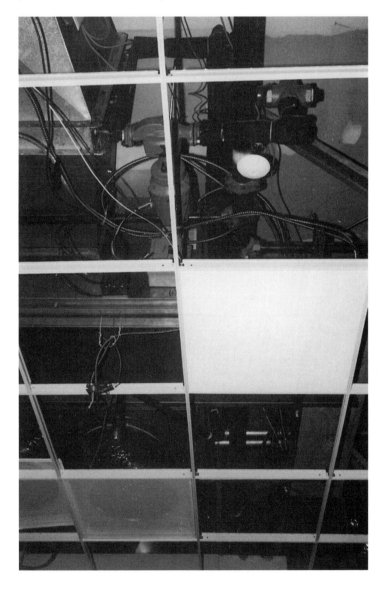

Figure 11-1 Suspended ceiling with equipment above

Because they are not usually encumbered with elements that can block the illumination from light sources, smooth, light-colored ceiling planes reflect light efficiently. When directly lit from below or the side, the ceiling surface itself can become a broad surface of soft illumination.

The ceiling represents the largest unused surface of a room, so its form and texture can have a significant impact on the room's acoustics. The smooth, hard surfaces of most ceiling materials reflect airborne sound within a space. In most situations, this is acceptable, since other elements and surfaces in a space can be sound-absorptive. In offices, stores, and restaurants, where additional sound-absorptive surfaces may be required to reduce the reflection of noise from numerous sources, acoustical ceilings can be employed.

Ceilings affect the way heating and cooling systems work. Warm air rises while cooler air falls; thus, a high ceiling allows the warmer air in a room to rise and cooler air to settle at floor level. This pattern of air movement makes a high-ceilinged space more comfortable in warm weather but also more difficult to heat in cold weather. Conversely, a low-ceilinged space traps warm air and is easier to heat in cold weather, but can be uncomfortably warm in hot weather.

Figure 11-2 Acoustically reflective materials

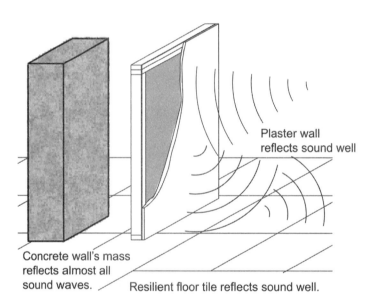

Plaster wall reflects sound well

Concrete wall's mass reflects almost all sound waves.

Resilient floor tile reflects sound well.

Figure 11-3 Painted ductwork blends into painted ceiling above.

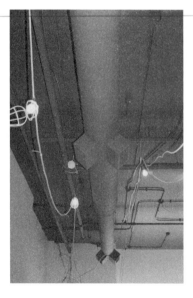

Ceilings can attract dust and dirt from heating, ventilating, and air-conditioning (HVAC) systems and from activities in the room below. High ceilings are especially hard to keep clean, and exposed ductwork and HVAC grilles can show dirt. Color choices for ductwork that hide dust and dirt can help. Well-maintained HVAC systems create fewer problems.

CEILING FORMS

Ceilings supported by the floor structure above them are normally flat. When created by a roof structure, however, a ceiling can take on other forms that reflect the shape of the structure, add visual interest, and give direction to a space. A single slope or shed form may lead the eye upward toward the ridge or down toward the eave line, depending on the patterns of daylight within the room. (See color plate C-65, sloped ceiling.)

Gabled ceilings expand space upward toward the ridgeline. Depending on the direction of any exposed structural elements, the gabled form may direct attention to the height of the ridge or to its length. A pyramid ceiling directs the eye upward to its peak, a focus that can be accentuated further with a skylight.

Figure 11-4 Coved ceiling with curved edges

Figure 11-5 Coffered ceiling

A coved ceiling uses a curved surface to soften the way it joins the surrounding wall planes. The resulting merger of vertical and horizontal surfaces gives the enclosed space a plastic, mobile quality. Coved ceilings can be designed to accommodate lighting fixtures for light that surrounds the space and illuminates the ceiling. Ceiling lighting coves are sometimes installed below skylights, with vertical surfaces sloping upward and outward. The illumination of the sidewalls at night helps to keep the skylight from looking like a black hole. Ceilings can be set back from the edges of a room to leave a recessed cove at the room's perimeter. Linear air diffusers can be installed in the recessed areas to leave the center of the ceiling unobstructed. Coved ceiling details are also used above wall cabinets to illuminate the area above. Where part of a ceiling is dropped lower, an indented cove can accommodate air-return grilles.

Increasing the scale of a curve leads to vaulted and domed ceiling forms. A vaulted ceiling directs the eye upward and along its length. A dome is a centralized form that expands space upward and focuses the attention on the space beneath its center. Free-form ceilings attract attention by contrasting with the planar quality of walls and floors.

Whether curvilinear or angular, decorative ceilings can dominate the other elements of interior space. Coffered ceilings attract attention with their detail and scale, and diffuse sound well.

EXPOSED CEILING TREATMENTS

By using the underlying architectural structure and materials as the finished ceiling, it is often possible to gain significant amounts of vertical space. Exposed ceiling treatments reveal mechanical equipment, plumbing, electrical conduits, sprinkler systems, lighting fixtures, and other elements that are ordinarily hidden above a ceiling, and permit easy access to all of these components.

Exposing the structure eliminates the cost of installing a ceiling. However, the cost of designing heating ducts to present a finished appearance may offset some of the savings. In some cases, upgrading electrical wiring to meet fire safety codes can be greater than the cost of installing a suspended ceiling. Exposed ceilings and their equipment may need to be painted as well.

Exposed Wood Structure

Any ceiling pattern tends to attract attention and appear to be lower than it is because of its visual weight. Since linear patterns direct the eye, they can also emphasize that dimension of space to which they are parallel. Linear members can create parallel, grid, or radial patterns.

Exposed beams bring the ceiling plane closer to the observer while drawing attention to the upper part of the room. The combination of high ceiling height with lower structural elements balances spaciousness with proportion.

Exposed wood structural members may be huge, roughly finished timbers or carefully finished wood beams. The exposed underside of a roof or floor above may also be either rustic or refined. In some cases, the exposed architecture showcases a building's craftsmanship. In other cases, the space above is full of mechanical and lighting equipment and is better kept hidden.

Exposed wood structures in older buildings reveal the architectural history of the space and provide the basis for unique interiors. Older wood structures often introduce textures and details that enrich the interior.

Exposed Concrete Structure

Exposed concrete structures make the most of floor-to-ceiling heights. Mechanical and electrical systems are exposed to view and may need to be coordinated for appearance as well as function. Concrete is not a warm, friendly material, but it can project the strength and function of a space.

The undersides of concrete slabs reflect the structural system used through the type and arrangement of their ribs.

- *One-way slabs* have thicker reinforcing ribs running in a single direction and are cast with their own parallel supporting beams.
- A *one-way joist or ribbed slab* has closely spaced joists that are in turn supported by parallel sets of beams.
- A *two-way slab* is often cast with supporting beams and columns on all four sides of approximately square bays. Two-way *waffle slabs* are reinforced by ribs in two directions. The coffered underside is usually left exposed.
- A *flat plate* is a concrete slab of uniform thickness supported directly by columns without beams or girders. Some slabs have drop panels—thicker areas around a column head for additional shear resistance. The column capital may also be thickened.

Figure 11-7 Waffle slab

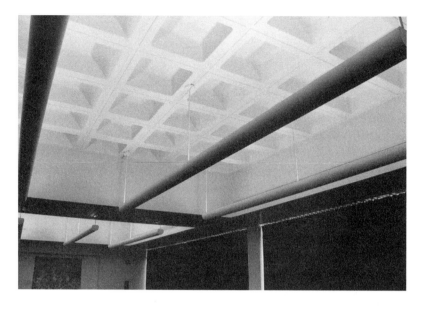

Exposed concrete structures are often left with their natural finish, but they can also be painted. Islands of acoustical ceiling treatments are suspended below the otherwise exposed concrete to lower sound levels and create more intimate spaces.

Exposed Metal Decking

On roofs, corrugated steel decking forms the structural platform for insulation and roofing material. Cellular or corrugated steel decking also provides permanent formwork and reinforcement for concrete when forming composite floor slabs. The underside of steel decking can be left exposed as the ceiling surface. Together with *open-web steel joists*, steel decking defines ceilings with a linear, textural quality.

Open-web joists are lightweight, shop-fabricated steel members used to carry floors across open spaces. The open-web joist is assembled from upper and lower chords with a bent steel bar running in a zigzag pattern between them. While remaining utilitarian,

Figure 11-8 Concrete column capital. Structural concrete columns are usually made with thicker tops that collect the load from the floor above.

Figure 11-9 *Steel decking*

the effect is more lightweight and smaller in scale than concrete or large wood beams. Exposed steel web joists, like other exposed structural materials, reveal building equipment. The openings in the webs allow pipes and ducts to be integrated into the ceiling structure, rather than hung below it.

Where open-web joists support steel floor decking without additional acoustical treatments, impact sounds, such as footfalls, will travel and even be amplified in the space below. Many times this leads to the installation of carpeting above and suspended acoustic ceilings below.

Where the metal decking is exposed to the space below, the corrugations that add to its stiffness and spanning strength will be visible. Cellular decking is manufactured by welding a corrugated sheet to a flat steel sheet, forming a series of spaces for wiring. Perforating the cells and filling them with acoustic insulation improves the deck's acoustical properties.

Steel ceiling components must be treated for rust resistance, and interior ceilings are normally painted. Open-web joists will collect dust.

WOOD CEILING TREATMENT

Beadboard, 5/16 inch (8 mm) thick and around 3–1/2 inches (89 mm) wide, can be used for ceilings. A routed groove down the center of each plank creates the illusion of two narrow planks when installed. Beadboard is installed at right angles to the ceiling joists. Edges at walls are easily trimmed with molding.

Wood decking or planks span beams to form the structural platform of a floor or roof. The underside of the planks may be left exposed as the finished ceiling. Wood planks are normally 5–1/4 in. (13 cm) wide and have V-shaped tongue-and-groove joints. Channel groove, striated, and other machined patterns are available. There is no concealed ceiling space with such a system.

Wood ceilings are often finished with stains and varnishes. A dark ceiling finish, especially a shiny one, may appear lower than it actually is. If a dark wood ceiling is combined with a dark floor and separated by light-colored walls, the effect can be that of a tuna sandwich on pumpernickel bread: horizontal and flat.

Wood ceilings made from light-colored or highly patterned woods, like knotty pine, can add warmth and character to a space. In some cases, wood ceilings are painted, either to reflect more light or to obscure unattractive wood.

Wood ceilings are usually highly sound-reflective. Sometimes, designers use lattices or baffles of wood in an attempt to improve sound absorption. Such efforts improve sound diffusion but must be topped with acoustic materials in order to significantly increase sound absorption.

Figure 11-10 Beadboard ceiling. Each rib is one-half of a board.

Ceiling panels with real wood veneer finishes are also available. Perforated wood-finished panels can have acoustically absorbent material inside. The panels are edge banded and open downward for ease of access.

Manufacturers of ceiling finishes provide wood and wood-look options. Standard 2 × 2 foot metal ceiling panels can be inexpensively finished with realistic printed images of wood as a powder-coated finish.

Suspended wood linear ceilings are attached with clips to a rail. They are available in a variety of wood species, including oak, ash, maple, poplar, and red cedar, with factory-applied finishes.

Figure 11-11 Wood ceilings tend to reflect sound.

Ceilings can be illuminated by daylight or by electric light. Illuminated ceilings may be designed as a modular lighting grid, or consist of skylights that open a space to the sky. Energy conservation restraints have made the totally illuminated ceilings of the twentieth century generally unfeasible; in any case, huge expanses of even fluorescent lighting tended to create characterless interior environments that isolated people from the variations in light and shadow that characterize natural environments. Current preferences for transitions from ambient to task to accent lighting call for more sophisticated lighting approaches.

Illuminated ceilings do have a part to play in coordination with daylight. Stained-glass designs set below sealed skylights add daylight and color without glare. When combined with perimeter lighting fixtures in the skylights, the effect is available for all times of day and types of weather. The use of energy-efficient LED or fiber-optic lighting makes it easier to maintain light sources in hard-to-reach locations.

Custom-printed fabric systems that hide an energy-efficient light source are available. These provide a softly textured illuminated ceiling.

Polycarbonate sheets assembled in structured panels are very lightweight and almost unbreakable. Their weather and UV resistance makes them appropriate for skylights, greenhouses, sunrooms, and interior applications where their transparency level (about 80 percent) diffuses direct sunlight.

ILLUMINATED CEILINGS

Plaster and gypsum board provide uninterrupted ceiling surfaces that can be finished smooth, given a texture, painted, or wallpapered. Plaster also affords the opportunity for merging ceiling and wall planes with curved coves. Both plaster and gypsum board require a supporting framework of wood or metal that is attached to or suspended from the roof or floor framing.

PLASTER AND DRYWALL CEILINGS

Figure 11-12 Curved gypsum board ceiling. The worker is applying a coat of veneer plaster. Photo courtesy of National Gypsum Company

Figure 11-13 Soffit framing

Figure 11-14 Soffit and drywall ceiling. This ceiling is hung below an uneven plaster ceiling, providing room for recessed lighting fixtures.

When the lath supporting plaster ceilings is nailed directly to the wood joist structure above it, the plaster is likely to crack as the wood expands and contracts. By suspending a plaster ceiling from flexible hanger wires, the ceiling is able to move independently of the supporting floor or roof structure. This method also creates a space in which to conceal mechanical and lighting equipment.

Plaster ceilings are supported by main runner channels spaced up to 4 feet (1.2 m) apart. Crosswise furring channels are attached to the main runners, and metal lath is attached to the furring at 6-inch (15-cm) intervals. The coats of plaster are then applied to the lath.

Gypsum board sheets may be attached directly to a building's structure, or suspended by hanger wires. Using resilient-furring channels to attach the gypsum board reduces the amount of sound transmitted to and from the space above. Type X gypsum board is used for fire resistance. Gypsum board may also be supported by furring channels and hung as a suspended ceiling. It may be finished with joint compound and joint tape, and then painted, or the gypsum board may serve as a substrate for a skim coat of plaster.

Acoustical barrier ceilings are composed of two layers of 5/8-inch (16 mm) gypsum board screwed together with staggered joints. Perimeters and penetrations are carefully sealed. Their significant mass and sealed openings act as sound barriers, blocking noise from the floor above. In combination with isolated wall and floor design, they also are able to contain noise within music practice rooms and other spaces.

ACOUSTICAL CEILING TILES

Although the terms are often used interchangeably, *acoustical ceiling tiles* and *acoustical ceiling panels* are technically different products. Acoustical ceiling tiles are used in concealed spline ceilings, where the narrow metal spline that supports them is not visible on the surface, or directly stapled or glued to a substrate. The space above an acoustical tile ceiling is not easily accessible without damaging the tiles. (Easily accessible suspended ceiling systems are discussed later in this chapter.)

Acoustical ceiling tiles are usually smaller than what are properly called acoustic panels, 12 inches (30.5 cm) square with kerfed (grooved or notched) or tongue-and-groove edges. Because they are either attached directly to the structure above or set into concealed support grids, they offer less access to the space directly above them. Acoustical ceiling tiles have a mineral fiber or glass fiber base; some for residential use are made of cellulose. The efficacy of acoustical ceiling tiles for sound absorption depends on how they are mounted.

Acoustical tiles are available with fissured surfaces (in fine, medium, and heavy), and with perforated holes. Vinyl finishes are used in food preparation areas. Tiles are normally white, although some are available in color. Acoustical tiles can be spray-painted, which results in some loss of acoustic capability. Acoustical ceiling tiles are available with special finishes that are resistant to chemical fumes and scrubbing.

Most ceiling tiles have square or beveled edges; kerfed tiles conceal suspension grids. Tile edges may be damaged when removed. The slight shadow line created by beveled edges minimizes edge damage.

Ceiling tiles absorb sound within a space and can reduce the amount of sound transmitted to other spaces. However, they are not designed to keep sound from entering a space from above. Tiles in systems suspended several feet below the floor structure do a better job of stopping impact noise from the floor above than those adhered firmly to the structure.

Manufacturers of acoustic materials offer contoured ceiling panels (frequently called tiles) in a variety of patterns and colors. The 2-foot square tiles can be mounted into any standard ceiling grid, and the soft, pliable base material can be cut easily and smoothly to accommodate corners, sprinkler heads, or heating and lighting fixtures.

Sound barrier ceiling tiles are designed to reduce sound transmission and control reverberation. The 1-inch-thick (25.4 mm) dense fiberglass tiles are sealed on the back with an aluminized sound barrier.

Ceiling manufacturers offer an ever increasing variety of forms. Acoustical canopies are hung from ceilings to provide spot absorption and help to define interior spaces. Their gently curved surfaces are finished to enhance light reflectance. Acoustical clouds work in a similar manner, to reduce reverberation time, control noise, and increase speech intelligibility.

METAL CEILINGS

Corrugated steel decking forms the structural platform for the insulation and roofing material. Cellular or corrugated steel decking also provides permanent formwork and reinforcement for concrete when forming composite floor slabs. The underside of steel decking can be left exposed as a ceiling surface. Together with open-web steel joists, steel decking defines ceilings with a linear, textural quality.

Stamped metal ceilings are sometimes found in older buildings, where they may be hidden under a newer hung ceiling. They bring an old-fashioned, textured look and a pleasing scale to ceilings. Older stamped metal ceilings can be rescued by carefully patching them with pieces of matching material retrieved from places where it will not be seen in the new design. New stamped metal can be purchased in sheet or modular tile forms. Stamped metal ceilings can be painted; most are bordered by matching coves at the wall joints. They will reflect sound within a room.

Figure 11-15 Stamped metal ceiling. Many of these ceilings are hidden under suspended ceilings.

It is difficult to open most stamped metal ceilings in order to install electrical conduits and fixtures, so the electrical design must be planned before installing the ceiling. Sometimes the equipment is left exposed and painted to match, blending inconspicuously into the ceiling pattern.

Stamped metal ceiling tiles can be inserted into standard, 24-inch (.6-m) square ceiling suspension systems. These tiles simplify installation and access for equipment. If the ceiling is to be painted, any grilles mounted in the grid should be painted to match. (See color plate C-66, Stamped metal tile in grid.)

SUSPENDED CEILING SYSTEMS

Ceiling systems that suspend finish materials below the structure of the floor above provide space for mechanical and lighting equipment. A *plenum* is the open area between a finished ceiling and the floor above it. The suspended ceiling units are designed to accommodate mechanical system distribution grilles, lighting fixtures, and fire-suppression sprinkler heads.

Many commercial spaces suspend acoustical ceiling units in a grid hung from the structure above. Lay-in panels (also referred to as tiles) in exposed grids are the easiest to lift out for access to equipment above them.

Because a dropped ceiling is usually suspended from the floor or roof structure above its form can either echo or contrast with the shape and geometry of the space. Modular ceiling materials are normally supported on a metal grid suspended from a roof or floor structure. Acoustical ceiling panels are larger than acoustical tiles and are laid in visible grids that establish a scale for the space. Long, narrow metal panels form a linear, directional pattern on a ceiling. In both cases, light fixtures, air diffusers, and other equipment can be integrated into the modular system.

A suspended ceiling creates a concealed space that can be used to house electrical or mechanical lines, recessed lighting fixtures, and insulating materials. The effect of a suspended ceiling can also be created with nonstructural elements, such as fabric or a series of suspended lighting fixtures. In a room with a high ceiling, all or a portion of the ceiling can be dropped to lower the scale of the space, or to differentiate an area from the space around it.

Acoustical Panels

The term acoustical panels—as opposed to acoustical tiles—is properly used for units that fit into a suspended ceiling. Acoustical panels are modular units of glass or mineral fiber that are excellent absorbers of sound. They are available in a variety of square and rectangular styles. Some may have aluminum, vinyl, ceramic, or mineral faces. Edges may be square, beveled, or *rabbeted* (i.e., with a rectangular groove cut into the edge to receive the support). Panels with recycled material content are increasingly available, and manufacturers are addressing the recycling of old ceiling panels.

Acoustical panels come with perforated, patterned, textured, or fissured faces. Some tiles are fire rated, and some are rated for use in high-humidity areas. Mylar-faced panels are used in clean rooms, food service areas, and other places where cleanliness is a priority. Mylar and vinyl surfaces have reduced acoustic properties.

The most common edge details are square or *tegular* edges, which facilitate drop-in installation and can be easily pushed up for access. Square-edged panels are economical, but the suspension system is wholly visible. Tegular-edged panels extend below the suspension system, minimizing the visibility of the grid and creating a shadow line or reveal. They come in a variety of profiles, including square, angled, beveled, and stepped. Some panels partly or completely hide the suspension grid.

Acoustical panels are most commonly available in 24-inch (61-cm) squares and 24 × 48 inch (61 × 122 cm) rectangles. Larger panels are available in rectangular and square configurations up to 60 × 60 inches (152 × 152 cm).

Acoustical panels are given acoustic ratings.

- *Ceiling attenuation class* (CAC) rates a ceiling's ability to block airborne sound transmission between spaces and from above-ceiling elements.
- *Noise-reduction coefficient* (NRC) ratings measure sound absorption at four specific frequencies.
- *Articulation class* (AC) ratings relate to the intelligibility of the spoken word within a space and are used in open office spaces with partitions of less than full height.

Acoustical panels, as well as acoustical tiles, are also rated for their ability to reflect light. High levels of reflectance correlate with smooth rather than textured surfaces. In general, the white finish of most acoustical tile ceilings contributes to the diffusion of light within the space, which in turn allows lower overall lighting levels and results in energy savings.

Acoustical panels are available with special humidity-resistant properties for use in high moisture areas, such as locker and shower rooms, indoor pools, and some laboratory spaces. They are usually composites of ceramic and mineral fibers, and can be treated with antimicrobial inhibitors to resist mold and mildew growth.

Acoustical panel systems, including both the panels themselves and their suspension systems, usually must have a class A fire rating to be installed on a commercial project. Systems are available with one-, two-, three-, or four-hour ratings.

Suspended acoustical ceiling grids are supported by hanger wires that provide flexibility and lightweight support. Special isolation hangers can be used to prevent supporting wires from transmitting noise to the building structure.

Suspension systems are designated for light-duty, intermediate, or heavy-duty use. Light-duty systems are suitable only for residential and light commercial use. Intermediate systems are designed to support moderate loads from light fixtures and ceiling diffusers and are used in many commercial applications. Only heavy-duty systems can

Figure 11-16 Tile rigidly fastened to the ceiling structure or furring is not very effective for acoustic absorption.

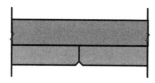

Rigidly fastened to concrete

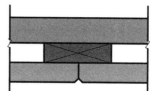

Nailed to furring

Figure 11-17 Properly suspended from the structure and away from the walls, acoustic tile combines with the open air above for maximum sound absorption.

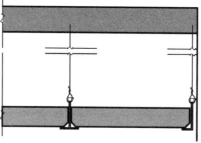

Suspended from ceiling and walls

Figure 11-18 The panels laid across this corridor ceiling are riddled with airspaces that effectively absorb sound.

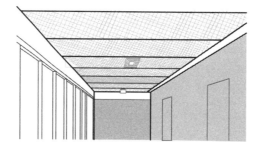

support additional loads hung from the suspended grid. Interior designers should avoid creating design elements that are suspended from ceiling grids unless the system was designed to support them.

Suspension grid systems are composed of main beams installed on hanger wires, which in turn support cross tees. Perimeters are supported by angle- or channel-shaped moldings.

Linear Metal Ceilings

Linear metal ceilings offer a strong linear design, durability, and ease of maintenance. Made in steel, aluminum, or stainless steel, panel options include slat size, metal coating type, texture, color, and acoustical insulation. They are typically installed as snap-in units on concealed suspension systems.

Three-dimensional metal ceiling panels of lightweight aluminum are available in a variety of designs and depths. They are installed in both narrow profile and standard ceiling suspension systems. Panels are available with perforations and acoustic fillers.

Some systems are designed to accept lighting fixtures and HVAC grilles. Open slots permit sound to be absorbed by backing of *batt* (thick, blanketlike) *insulation*. Perforated metal pans backed by fibrous batts are available for use with suspended ceilings. With the acoustic backing removed, they can be used for an air return. Panels can usually be cut in the field to accommodate grilles and lighting fixtures.

Linear metal panels typically vary from 2 to 8 inches (5 to 20 cm) wide. They ordinarily come in 12- and 16-foot (3.6- and 4.8-m) lengths, with custom lengths

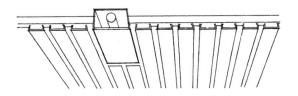

Figure 11-19 Linear metal ceiling. Acoustically absorbent insulation can be installed above the metal strips.
Reproduced with permission of the publisher from Francis D. K. Ching and Corky Binggeli, *Interior Design Illustrated*, 2nd ed. (Hoboken, NJ: John Wiley & Sons, Inc.), © 2005 by John Wiley & Sons, Inc.

available. Panels vary in depth, with greater depths having greater linear effect. Edge details aid in attaching the panels evenly to the suspension system. Roll-finished edges add to the support of interior panels, which can be shaped as flat pans, planks, tubes, blades, and baffles.

Linear metal panels are available smooth, perforated, or textured. Linear metal panels are most commonly made of roll-formed aluminum. Aluminum panels are preferred for high-humidity areas and where the environment is variable, including exterior applications. They are available mill finished, anodized, or colored with baked enamel. Roll-formed steel panels may be less expensive, but require more maintenance. Steel panels are available with baked enamel, powder coat, or electroplated finishes. Stainless steel performs well but is more expensive; it comes in brushed and mirror finishes.

The suspension systems for linear metal ceilings are similar to those used for acoustical tile. They are available in intermediate and heavy-duty classes. Many manufacturers incorporate recycled materials into metal panel ceiling assemblies.

Perforated Metal Pans

Perforated metal pans backed by fibrous batts are available for use with suspended ceilings grids. They come in many finishes and colors, and are both durable and easy to maintain. Acoustical metal pan ceiling units enclose sound attenuation pads for acoustical control. With the acoustic backing removed, they can be used for an air return. Metal pan ceilings are either snapped or hooked in place on a concealed suspension system. They may also be laid into traditional exposed ceiling suspension systems. Pans with detailed edges create narrow reveals with semiexposed grids. Air diffusers and light fixtures can be integrated into the systems.

Acoustical metal pan ceilings are made of steel or aluminum in a variety of sizes, metal coatings, colors, textures, perforation patterns, and acoustical insulation pads. Sizes vary from 12 × 12 inches (30.5 × 30.5 cm) square to 24 × 24 inches (61 × 61 cm) square, with some larger sizes available in planks or squares. The space above metal pan systems is accessed through either hinged panels or by removing the pan units. Steel pans are either galvanized or finished with baked enamel or powder-coated or electroplated finishes. Aluminum pans are mill finished, anodized, or painted. In addition to the standard flat panels, curved and corrugated units are also available. Suspension systems are similar to those available for acoustical panel and tile installations.

The acoustical properties of metal pans vary with the type of pan, the type and amount of perforations, and the conditions on-site. Sound passes through the perforations and is trapped in the acoustic materials behind them. Sound attenuation pads are often made of fiberglass; they are usually encapsulated to prevent stray fibers from becoming airborne. When installed without acoustic treatment, a black backing scrim is included to hide the view through to the ceiling above. Mineral fiber inserts limit the ability of sound to pass through to spaces above even better than fiberglass units. Some metal pan ceiling systems include recycled materials.

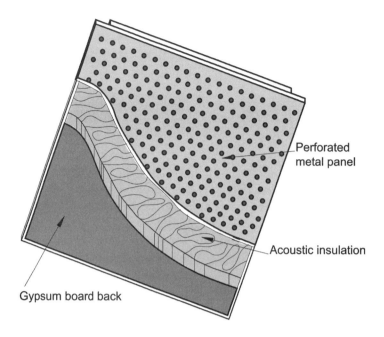

Perforated metal panel

Acoustic insulation

Gypsum board back

Metal mesh 2 × 2 foot lay-in panels are available in a wide range of welded wire, woven wire, and expanded metal mesh patterns. The panels are made with 25 percent recycled steel and use standard ceiling suspension systems.

Suspended Decorative Grids

Open framework grids are suspended from the structure above them, creating a lower ceiling plane that screens elements above. They allow lighting, sprinkler, and HVAC systems to be reached easily.

Suspended decorative grids are made of U-shaped blades of roll-formed sheet metal assembled into modular units and suspended from systems similar to those for acoustical ceilings. Some grids are able to support lighting fixtures, signs, speakers, and other ceiling elements, while additional support is needed with other systems. Light fixtures are often supported separately from the structure above.

Grid systems consist of beams or frames customarily at least 1 inch (25 mm) in width. The beams form grid modules that are usually 2 × 2 feet (6 × 6 m) or 2 × 4 feet (6 × 12 m). Smaller grid units, called *cells*, can be inserted into these modules. Various combinations of grid units and cells allow for a design with a diversity of scale and openness. Beams are made of aluminum or galvanized steel. Some systems use T-shaped steel with wire mesh units instead of cells. Anodized or colored aluminum blades with a baked enamel finish are available for grid systems. Steel blades are colored with baked enamel or powder-coated or electroplated finishes. Stainless steel blades are available with a mirror finish.

Most grid systems are installed in rectilinear configurations, but some are available with curved perimeters. The grids are often fabricated to move downward for access to the space above. The open grids do not block or absorb sound. Suspension systems for commercial spaces are intermediate and heavy duty.

STRETCHED CEILING SYSTEMS

Stretched ceiling systems consist of large, smooth, lightweight ceiling planes of flexible PVC membrane or woven fabric, both of which can be printed with designs or lettering. The fabric is stretched across a perimeter rail and attached to the rail with special fittings. Stretched ceiling panels can have flat or curved surfaces or perimeters, and can be installed over other ceilings and allow access to equipment above.

Stretched ceiling systems offer great diversity and flexibility to ceiling design. Typical spans range up to 16 × 40 feet (5 × 12 m). The rail mounted around the perimeter of the fabric can be straight or curved. Wood or metal frames are used at the edges of curved installations. Few intermediate supports are required to span large distances with lightweight systems. Components are usually recyclable.

Stretched ceiling systems can be printed with photographic-quality artwork. The PVC membranes are available in more than 100 colors, and in matte, satin, suede, metallic, and reflective finishes. Although the fabric can be backlit, this may cast shadows of the frame onto the fabric.

A stretched ceiling system can be installed quickly by experienced professionals. Penetrations for lighting and equipment are cut at the job site. These systems permit access to the equipment above them, and can be installed over other ceilings. Installations can be treated with antimicrobial and antifungal treatments for hospital, laboratory, and food preparation spaces.

Suspended cloud ceilings with acoustic panels are edged with metal frames, some of which accomodate lighting fixtures. Perforated metal sheets or panels can be suspended in curved or angled designs.

Hanging an acoustically absorbent material from the ceiling of a room with all sides exposed is the best way to capture sound waves. The softly sculptured surface pattern on both sides of *acoustic baffles* is designed to absorb sound in a wide range of frequencies. Baffles are available 24 × 48 inches with 3-inch thickness.

BANNER MATERIALS

The advent of techniques for lower-cost large-scale graphics has created a demand for banners in building interiors. Vinyl laminate fabrics, constructed of polyester, nylon, or fiberglass scrims between two layers of vinyl, take printing well and are generally fire-resistant. Although colors are somewhat limited, and the vinyl fabric lacks drapeability and an appealing feel, vinyl fabrics are easy to assemble into relatively heavy, opaque banners.

Stretched fabrics can be used to articulate interior space and to reflect or diffuse light. Fire-resistant materials are suspended either from points on ceilings and walls or from the manufacturer's space frame supports.

Millwork, Furniture Materials, and Textile Comparisons 12

There are several terms used to refer to the built-in components of interior architecture.

- *Fixed equipment* encompasses such items as food service kitchen equipment, laboratory casework and benches, library shelving, classroom and auditorium seating, and audiovisual equipment, all of which are physically connected to the building and require specialized construction or engineering.
- *Casework* is the term used for cabinetry that is attached to the wall.
- *Millwork* is the term applied to the "wood interior finish components of a building, including moldings, windows, doors, cabinets, stairs, mantles and the like" (Edward Allen and Joseph Iano, *Fundamentals of Building Construction*, 4th edition, John Wiley & Sons, Inc., 2004, Glossary).
- *Cabinetwork, cabinetmaking,* and *cabinetry* are all used to refer to the making of fine furniture or other woodwork.

As a built-in interior component, casework is expected to last a long time without showing undue wear. Casework is selected to accommodate the type of use—or abuse—that it is likely to receive. In residential settings, casework finishes are selected for exposure to acids and chemicals found in foods and cleaning materials. Laboratory casework is exposed to even more damaging chemicals. Depending on its location and use, the design of casework must strike a balance between durability and appearance. Where it is regularly exposed to moisture, materials must be selected to resist water damage and joined so as to allow expansion and contraction.

Casework and millwork can add up to a substantial percentage of the total construction budget, and costs can easily get out of control. Design decisions that affect details or materials can change the cost significantly. New products, innovations in materials, and developments in construction methods all affect the design and the cost. The complexity of casework details raises the importance of working with reputable manufacturers, fabricators, and installers. The interior designer must review shop drawings and finished work carefully for correspondence to specifications.

Some general features to look for in good-quality cabinets include:

CABINETS

- A melamine backer should be used on the underside of all countertops.
- Cabinet panel face materials should be balanced with a similar material on the back to prevent warping.
- High-pressure plastic laminates should be adhered to industrial particleboard on an MDF substrate or equivalent construction.
- Drawer bottoms should be set securely into grooved *dado* construction on all four sides.

Figure 12-1 Kitchen cabinets installed

Reproduced by permission of the publisher from Edward Allen and Joseph Iano, *Fundamentals of Building Construction: Materials and Methods*, 4th ed. (Hoboken, NJ: John Wiley & Sons, Inc.), © 2004 by John Wiley & Sons, Inc.

- The wood grain pattern on cabinets should be lined up vertically, carrying over to drawer fronts.
- Joints for drawers should be dovetailed or doweled.

Cabinets are usually either purchased from a store or manufacturer or built locally in a shop. The term *custom* is applied to all sorts of cabinetry and is not useful as an indicator of either type or quality. Cabinets produced elsewhere and bought from a store or distributor range from low-end or economy examples to high-end European cabinets.

Store-bought cabinets are designed to work best in specific layouts, and are often shown that way in showrooms. Getting them to fit into an existing interior is another matter, and may require large blank fill strips where they meet the walls. Specific accessory pieces such as wine racks may not fit in actual installations. Although the purchasing process is relatively simple compared to shop-built cabinetry, delays for certain pieces may take as long as for shop-built pieces. Costs will rise when sales tax, delivery, and installation are included.

Shop-built cabinetry is usually superior to lower-quality store-bought pieces in both fit and finish. Production shops work like factories, with little difference between one project and the next. Factory cabinet door styles offer limited variations from basic styles, materials, and layouts. The people who do the work in a production shop may never see the job site, and may have a limited understanding of the designer's intent. Alternatively, cabinets can be built individually for a single project.

Face frame–style cabinets consist of a hardwood frame that is fastened to the front of the cabinet's inner box. *Face frame cabinets* have large spaces between cabinet doors and drawer fronts, and are often built in large, multicabinet sections. This style of cabinetry is still used but is being replaced by frameless or European- (Euro-) style cabinetry.

Frameless cabinetry uses hinges that mount on the sides of the cabinet's box rather than on the front of the face frame. The type of hardware used allows the doors to be very close to or touching adjacent doors and still open without binding. Frameless cabinets are built in smaller modular units with edges capped with glued-on tape or hardwood trims. The door and drawer faces on frameless cabinets are usually separated by narrow shadow lines (*reveals*) of around 1/8 inch (3 mm). Flush overlay frameless

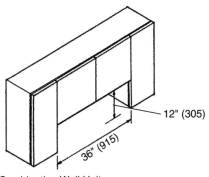

Combination Wall Unit
- For use over sinks and ranges
- 60" to 84" (1525 to 2135) long
- 30" (760) high

Figure 12-2 Wall cabinets
Reproduced by permission of the publisher from Francis D. K. Ching and Cassandra Adams, *Building Construction Illustrated*, 3rd ed. (New York: John Wiley & Sons, Inc.) © 2001 by John Wiley & Sons, Inc.

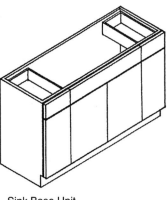

Sink Base Unit
- 54" to 84" (1370 to 2135) long in 3" (75) increments

Figure 12-3 Base cabinet sink unit
Reproduced by permission of the publisher from Francis D. K. Ching and Cassandra Adams, *Building Construction Illustrated*, 3rd ed. (New York: John Wiley & Sons, Inc.) © 2001 by John Wiley & Sons, Inc.

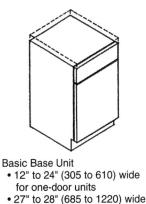

Basic Base Unit
- 12" to 24" (305 to 610) wide for one-door units
- 27" to 28" (685 to 1220) wide for two-door units
- 23" or 24" (585 to 610) deep

Figure 12-4 Basic base unit
Reproduced by permission of the publisher from Francis D. K. Ching and Cassandra Adams, *Building Construction Illustrated*, 3rd ed. (New York: John Wiley & Sons, Inc.) © 2001 by John Wiley & Sons, Inc.

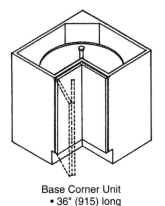

Base Corner Unit
- 36" (915) long

Figure 12-5 Base corner unit
Reproduced by permission of the publisher from Francis D. K. Ching and Cassandra Adams, *Building Construction Illustrated*, 3rd ed. (New York: John Wiley & Sons, Inc.) © 2001 by John Wiley & Sons, Inc.

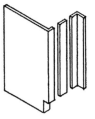

Finished end and final panels are available

Figure 12-6 Finished end and filler panels Reproduced by permission of the publisher from Francis D. K. Ching and Cassandra Adams, *Building Construction Illustrated*, 3rd ed. (New York: John Wiley & Sons, Inc.) © 2001 by John Wiley & Sons, Inc.

cabinet faces cover the edges of the box. Less common flush inset faces set door and drawer fronts into the opening of the box.

These basic styles are often combined in high-quality installations. When face frame cabinets are flush inset, as in what is commonly called the *craftsman style*, the clearance around the door is only 1/16 inch (1.6 mm). Mixing face frames with faceless frames can be done with experience and skill in design. Attention to detail is critical.

The designer of individually built cabinetry must work with the cabinetmaker to make sure the cabinets fit properly into the room. High-quality cabinets are designed to accommodate the variations in the room so that cabinets fit closely to walls and

Table 12-1 Grades of Casework Construction

Grade	Materials	Relative Cost	Production	Quality	Design
Economy Store Bought	Lightweight materials reduce shipping costs.	Low budget	Factory-built by low-skilled workers	Uneven construction and hardware	Options limited.
High-end Store Bought	Lightweight materials reduce shipping costs.	May cost more than locally shop-built.	Imported from Europe. Check availability of parts and service.	May have exceptionally well-designed and well-made details.	Replacement parts subject to changes in styles.
Production Shop Built	Factory-produced doors and drawer fronts on locally built cabinets.	Moderate	Cabinet box built locally; doors from factories; finish applied at shop.	Technical quality good, but workers may not visit site; design details may suffer.	Some style choices, but layouts may be limited.
Individually Shop Built	Potential to use highest-quality or exotic materials.	High	Custom-built locally by highly skilled craftspeople.	Very high quality, very hands-on. Unique details.	Close coordination between designer and builder.

are *scribed* (carefully fit to) the inevitable variations. The cabinetmaker must visit the job site to monitor these variations as the space is being built. Adjustments should be kept to a minimum and balanced between walls.

Cabinets have to be installed level and true; twisting distorts the box and causes alignment problems with doors and drawers. It is difficult to lay out and install cabinets without trim to cover discrepancies between the cabinetry and the built space; this is a detail that, when addressed, conveys high quality. It is easier to cover the edges of cabinetry with wide scribe strips and overlaid trim.

Specifications for cabinets rarely include countertops or fixtures such as sinks and the attached plumbing. Cabinet pulls are often not included, as they are usually chosen at the end of the job; they can vary widely in price. The cabinetmaker will usually drill for and install the selected cabinet pulls.

Finishing work may involve a professional painter if this is not specified as part of the cabinetmaker's work. Although the cabinetmaker may vary the construction from the designer's details, the cabinets should match the appearance and quality of hardware and materials specified. Areas that affect the quality of the work include full-extension drawer glides and drawer side materials. Good-quality cabinet interiors are usually melamine or veneer plywood. Specifications should include types of nosings and other trims.

The selection of the wood and the way it is milled greatly affect the appearance of cabinetry. Rotary-cut veneers are less expensive than plain sliced. Random matching costs less than sequentially matched sheets. Working with high-quality and matched materials requires a high degree of control and skill; this may be hard to assure in a large production shop. Simplified details and good-quality materials and construction set the best work apart. Hardware for cabinets includes hinges and drawer slides. Those that are certified ISO 14001 identify the manufacturer as meeting the highest standards of environmental safety.

The term *countertop* usually refers to a horizontal work surface in food preparation and workroom areas. Countertops are often supported by base cabinets; they may also be wall hung. Standard kitchen countertops are usually about 25 inches (635 mm) deep and contain an integrated backsplash. They often have cutouts for installation of sinks, cooktops or ranges, or integrated drain boards or cutting boards.

Stone countertops are durable and beautiful. Their weight demands adequate support, which can usually be provided by base cabinets. Stone countertops are porous to varying degrees, and will stain if not sealed. (See color plate C-68, Soapstone countertop.)

Wood is another beautiful material for a countertop. In dry areas where they can be properly cared for, wood countertops can be treated like fine furniture. Wood cutting blocks are intended to show the wear and tear of years of use.

Concrete countertops are made of lightweight aggregates and additives (fiber reinforced, silica fume pozzolan, acrylic), and reinforced with structural steel, wire mesh, fiberglass, and/or fibers. Those constructed of lightweight concrete weigh less but are not as strong. Standard cabinetry can support the weight if it is distributed over a large area.

Concrete countertops are either precast or built on site. They are cast in molds and can include subtle textures and decorative glass, metal, fossils, or other objects. Some counters include cast-in raised metal strips for hot pots near the stove or sink. Precast counters are cured and sealed before installation. On-site installations are formed to fit conditions and can include radius edges and curved corners. They are cured and sealed in place.

Concrete countertops are usually either 1–1/2 or 2 inches (38 or 51 mm) thick when installed; they may present a thicker front edge to view. Edge options include the

COUNTERTOPS

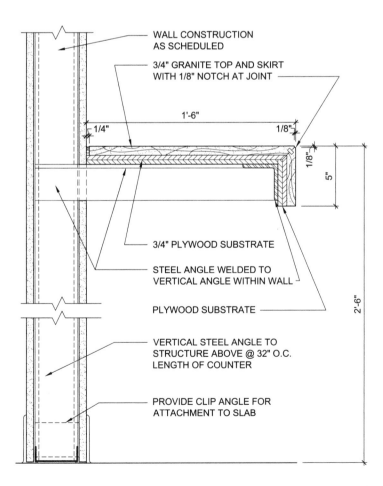

Figure 12-7 Wall-hung granite countertop detail
Reproduced by permission of the publisher from Maryrose McGowan and Kelsey Kruse, *Interior Graphic Standards* (Hoboken, NJ: John Wiley & Sons, Inc.), © 2003 by John Wiley & Sons, Inc.

Table 12-2 Countertop Materials

Material	Appearance	Durability	Maintenance	Cost*	Sustainability
Concrete	Unlimited colors. Exposed aggregate and other objects can be embedded. Nonstructural hairline cracks.	Very durable	Requires sealant to avoid stains. Waxing helps develop soft, burnished glow. Easy to clean.	$60 to 125 per sq ft, plus installation	Heavy; uses energy to transport. Can substitute 30% fly ash for cement to lower embodied energy. Recycles as slab or crushed aggregate.
Metal: copper	Turns rich golden brown with age. Impractical to keep polished bright.	Minimum 1/20 in. thick; prefer 1/16 in., to prevent dents and buckling.	Maintain natural finish with butcher's wax or beeswax. Soft; scratches easily.	$139 per sq ft on substrate, plus installation	Copper has high value as recyclable material. Copper mining is environmentally damaging and energy-intensive.
Metal: stainless steel	Silvery, high-tech.	Very durable and easy to clean. No. 304, government grade.	Scratches easily but marks not noticeable with random-grain finish. Brushed finish shows fingerprints.	$45 to $65 per sq ft	High recycled content available. Attach to substrate with mechanical fasteners. Most health codes require it in commercial kitchens.
Metal: zinc	Classic use in Parisian cafes. Originally shiny surface dulls to soft pewter-gray.	Prefer 1/16 in. to prevent dents and buckling.	Scratches easily but adds to patina. Wax like copper to maintain deep luster.	About $140 per sq ft	Recycles well.
Plastic laminate	Melamine-based color-through laminate eliminates brown edge.	Moderate durability; will scratch.	Easy to clean if stains wiped up quickly. Some finish textures and patterns hide scratches.	$25 to $50 per sq ft	Select recycled plastic, nontoxic glue, formaldehyde-free substrate. Use mechanical fasteners to enable recycling.
Solid surfacing: plastic (Corian)	Variety of colors, some with aggregates.	Very durable. May flex over time. Resists water and stains	Will stain if material dries on. Will scratch; sand scratches out; replace damaged areas with new.	$75 to 150 per linear foot installed.	100% acrylic or acrylic-polyester mix

Material	Appearance	Durability	Maintenance	Cost*	Sustainability
Solid surfacing: paper composite (Richlite)	Limited colors. Pleasant nonshiny surface.	Durable, impact- and heat-resistant. Colors may not be UV stable.	Easy to clean; can be scratched; light colors may show stains.	$50+ per sq ft	May contain high content of recycled paper, low VOC resins. Not recyclable.
Epoxy resin	Clear surface over a greater variety of materials	Extremely durable; resists chemicals well.	Requires skilled application.	Medium cost	Can be used over painted artwork on MDO.
Stone: engineered (Zodiaq, Silestone, Ceasarstone)	No visible seams. Silky texture. Without fissures, veins, or imperfections. Many colors.	Very durable; will not scratch or stain.	Easy to clean.	$110 to $250 per linear foot installed	Best-quality composites are about 90% quartz particles and 10% acrylic or epoxy binder. Those derived from marble or other stones are softer, and may need sealing.
Stone: granite	More than 100 types of granite.	Very durable. Seal every six months to avoid stains.	Easy to clean. Weight may require extra support.	$100 to $150 per linear foot installed	Heavy; select locally quarried materials.
Stone: lavastone (Pyrolave)	Glazed with custom-colored enamel; fired in kiln for glossy, crackled surface.	Extremely hard surface.	Easily maintained.	$260 and up per sq ft	Quarried from natural volcanic lava in France.
Stone: limestone	Honed surface	Porous; stains easily	Acids will dissolve unsealed surface.	$85 to $125 per linear foot	Heavy stone; use local source.
Stone: marble	Veining; polished finish. Cold surface for rolling out pastry.	Acidic foods will etch surface; red wine will stain.	Easy to clean. Weight may require extra support.	Varies widely with type	Heavy; select locally quarried materials. Slabs and crushed stone are recyclable.
Stone: slate and soapstone	Slate gray, black, or green. Soapstone similar but with light striations of quartz.	Scratch and chip easily, especially edges.	Marks can be sanded out or left in. Sealing not necessary. Mineral oil will make them glow.	Slate: $50 to $100 per sq ft Soapstone: approx. $44 per sq. ft.	Found closer to surface; softer stones use less energy to quarry.
Stone: travertine	Small holes must be filled for use.	Heat-resistant. Must be sealed.	Avoid acid stains. Stains can be sanded and resealed.	$4 to $25 per sq ft	Heavy; use locally quarried stone.

(Continued)

Table 12-2 (Continued)

Material	Appearance	Durability	Maintenance	Cost	Sustainability
Terrazzo	Available as tiles or poured-in place.	Very durable; resists stains and burns.	Easy to clean.	$20 to $50 per sq ft for slab	May use recycled aggregate. Epoxy or cement binders. Heavy; uses energy to transport.
Tile: ceramic and porcelain	Handmade tiles are beautiful but may make uneven surface; prefer to use as backsplash.	Very durable; resists stains and burns. Impervious to heat. May be scratched.	Low maintenance, especially with large tiles and tight grout joints. Seal grout.	Ceramic: $10 to $20 per sq ft Porcelain: $5 to $12 and up per sq ft	Select tiles with high recycled content. High embodied energy. Heavy; energy used for transport.
Tile: glass	Wide range of light-catching colors.	Durable, but more practical on backsplash than on countertop. Resists stains and burns.	Large tiles reduce number of grout joints. Seal grout to avoid stains, trapped dirt. Smooth surfaces may scratch.	$15 to $40 per sq ft; more for custom Field tiles, $7 to $16 per sq ft	Tiles often have high recycled content. Heavy; transport uses energy. Sintering process uses less energy than conventional melting. High embodied energy to make tiles.
Wood chopping surfaces: rock maple, oak	Endgrain butcher block is dimensionally stable.	Durable but burns and scratches easily. May harbor bacteria.	Requires regular cleaning and sealing. Remove burns and scratches by sanding.	$50 to $75 per linear foot	Select certified wood. Avoid product laminated with formaldehyde. Recyclable. Low embodied energy, especially if local. Can be mechanically fastened; avoids glue.
Wood: cherry, walnut, mahogany	Beautiful, but need protection. Wide planks may move or warp.	Require care to prevent damage. Avoid moisture.	Keep oiled or sealed and treat gently.	Varies with type and construction details	Select certified wood.
Wood: teak	Rich deep brown.	Natural water-shredding resins	Too dense to use as chopping surface.	Expensive and rising.	Select certified wood.

Figure 12-8 Granite countertop at Greers Seafood, Belmont, Massachusetts.
Photo by Douglas Stefanov. Corky Binggeli Interior Design.

standard eased edge, basic bevel, quarter round, back bevel, bullnose, and ogee. They weigh around 18.75 pounds per square foot, somewhat more than granite. Maximum size depends on structure, shipping, and handling limitations, with standard sizes often limited to 10 feet long or 20 square feet. Larger sizes require seams, which can be filled with clear silicon sealer or used as design elements.

Figure 12-9 Wood butcher block
Courtesy of John Boos + Co., Effingham, Illinois;
www.johnboos.com.

Designers and clients may have to pay fabricators from $25 to $50 for color samples, and more for custom colors. Undermount sink cutouts, drainboards, edge details, patterns, backsplashes, and concrete sink basins all cost extra. The contractor's price typically includes construction, shipping if required, and installation.

The surfaces of concrete countertops are often ground for increased durability and beauty. They are always sealed; epoxy sealers work well for kitchens but are very expensive and take over a week to apply two coats. The only maintenance required is the application of a good water-based liquid wax every nine months to a year.

High-pressure decorative laminate (HPDL), commonly called plastic laminate, is widely used for less expensive countertops in homes and other projects. For light to medium use, plastic laminate wears reasonably well, and comes in a huge selection of continually updated colors and patterns. ANSI A162.2, Performance Standard for Fabricated High-Pressure Laminate Countertops, establishes procedures for using plastic laminate. The plastic laminate is adhered to the substrate with an adhesive. The substrate may be particleboard, which is often preferred for its fine grade and smooth surface. An alternative, exterior-grade plywood, is bonded together with a water-resistant adhesive, and is preferred for wet areas and locations subject to high humidity. (See color plate C-67, Plastic laminate "Boomerang" countertop.)

A backer sheet is installed on the unexposed underside of the substrate to increase dimensional stability and resist warping induced by changes in temperature or humidity. The countertop edge detail should take into consideration the visible dark line of the plastic laminate's edge and the edge quality and workability of the substrate. Plastic laminate edge strips often peel off or break under continued use. Metal or wood edges are more durable, and wood can be refinished as it wears. (See color plate C-69, Curved plastic laminate countertop.)

Color-through laminates are high-pressure decorative laminate sheets in solid colors, without a brown Kraft paper core visible along cut edges. Color-through laminates are available from 0.05 to 0.06 inch (1.3 to 1.5 mm) thick. They have a high melamine resin content, and may buckle with temperature and humidity changes.

Postformed plastic laminate countertops are factory-produced with a single thin sheet of laminate, curved and glued over medium-density fiberboard or other substrate. The base material is shaped to provide an integrated front edge, work surface, and

Figure 12-11 Resin and glass countertop. This countertop is made with recycled glass. Photo by Emily Michot. Courtesy of EnviroGLAS.

backsplash, and on the job site need only be cut to length before installation. Factory-made miter-cut pieces are also available for inside corners.

Solid surfacing materials are known primarily by their trade names, among them DuPont's Corian, Wilsonart's Gibraltar, Nevamar, and Fountainhead. They offer uniformity of pattern and color, and can be cut like wood to many edge forms. Solid surfacing is available as counters with integral sinks, eliminating the seam between sink and counter. It is, unfortunately, not heatproof and can be damaged by a hot pan, as well as by materials containing acetate. It also is generally expensive to fabricate and install, although prefabricated countertops are available at more modest prices.

Solid surface materials are usually prefabricated at the installer's shop and then assembled on-site. The plastic material is glued, and the glue joints are sanded, leaving almost no visible trace of the joint. The edge treatment for solid-surface countertops can be very elaborate. The material itself is usually only about 1/2 inch (13 mm) thick; a built-up edge is usually created by stacking up two or three layers of the material, shaped to a rounded edge, or ogee. Fancier edge treatments are, of course, more expensive.

Engineered stone surfacing is made from natural quartz and held together with a plastic resin, making it nonporous and scratch-resistant. Manufactured under trade names such as Silestone and Zodiaq, it is stain-, abrasion-, and impact-resistant and does not require sealing. As with solid surface countertopping, the materials are prefabricated and installed by professionals. Thicknesses may be 3/4 inch (2 cm), 1–1/4 inches (3 cm), or 1–1/2 inches (4 cm).

Like engineered stone, terrazzo provides a very durable countertop surface. Terrazzo countertops are made with recycled glass particles for aggregates in a resin matrix.

Tile countertops are durable and colorful. The tiles chosen need to be flat and evenly set to keep a surface even enough for dishes and glassware. The grout lines should be as thin as feasible, and sealed to prevent accumulation of moisture and dirt. Tiles with irregular surfaces, such as most glass mosaic tiles or those with relief designs, are best used for backsplashes. (See color plate C-70, Tile countertop.)

Epoxy resin is an extremely durable finish that resists chemicals well. The resin requires skilled application for a smooth, thin finish, adding to its expense. However, it is an excellent material for use in laboratories and as a finish for restaurant tables and bartops, sealing and protecting an almost unlimited variety of materials under its clear surface.

Sink Installation

Self-rimming sinks sit in holes cut in the countertop (or substrate material) and are suspended by their rim. The rim forms a fairly close seal with the top surface of the countertop, especially when the sink is clamped into the hole from below.

Most materials, other than plastic laminate, also allow the installation of a bottom-mount or undermount sink. With these, the carefully finished edge of the countertop material is exposed at the hole created for the sink. The sink is then mounted to the bottom of the material from below. Silicone-based sealants are usually used to assure a waterproof joint between the sink and the countertop material. Undermount installations are more expensive than self-rimming sinks.

There are several standard edge details that are used on wood, stone, engineered stone, and solid surfacing countertops. The edge is often made thicker than the horizontal surface of the counter, usually by building up layers of material, so that the edge profile's proportions work well with the overall design.

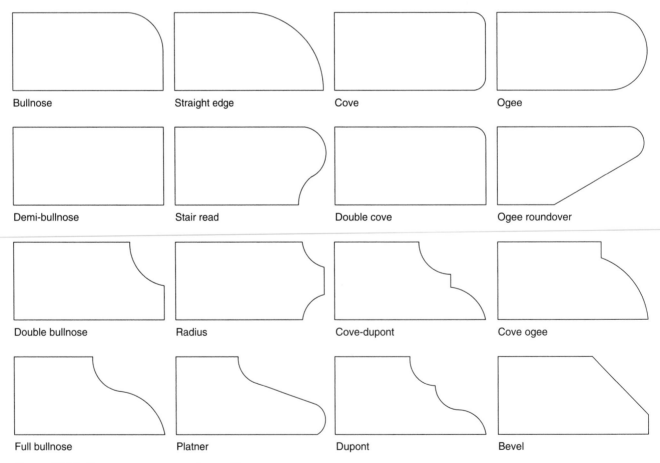

Figure 12-12 Common countertop edge profiles
Reproduced by permission of the publisher from Maryrose McGowan and Kelsey Kruse, *Interior Graphic Standards* (Hoboken, NJ: John Wiley & Sons, Inc.), © 2003 by John Wiley & Sons, Inc.

Toilet partitions can be designed and made from any solid material that will preserve privacy, permit sanitary maintenance, and endure the almost inevitable abuse. Wood, stone, and other materials have all been used to build toilet room stalls. The majority of toilet partitions are manufactured, rather than custom-built, and are ordered as prefinished parts that are assembled to fit the space. Table 12.3 compares the most common materials.

Table 12-3 Toilet Partition Comparisons

Material	Appearance	Durability	Cost	Maintenance
Color-through phenolic	Available in all styles and attractive colors. Color consistent throughout product	Impact-, scratch-, and graffiti-resistant; also has excellent screw-holding power	More expensive than baked enamel on steel	Scratches can be sanded out.
Phenolic black core	Full-color spectrum with black edges	Withstands severe moisture conditions from showers, pools, and saunas. Resists vandalism.	More expensive than baked enamel on steel	Clean with a mild liquid soap, then wipe and dry.
Phenolic core; melamine finish	Black or brown core is exposed on edges and when the material is damaged by scratches.	Resists damage from moisture, impacts, chemicals, urine, stains, and abrasion.	More expensive than baked enamel on steel	Remove slight scruffs, scratches, and graffiti with abrasive pad, then 1000-grit sandpaper.
Plastic laminate on particleboard	Wide variety of colors and textures. Plastic laminate can be pried off the particleboard core.	Resistant to acids, alkalis, and stains if removed promptly. Resists abrasion; can be scratched.	Costs slightly more than baked enamel on steel	Clean with mild liquid soap, then wipe dry. Prolonged moisture or high humidity can cause delamination.
Baked enamel finish on steel	Broad range of colors	Highly resistant to corrosion, grease, acids, caustics, mars, and stains. Resists wear, fading, staining, scratching, and scuffing	Economical	Easily cleaned with mild soap; wipe dry.
Solid polymer: high-density polyethylene (HDPE) or polypropylene (PP)	Offered in a wide variety of contemporary colors.	Resists moisture and impact damage well, as well as marks and stains; nearly graffitiproof. High temperatures may cause warping.	Similar to phenolic core partitions	Panels will support combustion. Fire dangers can be reduced by the addition of metal heat-sink strips. Clean with mild liquid soap, then wipe dry.
Stainless steel: Type 304 stainless steel	Satin or textured finish.	Impervious to just about any substance.	Higher cost	Easily maintained; scratches can be buffed out.

DEMOUNTABLE PARTITIONS AND OFFICE SYSTEMS

Offices and other facilities with frequent layout changes use *demountable partitions* to create divisions within larger spaces. Designed to be easily installed and taken apart, demountable partitions provide some, but not a great deal of, sound isolation and visual privacy. Surfaces are often covered with vinyl wallcovering, although other fabrics and finishes are sometimes used.

FURNITURE MATERIALS

Ash, cherry, maple, oak, pecan, teak, rosewood, walnut, mahogany, and poplar are all used to make furniture. In the softwood category are cedar, cypress, fir, pine, and redwood. Several different woods may be used in the same piece of furniture. For example, the term "solid cherry" or "solid mahogany" means that all exposed parts of the piece are made of solid wood. The frame or other parts not visible to the eye might be of another wood such as gum or poplar.

Furniture is often veneered with an attractive and carefully selected wood over a utilitarian wood or wood composite base. The process of applying veneer to good-quality furniture is labor-intensive and requires a high level of skill.

 Note: The furniture/wood manufacturing and refinishing industry uses many solvents. Many wastes generated from the use of paints, wood treatments, stains, varnishes, polishes, and adhesives may be ignitable or may fail the Toxicity Characteristic Leaching Procedure (TCLP) test. Sawmills and planing mills may generate wastewaters that fail the TCLP test.

Casters help preserve floor surfaces. When specifying office chair casters, designers have a choice between nylon or rubber, and hard or soft casters. Hard casters with slightly rounded wheel edges are preferred for spaces with carpet or carpet tile. Soft casters are usually matched to either hard or resilient flooring materials, where the extra friction helps control chair roll. Hard rubber casters are more likely to leave marks on carpet than plastic casters.

Wood Bonds for Furniture

Because trees don't grow in the shapes and sizes required for making furniture, pieces of wood are bonded together in different ways to achieve the necessary sizes and shapes. Four types of bonding are often used:

- Wide boards cut into long narrower planks and bonded back together. In solid wood furniture, strips are carefully glued together to form the tops, sides, and door panels. The interior may be of another wood.
- Shaping is achieved by gluing blocks of wood together. These blocks can be machined for a deep carved pattern or turned and shaped into a leg, pedestal, or post.
- Combination wood panels are made by mixing wood particles, chips, or flakes with resins and binding agents formed under extreme heat and tremendous pressure. These are exceptionally strong, stable, and resistant to warping. Called chipboard, particleboard, fiberboard or engineered wood, they are used on the backs of cabinets and doors or as cores for tops and panels.
- Ply construction is achieved by adding layers, placed at cross grain, to a solid wood or particleboard core. Adhesives are placed on each layer and permanently bonded under high pressure. This type of bond is very strong and resistant to warping.

Table 12-4 Furniture Materials Compared

Material	Finish Layer	Durability	Maintenance	Sustainability	Cost
Medium-density fiberboard (MDF)	Laminates or wood veneers	Moderate	Easy to clean with soft cloth.	May use recycled material.	Low; reasonably light to ship.
Solid wood: oak, maple, cherry hardwoods. Select pine.	Strong, protective finishes	Durable, strong, wears well, constructed with dovetailed joints, wood drawer glides	Varies with finish. Furniture wax, buffing	Specify certified wood.	High for same wood on exposed areas throughout; medium for mixed woods.
Rubberwood (para-wood, tropical hardwood)	Strong, protective finishes	Durable, strong	Varies with finish. Furniture wax, buffing	Trees formerly used for latex production harvested at end of life.	Up to 40% less than other hardwoods
Wicker: rattan, reed, willow, bamboo	Clear varnish, shellac, lacquer, or paint. Apply thin layer of liquid wax.	Indoor heat dries; cracks wicker. Avoid rain, direct sun, dew.	Prefers humidity; wipe with damp sponge. Vacuum, brush, dry suds. Do not wet. Use seat pads.	Renewable resource	Inexpensive material, cost varies with labor and design.
Metals	Anodized (for aluminum), brass- and chrome-plated, plastic, painted finishes	Very durable, but steel and wrought iron may be heavy.	Minimal	See individual materials in Chapter 7.	Medium
Synthetic materials	Plastics, foams	Most are very durable.	Minimal	Petrochemicals. Durability means longer life.	Low

An appropriate finish adds to the beauty and protection of wood furniture. A protective finish generally requires the application of several coats of oil, wax, lacquer, or paint to the surface. Clear finishes allow the markings and grain variations of naturally beautiful woods to show through. Tinted or opaque finishes change the color of the wood and can make two different woods appear to be the same. Finishes can vary the look of a piece, making it appear smooth and sophisticated or rough-hewn or rustic. Distressing is a technique for aging new furniture by beating or battering it before the finish is applied. Painted pieces show every flaw, and can be more expensive than those with natural finishes.

The *joins*—places where two pieces of wood connect—determine whether a piece will stand firm and strong, or wobble with use and age. In a piece of quality furniture,

Table 12-5 Decorative Finishes for Wood Furniture

Process	Appearance	Uses	Material Preparation
Stripping	Removes all old finish.	Before refinishing	Sand as smooth as possible before applying any finish.
Bleaching	Lightens wood's natural color.	Removes undesirable stains.	Commercial wood bleach
Staining	Colors the wood and emphasizes its grain.	Makes one type of wood look like another to create uniform color in a piece that is made up of more than one kind of wood, or to tint patched areas to match the rest of the piece.	Penetrating resin stain. Pigmented oil or wiping stains. Used only over bare, smoothly sanded, clean, dry wood.
Paste wood fillers	Fills pores in wood for smooth finish.	Open-pore woods, such as walnut, oak, and mahogany.	Available in colors or tint with pigment.
Linseed oil	Mellow luster	On bare sanded wood.	Will withstand hot dishes, but not water-resistant.
Enameling	Wide range of gloss levels; many colors.	Inexpensive unpainted furniture, children's furniture.	Oil-base enamel paint better for furniture than latex. Over bare or painted wood.
Milk paints (See color plate C-72, Milk paint on corner cupboard.)	Country colors.	Antiqued, patina, ragged, or rolled finishes. Use as stains or paints.	Premixed paints made with acrylics, in cans. Authentic milk paint with casein does not keep.
Distressing	Wood is marked to mimic signs of use.	Usually sanded. May use hammers, nails, screws, old hardware.	Apply flat coat, dry, then paste wax. Apply glaze, sand within 24 hours.
Antiquing (See color plate C-71 Wood finishes on chest.)	Simulates signs of slight wear on raised panels and moldings.	Sanding combined with glazing or two colors of paint.	Apply white pickling glaze, then wood stain
Glazing	Puts a wash of translucent color over base color.	Translucent color applied to surface then rubbed off.	Sponging applies glaze with damp sea sponge or soft cloth.
Strié or dragging	Fine lines in glaze reveal base color underneath.	Dry (brush) is dragged through glaze.	Glaze applied with small roller over base coat.
Wet color blending (See color plate C-74, Custom painted wall and C-73, Paint finish on wood.)	Subtle variations in color; soft natural glow	Blend colors smoothly.	Apply second coat of water-based stain/paint to wet first coat, brush out with dry bristle brush

wherever two or more pieces of wood join, the grains should match up. Corner blocks, triangular wood blocks that are cut to fit corners and then glued or screwed into place, should be used to further secure weight-bearing joints, especially those found in chairs.

Wicker furniture is made from a variety of materials, including willow and rattan. Well-made wicker furniture is relatively sturdy, but requires protection from the elements. Wicker-style pieces are now being made in nearly indestructible resin.

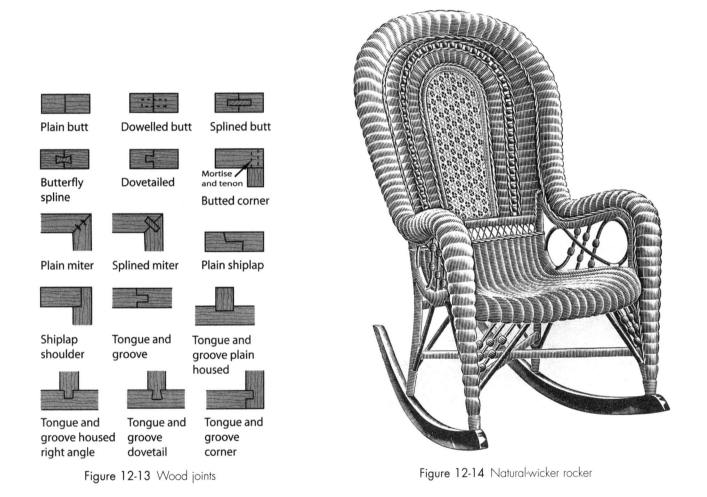

Plain butt   Dowelled butt   Splined butt

Butterfly spline   Dovetailed   Mortise and tenon / Butted corner

Plain miter   Splined miter   Plain shiplap

Shiplap shoulder   Tongue and groove   Tongue and groove plain housed

Tongue and groove housed right angle   Tongue and groove dovetail   Tongue and groove corner

Figure 12-13 Wood joints

Figure 12-14 Natural-wicker rocker

The invention of upholstery inaugurated a new era of comfort in furniture. The principal components of upholstered furniture are the frame, the suspension system, the cushions, and the upholstery material. The workmanship in upholstered furniture is often hidden, making it difficult to judge quality and durability.

UPHOLSTERED FURNITURE

Figure 12-15 Chair frame detail
Photo by Edward Addeo
Courtesy of Donghia

The frame provides the structure and form for an upholstered piece. Frames of kiln-dried hardwood resist warping and shrinkage. The use of *mortise-and-tenon* and *double-doweled joints* provides the most durable assembly, but screws, nails, staples, and glue are also used. Seat joints are reinforced, and corner blocks are glued or screwed into place for added strength. The exposed portions of a frame are machine-sanded and, for the finest furniture, hand-sanded to a smooth, flawless surface.

Manufacturers may apply a stain to a sanded wood frame to check for scratches; this prestained surface must be completely sanded off before a final stain is hand-applied. Sealer is then applied, followed by the finish coats. Catalyzed urethane is an extremely hard finish for fine wood furniture; it is water-, alcohol-, and scratch-resistant. A piece may be sanded between coats of finish to raise the wood's grain and improve the finish's adhesion. Coil, flat, and S-shaped springs are used for furniture seats and backs. Flat and S-shaped springs are used with metal, rubber, or plastic webbing to minimize bulk. Coils attached to steel bands or webbing and tied together at their tops, to resist

Figure 12-16 Chair springs. S-shaped springs give support to the chair back. Coil springs in the seat are hand-tied in complex patterns for solid support.
Photo by Edward Addeo
Courtesy of Donghia

twisting and interlocking, take up more room than flat springs. Marshall or innerspring units contain springs within individual pockets of muslin or burlap, and the units are joined together, ready for use.

The cushioning of upholstered pieces is supported by springs that add resilience.

Webbing systems are most often used to support the upholstery of commercial seating. Sagless or sinuous springs zigzag across a frame, connected by small, coiled springs. Rubberized woven decking can also be stretched tightly across a frame and stapled in place to provide a firm, resilient cushion support. Interwoven webbing tape of jute, cotton, or rubber can be used either to support cushions directly or to support spring systems. Corrugated steel bands are often used to support coil springs; plastic-covered wire mesh grids are a less expensive alternative.

Cushions and padding are layered over springs to aid comfort and appearance. A sheet of burlap is usually placed between the springs and the cushioning materials to keep them apart. Cushioning may be made from feathers, down, cellular foams (especially polyurethanes), polyester fiberfill, or combinations of these.

Polyurethane is often the first choice for upholstered furniture cushions. The durability and support provided by polyurethane foam is dependent on its density. Foam density is a measurement of the foam's mass per unit of volume, in pounds per cubic foot or kilograms per cubic meter. Density does not directly correlate with softness, and high-density foam can still be quite soft. High-density foam is often more expensive than lower-density foam. By bonding together multiple layers of foams of varied grades and densities, the cushion can be customized to the desired softness or firmness.

Polyurethane foam specifications may refer to *indentation force deflection* (IFD), a measure of the amount of force needed to indent the surface of a foam sample 25 percent of its thickness. The *compression modulus* is a measure of the quality of support, and is usually due to the type of foam used.

Polyurethane foam used in cushions and upholstered furniture emits toluene diisocyanate (TDI) and phenol, with emissions decreasing over time. Other chemicals have replaced chlorofluorocarbons (CFCs) for upholstery foams and insulating foams. One type of replacement, known as HCFC, is considered a greenhouse gas.

Upholstered furniture coverings are either permanently attached to the piece or removable for cleaning. Upholstery fabrics should be selected to withstand the normal wear of their intended use. Commercial-grade fabrics are labeled for wear, sun sensitivity, and fire resistance.

Designers purchase upholstery fabrics from the furniture manufacturer or specify them as *customer's own material* (COM) or *customer's own leather* (COL) purchased from a textile manufacturer. The furniture manufacturer's written approval is usually required to verify that an upholstery fabric order is acceptable. The "customer" in question is always whoever places the order with the manufacturer—not necessarily the end user. Ordinarily, it is either the furniture dealer or the interior designer. The fabric for reupholstered projects may be ordered by the upholsterer (to the designer's specification) or by the interior designer, for delivery to the upholsterer. Material sometimes varies from the standard 54 inches (137 cm) width.

Fabrics are traditionally applied to upholstered pieces running vertically from top to bottom, a *run-right*, or *up-the-bolt application*. This limits the width of materials available without a seam, and may waste fabric when laid out on some pieces. However, up-the-bolt application is required for fabrics with dominant directional designs that must be run vertically.

Railroad application often requires less fabric. The cushions are upholstered side to side with the *selvage* (side) edges of the fabric parallel to the seat cushion edge. Some fabrics accommodate both up-the-bolt and railroad application, while others must be used specifically with one or the other. The interior designer must specify which application is to be used.

For fabrics with large patterns, the design should be centered on each seat and back cushion and continue down the seat front and sides. Fabrics with a repeating pattern (*repeat*) or manufactured in narrower widths require more yardage.

Upholstered furniture can be reupholstered when worn, although this is usually only justified when the piece is an antique or has a unique value, or when it can be done for significantly less than the cost of a replacement. Slipcovers made of washable, tightly woven fabric can cover wear, and can be changed seasonally or replaced inexpensively for a new look.

TEXTILES

Textiles cover systems furniture panels and serve as stretched dividers. Draperies, shades, and blinds all utilize textiles to provide shade, warmth, and privacy with flexibility. Manufactured furniture, custom-upholstered pieces, and reupholstered and slip-covered furniture all use fabrics. Leather is also used as an upholstery material and finish material for fabric.

The term *textile* applies not only to woven fabrics, but more generally to a fiber, yarn, or fabric, or a product made from one of them.

- A *fiber* is an elongated, stringy, man-made, or natural material.
- *Fabric* can be rather loosely described as an artifact made by weaving, felting, knitting, or crocheting natural or synthetic fibers.
- *Yarn* is an assemblage of fibers twisted or laid together to form a continuous strand that can be made into a textile. Simple yarns are uniform in diameter throughout their length and may be made of a single yarn strand or of several pieces of

Figure 12-17 Leather desktop

yarn twisted together. Yarns can also be made with loops, curls, or irregular textures for tactile and visual interest. Yarns are sold by weight and classified by the relationship between their length and weight.

Textiles are evaluated for a variety of characteristics that affect their suitability for use in interior applications. A textile's durability includes its abrasion resistance, which is related to flexibility. *Tenacity* is tensile strength, and depends on whether the textile is wet or dry. *Elongation* is the degree to which the textile can stretch without breaking.

Fabric absorbency is categorized as *hydrophilic* ("water-loving"), *hydrophobic* ("water-fearing"), or *hygroscopic* (having the ability to absorb moisture without feeling wet). Moisture absorption helps control static buildup.

Resiliency is a textile's ability to return to its original shape after being bent, twisted, or crushed. Dimensional stability, shrinkage resistance, and elasticity are other important qualities. A textile's resistance to chemicals and light affects how it can be cleaned and its ability to be used as a window treatment.

Textile Selection

Textiles are selected based on many factors: their aesthetics, durability, comfort, safety, how well they retain their appearance, what is involved in their maintenance, the impact their manufacture and disposal have on the environment, and their cost. The desired appearance of a fabric depends on both its intended use and the preferences of the user. Textiles affect the transfer of heat, air, and moisture. The human body interacts with a textile: it is felt as well as seen. Its absorbency and temperature-regulation properties are important to comfort.

The way a fabric feels and hangs is as important as how it looks. *Hand*, or drapeability, refers to how a fabric hangs. A fabric's hand is affected by the type of fiber and yarn it is made of and how it is constructed. The scale of any pattern, whether woven or printed, will affect how the fabric can be used. An interior designer must calculate how much extra fabric to order for large-scale designs with a long repeat.

The ability of a fabric to retain its original appearance during use and care affects how long it will last. Commercial fabrics are rated for wrinkling, shrinkage, abrasion, soiling, stretching, pilling, sagging, and fading. Some fabrics need to be treated to preserve their appearance and resist dirt. The type, cost, and amount of care needed affect the practicality and life-cycle cost of a fabric.

Most of the fabrics specified for interior design projects are selected from a fabric manufacturer's standard line, which is usually available in various patterns and colors. A *colorway* is a group of products from a manufacturer grouped by color. When specifying furniture coverings, interior designers may select from a manufacturer's standard fabrics or specify a fabric of their own selection. In the latter case, the fabric is called the customer's own fabric (COM), and may involve additional charges and require special approval for use in public spaces. Interior designers sometimes request custom fabrics, which are modified from an existing product and manufactured for a specific project. Custom fabrics take extra time and effort to manufacture, and must usually be ordered in minimum quantities.

The production, use, care, and disposal of textiles—and products used in their manufacture—can have a significant negative effect on the environment. Care recommendations may also be problematic. Some fabrics can be recycled or will decompose naturally. Others are made using recycled materials. Therefore, interior designers must consider the textile's environmental impact on raw material sources during manufacturing, in transport, in use, and at the end of its useful life. The life-cycle cost of a fabric includes its initial purchase price; any treatment added to it; its transformation into a final form, such as upholstery or drapery; and maintenance costs, disposal, and replacement.

Textile Appearance

Although functional factors such as durability determine the suitability of a fabric for a specific use, fabrics are often selected and appreciated for their aesthetic qualities. The way that light waves break and reflect on the surface of a fabric is referred to as its *luster*. The preservation of a fabric's appearance depends on performance factors, including whether it begins to lose its luster, or frays, or changes color. A fabric's hand and the degree to which it attracts lint also affect how a fabric looks and feels.

Silk is a lustrous fabric, as compared to wool's texture, which diffuses reflected light. Fabric construction and finishing affects a fabric's luster, so that plain-woven cotton may be relatively unreflective, but with special finishes has the luster of chintz. Many fabrics will release fiber ends that become surface fuzz. Angora yarn is delightfully soft and fuzzy.

Figure 12-18 Luster of silk

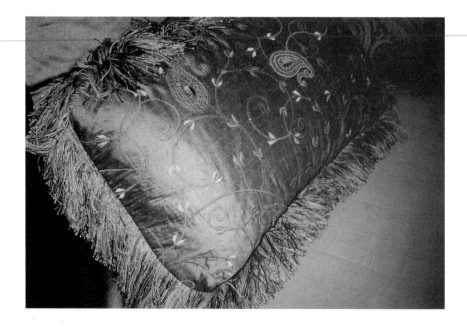

Pilling occurs when long, tough fibers roll into little balls that stay attached to the fabric's surface. Some fabrics attract dust, thread, hair, and lint through static electricity. Nonabsorbent materials are especially likely to cling to these fabrics.

Many fabrics fade when exposed to the sun's ultraviolet rays, while others are damaged by artificial light or air pollution. Some dyes can be displaced through rubbing or wear, a problem called *crocking*. Cleaning agents can cause color loss. Designers check on this by referring to the manufacturer for information or by testing a sample.

Any process that is used to add color and to augment the performance of unfinished fabric is referred as *finishing*. *Gray goods* (also called grey goods, greige goods, and loom-state goods) are fabrics of any color produced without any finish. Converted or finished goods are those that have been treated by bleaching, dyeing, or embossing. Mill-finished fabrics are sold and used without further treatment.

Textile Fibers

A fiber is any substance—natural or manufactured—with a high enough length-to-width ratio that it can be processed into fabric. The smallest hairlike component that can be separated from a fabric is a fiber. Fiber properties include abrasion resistance, cohesiveness, drape, luster, *feltability* (its ability to mat together), and *loft* (its compression resilience, or ability to spring back to its original thickness).

Fiber length varies from less than an inch to several miles. Longer fibers are, in general, stronger. Strong fibers help to make strong, abrasion-resistant textiles. They may be smooth, like silk fiber, or bulked or crimped, like cotton and wool fibers. The choice of a fiber affects a textile's appearance, durability, comfort, appearance retention, care, environmental impact, and cost. Fiber availability and supply affect whether a specified product will be available on schedule.

Large-diameter fibers are crisp, rough, and stiff, and resist crushing. Fine fibers are soft and pliable, and drape well. Fineness is a sign of manufacturing quality, and fibers should be uniformly thick or thin. Fineness is measured in *denier*, or *tex*. Denier is the fiber's weight in grams per 9,000 meters of fiber or yarn. A smaller denier number indicates a finer fabric. Tex is the fiber's weight in grams per 100 meters of fiber or yarn.

Fibers are classed as either staple or filament fibers. All natural fibers except silk are staple fibers. Natural fibers are not uniform and are generally short. Filament fibers, including silk and synthetic fibers, are long, continuous, and generally stronger than staple fibers; they can be cut to staple fiber lengths. Fibers may either be made of single filaments (*monofilament*) or many filaments (*multifilament*).

Textile Fiber Sources

Fiber sources are considered to be either synthetic or natural. Synthetic fibers are derived from natural resources such as wood or petroleum, but require industrial processing to achieve a usable fiber form. Fibers are further categorized as cellulosic, protein, or mineral fibers.

Cellulosic fibers are derived from plant sources. Linen is a natural cellulosic fiber that is made from the flax plant. Cellulosic fibers from wood and cotton are also processed into the synthetic fibers rayon, acetate, and triacetate.

Fibers from animal sources are referred to as *protein fibers*. Silk is made from the material secreted by the silk moth larva for its cocoon. Sheep, Angora goats, cashmere goats, Bactrian camels, alpacas, llamas, and vicuñas produce wool, mohair, cashmere, camel's hair, alpaca, llama, and vicuña fibers, respectively. Angora yarn is spun from the soft hair combed from Angora rabbits. Horsehair, a popular fiber in Victorian times, is made from the manes and tails of horses.

In addition to cellulosic and protein fibers, there are mineral fibers and elastomers. *Mineral fibers* include natural asbestos fibers from rocks, as well as man-made glass and metallic fibers. Rubber is considered an *elastomer* and is derived either naturally from rubber tree sap or manufactured from chemicals resulting in synthetic rubber, spandex, and other fabrics.

Synthesized man-made fibers are manufactured polymers derived from petroleum or natural gas. They include acrylic, aramid, modacrylic, nylon, olefin, polyester, saran, vinyl, and vinyon. Table 12-6 has a more complete listing of fibers.

Natural Cellulosic Fibers

Cotton fibers are fairly uniform and dimensionally stable when compared with other natural fibers. Cotton fibers wick away moisture along their length. Because cotton is not inherently flame-resistant and wrinkles easily, it is often treated when used in commercial interiors.

- *Organic cotton* must meet state-certified standards and be grown with no synthetic or chemical pesticides or fertilizers.
- *Transitional cotton* is similar, but is grown on land that has been organically farmed for fewer than three years.
- *Green cotton* is washed with mild soap and not bleached, although some dyes may be used.
- Everything else is called *conventional cotton*.

Long-staple cotton has added luster. Mercerized and ammonia-treated fabrics have a soft, pleasant, lustrous finish. Cotton sateen gets its luster from the fabric structure and finish. Batiste is soft and sheer, and voile is a crisp, sheer white.

Linen was widely made from flax in ancient Egypt, and is still popular today. Linen's strength and durability, as well as its comfort and beauty, make it suitable for use in interiors.

Ramie is an exceptionally strong fiber. It is stiff, inelastic, and brittle; therefore, it is often blended with softer fibers, including cotton and rayon. Ramie has been used in China for several thousand years and is now produced in China, the Philippines, and Brazil.

Hemp is as old as flax. It is produced in China, the Philippines, Italy, France, Chile, Russia, Poland, and India. Hemp is produced from a variety of the *Cannabis sativa* plant, another variety of which is used to produce marijuana and hashish. *Cannabis sativa* is considered a controlled substance in the United States and its commercial production is banned.

Figure 12-19 The strength and durability of linen make it appropriate for many uses, despite its tendency to wrinkle.

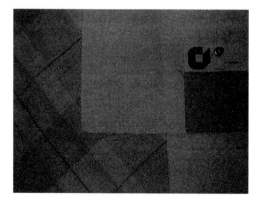

Table 12-6 Textile Fiber Comparisons

Fiber Type	Fiber Name	Varieties	Characteristics	Interior Uses
Cellulosic	Cotton	Organic cotton Long-staple cotton Cotton sateen Batiste	Easy to finish and dye. Naturally comfortable and attractive, durable, and spot cleanable; retains appearance well. Cotton fiber blends well with both natural and synthetic fibers. Low elasticity and resilience, and very dense.	Draperies, curtains, upholstery fabrics, slip covers, rugs, and wallcoverings
	Linen		Extremely strong and does not fray or produce lint. Mildew-resistant and dimensionally stable. Less absorbent than cotton and usually not as soft. Creases and wrinkles easily.	Window treatments, and bed, table, and bath items Upholstery fabrics must be steam-cleaned carefully to avoid shrinkage. Linen wallcoverings are woven up to 10 ft (3 m) wide, with a desirable irregular texture that masks the flaws in a wall's surface.
	Ramie (China grass, grasscloth)		Silk-like luster. Finely textured ramie fabrics resemble linen, and heavier textiles are similar to canvas.	Window treatments, pillows, and table linens
	Hemp		Naturally creamy white, brown, gray, green, or nearly black.	Household accessories
	Silk Tasar, wild silk from India Tussah, a dark, coarse wild silk	Wild silk fiber is brown, yellow, green, and orange. Dupioni silk's irregular, thick-and-thin fiber is used in linenlike silk fabrics such as shantung.	Fabrics range from sheer gossamer chiffons to heavy brocades and velvets. Strongest natural fiber. Resists wrinkles and tolerates cleaning solvents, but deteriorates under sunlight's ultraviolet radiation. Moderately abrasion-resistant. Dupioni silk is produced when two silkworms spin their cocoons together.	Upholstery, wallcoverings, and wall hangings; sheets and blankets The natural texture of wild and dupioni silks make good coverings for ceilings and walls. Window treatments and upholstery fabrics have a soft luster and drape.
	Jute	Burlap or hessian fabric	Weak creamy white to brown fiber	Carpet backing, window treatments, wall coverings, and area rugs.

(Continued)

Table 12-6 (Continued)

Fiber Type	Fiber Name	Varieties	Characteristics	Interior Uses
Natural protein fibers	Wool and wool blends	Virgin wool Ordinary wool Recycled wool Mohair	Durable; retain their aesthetic appeal, and are naturally flame-resistant. Wool from domesticated sheep is resilient, elastic, and flexible	Upholstery textiles, carpets Mohair: sound-absorbing drapery
Synthetic fibers	Nylon	Microfibers Wool blends	One of the strongest synthetic fibers, with good elasticity. Has low absorbency and dries quickly, but may build up static electrical charges. Nylon retains its appearance and shape during care; resists wrinkling as well as mold, mildew, rot, and many chemicals.	Carpets and commercial upholstery fabrics
	Polyester	Microfibers Cotton blends	Strong and resilient; abrasion-, moisture-, and wrinkle-resistant. Also has excellent dimensional stability. Easy to maintain, but pills.	Microfibers: Quilts, bedspreads, blankets, and padding for furniture, futons, mattresses, and fiberfill. Cotton blends: Used for sheets, blankets, sheer curtains, drapes, mattress ticking, and table linens. Nonwoven polyester fabrics used for interfacings and interlinings, and as base fabrics for coatings and laminates. Wallcoverings and upholstery.
	Olefin		Lightweight and elastic, and resists stains and crushing. Durable, strong, abrasion-resistant, inexpensive, chemically inert, thermoplastic, and static-resistant. Usually shrink-resistant, but when heated, it will shrink and melt. Air-dries quickly when washed; dry-cleaning is not recommended. Oily stains can be hard to remove.	Used alone or blended for upholstery, drapes, and slipcovers. It offers an inexpensive alternative for fabric wallcoverings. Also used for nonwoven furniture webbing and antimicrobial, antifungal woven mattress covers.

Fiber Type	Fiber Name	Varieties	Characteristics	Interior Uses
	Acetate	Cotton blends Satins Brocades Taffetas	Flexible, and produces fabric that drapes well. Thermoplastic fiber is easily damaged by heat; wrinkles easily.	Carpets, draperies, window treatment interlining, pillow fillings
	Rayon	Viscose rayon	Absorbent and dyes well. Can resemble cotton, linen, silk, or wool. Not very strong when dry and even weaker when wet; not very resilient, and wrinkles easily. Silverfish and mildew can damage it.	Drapery and upholstery
	Vinyl (polyvinyl chloride, vinyon)	Simulated leather and suede. Vinyl-coated mesh fabrics have a small-scale open-weave design that allows air to pass through. Vinyl-coated polyester fabrics are made by coating a polyester scrim with liquid vinyl, and then curing with heat.	Additives to the vinyl coating offer color, flame retardance, and resistance to ultraviolet light, water, and mildew. Acrylic-coated polyester is dimensionally stable and available in a wide range of colors. Because it accepts silk-screen printing, appliqué, and handpainting, it can be used for a wide range of aesthetic purposes.	Lightweight nylon banner fabrics are translucent and drape well, while heavier nylon is used for outdoor applications. Nylon colors can be blended, and the fabric accepts printing, appliqué, handpainting, and vinyl film applications.
	Acrylic		Exceptionally light and bulky, and blends with other fibers. Accepts dyes well and can be made to look like wool and feel like silk; but when abraded, the long fibers in acrylic fabrics tend to pill. Has good durability and stain resistance.	Fluffy, wool-like insulating material. makes it attractive for upholstery fabrics and for wool-like flat weaves or velvets. Some acrylic drapery fabrics resist sunlight and weathering.
	Modacrylic		Flame-retardant, strong, warm, soft, and resilient, but less durable than acrylic, and may pill. Does not readily absorb water and is flame-retardant without being dense, so fluffy fabrics remain lightweight. Retains color well and resists acids, weak alkalis, and most organic solvents. Resists moths, mold, sunlight, and flames.	Modacrylics are used for outdoor fabrics, awnings, and in marine applications, as well as for upholstery, window treatments, and blankets, and to make fake fur.

(Continued)

Table 12-6 (Continued)

Fiber Type	Fiber Name	Varieties	Characteristics	Interior Uses
	Lyocell		Opaque, absorbent, durable, and strong (both wet and dry), and has a soft, fluid drape. Blends with wool, cotton, and manu-factured fibers. May fuzz when abraded, and will wrinkle, but not as much as rayon. Subject to mildew and some insect damage.	Upholstery and window treatment fabrics
	Polybenzimidazole, or PBI		Aromatic, polymer-based manufactured fiber that neither melts nor burns, and remains intact and supple even when charred.	Upholstery, window treatment fabrics, and car-pets for aircrafts, hospitals, and submarines
	Aramid		Strong, fire-resistant, virtually impervious to alkalis, acids, and solvents. Has no melting point, does not burn easily, and maintains good integrity even at elevated temperatures. May degrade when exposed to sunlight, and sensitive to moisture and salts.	Liners under upholstery fabrics to protect furni-ture from fire
Metallic fibers	Gold, silver, and aluminum		Weak and soft; often made stronger with a core fiber. Aluminum fibers can be coated and colored.	Upholstery fabrics, stainless steel fibers in conductive carpets
Elastomeric fibers		Latex Spandex Elastoester	Stretch to over twice their original length and return quickly to their original shape.	New uses include microbead pillows, uphol-stery, door panel fabrics, bed bottom sheets
Textiles with integrated sensors	Photochromic tex-tiles become dark when exposed to light and can be made clear again by removing the light source or exposing them to light of another wavelength.	Piezoelectric tex-tiles are being developed for sens-ing fabrics, wear-able monitoring devices, motion-capture garments, and other military applications.	Thermochromic textiles react to temperature changes; electrochromic textiles react to elec-trical charges. Have shape memory: ability to return to a previous shape after being deformed.	Applications for furniture, clothing, medicine, and technology

Silk, produced by the larval form of a moth, has been cultivated in Asia for many centuries. The cocoons are boiled (with the larvae in them) and unwound into long silk fibers. Wild silkworms eat wild oak and cherry, producing less uniform fiber colors and textures. Harvested after the moth matures and leaves its cocoon, wild silk cannot be reeled (unwound from the cocoon), and is used as spun silk. Silk is the strongest natural fiber and varies in length from 1,000 to 1,700 yards (900 to 1,550 m). Current research is investigating the cultivation of colored, nondyed silk. Cultured silk larvae eat mulberry leaves that grow on land that is not otherwise arable, and aid in soil retention. The dyes used on silk often have negative environmental impacts.

Jute is a very low-cost, weak fiber in use since biblical times. It is commercially grown in India and Bangladesh. Jute deteriorates when exposed to water.

A variety of grasses are used in window treatments and wallcoverings, and as decorative elements applied to wall treatments. Grass fibers are often given a flame-resistant treatment and colored.

Natural Protein Fibers

Natural protein fibers are hygroscopic, and become weakened when wet. They are generally resilient, and tend to feel fluffy or light for their thickness. Natural protein fibers are usually self-extinguishing; they do not burn easily. They may, however, be damaged by detergents, sunlight, chlorine bleach, and dry heat.

Wool is widely used by itself and in blends with other fibers. Wool is washable, easily dry-cleaned, or refreshed with a soft, firm brush. Finishing treatments are available to prevent damage by moths. *Virgin wool* has not been previously processed. *Ordinary wool* may include reclaimed scraps from knits, broken threads, and other sources that may have damaged fibers. *Recycled wool* is new wool or felted fabric scraps that are shredded and reused. Wool fabrics can be blocked or shaped while drying. They range from sheer wool voile to medium-weight printed wool challises, flannels, and tweeds to heavier upholstery fabrics.

The legal definition of the term *wool* also includes the fibers from Angora and cashmere goats, camels, alpacas, llamas, and vicuñas. Specialty wools include mohair from Angora goats in South Africa, the United States, and Turkey. Mohair is resilient, with each hair having fewer scales than wool and no crimp. It is smoother and more lustrous than wool. Mohair is strong and resists crushing when made into flat and pile upholstery fabrics.

Synthetic Fibers

Manufactured fibers can be solution-dyed for color; stabilizers can also be added. Synthetic fibers are subject to heat sensitivity, pilling, and static electricity. They are *oleophilic*, meaning they have a high affinity for oils and greases, which are difficult to remove.

Nylon microfibers used in furnishings are water-repellant, wind- and wear-resistant, vapor-permeable, and comfortable. Nylon is also used in wool and cotton blends.

Polyester is often blended with other fibers, including cotton, to enhance their performance. Polyester microfibers in furnishings are versatile and durable, drape well, and have a good hand. Polyester is subject to pilling. Some low-pill fabrics and treatments are available.

Olefins are extremely durable, and are used to make indoor-outdoor carpet, as well as upholstery fabric. Contemporary olefins have an improved appearance, and are solution-dyed in a wide range of colors.

Rayon, acetate, and triacetate are cellulose-based synthetic fibers. Viscose rayon blends well with other fibers. Acetate fibers are flexible and produce fabric that drapes well. As a thermoplastic fiber, acetate is easily damaged by heat and wrinkles easily.

After sunlight-resistance modifications, acetate satins, brocades, and taffetas can be used for lining fabrics and drapery fabrics. Blended with cotton, acetate is used in bedspreads and quilts. Triacetate is chemically similar to acetate, but is processed into a fiber with greater stability and abrasion resistance. Triacetate can be permanently pleated. However, its production is being phased out, largely for environmental reasons.

Acrylic was introduced in 1950 under the trade name Orlon. Its light and bulky texture is fluffy like wool, but the long fibers will pill.

Modacrylics were the first inherently flame-retardant synthetic fibers. Modacrylic looks similar to acrylic, with a soft, matte luster for wool-like fabrics and a bright luster for fur. The environmental impact of modacrylics is similar to that of acrylics. They do not break down naturally. However, the acetone solvent used in their spinning process can be easily recovered for reuse.

Vinyl, or polyvinyl chloride, is officially known as vinyon. Vinyl is a durable, easy-to-clean material for commercial upholstery, and is used for simulated leather and suede.

Lyocell was introduced in the 1990s out of concern over rayon's impact on the environment. This man-made fiber is manufactured in the United States and Europe entirely of solvent-spun cellulose from trees farmed for this purpose, with 99 percent of the solvent recovered for reuse. Unlike most synthetics, it will degrade in a compost pile.

Special-Use Fibers

Aramid (the name derived from aromatic polyamide) is a synthetic fiber developed in 1961 for aerospace and military applications, bulletproof body armor, and as a substitute for asbestos. Kevlar, by DuPont, is perhaps the best-known aramid.

Mineral fibers include glass, which has been produced as a fiber since the middle of the nineteenth century. Because it is unaffected by fire, glass fiber is sometimes used to sew upholstery fabrics to meet the requirements in California Technical Bulletin 133. Glass fiber material is used for sheer window treatments. It is known under the Owens Corning trade name Fiberglas.

Elastomers are fabrics that will stretch and return to their original form repeatedly.

- Latex is natural rubber from the rubber tree.
- Spandex, which has better durability than rubber, was introduced by DuPont in 1958. It takes dye and does not need cover yarns. Spandex can be used directly as a filament or as a core or wrap for other fibers, and is often mixed with other materials in apparel. It is used in furnishings for elastic webbing, slipcovers, and bottom sheets.
- Elastoester is less elastic than spandex, moderately resistant to bleach, and has a more silklike hand. It is manufactured under the trade name Rexe, by the Japanese textile firm Teijin Ltd., and is used for fitted furnishings.

High-Tech Textiles

Crypton is a type of engineered fabric widely used for commercial projects that need a stain-, water-, and bacteria-resistant fabric. By using a patented weaving process and barrier system, Crypton prevents other materials from going through its surface. Crypton is available in products from a variety of textile manufacturers.

Interior design fabrics available today include textiles that incorporate fiber-optic yarns. The cutting edge in textiles is the development of fabrics with integrated or embedded sensors. Smart and interactive applications, most developed for the military and medical industries, include smart shirts, sensor fabrics, bactericidal fabrics, self-tensioning shelters, and chameleon fabrics, otherwise known as camouflage

Fiber Care

- *Acetate*: Dry-clean, or gently hand-wash, warm; bleach okay. Dry low, iron very low. Avoid nail polish remover.
- *Acrylic*: Carefully follow label instructions, as basic acrylic fibers with different properties are used. Wash and wear, except furlike fabrics. Bulky yarns may need to be machine dried to retain shape after washing, or they become large and misshapen. Some can be dry-cleaned; read the label. Steam-clean draperies but not upholstery, which may shrink.
- *Cotton*: Wash with detergents in cool water. Whites can be washed in hot water. Warm water preserves color. Chlorine bleach weakens fibers. Cotton drapes should be dry-cleaned. Cotton upholstery should be steam-cleaned with caution, as it may shrink and split. Store cotton fabrics clean and dry, to avoid mildew. Bleach removes odor from mildew, but spots may be permanent. Acids are harmful to cotton, and acid stains from fruit or juice should be cleaned with cold water. Cotton fabrics can be dry-cleaned. Sunlight yellows and degrades cotton, and some dyes may disintegrate in window treatments.
- *Flax*: Dry-clean or machine wash (hot), and use chlorine bleach. Crease-resistant finishes may decrease fabric strength and abrasion resistance. Store dry to avoid mildew.
- *Glass fiber*: Hand-wash, hot; bleach. Line-dry, or iron; store flat to protect fibers.
- *Hemp*: Machine wash and dry. Resists ultraviolet light, mold, rot from water.
- *Lyocell*: Dry-clean or launder warm, with minimal agitation; bleach; dry warm, iron hot.
- *Modacrylics*: Wash or dry-clean with special care; low heat.
- *Nylon*: Wash in warm water, on gentle cycle. Picks up color from other fabrics, dirt in wash water. Chlorine bleach may eventually cause yellowing. Dries quickly on line; don't use hot dryer. Static cling.
- *Olefin*: Launder warm; bleach okay; dry warm; iron very low.
- *Polyester*: Wash in warm water; machine dry medium; remove promptly, hang; steam iron touchup. Tends to retain oils.
- *Polyester cotton durable press*: Launder hot, bleach; dry warm; iron medium.
- *Rayon*: Subject to progressive shrinking and weakened by water, so must be dry-cleaned. When used in furnishings, uncertain if can clean with water; may shrink or waterspot, and lose color. Store dry to avoid mildew.
- *Silk*: Dry-clean or gentle hand-wash, warm. Furniture generally cleaned by dry extraction method. May waterspot. No bleach. Dry warm; iron medium.
- *Sisal*: Clean by dry extraction method.
- *Spandex*: Launder warm, no bleach; dry warm; iron very low.
- *Wool*: Damaged by most detergents, and must usually be dry-cleaned, or gentle hand-wash, warm. No bleach. Dry warm; iron medium with steam. Protect from moths; do not store in plastic bags.

fabrics. Emerging technology is on the horizon for smart fabrics in furniture and smart carpets.

Fabric Finishes

Fabric finishes are intended to improve the performance of a fabric. They can, nevertheless, decrease the fabric's ability to resist abrasions and absorb liquid, and cause it to stiffen and change color. Fabric treatments should be tested on a sample before being used.

Fabric Finishes and Treatments

- *Calendaring* is a mechanical finish operation during which fabric passes between a series of rollers to produce various finish effects.
- *Flame-retardant (FR) finishes* on cotton, rayon, nylon, and polyester add to the fabrics' cost and may cause problems with durability and care. There are two major types of flame-resistant treatments: salines and polymers. Salines, the less expensive of the two, are not as durable as polymer treatments, and sometimes discolor fabrics. They also increase fabrics' ability to absorb moisture, which can result in noticeable dimensional changes in long pieces, such as draperies. In addition, the chemicals in saline treatments can corrode metal tacks and upholstery staples. Fire-resistant coatings may decrease in effectiveness over time or if cleaned. Flame-resistant polymer treatments are reasonably durable, although they will wash out after about 20 dry cleanings. The fabric is rolled off the bolt into a chemical bath, and the treatment is then heat-set. Because shrinkage is not uncommon, most finishers request that the fabric sent for treatment exceed the amount actually needed by about 5 percent. Not all fabrics react well to polymer treatments, which may result in color changes or stiffness. It is advisable to always have a sample tested before treating the entire fabric.
- *Heat insulation* is the process by which drapery fabrics are sometimes treated with plastic and aluminum adhesive coatings to help keep heat in a building during the winter and to reflect the sun's heat in the summer.
- *Mercerization* treats cellulosic fibers and yarns with alkalis or caustic sodas.
- *Mothproofing* upholstery fabric fibers maintains protection for the fabric and is not diminished by cleaning. Newer mothproofing methods attempt to reduce the attraction of the moth larvae to the wool. Bacteriostatic and antimicrobial finishes can be applied to fabric yarn or added during fiber manufacture to resist the buildup of fungi, microbes, and bacteria, and the spread of mildew, mold, and rot.
- *Sizing, or starching,* adds stiffness, weight, and body to fabric, but washes out.
- *Stain-resistant treatments* are usually sprayed on and can typically be used with fabric treated for fire resistance. After treatment, fluids will bead on the surface of the fabric without being absorbed or spreading, and can then be easily removed. Stain-resistant treatments do not usually change the appearance or feel of a fabric.
- *Water-resistance treatments* should be chosen with care, as some have harmful effects on human health and the environment. Treatments for stain-resistance protect against both oil- and water-based stains. They are usually applied as a spray and are commonly compatible with fire-resistance treatments. Stain-resistant treatments cause spills to bead up on the surface, rather than being absorbed into the fabric. They are generally odorless and not harmful to people or the environment; nor do they ordinarily change the hand of the fabric.
- *Whiteners* include bleach (which damages fibers), optical brighteners, and fluorescent whitening compounds, which mask yellow and can be used with bleach.

Finishing processes for fabrics have important environmental effects, as they use a great deal of water and energy. Fabric finishing processes are, however, being improved to control air pollution and hazardous waste disposal. Potentially hazardous chemicals are being replaced by biodegradable finishes. A *permanent finish*, such as mercerization, lasts the life of the item. A *durable finish*, such as wrinkle resistance, may diminish in

Figure 12-20 Durable cotton upholstery fabric

effectiveness with age. *Temporary finishes* last until the textile is washed or dry-cleaned. *Renewable finishes,* such as water repellants, can be applied and reapplied by the consumer or dry cleaner.

Fire resistance in fabrics is important in the home and in commercial uses. The fire resistance of a fabric is related to the fiber from which it is made and the density of its manufacture. Sheer, lightweight, napped, pile, and tufted fabrics burn quickly. More open fabrics tend to burn more freely than tightly woven ones. Some jurisdictions require fabrics in public spaces to meet stringent fire-resistance standards. If an interior designer is unable to identify an inherently flame-resistant fabric that meets design requirements, local authorities may accept another fabric that has been treated with a flame-resistant chemical.

An alternative that does not involve chemical treatment and that meets the high standards of California Technical Bulletin 133 (CAL 133) is the *lamination* of aramid fabrics to the back of the upholstery fabric. Lamination is faster and less expensive than upholstering the piece with an aramid, and again with the finish fabric; and the flame-resistant properties of aramid fabrics still protect the upholstery foam from fire.

Stain-resistant treatments are frequently applied to both residential and commercial fabrics for resistance to oil- or water-based stains. Some environmentalists cite two fluoroplastics, Teflon by DuPont and Scotchgard by 3M, as leaving long-term residues in the environment or in the human body.

 Note: Leather, in addition to its use in upholstery, can be employed as a tile finish on walls and floors. Tooled leather has been used since medieval times as a wallcovering. Woven leather rugs and animal hides are used as rugs.

Basic Weaves and Fabrics

Most of the fabrics used in interiors are woven of interlaced yarns on a loom. The *warp* of the fabric consists of a set of carefully spaced continuous yarns that run the length of the fabric. The yarns woven across the warp are called the *weft* (or, sometimes, the woof or filling yarns). (See color plate C-75, Loom-woven rug detail.)

The selvage of a fabric is the tightly woven edge produced when the weft yarns are turned and reinserted for another row of weaving. The selvage resists stretching, increasing a fabric's dimensional stability, and prevents it from unraveling during processing and fabrication. Selvages often carry printed information about the fabric's

Figure 12-21 Woven leather rug
Photo by Jessica Burko. Courtesy of
Claudia Mills Studio.

pattern and manufacturer, and for printed fabrics, include sample squares of all the colors used.

A material may have the ability to stretch along its *bias*, the 45-degree angle between the warp and the weft. Fabrics hung along the *bias* allow greater movement and fluidity, but will stretch out of shape in many applications. Using a fabric on the bias usually results in waste.

Archeologists have found remnants of knit fabrics from 250 CE on the borders of ancient Palestine. In 1589, Reverend William Lee invented the knitting machine in England. In 1851, Joseph Marie Jacquard invented a loom capable of producing detailed woven patterns. Its use of punched cards is considered the predecessor to the invention of the computer. The *jacquard loom* is used for expensive tapestries, brocades, and damask. In 1863, William Cotton invented a knitting machine that could add or drop stitches to create finished, three-dimensional products. (See color plate C-76 Hand-loom woven cotton runner.)

Knitted fabrics are either weft knitted, a process based on hand-knitting techniques, or warp knitted. The gauge or cut of a knit measures the fineness of its stitching. There are knit counterparts for most woven fabrics. Knits trap air well for insulation, but need a windbreak. Knits can run or unravel. Some knits are also prone to problems with sagging, skewing, shrinking, and snagging interwoven loops.

Fabrics made from fibers without the use of yarn include felt, tapa cloth, and fiberweb structures. Felt and tapa cloth are traditional techniques, while fiberweb structures use sophisticated technologies.

Table 12-7 Textile Fabrication Methods

Dobby weaves	Used to create woven-in shapes and textures by raising and lowering warp threads mechanically. Fabrics ornamented with dots or other raised shapes, as well as piqué, waffle cloth, and huck toweling, are all produced by dobby attachments on mechanical looms.
Matelassés	Fabrics that appear puffed or quilted due to being woven with double sets of yarns.
Crepes	Woven with yarn twisted so tightly that it has a crinkled or pebbled appearance.
Woven pile fabrics	Create depth by weaving an additional set of warp or filling yarns into the basic or ground yarns.
Pile weaves	Include velvet, velveteen, and corduroy fabrics.
Single-filling knits	Tend to run, especially if they use filament yarns.
Double-filling knits	More stable, and include double-knit jerseys with ribs and interlock structures, as well as jacquard double knits.
Sliver-pile knits	Deep, furlike pile.
Weft-insertion jersey	Laid-in weft for three-dimensional effects, as in fleece and French terry.
Weft knitting	Flat or tubular fabrics known as single or double knits.
Warp knitting	Made on fast knitting machines; produces many weights and types of knit fabrics for a great variety of uses.
Felt	Nonwoven fabric made of animal hair such as wool without yarn.
Tapa cloth	Bark fiber fabric made by pounding soaked fibers.
Fiberweb fabrics	Contemporary nonwoven fabrics bonded mechanically or by resins, heat, or chemicals. Fiberwebs are used to back quilted fabrics, as interlining, and as base fabrics for laminating or coating. Spun-bonded webs are fused as they come from spinnerets for carpet backings, wallcoverings, and house-wrap vapor barriers. Hydroentangled or spun-lace fabrics, also called water-needled fabrics, become interlinings, mattress pads, table linens, wallcoverings, and window treatment components. Melt-blown fiberwebs are used in hospital and medical products.

Dyeing and Printing

Textiles can be dyed as fibers, yarns, or woven pieces. Integral color is added to raw natural fiber, molten polymer, or fiber solution.

- *Fiber dyes* are more likely to be colorfast because the color penetrates throughout the fiber.
- *Yarn dyeing* is done after spinning and before weaving.
- *Piece dyeing* is an inexpensive and simple way to manufacture solid-color fabrics; but unless the fabric is composed of only one type of fiber, the distribution of the dye may be uneven.
- *Polychromatic dyeing* involves applying dyestuffs at varying speeds and in different directions through jets or rollers. Patterns are often controlled by computers.

Level color is uniform throughout a product. Colorfast dyes and prints will not shift hue or migrate onto other materials. Color is affected by minor irregularities in fiber, yarn, fabric, and finishing. Detergent, perspiration, dry-cleaning solvents, and sunlight can all degrade color.

Metamerism is when two colors match under one light source but not under another. The *Bezold effect* is when two or more colors merge to make a new color, as with small-scale prints and yarn-dyed fabrics when seen from a distance.

Table 12-8 Textile Dyeing and Printing Processes

Technique	Process	Advantages	Disadvantages	Comments
Solution dyeing, gel dyeing, or mass pigmentation	Dyes may be added before fibers are formed.	Color is permanent part of fiber.	When fibers are dyed, color varies with the fiber.	Mixed fibers create heathers.
Yarn dyeing	Yields good penetration and high-quality results.	Used for plaids, stripes, and other patterns.	Expensive	
Fabric dyeing	Yards of fabric dyed.	Inexpensive and can be done in smaller quantities.	Color may be irregular.	
Dyeing finished sewn products	Finished articles dyed.	Least expensive to dye.	Difficult to match all parts of an item, so a distressed look may result.	
Dyes and Pigments				
Textile pigments	Insoluble color particles held to the surface of a fabric by a bonding agent.	Quick, simple, and economical to apply. Pigment colors are easier to match than dyes because they do not mix chemically with the fiber, which can cause hue shifts.	May stiffen, crock, or fade. Dyes vary in brightness, cost, and the range of colors in which they are available.	Many types of textile pigments; some work better on natural fibers, others on synthetics.
Textile dyes: natural, reactive, and vat dyes	Absorbed into the fibers.	Dyes have great color strength, and a small amount can color a large quantity of fabric.	Unused particles left on the outside bleed and rub off.	Fluorescent dye absorbs light at one wavelength and emits it at another to make whites whiter and fabrics glow in the dark.
Natural or vegetable dyes	From plant, animal, and mineral sources.	Used primarily with natural fibers.	Colorfastness varies, and these dyes are available in limited colors.	
Reactive or fiber-reactive dyes	Bright dyes that combine chemically with fibers, including cotton and other cellulosics, wool, silk, and nylon.	Have good light resistance, and remain colorfast after washing	Are sensitive to chlorine bleach.	

(Continued)

Table 12-8 (Continued)

Technique	Process	Advantages	Disadvantages	Comments
Vat dyes	Used for drapery fabrics, cotton, and some cotton/polyester blends.	Insoluble in water, and reasonably lightfast and colorfast.	Come in an incomplete color range.	

Printing Techniques

Technique	Process	Advantages	Disadvantages	Comments
Fabric printing	Adds a design in color on top of the base fabric.	Some firms allow custom color to be specified in a print. With computer-aided design and manufacturing, a design can be created on screen, manipulated, and colored in various ways.		Direct imaging is available; customers can select or design their own patterns, which are then printed on fabric. Small yardages are feasible.

Resist Printing:

Three commercial methods are direct, screen, and discharge printing.

Patterns depend on certain parts of the fabric being made resistant to the dye.

Technique	Process	Advantages	Disadvantages	Comments
Direct printing (also called roller, calendar, or cylinder printing)	Fabric is passed between etched color rollers, with each color applied by its own roller.	Direct-printed fabrics often have a white background.		*Block prints* are a method of direct printing with inked, carved blocks. *Flatbed printing* is a variation on block printing that uses large blocks for small runs of large pattern repeats.
Screen printing	Forces dye through a stencil, with a different stencil used for each color.	Flatbed screen printing uses a squeegee to push dye through the stencil onto fabric that has been stretched flat.		Rotary screen printing uses a perforated cylinder screen to apply color, and is faster than flatbed method.
Discharge dyeing	Removes dye from a colored fabric with bleach or a chemical dye remover.	Often used for polka dots or small floral prints, and can be combined with color printing.		
Hand-dyeing techniques	Includes *ikat*, in which the fiber is dyed in a pattern before weaving, and *tie-dyeing*.	Some of these dyeing techniques are being translated into woven fabric designs produced by highly skilled specialty weavers.		

Appendix:
Woods Used in Interiors

The wood species listed in this table are limited to those currently available for use in interior environments. Availability and sustainability of resources are subject to change.

*Species marked with an asterisk (*) are illustrated in color plates.

Species	Names	Appearance	Qualities	Sources	Uses
Horse chestnut (A. hippocastanum)		Very fine texture, spiral grain. White, some light gray streaks	Lightweight; low decay resistance, stiffness. Steam-bends well	European native; Europe, India, China, Japan, and North America	Interior trim, decorative veneers. Substitute for holly
Afzelia (Afzelia spp.)	Pod mahogany, doussie, chanfuta, apa, aligna, mkora, mbembakofi	Pale straw sapwood; brown heartwood	Coarse texture; heavy, stable; strong; Difficult. Takes a high polish.	Hardwood: tropical Africa and Asia	Joinery, window frames, floors, stair-cases, furniture, doors, and chests
Agba (Gossweilerodendron balsamiferum)	Egba, nitola, ntola, tola, white tola, moboron, mutseka-mambole, Nigerian cedar	Pale straw to reddish-brown heartwood; lighter sapwood. Looks like mahogany.	Soft, low stiffness, shock resistance; strength; stable; decay resistance.	Hardwood: tropical west Africa	Interior joinery, paneling, table and chair parts, flooring, decorative veneer
Albizia* (Albizia spp.)	Okuro, ayinre, sifou	Coarse texture, red- to chocolate-brown, purplish	Heavy, high strength. Finish needs grain filling.	Hardwood: southern Africa	Flooring, veneer, furniture, construction.
Alder (Alnus)	Common alder (Alnus glutinosa; black, gray, or red alder)	Orange-brown wood	Lightweight, soft, stable. Straight grained, fine textured	Hardwood: Europe, Russia, Africa, Asia	Cabinet work, veneer
	Red alder (Oregon, or western alder)	Pale yellow to reddish-brown		Hardwood: Pacific Coast America	Furniture, sashes, doors, millwork
Ash (most commonly Fraxinus)	White ash (F. americana)	White, strong, straight-grained wood	Hard, tough, strong, elastic	Hardwood: Eastern North America	Furniture, plywood, veneer
	Black Ash (F. nigra; brown, swamp, basket, hoop)	Straight grain, coarse texture. Grayish-brown to light brown	Softer, weaker, lighter than white ash. Steam-bends. Decays.	Northeastern US and Canada	Porch furniture, cabinets

304

Species	Names	Appearance	Qualities	Sources	Uses
Araucaria species	Moreton Bay pine (A. cuninghamii); hoop, colonial, Richmond River, or Queensland pine. Alloa, Ningwik, Pien	Light, even-texture	High-quality. Most natural stands were depleted by logging. Now produced on timber plantations	Softwood conifer: Australia and New Guinea. Not a true pine	Plywood, furniture, veneer, joinery
	Paraná pine (A. angustifolia)	Straight grain, uniform texture. Yellowish; heartwood shades of brown, often with bright red streaks	Holds paint well. Heartwood not durable	Softwood conifer: Brazil, Paraguay, Argentina native	Trim, sashes doors; furniture, case goods, veneers, staircases
Ayan (Distemonanthus benthamianus)	Movingue, Nigerian satinwood, barre, ayanran, bonsamdua, ejen, and okpe	Fine texture; high luster. Lemon-yellow to brown sapwood; cream to golden heartwood	Straight to wavy grain. Heavy, dimensionally stable. Glues, stains, polishes well	Hardwood: West Africa	Cabinetry, windows, door frames, flooring, veneers
Bamboos: woody perennial, evergreen grass plants Poaceae* Not true wood	91 genera and about 1,000 species of bamboo	Pale yellow. Straw-yellow or brown when carbonized.	Lightweight, fast growing wood substite. Consider sustainable farming practices and use of synthetic resins.	Asia, Australia, subSaharan Africa, and from southeast United States to Chile	Flooring, furniture, accessories
Beech (Fagus) Fine, short grain; dense, hard, and brittle; not tough	European beech (F. silvatica)	Wood is cream to medium brown	Easy-to-work utility wood; soaks and dyes well, steams well. Accepts excellent finish; rots easily unless protected	Hardwood:	Furniture, parquet flooring, staircases, decorative veneers
	American beech	Reddish-brown to light orangey-tan. Fine grain, small rays	Heavy, hard, tough, and strong wood	Native to North America	Flooring and interior furniture

Species	Names	Appearance	Qualities	Sources	Uses
Birch (*Betula*)	Paper, canoe or American white birch	Resembles maple	White, soft wood of low value	North America	Furniture, floors, OSB, plywood, veneer, paneling
Deciduous hardwood	Yellow birch	Light tan with hint of yellow	Hard; sapwood: white to cream, heartwood: light reddish-brown	Native to eastern North America	Flooring and cabinetry
	(*Betula pendula*) European silver or warty birch	Creamy white to pale brown wood	Straight grained and fine textured. Resembles maple; used interchangeably	Grows throughout Europe	Furniture, veneer, plywood, paneling, cabinetry, flooring
Blackbean	*Castano spermum australe* or Moreton Bay chestnut	Deep browns with wavy streaks, coarse texture	Soft, fine-grained lumber resembles walnut and takes polish well, but is less durable	Hardwood: Australia, Oceania	Furniture, cabinetry, joinery, veneer
African blackwood	*Acacia melanoxylon*, mpingo	Dense reddish to pure black lustrous heartwood; bright yellow sapwood	Extinct in Kenya and severely threatened in Tanzania and Mozambique	African hardwood, it has been harvested at an unsustainable rate	Furniture, since ancient Egypt. Very expensive
Australian blackwood	Family Leguminosae; black wattle	Straw-colored sapwood; reddish-brown to black heartwood with attractive bands	Heavy, strong, stable in service. Steam-bends very well; polishes very well Straight grained, sometimes with a fiddleback ligure; lustrous.	Hardwood: Australia, Africa, Asia, Europe, Oceanic countries, South America, U.S.	High-quality furniture, cabinets, paneling, veneering, joinery
Bubinga	*Guibourtia tessmannii*; kevazingo, akume, bingbinga, essingang, ovang, waka	Fine grain; hard, heavy; lustrous finish. Light red or violet with evenly spaced purple stripes.	Population within its natural habitat has not been officially assessed. Some from environmentally responsible sources.	Hardwood: Cameroon, Gabon, Ivory Coast, perhaps Zaire	Veneers, inlaid work, flooring, high-end furniture
Brazilwood	*Caesalpinia echinata*; Bahia, para, or pernambuco wood, Braziletto and Brazilian ironwood	Fine texture, natural luster. Nearly white sapwood. Bright orange heartwood matures to deep red	Very hard and heavy, with exceptional bending strength. Highly resistant to decay, very stable. Very smooth, lustrous finish	Hardwood: grows in eastern Brazil	Parquet flooring, decorative veneers

Species	Names	Appearance	Qualities	Sources	Uses
Butternut	*Juglans cinerea*; white walnut, oilnut, tropical walnut, nogal blanco, tocte	Resembles black walnut when stained but lacks its strength or stiffness	Light brown heartwood with darker streaks and nearly white sapwood. Soft, Straight grained and coarse textured with a satiny luster.	Hardwood: U.S. and Canada	Furniture, cabinets, paneling, interior trim, veneer, and millwork
Carapa (*Carapa guianensis*)	Andiroba, crabwood, figueroa, Brazilian mahogany	Coarse texture, highly figured, or plain grain. Reddish or dark red-brown	Soft, durable, insect-resistant. Heavier than mahogany. Overexploited in Brazil	Hardwood: South America and Africa	Furniture, cabinets, flooring, millwork, decorative veneers, architectural paneling
Cedar (*Cedrus*)	Cedar of Lebanon, Atlantic, Atlas, and deodar cedar	Straight grained; Atlantic and Lebanon cedars often knotty. Fine textured. Heartwood light brown and resinous; sapwood pale colored	Decay-resistant heartwood and oil are natural moth repellants. Polishes well. Extensive reforestation	Softwood conifer: western Himalayas, Mediterranean region, Northern Africa, Middle East, and India	Paneling and decorative veneers, furniture, cabinetry, doors, interior joinery, construction, and outdoor furniture
South American cedar / Not a true cedar / Cedrela species are scarce and infrequently used	*Cedrela*; Brazilian, Peruvian, Honduras, Mexican, and Tabasco cedar, cedro.	Similar to cherry. Red-brown with light streaks.	Moderately heavy, stable in service. Heartwood is very decay-resistant	Hardwood: Central and South America.	Fine furniture and cabinetry, chests, decks, construction, plywood, and decorative veneers
Spanish cedar (*Cedrela odorata*)	Related to mahogany	Reddish brown to light pink. CITES-listed	Lightweight fragrant wood with very good resistance to insects	Hardwood: Mexico south to Argentina	Construction work, paneling, and veneer
Alaska-cedar (*Chamaecyparis nootkatensis*)	Alaska yellow, yellow, and white cedar. Nootka false, yellow, Alaska cypress, or sitka cypress.	Straight grained, even texture. Bright, clear yellow heartwood; yellowish sapwood	Light and soft, very high decay resistance and dimensional stability. High acid resistance. Takes a fine finish, wears smooth	Softwood: Pacific Coast of North America	Interior and exterior finish, furniture, cabinetry, doors, veneer

Species	Names	Appearance	Qualities	Sources	Uses
Port-Orford cedar (*Chamaecyparis lawsoniana*)	Port Orford white, white, or Oregon cedar, false cypress, Lawson cypress	Yellowish-white to pale brown heartwood; pale yellowish-white sapwood	Lightweight, very good acid and decay resistance. Accepts finishes very well. Gingerlike odor	Softwood: northern Pacific Coast of U.S. Asia, Europe, New Zealand	Mothproof boxes and closets, chests, millwork, furniture, paneling. Now in short supply due to overharvesting without replanting
Incense-Cedar (*Libocedrus decurrens*)	Pencil and Californina incense-cedar	Straight grained, medium texture. Light brown heartwood with red, nearly white sapwood	Light, soft, very good decay resistance easy to work; finishes very well	Softwood; grows in northwestern United States	Venetian blinds, chests, trim, millwork, and plywood
Cherry (*Prunus*) Deciduous hardwood fruit tree	(*Prunus serotina*) Black, wild, wild black, rum or Cabinet cherry, capulin, New England mahogany	Straight grained; uniform texture and a rich luster. Reddish-brown heartwood, white sapwood	Hard, heavy, strong, good decay resistance. Steam-bends well, stains easily, and polishes to excellent finish. Darkens with age	Canada, U.S., and Central America	Cabinetry, interior furniture, paneling, architectural woodwork
	(*Prunus avium*) European or wild cherry, gean, mazzard, merisier, kers		Small gum pits. Variations in color are common.	Europe and southeast Asia	Cabinets, furniture, paneling, veneer, woodwork
Chestnut (*Castanea*) Similar to oak; Hardwood in the beech family, native to the northern hemisphere	American chestnut (*Castanea dentate*)	Straight grain. Holes in wormy chestnut caused by insects.	Strong, easy to split, high decay resistance.	Chestnut blight fungus has almost wiped out species; scarce	Furniture, interior trim, shingles. Often reclaimed from historic barns
	Sweet chestnut (*Castanea sativa* Spanish chestnut)	Yellow-brown heartwood and narrow, pale sapwood	Splits and warps when it dries. Polishes well. Natural acidity causes blue-black stains when in contact with iron	Grows in southwest Europe, North Africa, and western Asia	Furniture, veneer

Species	Names	Appearance	Qualities	Sources	Uses
Coachwood (Ceratopetalum apetalum)	Scented satinwood or tarwood	Often highly figured; caramel odor; pale pink to pinkish-brown	Light and easily worked. Straight grain and even, fine texture	Hardwood: New South Wales and Queensland	Flooring, furniture, cabinetry, plywood, paneling, veneers
Cocobolo (four species of Dalbergia)*		Fine texture, oily look and feel. Orange, with dark figures changes color after being cut	Stands up well to repeated handling and exposure to water; extraordinarily dense; produces a clear musical tone if struck.	Hardwood: Central America. Heavily exploited and in danger of extinction	Inlay work, decorative and figured veneers. Expensive, rare
Cypress	Yellow cypress	Very distinct leafy grain. Pale yellow to yellowish-red, often salmon-colored	Strong and light, very durable, and naturally resistant to decay. Soft; easy to work, finish	Softwood: southeast United States	Outdoor applications, furniture
	Bald cypress (Taxodium distichum; swamp cypress)	Naturally rot and disease resistant	Usable prehistoric bald cypress wood is often found in New Jersey swamps and occasionally in New England	Native to the United States	Flooring (relatively soft) Construction Furniture
	Nootka cypress (Callitropsis nootkatensis; yellow or Alaska cypress)	Straight grain, fine texture. Sapwood slightly lighter than bright, clear, yellow heartwood	Hard, durable wood has good dimensional stability; resists acid, weather, insects and exposure to soil. Takes a finish well, wears smoothly over time.	Slow-growing evergreen hardwood native to the Pacific Northwest. Overexploited in the past	Paneling, cabinetry, millwork, and saunas Expensive. Substitute for western red cedar and bald cypress
	Hinoki cypress	Lemon scent, light color, and rich short grain	Highly resistant to rot	Native to Japan	Traditional Japanese buildings
	Mediterranean cypress (Cupressus sempervirens)	Scented wood	Very durable, scented wood.	Mediterranean, California, Pacific Northwest, South Africa, Great Britain, Australia, New Zealand	Furniture
Degame (Calycophyllum candidissimum)	Lemonwood and lancewood	Broad sapwood, white to brownish-white, with variegated dark brown heartwood	Hard, heavy, tough, and resilient. Very good steam-bending and turning properties; stains and finishes well. Straight grained, fine texture	Hardwood: grows in Cuba, Central America, and South America	Flooring and cabinetry

Species	Names	Appearance	Qualities	Sources	Uses
Ebony (*Diospyrus* species) Darkest wood, extremely dense, will sink in water. Due to overharvesting, many species of ebony are now considered threatened	Ceylon ebony, Andaman marble from India, Ebène mabre from Maritius in East Africa	Pure black, may have brown streaks	Heartwood is dense and hard, polishes to smooth finish.	Hardwood native to South India and Sri Lanka. Endangered in Africa and Asia.	Craft work, musical instruments
	Black Macasser ebony*	Black with heavy brown streaking		India and East Indies	Cabinetmaking
	Calamander wood (*D. quaesita*); Coromandel wood, variegated ebony	Hazel-brown wood striped with black or shades of brown; very hard		India, Ceylon. Considered threatened, vulnerable	Furniture
	Persimmon (*D. virginiana*); white ebony, date plum, possum, boa, or butter wood, barabara	Older persimmon heartwood is black or dark brown. Creamy white sapwood mottled, gray spots, dark brown core	Polishes well, retains smoothness under heavy use. Very heavy and dense, hard, tough, strong. Straight and fine-grained	Hardwood fruit tree: United States	Paneling in traditional Korean and Japanese furniture, veneers
	East Indian Ebony (*D. ebenaceae*); Indian golden, or Macassar ebony, camagon	Heartwood medium brown to jet black to gray. Light gray sapwood	Very heavy, hard, strong, and stiff with high shock and decay resistance. Steam-bends reasonably well but wood is brittle. Takes an excellent finish. Metallic luster	Hardwood: Sri Lanka and southern India	Luxury furniture, inlay, and decorative veneer
European elm (*Ulmus* spp.);*	English, smooth-leaved, French, Flemish, Dutch elm, or Scotch elm, and wych	Cross-grained with dull brown heartwood (often with reddish tinge); pale sapwood	Moderately heavy and hard; steam-bends very well. Resists decay when permanently wet	Hardwood: temperate regions of Europe and western Asia	Flooring, chair seats, cabinets, decorative veneers, paneling, and chopping blocks
	American Elm (*Ulmus Americana*); white, water, soft and gray elm	Light brown to brown heartwood with reddish tinge; light sapwood	Wear-resistant. Steam-bends very well, coarse texture	Hardwood: eastern half of U.S. and southern Canada	Furniture (bent parts), plywood veneers, flooring

Species	Names	Appearance	Qualities	Sources	Uses
Entandrophragma species Deciduous hardwood trees of the mahogany family, native to tropical Africa	E. angolense (mukusu in Uganda, tiama in Ivory Coast, edinam in Ghana, and kalungi in Zaire)	Heartwood, pink-brown to dull uniform red; darkens to deep red-brown; sapwood, pale	Tends to warp. Interlocked grain produces broad stripes. Medium to coarse texture	Africa	Furniture, joinery, cabinetmaking, decorative veneers and plywood
	E. candollei (kosipo, omo in Nigeria, candollei in Ghana)	Heartwood, dull or purplish-brown; sapwood, pale	Coarse textured; slow drying with tendency to warp	West Africa to Congo and Angola	Furniture, cabinetwork, flooring, decorative veneers, plywood
	Sapeli (E. cylindricum) aboudikro, penkwa, muyovu, Sapelli, Libuyu	Red-brown to purple-brown heartwood; pale sapwood	Fine textured and lustrous, with a cedarlike scent; grain sometimes wavy, shows figures on quartered surfaces	Africa	Furniture, cabinetwork, veneers, plywood, joinery, flooring, paneling
	*Sipo (E. utile): utile, efuodwe, sipo, okeong, assie, kosi-kosi, mufumbi	Heartwood red-brown or purple-brown; faint cedar scent	Air-dries but tends to warp, but kiln-dries satisfactorily. Sipo lumber is corrosive to metals	Hardwood: West and Central Africa; Ivory Coast	Furniture, cabinetwork, joinery, decorative veneers, and plywood
Eucalyptus species Produce oil that burns readily; trees have been known to explode; regenerate quickly after fire. Alpine ash and mountain ash are killed by fire, leaving stands of mostly undamaged timber that could be harvested	Australian mountain ash (E. regnans)	Light reddish-brown or gray brown	Among the tallest trees in the world	Australia	Shipbuilding
	Lyptus (trade name for wood from hybrid eucalyptus plantations)	Dark red to light pink	Hardness similar to oak.	Produced in Brazil by Weyerhauser, may fail to meet LEED standards	Hardwood flooring, furniture, cabinets, and architectural millwork
	Karri (E. diversicolor)	Heartwood, reddish-brown; sapwood, paler; striped figure on quartered surfaces	Moderately heavy and very strong; finishes, polishes well. Avoid cracking and warping by slow drying. Wavy or striped figure	Nontropical hardwood: South Africa, western Australia	Indoor and outdoor furniture, cabinets, flooring, plywood, veneer
	Jarrah (E.marginata) west Australian eucalyptus	Light to dark red. Rich color, beautiful grains	Today, recycled from demolished houses	Australia	Flooring, furniture, joinery, veneers

Species	Names	Appearance	Qualities	Sources	Uses
Sold as Australian or Tasmanian oak but not a true oak. Includes three species marketed together.	E. delegatensis (alpine ash, white-top, woollybutt) E. obliqua (messmate or brown-top stringy-bark) E. regnans (mountain or Victorian ash, stringy or swamp gum)	Straight grained, sometimes interlocked or wavy, coarse texture, light brown heartwood with a pinkish tinge	Heavy, hard. Stains and polishes easily and can be brought to an excellent finish	Hardwood: southeastern Australia Australian oak	Joinery, building construction, flooring, furniture, plywood, veneer
Khaya (Khaya species)	African, Nigerian, Ivory Coast, and Gold Coast mahogany, Benin, degema, Lagos wood, acajou, khaya, akuk, bandoro	Creamy white sapwood and reddish-brown heartwood, purple cast	Stains and polishes well. Grain, often with a ribbon figure, moderately coarse texture	Hardwood: West Africa. Generally cheaper and more abundant than American mahogany.	Furniture, cabinetry, joinery, interior trim, paneling, plywood, veneers
Fir Softwood with a great many species. The wood is considered to be inferior in quality, so used for pulp, plywood, and rough timber	(Abies balsamea), Balsam, Canadian, eastern, and bracted balsam fir	Creamy white to pale brown	Light and soft, even grained, medium to fine texture	Grows in eastern half of United States and Canada	General construction, sashes, doors, trim, plywood
	Coast Douglas fir	Tan with dense darker growth rings	Moderately soft and grows quickly.	Pacific Northwest Will not grow in shade, clear-cut logging helps it thrive	Dimensional lumber, plywood, flooring, veneer, and furniture
	Rocky Mountain Douglas fir*	Similar to Coast Douglas fir	Exceptionally strong wood	Western North America	Plywood, dimension lumber, furniture, cabinets, doors, window frames
	(Abies concolor), White, western, concolor, Colorado, silver, white or lows, and white balsam	Whitish to yellowish-brown	Light, soft, stains, paints, and varnishes well. Generally straight and quite even grained	Softwood: United States	General construction, sashes, doors, trim, plywood

Species	Names	Appearance	Qualities	Sources	Uses
Freijo (*Cordia goeldiana*)	South American walnut, frei jorge, jenny or cordia wood	Heartwood is golden-brown maturing to dark brown	Resembles teak in appearance and strength properties. Moderately hard and heavy, coarse texture or rich, golden luster. Heartwood is resistant to white or brown-rot fungi.	Hardwood: grows in South America	Cabinetry, furniture, interior joinery, paneling, flooring, and veneers
Gaboon (*Aucoumea klaineana*)	Okoum, angouma, combogala, n'goumi, mofoumou	Natural luster, pinkish heartwood	Light, soft. Straight grained but sometimes wavy producing striping on quarter-sawn surfaces	Hardwood: grows in equatorial Africa	Plywood, joinery, moldings, trim, fine furniture, construction, paneling, veneers
Guarea (*Guarea cedrata*, *G. thompsonii*) Two species typically sold as one commercial species	*G. cedrata*: white or scented guarea, light bosse, obobonufua, *G. thompsonii*: black guarea, obobo, bosse, diambi, divuitii ebanghemwa	Mahogany-colored reddish-brown heartwood; wide, pale sapwood	Straight, sometimes curly grain	Hardwood: tropical west Africa, Ivory Coast and Nigeria	Furniture, joinery, flooring, veneer
Hackberry (*Celtis occidentalis*)	Sugarberry, nettle or hacktree bastard elm, hoop ash	Resembles ash, elm. Yellow-gray to light brown heartwood and greenishyellow sapwood	Soft and moderately heavy. Glues, stains and finishes well—natural finishes especially. Straight grain and fairly uniform texture	Hardwood: eastern half of U.S. and southern Canada	Millwork and interior cabinetry
Hemlock (*Tsuga* species)	(*Tsuga heterophylla*) Western and Pacific hemlock	White to light yellow brown.	Light, soft. Finishes and polishes well.	Hardwood: Northwest Europe Pacific Northwest	Joinery, doors, flooring, furniture, plwood, paneling, veneer
Hickory (*Carya* species)	(*C. illinoensis*) Pecan hickory pecan nut. Sweet pecan. Nogal, morado, pecanier	Pale to reddish-brown heartwood. Whitish sapwood	Very heavy, hard, strong, but flexible. Tight straight grain, coarse texture	Hardwood: U.S. and Mexico	Flooring; veneers; paneling; chair parts, furniture

Species	Names	Appearance	Qualities	Sources	Uses
	Shagbark, shellbark, white, scalybark, or red heart hickory	Brown to red-brown heartwood. Sapwood wide, white	One of the hardest, heaviest, and strongest woods in the United States. Excellent elasticity, good steam-bending, moderate dimensional stability, and low decay resistance. Polishes to a naturally smooth finish. Straight grained and coarse textured	United States and Canada	Flooring, furniture, paneling, veneer, building materials
American Holly (Ilex opaca)	Evergreen, white, Christmas, prickly, scrub, dune holly	Ivory white, stained white to imitate ebony	Fine texture	Hardwood: eastern half of U.S.	Marquetry, inlay, and furniture
European hornbeam (Carpinus betulus)	Hornbeam, avenbok, vitbok, haagbeuk	Fine, even texture. Dull white heartwood, gray streaked sapwood	Heavy, hard, tough. Similar to ash, strong. Resists splitting, steam-bends well	Hardwood: Southern half of Africa	Flooring, veneer
Iroko (Clorophora excelsa)	Kambala, mvule, odum, intule, tule	Light to dark brown heartwood; paler sapwood	May have hard Calcium Carbonate deposits in grain. Resists decay.	Hardwood: southern half of Africa	Joinery, countertops, tabletops, windows, doors, cabinetry, plywood, veneer
Juniper	Eastern juniper, eastern red, or aromatic cedar	Pinkish-red to brownish-red heartwood	Soft, brittle, light. Fragrant. Durable in contact with soil.	Softwood: North American	Clothes chests, closets
Katsura (Cercidiphyllum japonica)	Heart tree, cake tree	Light brown with darker growth rings.	Straight grained. High luster polishes well. Soft, light, stabile	Hardwood: Japan, China, Korea	Cabinetry, furniture, joinery, plywood, veneers
Kauri (Agathis australis)	Southern kauri, New Zealand kauri	Golden with highlights and feathery grains	Trees buried in salt marshes like new but lighter in color	Restricted use due to deforestation from logging	High-end furniture construction, panelling.
Larch (Larix species)	L. decidua European larch	Yellowish tan	Tough, waterproof, durable, flexible	Softwood conifer: Europe	Rustic furniture
	L. kaempferi, Japanese larch kara-matsu (Japan)	Reddish tan	Tough, durable	Softwood: Japan, British Isles plantations	General construction

Species	Names	Appearance	Qualities	Sources	Uses
	L. occidentalis Western larch	Medium tan with brown growth rings	Dense, very durable	Softwood: Western U.S. and Canada	Interior, exterior finishing
California laurel (*Umbellularia californica*)	Myrtle, Oregon, myrtle, myrtlewood, bay laurel, pepperwood, spice tree	Heartwood yellow-brown or olive, range blond to black. Sapwood pale brown.	Exquisite figure, color. Polishes very well. Slow growth takes centuries.	Hardwood: Oregon and California. No large stands remain, only small groves	One of the most expensive woods in U.S. Burls sliced into veneer. Trims, cabinetry, furniture
Limba (*Terminalia superba*)		Pale yellow to light brown, black streaks	Works very well. Exceptional color and finish	Hardwood: tropical West Africa. Over-harvested.	Furniture, musical instruments. Rare, expensive
Pacific madrone (*Arbutus menziesii*)	Coast madrone, madrona, madrono, arbuti tree	Pink to pale red-brown, resembles apple	Fine texture. Hard, strong. Stains, polishes well.	Hardwood: Pacific Coast of U.S., Canada	Inlay, paneling, furniture. Burl veneers
Magnolia (*Magnolia grandifolia*)	Evergreen, sweet, southern magnolia. Cucumber wood, bat tree, bull bay	Like yellow poplar, brown heartwood with yellowishgreen sapwood	Straight grain, close texture. Steam bends, finishes well	Hardwood: U.S. and Britain	Venetian-blind slats, cabinetry, furniture, doors, veneer
Mahogany Philippine mahogany is shorea, not mahogany. African khaya called African mahogany, is not mahogany.	*Swietenia mahogany:* West Indies, Spanish, Cuban, Honduras mahogany, Madeira redwood *S. macrophylla* Honduras mahogany	Reddish	Hard. Easy to work, stable, polishes well. All species of mahogany are listed by CITES and protected; illegal traffic continues, notably from Brazil	Hardwood: West Indies and South America	Furniture
Maple (Acer species)	*A. campestre* European or sycamore maple	White with silky luster. Wavy grain, prized as veneer	Hard wearing wide boards without heart.	Hardwood: Europe, North America, New Zealand, Falkland Islands	Furniture, flooring
	A. platanoides Norway maple	Yellow-white wood with reddish tint	Dense.	Hardwood: Eastern, central Europe, southwest Asia	Interiors finishes, furniture, flooring

Species	Names	Appearance	Qualities	Sources	Uses
	A. saccharum Sugar hard, country hard maple	Curly maple grain reflect light.	Very hard, durable, strong. Turns well. Natural luster finishes well. Figured maples.	Hardwood: Northeastern U.S. and Canada	Furniture, flooring, butcher blocks, cabinetry, paneling, countertops, veneer
	A. nigrum Black, black sugar, hard, rock maple	Reddish-brown	Hard, similar to sugar maple	Hardwood: Northeastern U.S. and Canada	Veneer, furniture
	A. rubrum, soft, natural red, silver maple, box elder	Cream to reddish-brown. Stained to look like cherry	Medium hard; good steam-bends, finishes well. Substitute for maple and beech	Hardwood: eastern U.S. and Canada	Furniture, paneling, millwork, kitchen cabinets, moldings, doors
	A. macrophyllum Bigleaf, broadleaf, Oregon, Pacific Coast, western or white maple	Pale pinkish-brown to almost white, grayish cast	Straight or curly grain. Stains, sands, and polishes well.	Hardwood: western North America. Marketed as soft maple.	Furniture, cabinets, plywood panels, veneer, flooring, interior construction
	Figured maples	Quilted maple (A. saccharinum)	Flowing three-dimensional figure	Most common in big leaf maple; native to the Pacific Northwest	
		Curly English sycamore	Has figured grain		
		Tiger maple	Priced by the degree of figure (low, medium, or high) and color		
		Spalted maple (A. saccharinum)	Mineral streaks and spalting lines. Spalt results from fungi attacks on decaying logs	Lumber is used after decay has started, but before wood becomes spongy	
	Bird's-eye maple* (A. Saccharinum)	Cream white to reddish-brown	"Eyes" are discreet circles scattered throughout wood	May result from stunted growth	Rare-veneer
Mesquite (Prosopis glandulosa)	Honey common, velvet mesquite, algarobo, honey pod	Tan sapwood; heartwood, brown with golden hue. May resemble mahogany	Heavy, hard, strong, brittle, outstanding decay resistance. Finishes, polishes well. Fine, wavy interlocked grain	Hardwood: western U.S., Central and South America	Fireplace mantels, flooring, and some furniture
Muhuhu (Brachylaena hutchinsii)	Muhugu, mubuubu, watho, mvumvo, mshenzi	Dark yellow-brown heartwood (some with darker streaks). Grayish sapwood	Straight grain, very fine texture. Very heavy, hard, dense, durable. Stains, polishes well	Hardwood: East Africa.	Heavy-duty flooring, door and window frames

Species	Names	Appearance	Qualities	Sources	Uses
Muninga (*Pterocarpus angolensis*)	Ambila, brown African padauk, bloodwood, kiaat, kajat, mninga, mukwa, mutete, and mututi	Often has attractive figure on quartered surfaces	Coarse, uneven texture. High decay resistance, dimensional stability. Finishes well.	Hardwood: south-central Africa	High-end furniture, cabinets, paneling, flooring, joinery
Oak (*Quercus* species) Hardwood: several hundred species.	*Q. alba*: white eastern white, stave, ridge white oak. Cucharillo, Encino, roble.	Straight grained with a medium-coarse to coarse texture. Light tannish heartwood; narrow, nearly white sapwood	Heavy, hard, strong; Very wear resistant, durable.	U.S. and Canada	Furniture, flooring, baskets, trim, millwork, veneers
	Q. bicolori Swamp white oak	Close-grained, light brown	Heavy, strong and hard. Knottier than white oak.	Hardwood: Eastern U.S. Canada. Sold as white oak.	Furniture, cabinets, veneers, finishing, flooring
	Q. robor Pedunculate English, English brown oak	Like white oak	Heartwood is hard, long lasting, and durable	Hardwood: Europe, Asia Minor, North Africa	Interiors and furniture
	Q. petraea Sessile oak	Pale brown	Fewer knots	Hardwood: Europe	Lumber, veneer
	Q. rubra Northern, eastern, American, Canadian, and mountain red oaks. Gray oak.	Light, reddish-tan heartwood; sapwood almost white.	Hard, strong, stiff. Finishes well but large pores may require filler.	Hardwood: United States, Canada, and Europe	Cabinetry, furniture, millwork, plywood, flooring, heavy construction
	Q. borealis Northern red oak	Very open grain	Best North American red oak	Hardwood: listed as an invasive species in Germany	Flooring, furniture, cabinetry, paneling, timbers, and millwork
	Q. falcate Southern red oak, Spanish oak	Light red	Hard, strong, coarse grain	Hardwood: Europe	Lumber, furniture, flooring
	Q. suber Cork oak	Bark is cork	Resilient, regrows	Hardwood: Mediterranean	Flooring and other applications

Species	Names	Appearance	Qualities	Sources	Uses
Okoumé (Aucoumea klaineana)	Angouma, gaboon	Light pink-brown.	Variable interlocked grain.	Hardwood: equatorial West Africa	Plywood, veneer paneling and furniture
Ovangkol (Guibourtia ehie)	Amazoue, amazakoue, anokye, ehie, and hyeduanini	Yellow-brown to chocolate-brown, with gray-black stripes.	Heavy, moderately hard. Finishes very well.	Hardwood: tropical West Africa, primarily Ivory Coast Ghana	Cabinetry, fine furniture, doors, trim, flooring, plywood, veneer, paneling
African padauk (Pterocarpus soyauxii)	Barwood, comwood, corail, African coralwood, muenge, mbe, mbil, mututi, ngula, vermillion, and yomo	Rich red to purple-red heartwood; pale beige sapwood	Coarse texture large pores. Hard, heavy, and strong, with exceptional decay resistance and dimensional stability. Finishes well without stain	Hardwood: central and West Africa	High-end cabinets, furniture, veneer, inlay, flooring
Palmwood (Cocos nucifera)	Palmwood is the commercial name for wood of the coconut palm tree	Golden to near ebony, with dark brown flecks	No knots, imperfections. Prepared by removing moisture and substituting nontoxic preservative oils. Alternative to endangered hardwoods.	Recently classified as a hardwood. Comes from farmed plantations of old coconut palms planted originally for coconut fruit	Medium density: walls, ceiling joists, and horizontal studs. Low density: wood paneling, internal trim, and ceilings
Pau marfim (Balfourodendron riedelianum)	Moroti, guatambu moroti, guatamba, farinha seca, pau liso, kyrandy, and ivorywood	Dense, fine textured, mostly straight grain, creamy white color	Heavy, tough, strong, stable. Excellent wear. Stains, finishes well. Used as a substitute for maple and birch	Hardwood: grows in Brazil, Paraguay, and Argentina	Flooring, cabinetwork, furniture, paneling, and veneer
Pear (Pyrus communis)	Peartree, pearwood, and common pear	Pinkish-brown	Heavy, hard, and tough, with dimensional stability. Stains and finishes extremely well	Hardwood fruit tree: Western Europe, North Africa across Asia, North America	Furniture, decorative veneers, paneling, marquetry, and inlay
Pecan (Carya illinoensis)		Pale reddish-brown, with dark streaks	Close grained	Hardwood: U.S.	Furniture, flooring

Species	Names	Appearance	Qualities	Sources	Uses
Pine (*Pinus* species) Softwood conifer with many species Highly combustible resin of some species is used to make turpentine. Pine has a pleasant but pronounced smell, and a very small number of people are allergic to pine resin; it can trigger an asthma attack	*Pinus radiatus:* Monterey pine, radiata pine	Light wood	Soft, coarse grained	Coastal California; New Zealand. Displacing native trees in Australia, and Chile.	Flooring, furniture plywood, reconstituted panel products
	P. resinosa: Red pine called Norway pine, incorrectly	Reddish	Strength between white and yellow pine	Softwood: northeastern North America	Interior wood trim, moldings
	P. sylvestris L: Scots Riga, Norway, Mongolian pine and—incorrectly—Scotch pine	Pale brown to red-brown	Considered an invasive species in Ontario, Canada, and Wisconsin in the United States	Softwood: West and north central Europe. New Zealand	General construction
	P. strobes Eastern white, northern white, soft, Weymouth pine	Knotty pine refers to the knots and color of white pine	Lightweight, straight grain, lacks figures, resists shrinking, swelling	Softwood: Eastern North America	Furniture, millwork, sashes, doors, trim, paneling, cabinetry, veneer
	Pinus echinata Southern, loblolly, longleaf, shortleaf pine	Yellow, resinous wood	Medium-hard wood	Softwood: Southern and eastern U.S. some salvage	Lumber and pulp, strong timbers, Veneer, plywood
	P. ponderosa Ponderosa, western yellow, California white, Oregon, bird's-eye, knotty, prickly, blackjack, and pitch	Prominent dark resin duct lines and numerous small but sound knots. Light reddish-brown heartwood; pale yellow sapwood	Straight grained, sometimes with a bird's-eye pattern. Light, soft, stable. May need sealer coat to handle resin	Softwood: western U.S. southern British Columbia	Millwork, building construction, furniture, paneling, plywood
Plane (*Platanus* species) Hardwoods grown in North America and Eurasia, from the Balkans to Iran	*P. occidentalis* American sycamore, American plane, buttonwood, buttonball, water beech	Reddish-brown heartwood; lighter-colored sapwood	Moderately light-weight, hard, stiff, and strong. Quarter-sawn lumber primarily.	Hardwood: eastern half of U.S.	Lumber, butcher blocks, interior furniture flooring, and veneer

Species	Names	Appearance	Qualities	Sources	Uses
	P. racemosa California sycamore, western sycamore, buttonball, buttonwood	Tough coarse-grained wood	Difficult to split or work	Hardwood: California	Butcher blocks
	P. orientalis L. Oriental plane	Highly figured	Ancient garden tree	Hardwood: Eurasia	Indoor furniture
Poplar (*Populus* species)	European black, Canadian, and balsam poplar, cottonwood, and various aspens	Creamy white to pale brown	Straight grained and woolly, with a fine, even texture. Soft, light, low strength. Staining can be patchy, but paints and varnish apply well.	Hardwood: North America, Europe, and Asia.	Furniture framing, interior joinery, plywood core stock, veneer
Purpleheart (*Peltogyne* species)	Amaranth, violetwood, coracy, pauroxo, pauferro, koroboreli, saka, nazareno, morado, and tananeo	Creamy white sapwood; vibrant purple heartwood that turns to dark purplish-brown when exposure to light	Very heavy, hard, strong, and stiff, with good decay resistance and stability in service. Polishes well with no staining required	Hardwood: tropical regions of Central and South America.	Inlay, marquetry, furniture, cabinets, flooring
Queensland walnut (*Endiandra palmerstonii*)	Oriental wood, walnut bean, Australian walnut, Australian laurel	Pinkish sapwood; brown heartwood, with pinkish, gray-green, or blackish streaks	Straight to wavy grain, fine, even texture. Polishes to an excellent finish. Resembles European walnut, but stronger	Hardwood: grows in northern Queensland, Australia.	Furniture, joinery, paneling, flooring, construction, veneers
Ramin (*Gonystylus macrophyllum*)	Ramin telur, melawis, lanutan-bagyo	Creamy white to pale straw. Straight to interlocked grain and fine, even texture	Moderately heavy and hard, with high crushing strength. Stains, paints, and generally finishes nicely, although grain filling may be necessary.	Hardwood: Sarawak, Malaysia. Listed as endangered. It is estimated that 90 percent of the trade in ramin is illegally logged.	Furniture, moldings, joinery, flooring, paneling, plywood, veneers, window blinds
Redwood (*Sequoia sempervirens*)	California, coast, sempervirens, and Humboldt redwood	Very prominent growth rings. Light red to deep reddish-brown heartwood; near-white sapwood	Straight grained. Light, soft; good decay resistance and stability. Accepts and holds paints exceptionally well	Softwood: Pacific Coast of U.S.	Building construction, outdoor furniture

Species	Names	Appearance	Qualities	Sources	Uses
Western Redcedar (*Thuja plicata*) Evergreen conifer in cypress family (not a cedar)	Arborvitae, giant arborvitae, giant cedar, canoe cedar, Pacific red cedar, and shinglewood	Pinkish-brown to dull brown heartwood; nearly white sapwood	Straight grained, coarse texture. Light, very good decay resistance and stability. Finishes well Weather- and moth resistant oils.	Softwood: Pacific Northwest, Hawaii, Europe, New Zealand	Saunas and decorative veneers: closet linings. Shellac confines its oils
Rimu (*Dacrydium cupressinum*)	(Formerly red pine)	Very slow growing with intricate veins, burls	New Zealand's government forbids felling rimu in public forests, but limited logging continues on private lands	Large hardwood evergreen conifer: native to New Zealand	High-quality wooden furniture
Rosa peroba (*Aspidosperma* species)	Red peroba, pink peroba, palo rosa, amargosa	Rose-red heartwood; yellowish sapwood	Fine textured, hard, heavy, very dense; durable heartwood. Stains and polishes well	Hardwood: grows in southeastern areas of Brazil	Joinery, furniture, flooring, paneling, decorative veneers
Rosewood* (*Dalbergia* species) Hardwoods	Brazilian rosewood *D. nigra*: Rio or Bahia rosewood	Richly hued brown wood, dark veins. Exudes strong, sweet smell	Strong, heavy wood that polishes exceptionally well.	Brazilian rosewood is CITES-listed, over-exploited	Furniture, cabinetry, paneling, marquetry, and carving
	Indian Rosewood (*D. latifolia*: East Indian or Bombay rosewood, Bombay blackwood, shisham, sissoo, biti, ervadi, and kalaruk	Interlocked grain, with a uniform, moderately coarse texture.Purple-brown heartwood with attractive dark streaks; yellowish-white sapwood, often with a purple tinge	Heavy, hard, and dense, with high bending and crushing strengths; good stability and steam-bending capability, and very durable heartwood.Finishes nicely, although filling is recommended	Hardwood: grows in southern India	Furniture, cabinetry, paneling, and decorative flooring
	Kingwood (*D. cearensis*)	Purple, with many fine darker stripes	Richly grained	Small area in Brazil	Inlays on very fine furniture
	Tulipwood (*D. decipularis*: Brazilian tulipwood)	Heartwood pinkish to yellowish with pronounced yellow stripes in violet, salmon, rose.	Very high-quality wood; very dense with a lovely figure. Available only in small sizes	Rarely used as a solid wood for luxury furniture	Inlays and marquetry in furniture
	Scented mahogany, aboudirko, penkwa, muyovu, libuyu, and sapele mahogany	Medium texture, high luster; pale yellow sapwood, and light red to dark reddish-brown heartwood	Sometimes wavy grain, distinctive roe figure on quartered surfaces. Stains well if grain is filled	Hardwood grows in West, Central, and East Africa	Furniture, cabinetry, veneers, paneling, flooring, joinery, window and door frames, doors

Species	Names	Appearance	Qualities	Sources	Uses
Sapele (*Entandrophragma cylindricum*)	East Indian satin-wood, buruta	Gold color, with a reflective sheen	Fine texture, sometimes wavy. Lustrous	Hardwood: Nigeria, Ivory coast, Cameroon	Luxury cabinets, fine furniture, joinery, paneling, inlay, veneer
Ceylon satinwood (*Chloroxylon swietenia*)		Heartwood light to golden yellow, lightens to soft brown	High luster. Turns, stains, and polishes well.	Hardwood: Philippines	Plywood sheets, veneers, door skins, and furniture
Shorea (*Shorea* species): 360 species of hardwood rainforest trees	Almon (*S. almon*)	Light red to pink wood	Moderately soft, easily worked.		Light construction and interior finish
	Balau (Philippine mahogany in North America)	Similar to teak	Very dense, oil-rich, strong, and weather-resistant	Southeast Asia	Outdoor furniture
	Meranti (lauan, meranti bukit and meranti bakau)	Light- to medium-weight hardwood; categorized as white, yellow	Very hard, stiff, does not turn well. Most is illegally harvested.	Malaysia, Sarawak, and Indonesia, Philippines	Light construction, veneers
	Lauan (meranti from the Philippines)	Red to near white. Red lauan is dark red-brown to brick red	Poor- to medium-quality wood	Philippines	Inexpensive plywood
	Sal (*Shorea robusta*)	Light color when freshly cut; turns darker with exposure to light	Hard coarse grain, good strength and elasticity	Native to south Asia	House super-structures
Snakewood (*Acacia xiphophylla*)		Very tight, wavy grain. Orange with black spots	Usually as very small trees.	Western Australian hardwood; rare	Veneer, inlays
Spruce (*Picea* species)	Norway spruce (Sprucewood, whitewood)	Near white, straight grain	Before the development of petro-chemicals, its resin was used to make pitch. Strong, lightweight.	European native	Lumber
	Sika spruce (*P. sitchensis*)	White wood is valued for traditional Japanese houses	High strength, lightweight, with regular, knot-free rings	Native to west coast of North America; Britain, New Zealand	General construction, flooring, paneling, furniture, cabinets, plywood
Coniferous evergreen softwoods					

322

Species	Names	Appearance	Qualities	Sources	Uses
Sugi (*Cryptomeria*)	formerly Japanese cedar but not a cedar	Wood is scented, reddish pink	Lightweight but strong, waterproof and decay resistant	Hardwood: forestry plantations in China and Japan	Construction work and interior paneling
Gum (*Liquidambar straciflua*)	Alligator tree, bilsted, redgum, sapgum, starleaf gum, liquidambar, hazel pine, and satin walnut	Reddish-brown heartwood (sold as "redgum"); creamy white sapwood (sold as "sapgum")	Figured grain may form ribbon stripe satiny luster. Finishes easily. Stained to simulate other woods, such as cherry	Hardwood: eastern half of U.S.	Interior furniture, veneer, trim, paneling
Teak (*Tectona* species)	Common teak (*T. grandis*: Burma, Rangoon, or moulmein teak, gia thi, jati sak, kyun, mai sak, rosawa)	Golden brown heartwood; grayish or white sapwood. Moderately hard	Straight grained, coarse, uneven texture; medium luster, oily feel. Heavy, excellent decay resistance and dimensional stability. Natural oils can cause adhesion difficulties.	Hardwood: Indonesia, India, Central America, China. Concern about the disappearance of old-growth teak	Furniture, joinery, flooring, paneling, plywood, veneers. Mature teak is very expensive.
	Dahat teak (*T. hamiltoniana*)	May be strongly figured	Hard, heavy, durable, carves well	Confined to Myanmar, where it is endangered	Veneer, furniture
	Philippine teak (*T. philippinensis*)	Golden brown to grayish white	High quality, durable	Exclusively native to the Philippines; endangered.	Furniture, joinery
	Rhodesian teak (*Baikiaea plurijuga*; Zambesi redwood, umgusi, mukushi and mukusi)	Red-brown heartwood, often with black flecks; much paler sapwood	Fine, even texture. Very heavy and hard. High bending and crushing strength, decay resistance, stability	Hardwood: Zambia and Zimbabwe	Flooring, furniture
Redwood	Coast redwood, California redwood	Red heartwood is best but is rare.	Light weight, resistance to decay and fire. Phenolics and resins in old-growth redwoods protect from termites and water damage	Only 3% of the existing redwood is old-growth, and not all of it is protected	Redwood burls are made into tabletops, veneers, and turned goods
Sequoia (*Sequoia sempervirens*)	About 100 species	Type of redwood	Fire rating of A1. Wood sinks in water; insect-resistant, very durable	Hardwood: native from Mexico through South America	Furniture, decking, and outdoor uses

Species	Names	Appearance	Qualities	Sources	Uses
Tabebuia (*Tabebuia caraiba*)	Poui, Ipê, Pau d'arco, Ipê roxo, and lapacho	Reddish brown, may have green tinge, light or dark stripes	Extremely hard and resistant to fire and pests. A1 fire rating	Commercially farmed hardwood. FSC certified ipe	Furniture, decking
Surinam greenheart (*Tabebuia serratifolia*)		Creamy white sapwood; pale, reddish-brown heartwood	Fine, uniform texture, straight grain. Very soft, lightweight, low strength	Hardwood: Asia, Europe, eastern North America	Furniture, millwork, venetian blinds and shutters, veneer
Tilia species	Basswood (*Tilia*: linden in North America, lime in Great Britain)	Creamy white heart-wood and sapwood	Soft, light. Generally straight grained, medium luster	Hardwood grows in Europe and eastern Asia	Venetian blinds, core stock, and decorative veneer
	European lime (*Tilia vulgaris*: European lime, tilleul and linden)				
Utile (*Entandrophragma utile*)	Abebay, afau-konkonti, assie, efuodwe, kosi-kosi, mebrou zuiri, oke-ong, and sipov	Light brown sapwood; reddish-brown, mahoganylike heartwood	Interlocked, irregular grain, often produces a striped ribbon figure. Hard and moderately heavy	Hardwood: Ghana and the Ivory Coast	Furniture, cabinets, joinery, interior construction, flooring, plywood, veneer
Walnut (*Juglans* species)	Black walnut (*J. nigra*) Eastern or American black walnut	Rich chocolate brown	Wood is dense, hard, tight grained, and polishes well. Heartwood, when kiln-dried, turns dull brown, but is rich purplish-brown when airdried	Hardwood: native from southeast Europe to Japan, Americas	Flooring, cabinetry and furniture, panels, veneer, joinery
	Persian walnut (*J. regia*) English walnut common walnut	Sapwood is creamy white; heartwood is chocolate brown	Very high-quality wood similar to black walnut. Introduced into western and northern Europe by Romans	Hardwood: Europe, North America	Furniture
	Butternut (*J. cinerea*) white walnut	Golden brown, beautiful grain	Lightweight polishes well. Much lower in value than black walnut; softer, coarser, less strong and heavy, and paler	Native to North America. Threatened by fungus.	Carving, cabinetry

Species	Names	Appearance	Qualities	Sources	Uses
Willow (*Salix* species)	Black willow, weeping willow, crack willow	Light brown wood with thin whitish sapwood	Lightweight, soft, perishable wood	Hardwood: Mostly native to the northern hemisphere	Wicker furniture, baskets, veneer, chairs
Yellow poplar (*Liriodendron tulipifera*) Not a true poplar.	American whitewood, tulip poplar, -tree, -wood, poplar, popple, white poplar, canary- canoe wood-; and saddletree	Straight grained, fine, texture. Yellowish-brown heartwood, ages green white sapwood.	Takes paint, stains, and other finishes well. Readily available and inexpensive	Hardwood: grows in eastern United States and Canada	Furniture components, sash, doors, shelving
Yew (*Taxus* species)	European yew (*Taxus baccata*: yew, common yew, and yewtree)	Narrow, whitish sapwood; orange-brown, red-brown, or purplish-brown heartwood ages to a golden brown	Straight grained, sometimes curly and irregular. Excellent steam-bending capability decay resistance. Polishes well	Softwood: grows throughout Europe, southern Asia, and northern Africa	Bent furniture, cabinets, joinery, doors, paneling, veneers
	Pacific yew (*Taxus brevifolia*: yew or western yew)	Even grained, with a very fine texture. Bright orange to rosered heartwood; light yellow sapwood.	Heavy, hard, strong, good steam bending and decay resistance. Oil-based finishes will turn heartwood to a chocolate brown	Grows in western Canada and United States. In relatively scarce supply	Bent work, paneling

Index

Page numbers in **bold** identify illustrations.

A

Aalto, Alvar 65, 104, 119, **120**
Abrasion resistance 206
Absorptance 84
Accessible design 5, 6
Acetate 176, 189, 192, 275, 287, 291,
   293–4, 295
Acetone 160, 294
Acid-etched 96
   Staining, concrete 47–8
Acoustic properties and materials 11,
   129, 152, 165, 169, **248**, 263
   Ceiling 248, 256–9, 261–3
   Flooring 195, 214–218
   Treatments 121, 134, 143, 212–3, 229–30,
     236, 247, 250, 253–4, 256, 278
ACQ wood preservative 109
Acrylic 176–8, 235, 244–5, 270–1, 291,
   C-51
   Coating or finish 40, 72, 154, 168,
     213, 113, 242–3, 269, 280
   Fiber 184–5, 189, 288, 295, 137, 291,
     294
   Flooring 206, 221
   Panel 185, 229
Acrylonitrile-butadiene-styrene (ABS)
   178–9, 184
ADA Accessibility Guidelines 2
Adaptive reuse **26**
Adhesive 106–7, 111–2, 117–22, 137,
   166, 173, 175, 178–80, 184–5, 192,
   206, 209–10, 214–5, 218, 231–2,
   234, 236–7, 274, 278, 296
Admixture, concrete **44–5**
Adobe 63, 64, 66, 137
African peduak wood 202, Appendix
Afromosia wood 202, Appendix
Aggregate 38, 42–45, 47, 61, 73, 75, 129,
   138, 158, 199–200, 230, 232,
   269–70, 272, 275
Airplane plywood 119, **120**
Ajanta caves, India 127
Alabaster 55, 130
Alarm glass 89

Alcohol 160, 178–9, 241–3
Alkaline 212, 214, 296
Alkyd 179, 184, 238 resin 241, 243
Allen, Edward 265
Alloy 149, 153, 156–7, 160, 162, 169–73
Alpaca 287, 293
Alpha-beta brass 165
Alumina 162
Alumino-borosilicate glass 82
Aluminum (Aluminium) 86, 149, 153–5,
   162, **163,** 164–6, 170, 172, 209–10,
   244, 257, 262, 279
   Brass and bronze (albronze) 165, 168
   Coating, face, fiber, foil 132, 140, 259,
     292, 296
   Oxide 154, 162, 206
Amboyna wood 103, 115, Appendix
American beech 202, Appendix
American Society for Testing and
   Materials (ASTM) standards 30,
   70–2, 90–1
   ASTM 1066, Vinyl Composition Floor
     Tile
   ASTM B 86-04 Zinc and
     Zinc-Aluminum (ZA) Alloy
   ASTM B339 Grade A Tin for the
     Manufacture of Tinplate
   ASTM B545-97 (2004) E1
     Electrodeposited Coatings of Tin
   ASTM C36 140
   ASTM D256 Impact Resistance
   ASTM D2583 Barcol Scale
   ASTM D760 Flexural Strength Test
   ASTM E-119, Fire Tests of Building
     and Construction Materials
   ASTM E-84 Tunnel test
   ASTM F 1303 Grades of Sheet Vinyl
     Floor Covering with Backing
   ASTM F-793 Classes
   ASTM G21, G22 Tests for Bacterial
     and Fungal Resistance 234
   ASTM Gypsum Wallboard
   ASTM-B633 Zinc
Ammonium 109, 288
   Chloride 168
   Oxalate 169
   Sulfate 168
Angora 286–7, 293

Anhydrite 130
Aniline dye 107, 243
Annealing 83, 87, 90, 96, 153, 172
Annular ring 105, 109
Anodizing 154, 162–4, 172–3, 262, 279
American National Standards Institute
   (ANSI)
   ANSI 137.1 (1988) Ceramic Tile
     Performance Standards 195
   ANSI 194.1 Cellulosic Fiberboard
     121
   ANSI A 162.2 Fabricated High-
     Pressure Laminate Countertops 274
   ANSI A156.18 Materials and Finishes
     153
   ANSI A208.1 Wood Particleboard 121
   ANSI HP-1 Hardwood and Decorative
     Plywood 119
   ANSI/ICPA SS-1-2001 Solid
     Surfacing Materials
Antimony 84, 169, 171
Antique brick 69
   Finish 153, 280, **C-71**
   Mirror 87
   Wood flooring 203
Antigraffiti film 244
Antimicrobial 259, 263, 290, 296
Antireflective glass 89
Antiskinning agent 238
Antron 189
Apple wood 103–4, Appendix
APT Bulletin, Association of Preservation
   Technologies 27
Aramid 189, 193, 288, 292, 294, 297
Articulation class (AC) 259
Architectural Metal Products (AMP)
   Division 153
   Bronze and brass 165, **C-43,** 166
   Hardware 166
   Millwork 106
   Resin panels 183, 229, **C-61**
Area rug 221
Armchair, plywood **120,** Architectural
   fabrics 178
Arsenic 84–5, 109, 169, 186
Art glass, mosaics 244, **C-55**
Asbestos 21–2, 131, 184, 214–5, 288
Asdin, Joseph 29

As-fabricated finish 154
Ash wood 105, 115, 202, 254, 278,
    Appendix
Ashlar 55, **63**
Aspen wood 120, Appendix
Asphalt 158
Assemblies 141, 223–4
Attenuation 11
Australian cypress wood 202, Appendix
Awning 184, 189
Azurite 166

B

B.F. Goodrich 176
Back-coated textile 235
Backer board 224–5, 230
    BKL backer 186
    Sheet 182, 274
Backing, carpet 216, 218–9
    Grade veneer 114
    Latex 236
    Vinyl sheet 214
Backsplash 269, 274–5
Baekeland, Leo Hendrik 176
Baffle 253, 263
Baked enamel 262, 277
Bakelite 176, 183
Baldwin, Francis 233
Baltard, Victor 151
Bamboo 122–3, 202, 210, 221, 279,
    Appendix
Banner 263, 291
Barcelona Pavilion 79
Bark 105, 299
Base 178–9, 231, **232**
    Cabinet **267**, 269
Basecoat 129, 132, 134, 137–8, 194, 223
Basralocus wood 202, Appendix
Batiste 288–9
Bauxite 162
Bead 231, **232**
Beadboard 253, **254**
Beam 110, 128, 151, 158, 161, 251, 262
Bed, iron **104, 157**
Beech wood 203, Appendix
Benedictus, Edouard 79
Bent glass, laminated wood 89, 120
Berber carpet 219
Berlange, H.P. 64
Bessemer, Henry, steel process 150–1
Beveled 96, 203, 257, 259, 273
Bezold effect 200
Bias 298
Bibliothèque, Paris 78
Bicheroux, Emil 79
Binder 29, 175, 181, 184, 215, 237, 243,
    278
Biomass 69

Birch wood 103, 105, 202–3, Appendix
Bird's-eye maple 115, Appendix
Bituminous coating 166
Black cherry wood 202, Appendix
    Locust wood 105, Appendix
    Lung disease 158
    Walnut wood 202, Appendix
Blast furnace 150, 152, 157–8
Bleach 280, 287, 294–6, 300–1
Blind glass 96
    Window treatment 95, 284
Blown glass 77, 82, 85
Blue board 140, 143, 145, 224
Bluestone 58
Board feet, flooring 110–1, **205**
Body-tinted glass 86
Bokhara rug 221
Bolt 159–60
Bonded terrazzo 201
    Polyurethane foam 220
Bonderizing 155
Bonding agent, adhesive 134, 219, 300
Bone inlay 102
Book matching 116, **117,** 228
Borate, boric acid, boron 109, 146, 210
Borosilicate glass 82
Bow **107,** 109, 209
Box wood 103, Appendix
Braided rug 221–2
Brandenberger, Jacques Edwin 176
Brass and bronze 62, 79, 103, 149, **150,
    152,** 155, 164–6, 171, 201, 279,
    C-44, C-46
Brazilian rosewood or cherry 111, 115,
    202, Appendix
Brazing 166
Breeze block 73
Brick 62, 64, **68, 70,** 71, 97, 104, 116,
    129–30, **132,** 134–5, 139, 199, 223
Brindle tufts 101
Broadloom carpet 217–8
Brocade 289, 291, 294, 298
Broom finish, concrete 49
Brown coat **131–133,** 140
Brownstone 58, 130
Buckskin 193
Budget, materials 8–10
Buffed finish 152, 154, 164, 168, 194,
    206, 279
Built-in 265
Bullet- and burglar-resistant glass 91
Bullnose 231, **232,** 273
Bunshaft, Gordon 80
Burlap 283, 289
Burlington, Lord 127
Burl 115
Burnham, Daniel, 64
Butane 184
Butcher block 272, **273**
Butt joint or corner 159, **281**

Butterfly spline **281**
Byzantine 54, 77, 150

C

Cabinet, cabinetry, cabinetwork,
    cabinetmaking 106, 119–22, 228–9,
    265–**267,** 278
Cadmium 84, 149
CAL 116 and 117, 284
CAL 133, 189, 193, 284, 294, 297
Calcined 129, 227
Calcium hydroxide, oxide 48, 83, 146
Calendaring 179, 232–3, 296, 301
Calico 171
Cambium **105**
Camel hair 287, 293
Cane 121
Cannabis sativa 288
Canvas 289
Carbon 156–8, 160, 175, 177
    Black 34, 71
    Dioxide (CO_2) 16, 129, 159
    Disulfide 176
    Monoxide (CO) 16, 157, 284
    Steel 153, 155, 157
Carbonized bamboo 210
Carcinogen 158, 167, 170, 210, 237
Carnauba wax 241
Carothers, Wallace Hume 176
Carpet 178, 191, 195, 207, 216, 219–20,
    290–1
    Backing, pad 178–9, 181, 289, 299
    Fiber 178–9, 184, 189, 192, 217, 295
    Indoor-outdoor 184, 219
    Tile 217–9, 278
Carpet and Rug Institute (CRI) 218
    CRI IAQ 220
Carved leather 193
Case-hardening 153
Casein 175, 240, 280
Casework 265
Cashmere 287, 293
Casing bead 142
Cast 150
    Brass 165
    Concrete 200
    Glass 77, 83, **85,** 86
    Iron 156, 170
    Nylon 179
    Plaster ornaments 134
    Resin 185
    Zinc alloy 173
Caster 278
Catalyzed lacquer and urethane 112, 242,
    282
Category I, II, IV, V, VI wallcovering 236
Cathedral grain 118
Cathodic process 86
Caucasian rug 221

Caustic soda 176, 296
C-channel 185
Ceasarstone 271
Cedar 103, 109–10, 115, 149, 202, 207,
    229, 278, Appendix
Ceiling Attenuation Class (CAC) 259
Ceiling, cell 262
    Form 249, **265, C-65**
    GFRG 227
    Panel 254, 257
    Plaster and stucco 116, 127–8, 138
    Suspension system 134, 157, 185, 257,
    262
Celanese 189
Cellophane 176
Cellular foam 283
    Glass 77
    Steel decking 252–3, 257
Celluloid 175–6
Cellulose, cellulosic 122, 129, 175, 257,
    178–9, 287, 289, 293–4
    Acetate and acetate butyrate (CAB)
    184, 242
    Fiber and fiberboard 121, 288, 296,
    300
Cement, cementitious 29, **30,** 31, 36–7,
    112, 129–30, 140, 146, 158, 180,
    196, 200–1, 230, 272
Ceramic 86, 97, 173, 206, 259
    absorption levels 99
    glazes 66, 68, 98–9, **C-27**
    tile 33, 97, 100, 132–3, 195, 197–8 ,
    230–1, 272, **C-26, C-54**
Cerium 84
Certified wood 272, 279
Chair components 179, 184, **282**
Challis 293
Channel 161, 253, 256
Chapel of Notre-Dame-du-Haut,
    Ronchamp, France 42, **43**
Chartres Cathedral 53
Checks, checking 109, 118, 202
Chemical treatment, resistance 152–4,
    164, 166, 168, 193, 199
    Sensitivity, concrete 46
    Welding 215
Cherry wood 103–4, 202, 272, 278–9,
    293, Appendix
Chest, damascened 119, **150**
Chestnut wood 103, 105, Appendix
Chicago Century of Progress Exposition
    214
Chiffon 289
Children's space **C-3**
Chinese materials 97, 101, 119, 149, 221,
    242, 288
China grass 289
Chintz 286
Chipboard 112, 278
Chlorofluorocarbon 283

Chlorine 164, 300
Chrome 155, 166–7, 279
Chromated copper arsenate (CCA) 109
Chromium 84, 109, 149, 155, 157–8, 160,
    166–7, 170, 186, 193
Cigarette ignition test 284
Cinder 73, 152
Cladding 155
Classroom seating 265
Clay 66, 69, 72, 97–8, 112, 129–30, 168,
    237
    Porcelain 197–8, 240
    Tile 134, 223, 230
Clean room ceiling 259
Cleat, nailing 204
Cleft 59, 200
Clic flooring 209
Closed-loop 11, 121
Cloud ceiling 23
CLS cabinet liner 186
Coal 31, 69, 158
Coating 81–2, 163, 167–8, 178–80, 299
Cobalt 84
Cobweb paint finish 240
Codes 2–4, 137, 244
Codes Guidebook for Interiors 2
Coffers 134, **137,** 147, 226, **250**
Coil spring 282
Colburn, Irving 79
Cold-cut glass 77
    -Drawing 152
    -Rolling 154
    -Spray technology 172
    -Worked metal 152
Collagen 193
Color 2, 280, 293
    Coat, stucco 140
    Colorfast 299–301
    Colorway 286
Column, concrete 252
    Cover **146,** 147, 156–7, 226, 228
    GFRG 147, 227
    Iron 156, 150–1
    Plaster 134
    Wood 110, 237
Combing paint 240
Combustible 170, 172, 176
Comfort 10
Commercial bronze 165
    Glass 82
    Kitchen finishes 199, 228
    Non-vinyl wallcovering **237**
Commode 103
Common brick 62
    Wood 203
Composite or composition wood product
    106–7, 109, 111, 118–9, 184
Compression modulus 283
Concrete 37, **38, 39,** 104, 134, 157, 158,
    163, 248

Countertop and sink 269–70, **274**
Finishes 49–50
Formwork 122, 257
Slab, subfloor 80, 195, **200,** 201, 206,
    209, 215, 231
Structure 141, 251–2
Concrete block, brick, CMU 74, 134,
    138–9, 73–75, 223
Conductive materials 149, 152, 162, 167,
    171–2, 218, 292
Conifer 105, 175
Consolidated paint 240
Construction Specification Institute
    (CSI) 210
Construction-grade plywood 119
Construction waste 145
Contact cement 117, 185
Contraction, wood 202
Control joint 142
Conventional cotton 288
Conversion coating, varnish 112, 154,
    163–4, 168
Cooktop 269
Copper 62, 84, 87, 97, 107, 149, 155,
    164–5, 167–9, 171, 186, 270
    Alloy 153, 170
    Finish **C-47, C-48**
Core-formed glass 77
Corian **180,** 270, 275
Cork 185, 211–2, 220, 237, **C-57**
Corner joint 159
    Molding and reinforcing 142
Cornice 134, **135,** 137
Corrected grain leather 193
Corrosion 81, 131, 149, 155, 158, 160, 162,
    164–5, 167–3, 180, 199, 277, 296
Corrugated metal, 161, 252–3, 257, 283,
    C42
Cotton and blends, sateen 175, 221–2,
    245, 283, 286–9, 290–2, 294–6, 300
Cotton, William 298
Countertop 6, 46, 60–1, 83, 120, 122,
    177–8, 184, 186–8, 229, 265,
    269–70, 274–5
Cove base 201, 216, **232**
    Ceiling **249,** 250, 257
Crack filler 135
Crackle paint finish 240
Cradle-to-cradle 11
Craftsman style cabinet 267
Creosote 105
Crepe 299
Cristallo 78
Crochet 284
Crocking 287, 300
Crook **107,** 109
Crown glass 78, **82**
Crown molding 240
Crypton 294
Crystal Palace, London 78, **80,** 150, 157

Cup **107,** 108–9, 209
Cuprammonium method 192
Curb 231, **232**
Curing, concrete 44
Curtain 192, 289
Curtain wall 80
Curve radius 141
Curved plastic laminate countertop **C-69**
Cushion 214, 218–9, 283
Custom tile 231
Custom cabinet 266
Customers own leather (COL) 283
    Material (COM) 283, 286
Cut pile 217, 221, 298
Cutting block 269
Cyanide 181
Cylinder printing 301
Cypress 109–10, 207, 278
Cyproconazole 109

D

Dacron 192
Dado 266
Damascening **150**
Damask 298
Darby, Abraham 150
Davis, Alexander Jackson 54
De Key, Lieven 127
Deal (pine) 103
Deciduous 105, Appendix
Decking 110
Decorative laminates 120–1
    Stucco 138
    Thin wall tile 230
Deflocculents 66
Delamination 210, 219, 277
Demolition 18–9, 45, 145
Demountable partition 145, 224, 229, 278
Denier 287
Densified prime polyurethane foam 220
Dhurrie rug 221
Diamond matching 116, 228
Dichroic coatings 96
Didecyldimethylammonium chloride
    (DDAC) 109
Die and die casting 68, 152, 163, 173
Diffusion 11
Dimension lumber 106, 110
    Stone 231–2
Dimensions, functional **6, 7, 8**
Dimensional stability 113, 121, 203, 208,
    210, 218, 233, 274, 285, 296
Direct printing 301
Discharge dyeing 301
Distressed finish, distressing 205, 279,
    280–1, 300
Divider strip 201
Dobby weave 299

Documentation, building conditions
    24–5, 27
Dome 147, 226–7, 250
Door 119–20, 150, 178, 265, **C-44**
    Frame 122, 149, 162, 165, 281, 292
Double doweled joint **282**
    Glue-down 218
    Knit jersey 299
Douglas fir 119, 202, Appendix
Dovetail joint 104, 266, 279, **281**
Dow Chemical 177
Dowel joint 266, **281**
Down 283
Dragging 280
Drainboard 269, 274
Drapeability 285
Drapery 95, 127, 184, 192, 284, 286,
    289–91, 294–6
Drawer 178–9, 184, 266, 268, 279, 281
Drawn metal 152
Dressed size 106, 111
Drier, paint 238
Drop 232
Dropped ceiling 258
Dryclean 295, 297, 299
Dry-set mortar 231
Drywall 112, 130, 134–5, 140, 143, 145,
    247, **256**
Ductility 149, 153, 156, 167, 170–3
Ductwork 248, **249**
Dupioni silk 289
DuPont 176–7, 193, 275, 294, 297
Durability, durable finish 2, 10, 296
Durable cotton upholstery fabric **297**
Dust pressed tile 198
Dye 48, 107, 182, 184, 193–4, 214, 237,
    240, 243–4, 287, 289, 291, 293–5,
    299

E

Earle Theater **23**
Earthen plaster 129
Earthenware 98
Eased-edge 203, 273
Ebony wood 103, 115, Appendix
Economy cabinet 268
Edge 159, 186, 205, 269, 274–5, **276,** 277
Efflorescence 40, **71**
Eggshell finish 238–9
Egypt 29, 77, 97, 101, 119, 125, 149,
    193, 283
Eiffel, Gustave 151
Elastane 189
Elasticity 2
Elastoester 294
Elastomer, elastomeric 173,189, 283,
    292, 294
Electrically heated glass 88

Electrochemical finish 152
Electrochromic 89, 292
Electrodeposition 155, **C-39**
Electrolysis, electrolytic 155, 164, 170
Electroplating, electropolishing 155, 167,
    170, 262
Elevator cab 166
Elm wood 103, Appendix
Elongation 285
Embodied energy 14, 111, 162, 272
Embossing 150, 194, 287
Emission control system 158
Emulsion paint 238, 240
Enamel 87–8, 155, 271, 280
Encyclopedia of Cottage, Farm and Village
    Architecture, The 37
End match 228
Energy use 14, 31, 255, 270, 296
Engineered chrome 166,
    Stone 60, 61, 232, 275–6, **C-15**
    Wood 208–111, 112, 121, 278
Engraving 50, **51,** 88
Environmental criteria 12
Environmental Protection Agency (EPA)
    109–10, 145
Environmentally preferable product
    (EPP) 13
Epoxy 50, 72, 96, 155, 175, 180, 184, 196,
    199, 201, 231, 271–2, 274–5
Equipment 155, 170
Etched finish 154
Ethane 184
Ethylene, ethyl acetate, benzene, resins
    112, 184–5, 191, 214
Evergreen Recycling Program 190
Evergreen tree 105
Exotic wood 202
Expanded metal mesh 161, 131–2,
    133, 262
Expansion joint 142
Expansion of materials 202, 208–9, 212,
    256, 265
Explosion 159, 172, 242
Exposed beam, ceiling 116, 250, **251**
Extender 177
Exterior plywood 119
Extruded metal 152, **153, 154**
Extrusion process tile 198

F

4-phenylcyclohexene (4-PC)
Fabric 180, 229, 255, 258, 262, 284,
    295–6, 300–1
Face frame cabinet 266–7
Faced blocks 74
Facing brick 62, 64, 68, 72
Factory built 268
Fade 300

Faience 97
Fake fur 291
FDA approved, compliant 187–8
Feather 283
Feldspar 98, 171
Felt, felted 121, 166, 206, 220, 231, 284,
        287, 293, 298–9
Ferrous 149, 155–6, 159, 161
Fiber 173, 178, 188, 222, 284–5, 285,
        287, 289, 295–7
    Carpet 190, 217
    Dye 299–300
    Filling or cushion 182, 192, 220
    Optic 255, 294
Fiberboard 112, 118–9, 121, 278
Fiberglass, Fiberglas 179, 185, 224, 228,
        230, 245, 263, 269, 294
Fiberglass reinforced gypsum (FRG or
        FGRG) 147, 225–6
    Reinforced concrete 269
    Reinforced plastic (FRP) wallcovering
        236, 257
Fiberweb fabric 298–9
Fibrous cement 112
Fieldstone 55, 60
Figured wood 114–5, Appendix
Filament yarn 299
Filigree 150
Filled cell insulation 73
Filler 177, 181–2, 213, 220, 239, 280
Filling yarn 297
Film for glass 97
Fine ceramics 98
Finger joint 104
Finish coat 111, 251
    Fabric 287
    Flooring 195, 205–6
    Metal 152, 154, 162
    Plaster **131,** 132, **133,** 134, 140
    Wood 184
Fir, wood 119, 202, 278, Appendix
Fire and flame resistance 10, 38, 74, 89,
        131–2, 140, 146, 150, 189, 192–3,
        223–4, 227, 236–7, 244–5, 256,
        263, 283–4, 288, 290–1, 293–4,
        296–7
    Safety 181, 277
    Rated 183, 199, 259
    Suppression 137, 258
Fireplace 46, **47,** 61, 69, 99, 227, 265
Fissured ceiling panel 259
Fitness club flooring 213
Fixed glazing 244
Fixed equipment 265
Fixture, plumbing 171
Fixture, store 179
Flagstone 198
Flakeboard 118–9
Flamed finish 59, **61,** 199
Flannel 293

Flash cove 214
Flat cut or sliced wood 106, 115, 228
    Glass 79, 96
    Grain 205
    Paint 238–9
    Plate 251
    Wire 218
Flatbed screen printing 301
Flax 213, 231, 288, 295
Fleece 299
Flexible wallcovering 232
FlexiGuard 244
Flitch 113, 116, 228
Float or floated finish, concrete 49, 138
Float glass 77, 80, 82–3, 86, 91–3, 96
Floating floor installation 204, 208–9, 211–2
Flocculant 66
Flocking 192
Flokati rug 221
Flooring, metal 169,
    Vinyl 177–8, 180–182, 184–5, 188
    Wood 106, 119, 121, 150
Fluid-applied athletic flooring 199
Fluorescent lighting 255
    Whitening compound 296
Fluoroplastic 178–9, 193, 297
Flush cabinet face 266–7
Flux 67
Fly ash 30, 46, 69, 139, 270
Foam products, glass, rubber, plastic 77,
        184, 214, 220, 279, 283, 297
Foil, Foil-backed 87, 140
Food processing, service area 199, 257,
        259, 263, 257, 270
Forest Stewardship Council 110
Forge 152
Form 2
Formaldehyde 20, 46, 112, 121–2, 176,
        178–9, 181, 185, 210, 242, 270, 272
Formica 176, 185
Formwork 131
Fortel 192
Fossil 269
Fountainhead 275
Fourcault, Emile 79
Frameless cabinet 266
Frazee, John 55
French terry 299
Frieze carpet 219
Frit 67
Frog 68
Fuel, fossil 14–5, 31, 130, 183, 210
Functional criteria 10
Fundamentals of Building Construction 265
Fungicide 109–10
Furan 34, 180
Furnace 158
Furness, Frank 213
Furniture materials 121–2, 188, 228, 265,
        278–9, 292, 295

Concrete **47**
Glass 88, 95–6
Hardware and accessories 165, 206–7
Metal 149–51, 156–7, 170
Outdoor 154, 156, 162, 182, 187,
        178–9, 181, 184, 189
Plastic 177–8, 182
Plywood 113, 119
Stone 60
Furring 131, **132,** 133, 141, 256
Fused glass 83–4
Fusion-bonded carpet 217, **218**

G

Gaineswood, Demopolis, Alabama **128**
Galena 169
Galvanic corrosion 149, 164, 166
Galvanized 131, 142, 155, 161–2
Gas, natural 181, 183–4, 288
Gauge, knitting 298
Gauging plaster 129
Gel coat 214, 300
Gibraltar 275
Gilded, gilt 127, 134, 150
Glass 77, 83–4, 92, 96–7, 150, 154,
        166–7, 170–1, 173, 238–9, 269
    Ceramic 77, 82
    Fiber, textile, wool 77, 82–3, 129, 132,
        138, 179, 226–7, 237, 259, 257, 295
    Glass block and brick 77, 86, **87**
    Mosaic tile 116, 150, 195, 198, 231,
        275
Glass fiber reinforced concrete
        (GFRC) 46
    Gypsum (GFRG, GRG) **146,** 147,
        226, 227, 288
    Lumber 186
    Polyester 177
Glazed brick 72
    Ceramic tile 196–198, 230
    Concrete masonry units (CMUs) 73
Glazes, ceramic 97–8
Glazing, electrochromic switchable
        privacy 89
    interior 78–9, 93, 95, 134, 178–9, 244,
        280
    safety 177, 184
Global warming 181
Glue 121, 211, 219, 234, 257, 270, 275,
        282
    -Chip glass 96
    -Down floor 204, 209, 212, 214, 218,
        220
    -Laminated (glulam) timber 112
Glueless locking system 209, 212
Glycol 183, 243
Gold 78, 84, 116, 149–50, 155, 168, 292
Good-grade veneer 113

Gothic 53, 64, 78, 101, 116
Grades of casework construction 268
Graffiti resistant 277
Grain, 152, 200, 210, 280–2
    Wood 105, **106,** 108, 111, 202, 243, 266
Granite 34, 45, 54–6, 59–61, 98–200, 271, **273**
Grass fiber, cloth **235,** 289, 293–4
Grass grid paving units 74
Gravel 45
Gray (grey, greige) goods 287
Greek 53, 101, 116, 221, 240
Green body ceramics 98
Green cotton 288
Green products 13, 15
Greenboard 140, 224, **C-59**
Greenhouse gases 13–4, 16, 283
Greenpeace International 111
Gregor, William 172
Grid system 262
Grille 157
Grog 66, 69
Gropius, Walter 64
Groundwater contamination 158
Grout 31–2, **33,** 99–100, 180–1, 196, 199, 231–2, 275
Growth ring **105**
Gum wood 278, Appendix
Gunmetal 165
Gymnasium flooring 199
Gypsum, cement and concrete **127,** 129–30, 230
    Board 112, 125, 140–1, 143–4, 224–5, 231–2, 234, 255–6
    Lath 132, 142, 225
    Plaster 125, 129, 132, 231, 234
    Wallboard (GWB) 130–1, 134, 140–1, 146, 173, 224, 225, **226**

H

Hackberry wood 105, Appendix
Haddon Hall, Derbyshire 127
Hagia Sophia, Istanbul, Turkey 53
Hair and hide 129, 194, 297, 299
Half-round slicing 115
Hand 285–6
    –dyeing 301
    -forged iron 160
    Layup GFRG 227
    –loom woven cotton runner **C-76**
    -made rug, tile 221, 231
    painting 291
    –scraped hardwood flooring 205
    –spun wool 221
Handbook for Ceramic Tile Installation 100
Hanger wire 256, 259
Hard chrome 166
Hard finish 129

Hard floor covering 195, 278
Hardboard 112, 118–9, 121, 228
Hardness, wood 202
Hardware 156–7, 162, 165, 167, 266, 268, 281
    Cloth 161
    Finishes **C-55**
Hardwood 105–6, 110, 279
    Flooring 202–3, 205–6
    Veneers 113–4, 119, 228
Hardwood Plywood Manufacturers Association 119
Hazardous waste 167
Heart pine wood 202, Appendix
Heartwood **105,** 108
Heat treatment 153, 241
    -Shielding, strengthened glass 81, 87, 90
    -Welding, fusion bonding 215, 220
    Insulation fabric 296
Hematite 149
Hemlock wood 207, Appendix
Hemp 112, 175, 208, 288–9, 295
Herringbone matching 116
Hessian 289
Hexavalent chromium plating 167
Hickory wood 104–5, 202, Appendix
High–abuse gypsum wallboard 224
    -Density fiberboard (HDF) 209
    -Density overlay (HDO) 121–2
    -Density polyethylene (HDPE) 110, 122, 182–3, 186, 277
    -Early-strength concrete 44
    End cabinet 268
    –Impact gypsum wallboard 224
    Pressure decorative laminate (HDPL and HGS, HGP) 182, 186, 265, 274
Historic buildings 22, 25
Hollow brick 68
Homasote 112
Homogenous sheet vinyl 214
Honed finish 59, 198–9, 271
Honeywell nylon 190
Hooked rug 221
Horsehair 287
Hospital finishes 263, 292
Hot-rolled, -worked metal 152
Human factors 4, **5**
Hunter, Matthew A. 172
HVAC 248
Hyatt, John Wesley 176
Hydrated calcium sulfate and lime 129
Hydration 39, 44
Hydraulic cement 30
Hydrocarbon 181
Hydroentangled fabric 299
Hydrofluoric acid 81, 96
Hydrofluorocarbons (HFCs) 16 HCFC 283
Hydrogen, hydrogen sulfide 31, 145, 175
Hydrologic cycle 17
Hydrophilic, hydrophobic, hygroscopic 285

I

Iano, Joseph 265
Igneous rock 45, 55–6, 200
Ikat 301
Illuminated ceiling 255
Illumination 247, 248, 250
Impact sound 11
Impervious 186, 197–8, 230, 277
Impression glass 88
Incan stonework 54
Indentation force deflection 283
India 97, 128, 138, 149, 221, 289, 293
Indoor air quality (IAQ) 1, 12, 19, 220, 234
Infrared (IR) 81, 86
Ingot **152,** 157, 163, 168, 171
Inlaid wood **102,** 103, 214
Innerspring 283
Insecticide 109
Institutional flooring 199
Insulae 42
    Insulation, insulating 15, 112, 132, 178, 180–2, 189, 212–3, 229, 237, 247, 255
    Building panels 184
    Concrete forms (ICFs) 51
    Glass unit (IGU) **85,** 86, 91, 94–96
    PET 191
Intarsia 102
Integral wall base 214
Interior architectural façade 188
    Plywood 119
Interlayer 179, 181, 214, 244
Interlining 299
Invista Nylon 190
Iroko wood 115, 202, Appendix
Iron 149–50, 153–8, 160, 165, 168, 170, 240
    Oxide 84, 157–8, 243
Ironwood (Ipe) 106, 110, Appendix
Islamic design **4,** 53–4, 97, 101, **102, 116,** 138, 150
ISO 14001 268
Isocyanate resin 210
Isolation hanger 259
Italian plaster 138
Ivory 102–3, 176

J

Jacquard, Joseph Marie and loom 298–9
Jahan, Shah 54
Jandl, H. Ward 28
Japan 103, 242, 294
Jarrah and Jatoba wood 202, Appendix
Johnson Wax Building, Racine, Wisconsin 67
Joint or join 47, 240, 266, 279
    Compound and tape 141, 143–4, 224–5, 256
    Sealant 181

Welded 159
Wood 103, 106, **281**
Joist 110, 131, 161
Jones, Inigo 127
Jute 213, 219–221, 283, 289, 293

K

Kahn, Louis 65
Kaolin 66, 98–9
Karnak, Egypt 53
Kazakhstan rug 221
Keene's cement 129
Kelly, William 150
Kent, William 127
Kerfed 232, 257
Ketone 181, 185
Kevlar 189, **190**, 294
Kilim rug 221
Kiln **66**, 68, 69, 98–9, 141, 210, 271, 282
Kitchen cabinets installed 266
Knit fabric 284, 298–9
Knot 105, 111, 113–4, 202–3, 221, 239
Knotty pine 253
Kodel 192
Kroll process 172

L

Laboratory casework, finishes 199, 259, 263, 265, 276
Labrouste, Pierre-François-Henri 78, 151
Lacquer 107, 113, 155, 166, 179, 242, 279
Lambot, Jean-Louis 37
Lamination and laminated 81, 86, 193, 297, 299
    Coating 168, 279
    Decorative 113, 275
    Flooring 209–10, 213
    Glass 88, 90, 244
    Parquet 208
    Safety glazing 184
    Veneer lumber (LVL) 112
    Vinyl 179
    Wood 104, 111, 272
Lap joint 159
Larkin Building, Buffalo, New York 64
Latex 34, 147, 178–9, 219–2, 232, 236, 279, 280, 292, 294
    Paint 238, 240
    Resin flooring 199
    –Portland cement mortar 231
Lath 128–9, 131–2, 134–5, 137, 139, 161, 223–5, 231, 256
Lavastone 271
Lay-in panel 258
Le Corbusier 42, 65, 151
Lead, leading 22, 78, 3, 85, 88, 149, 155, 165, 169–71, 173
Leadership in Energy and Environmental Design (LEED) 15, 17–8, 210

Leather 151, 166, 173, 175, 184, 193, **194**, 221, 284, **285**, 297
LeBrun, Charles 127
LED lighting 255
Lee, William 298
Lehr 83, 87
Leiden Town Hall 127
Lepenski Vir, Serbia 29
Les Halles Centrales 51
LeVau, Louis 127
Level color 299
Lever House, New York 80
Lexan 244
Libbey-Owens Glass Company 79, 83
Library at Viipuri 105 shelves 265
Life-cycle cost 5, 8, 285–6
Light framing 110
Light reflectance 223, 259
Lighting equipment, fixture 82, 162, 171, 177–8, 227, 247, 250, 256, 258, 262
Lightweight framing 112
Lime 46, 127, 138, 160, 193, 237, 240
    Moldings 134
    Mortar, plaster, putty and stucco 32, 128–9, 138
Limestone 30, 45, 57–61, 82, 125, 130, 198, 200, 213, 277
Linear metal panel 258
Linen 287, **288**, 289
Linoleum 185, 195, 211–3
Linseed oil 103, 213, 238, 241, 243, 280
Lintel blocks 74
Liquid crystal glazing 89
    Vehicle 237
    Resin system 244
Llama 287, 293
Locker room finishes 199, 259
Locust, black wood 109, Appendix
Loft 287
Long-staple cotton 288–9
Longstrip wood flooring, planks 209, 211
Loom state goods 287
    -Woven rug detail **C-75**
Loop pile 217, 219, 221
Lost wax process 77, 150
Loudon, J.C. 37
Low-emissivity (low-e) glass 86, 96
    -density polyethelene (LDPE) 182
    -iron glass 82, 93
    -pressure plastic laminate **182**
Lucite 178, 244
Lumber 106–7, 111
Lung disease 214–5
Luster 149, 166, 171, 173, **286**
Lyocell 292, 294–5

M

Machu Picchu, Peru 54
Mack's cement 129

Magnesium, magnesium oxychloride 83–4, 149, 155, 170, 199
Magnetic 156, 158, 240
Magnetron process 86–7
Mahogany wood103, 110, 202, 272, 278, 280, Appendix
Maisons Jaoul, Neuilly-sur-Seine, France 65
Majolica ceramics 97
Malachite 56, 167
Manganese, manganese oxide 77, 164–5, 170
    Industrial finish 199
Maple wood 203, 254272, 278–9, Appendix
Marble 34, 42, 45, 55, 57, 59–61, 79–80, 103, 105, 116, 127, 198–9**C-20, C-21**
    Finishes 200, 202, 233, 271
Marine varnish 241
Marl 30
Marquetry 103
Marshall Field Wholesale Store, Chicago 55
Martin's cement 129
Maryland State House **233**
Masonite 112, 121
Masonry, masonry cement 32, 53, 139, 141, 151, 163, 167, 231
Mass pigmentation 300
Matelassé 299
Material Safety Data Sheets (MSDS) 13–4, 210
McDonough Braungart fabric protocol 13
Medallion, ceiling 134, **137,** 227
Medium-density fiberboard (MDF) 106, 112–3, 121, 184, 228, 265, 274, 279
Medium-density overlay (MDO) 121–2, 271
Melamine 112, 121–2, 178, 181, 184–5, 209, 211, 265, 268, 270, 274, 277
Melmac 176
Merbau wood 202, Appendix
Mercerization 288, 296
Mesh fabric 291
Mesquite wood 202, Appendix
Metal 79, 83,99, 149, 153, 173, 269, 279
    Interior finishes and trims 186, 254, 258, 269
    Metal finishes 152, 154–5, 164
    Metal fume fever 159, 165, 173
    Metal lath **131, 132,** 142
    Mesh 262
    Metal oxide 86–7
Metallic 87, 96, 168, 200, 232, 240, 243, 253, 270, 282, 288, 292
Metal Finishes Manual 153
Metamerism 300
Metamorphic rock 55, 57, 200
Methane 16, 184
Methylene diphenyl diisocyanate (MDI) resin 112

Methylmethacrylate (MMA) flooring 199
Meyer, Adolf 64
Mezquita, Cordoba, Spain 54
Mica 171, 240
Microtopping 27
Microbeveled edge 209
Microfiber 290
Mies van der Rohe, Ludwig 79, 211
Mildew and mold 217–8, 224, 234, 236,
    238, 259, 289–91, 295–6
Milk paint 240, 280, C-72
Mill building 26
Mill finish 154, 287
Millwork 109, 265
Mineral fiber, oxide 199, 213, 257, 259
    287–8, 294, 300
    Spirit or oil 238, 243, 271
Mining 157, 167, 169, 171
Mirror 78, 86–7, 93, 103, 156, 178, 262
Miter 281
Modacrylic 288, 291, 294–5
Modular component, cabinet 103, 266
Modulus of elasticity 111
Mohair 287, 290, 293
Moisture-resistant gypsum wallboard 140,
    224
Mold cast 163
Molded glass or leather 83, 193
    Plaster 129, 134
Molding 121–2, 211, 227, 240, 265
Monofilament 287
Monolithic terrazzo installation 201
Mortar 31, 32, 74, 86, 157, 163, 199,
    231–2
Mortarless brick installation 69, 199
Mortise-and-tenon joint 104, 280, 281
Mosaic 77–8, 195, 197
Moth resistance 291, 295–6
Mother-of-pearl 78, 102, 150
Mud brick and plaster 116, 125, 128
Muffin pan 151
Mulberry wood 105, Appendix
Multifilament 287
Multilevel loop 219
Muntz metal 165
Murano 78
Music space finish 257
Muslin 283
Mylar 97, 259

N

Nail-down installation 204
Napped 297
National Association of Architectural
    Metal Manufacturers 153
National Fire Protection Association
    (NFPA) 2, 284
National Particleboard Association 119
National Terrazzo and Mosaic
    Association 34

Natural fiber, dye, rubber 176, 221, 236,
    287, 289–90, 293–4, 299, 300
Navajo rug 221
Neat plaster 129
Needlebar, needlepunching 216, 220
NEMA LD 3 Impact Resistance 187
Neoprene 166
Nepheline syenite 67
Nevamar 275
Nickel and nickel-silver 84, 149, 158,
    165, 167, 170–1
    Finish 155, 165, 167, 171, C-50
Nitric acid 160, 169
Nitrocellulose 113, 242
Nitrogen, nitrogen oxide 85, 170, 172,
    181
Nitrous oxide (NOx) 16, 31
Nobel, Alfred and Immanuel 119
Noble metal 149
Noise-reduction coefficient (NRC) 259
Nomex 189
Nominal dimensions and sizes 106, 111,
    195–6
Nonferrous 149, 155, 162
Nonvitreous 197, 230
Nonwoven fabric 290
North American design 103–4, 128, 138,
    221
Novolac 199
No-wax vinyl flooring 214
Nylon carpet, fiber, microfiber 129, 176,
    178–9, 184, 191, 216–9, 222, 288,
    290, 293, 295, 300
    Textiles 189, 263, 295–6
    Furniture components 206, 278

O

Oak wood 103–4, 109, 115, 127, 203,
    254, 272, 278–80, 293, Appendix
Octaborate tetrahydrate 109
Office finishes 248, 278
Ogee 273, 275
Oil 178–80, 238, 272, 279–81, 183–4,
    160, 166, 168, 193, 238, 241
    -Based paint, resin, stain 180, 208,
    238, 240–1, 280
Old House Journal 27
Old-growth forests 104, 111
Olefin fiber, carpet 191, 217, 219, 288,
    290, 293, 295
Oleophilic 293
Oleoresin 175
Olive wood 103, Appendix
One-way–cell foam 220
    Framework grid 262
    Slab, joist 251
    Steel joist 161, 252–3, 257
Optical glass 81, 83
    Brightener 296
Orange wood 103, Appendix

Ordinary wool 290, 293
Ore 157, 159, 167–71
Organic coating 155, 168
    Cotton 288–9
    Resin 155
Organisol 155
Oriental rug 221
Oriented strand board (OSB) 106, 112,
    119–20, 122, 184, 209
Orlon 189, 294
Ormolu 150
Ornamental plaster 129, 134, 137
Osage-orange wood 105, Appendix
Osnaburg 234
Overlayed materials 50–1, 121
Owens, Michael 79
Owens Corning 294
Oxidation, 149, 152–3, 157, 164, 238
Oxide 66, 77, 82, 84, 149, 160, 162, 166,
    170–2
Oxygen 159, 170, 172, 177, 212
Ozone 159, 212, 244

P

Paint 116, 130, 135, 138, 166, 169–70,
    173, 178–9, 180,238–9, 278
    On concrete and masonry 72, 239, 252
    On cabinets, furniture, leather 193,
    268, 279
    On ceiling 248, 250, 255, 257
    On floor 199–200, 205, 207, 208
    On GFRG 227
    On metal 153, 253, 257, 279
    On wall 236–7, 280, C-74
    On wood 253, 279–80, C-73
Palazzi 54
Palladio, Andrea 127
Paneling, plywood and solid wood 106,
    112, 122, 127, 130, 227–8
Panga panga wood 202, Appendix
Paper-backed lath 133
Papercrete 112
Parawood 279, Appendix
Paraxylene 191
Parian's cement 129
Parison 83
Parkes, Alexander and Parkesine 175
Parquet flooring 208
Particleboard 106, 111, 112–3, 118–20,
    121, 185, 208–9, 265, 274, 277
Partition 188, 135, 229, 277
Paste and paste wax 172, 241
Patina 149, 151, 153–4, 164, 167–9, 203,
    270, 280
Pattern matching 232
Patterned finish 83, 88, 93, 154, 244
Pavers 68, 70, 74, 116, 198
Paxton, Joseph 78, 150
Pear wood 103, Appendix
Pebbles 61, 116

Pecan wood 202, 278, Appendix
Peel-and-stick veneer 118
Peened finish 154
Pegboard 121
Penetrating sealer 205
Pennington, Josiah 233
Pentachlorophenol 109
Perfluorocarbons (PFCs) 16
Perforated acoustic tile, panel 254, 257, 259, **262,** 263
    Gypsum lath 132
Perlite 129
Permanent finish 296
Perriand, Charlotte 151
Persian rug 221
Peruvian walnut wood 202, Appendix
Pesticide 243
Petroleum, petrochemical 175, 177, 181, 183–4, 186, 191, 279, 287–8
Pewter 103, 169, 171
Phenol, phenolic resin 112, 122, 176, 181–2, 184, 241, 277, 283
Phenol-formaldehyde (PF) 112, 119
Phosphate 130, 155
Phosphorus, phosphoric acid 164, 169
Photovoltaic glass 87
Pickling 155, 160
Picture molding 240
Piece dyeing 299
Pietra dura 54
Piezoelectric 98, 292
Pig iron 157–8
Pigment 73, 87, 113, 128, 149, 166–7, 169–70, 172–3, 177, 181, 194, 199, 213–4, 237, 238, 240, 243, 280, 300
Pile 217, 219, 221, 297, 299
Pilkington, Alistair and Profilit 80, 86
Pillar 150
Pilling 189, 285, 287, 290–1, 293–4
Pilotis 42
Pine wood 103–5, 119, 202, 207, 278–9, Appendix
Pink brass 165
Pitch pocket 105, 114
Pith **105**
Pittsburgh Plate Glass Company (PPG) 79, 83
Plain butt joint **281**
Plain-sawn, -slicing **108,** 115, 205, 207, 228
Plank, laminated 110, 202–4, 209–10, 212, 253
Plaster 48, 64, 116, 125, 127, 129, 131, 135, 224, 232, 234, 247–8, 255–6
    Coats **133**
    Molding, cornice, or medallion 130, cornice **135, 137**
    Walls and accessories **137,** 142–3, 223
Plasterboard 140
Plasterwork, ornamental 127–8
Plastic 82, 86, 173, 175, 209, 279

Coating 296
Glazing 244
Laminate 121, 182, 185–6, 179, 181, 228, 270, 274, 276–7, **C-67**
Lumber 182, 186–7
Matrix terrazzo 201
Webbing 283
-Wood composites 110
Plasticity 2
Plasticizer 177, 181, 185
Plastisol 155, 232–3
Plate glass 79–80, 82, 93
Plating 171
Platinum 149, 155
Plenum **21,** 144, 167, 169, 258
Plexiglas 176, 178, 244
Plumbing 173, 177–9, 181
Plunkett, Roy 177
Ply 119, 208–9
Plywood 104, 106–7, 112–3, 117–8, **119,** 121, 166, 206, 209, 228, 231, 274, 278
Pneumoconiosis 158
Pointing 32
Polar fleece 191
Polishing 50, 152
Polyalkene 178–9
Polybenzimidazole (PBI) 292
Polybutylene (PB) 178–9, 184
Polycarbonate 90–1, 184, 244, 255
Polycarboxylates 33
Polychromatic dyeing 299
Polyester 34, 175–7, 179–80, 184–5, 187, 192, 213, 245, 299
    Carpet 217, 219
    Coating, finish 107, 113, 155, 194
    Fabric 263, 291, 293, 295–6
    Fiber, fiberfill, microfiber 283, 288, 290, 293
    Resin 229, 244
Polyethylene 178–9, 184, 191
Polyethylene terephthalate (PETE or PET) 182–3, 191, 219
Polymer, polymeric, polymerized **175,** 176–7, 181, 187, 219, 277
    Coating, oil 96, 241
    Dispersed liquid crystal (PDLC) 88
    Fiber 288, 292
    Fabric treatment 192–3, 296
    Panel 183, **C-52**
    Resin 187, 219
Polyolefin 178–9
Polypropylene (PP) fiber, carpet 178–9, 182, 184, 191, 217, 219, 222, 277
Polystyrene (PS) 178–9, 182, 184
Polytetrafluoroethylene 178–9
Polyurethane 184, 189, 192, 219, 243, 283
    Coating, finish, resin, varnish 107, 113, 117, 147, 155, 199, 205, 210, 237, 241
    Foam 180, 220

Polyvinyl acetate (PVAC) 178, 184, 179
    Alcohol (PVAL) 178 178–9
    Butyral (PVB) 88, 90, 178–9, 219
    Chloride (PVC) 122, 176–7, 179, 181–2, 184, 192, 211, 214, 219, 244, 245, 262–3, 291, 294
    Fluoride (PVF) 158, 178–9
Poplar wood 115, 120, 254, 278, Appendix
Poppy oil 103
Porcelain tile 97, 99, 197–8, 230, 272, 230, **C-53**
Porcelain Enamel Institute (PEI) 197
Portland cement, mortar, stucco 29, 33, 73, 112, 125, 129 138–9, 230–1
Postconsumer recycled material 17
Postensioned concrete 39
Potable water 43
Poured flooring 199, 201
Powder coating 155, 180, 254, 262 **C-40**
Pozzolan 29–30
Precast concrete 38, 45
Precatylized, postcatylized lacquer 242
Preconsumer recycled material 17
Predecorated gypsum board 225
Prefinished gypsum wallboard 140 panel 224, 228
Premium grade veneer 113
Preservation 23
Preservatives 109, 243
Pressed glass 85
    Metal 152
Pressure-treatment 108
Prestressed and pretentioned concrete 39
Primer 138, 143–4, 144, **226,** 232, 237–8, 240
Printing 171, 298–301
Propane 184
Properties of materials 2
Propiconazole 110
Protein fiber 175, 287
Public space finish **C-2**
Pulmonary fibrosis 162
Purpleheart wood 202, Appendix
Pyroelectric 98
Pyrolave 271
Pyrolytic process 86–7

Q

Quarry stone, tile 55, 59, 100, 198, **C-56**
Quarter cut, sawn, sliced 106, **108,** 228 **116,** 205
Quartz 34, 45, 57, 78, 98, 171, 199, 202, 271, 275
Quartzite 34, 57
Quenching 153
Quilted fabric or fiberglass wall panel (QFM) 230, 299

R

Rabbeted edge 259
Radiation 82, 169
Radioactivity 130
Rag rug 221–2
Ragged finish 280
Railing 154, 157, 228
Railroad application 283
Ramie 288–9
Random matching 116, **117,** 228, 268
Range 269
Rattan 279–80
Ravenscroft, George 78
Rawhide 193
Rayon 176, 192, 245, 287–8, 291, 293,
    295–6
Reactive dye 300
Ready-mixed concrete and plaster 38, 129
Reclaimed wood flooring 204
Reconstruction 24
Recycled and recycling 17, 20, 35, 230
    Carpet 216, 220
    Ceiling systems 259, 263
    Ceramic tile 100, 197, 272
    Concrete and aggregate 44–5, 270,
        272
    Fabric and fiber 220, 286
    Glass 69, 78, 82, 84–5, 98, 219, 275
    Gypsum board 145–6, 224
    Masonry brick and CMUs 69, 75
    Metals 157, 163, 166–7, 169–72, 262,
        270
    Nylon 189–90, 217–8
    Paint 240
    Plastics, PET, PVC, PVB 110, 122,
        181–3, 185–6, 191, 219–20, 237
    Resin, polyester 229, 272
    Rubber 211, **213,** 293
    Water 141
    Wood products 228, 272, 279
    Wool 203, 220, 290
Red brass 165
    Cedar 104, 254, Appendix
    Oak 202, Appendix
Redwood 109–10, 278, Appendix
Reed 116, 125, 279
Refinement 2
Reflectance 81
Reflected sound **11**
Reflective coatings, glass 87–8, 96
Refraction **81**
Refractory ceramics 97
Refrigerated area flooring 199
Rehabilitating Interiors in Historic Buildings
    27
Rehabilitation 24–5
Reich, Lilly 151
Reinforced concrete 38
    Sponge rubber 220
Reinforcing bars 39–**40**

Renewable finish 297
Renovation 26
Repeat 284–5
Reprocessed paint 240
Resiliency, resilient 285
    Furring channels 134, 143, 256
    Floor coverings 195, 211, 213–4, 248,
        278
    Wall base 240
Resin 61–1, 88, 90, 112, 120–2, 155, 175,
    177–180, 183–5, 209–213, 219,
    238, 241, 243, 275, 278, 280, 299
    -Based plaster 138
    Panel 229
    Countertop 275
Resist printing 301
Restaurant finishes 248, 275
Restoration 24, **C-1**
Reveal 137, 142, 236, 266
Rexe 294
Rib lath 131, **133**
    Slab 251
Richardson, Henry Hobson 55
Richlite 271
Rift cut or sawn 106, 109, 116, 228
Rivet 151, **160,** 168, 173
Rock, rock crystal, rock lath 53, 78, 131
Rolled glass 83
    Finish 280
Roller shade 245
    Printing 301
Romaine's Restaurant **228**
Roman 29, 40, 42, 63–4, 77, 101, 116,
    150, 193, 240
Ronchamp, Chapel 42, **43**
Rosewood 115, 278, Appendix
Rotary cutting, peeling, lathe **115,**
    118–9, 208, 228, 268
Rotogravure process 214
Rubber products 110, 173, 176, 207, 211,
    213–4, 216, 220, 278, 282–3, 288
Rubberwood 211, 279, Appendix
Rubble 55, **62**
Rubens, Peter Paul 127
Rug 184, 195, 216, 220–1, 289, 297
Run plaster 137
    –Right application 283
Rush 125
Russian design 101, 119, 221
Rust 151, 153, 155, 157, 160, 173, 238,
    253, **C-45**
Rustic terrazzo 201
Rya rug 221

S

SixAgain closed-loop recycling program
    190
Safety glass and film 10, 244
Sag-resistant gypsum ceiling board 140

Saline flame resistant treatment 192, 296
Salt-glazed brick 68
Salvaged material 17
Sand cast, cushion, finish 140, 163, 173,
    181, 199, 201, 237, 240
Sandblasting 88, 95–6, **C-24**
Sandstone 55, 58–61, **C-12**
Sanitary ceramics and base 99, 231
Santos mahogany 202, Appendix
Sapwood **105,** 108
Saran 177, 288
Sassafras wood 105, Appendix
Satin fabric, finish, spar 130, 238–9, 291,
    294
Sauna **229,** 277
Sawn face 208
Saxony carpet 219
Säynätsalo Town Hall, Finland 65
Scale on metal 155
Scotchguard 193, 297
Scott's cement 129
Scratch coat **131,** 132, **133,** 140
Screen printing 301
Screenwall block 74
Scribed 268
Scrim 233
Scrubber 31, 130, 141
Sealant 178, 184, 270
Sealer 49, 118, 120, 199–200, 205, 209,
    232, 237–8, 274, 282
Seamless quartz flooring 199, **202**
Security glass 90 film 244
Sedimentary rock 55, 58–60, 173
Selection criteria 1–2
Selective demolition 14
Selenite 130
Selenium 84, 168
Self-centering lath 131
    -Cleaning glass 89
    -Consolidating grout (SCGs) 33
    -Furring lath 132, **133**
    –Leveling compound 206
    –Polishing rubber floor 214
    -Stick vinyl and carpet tile 214, 218
Selvage 283, 297
Semigloss finish 238–9
Semon, Waldo 176
Senior housing, Weston, MA **C-4**
Serape rug 221
Serpentine stone 56
    Brick wall 69
Shade 284
Shale 45, 72, 198, 200
Shantung 289
Shape memory 292
Sheen 238
Sheet glass 82, 93
    Metal 160–1, 262
    Linoleum, rubber and vinyl 213–4,
        220
Sheetrock 140

Shell 103, 200
Shellac 117, 242–3, 279
Shelving 120, 281
Shiplap 208, **281**
Shop-built cabinet 266, 268
Shot blast 164
Shrinkage 285
Signage 178, 262
Silestone 271, 275
Silica sand 34, 83, 46, 77, 131, 154
   Fume pozzolan 269
Silicon 30, 34, 164–6
Silicone sealant 9, 181, 184, 196, 273,
   276
Silk 221, 286–7, 289, 293, 295, 300
   -Screened glass, printing 96, 291
Silver 78, 84, 86–8, 96, 103, 149–50, 155,
   168–9, 292
Simulated leather, suede 192
Single-filling knit 299
Sink, 47, **48,** 49, 156, **267,** 269, 274–5,
   275
Sintering 169, 272
Sisal 129, 221, 295
SITE architectural group 65
Sizing 237, 296
Skara Brae, Scotland 63
Skidmore, Owings and Merrill (SOM) 80
Skim coat plaster 143–4, 256
Skylight 177–8, 250, 255
Slag 30, 157, 152, 158, **159,** 169, 171
Slate 57, 60–1, 198, 200, 271, **C-22,**
   C-23
Sleeper 206
Slip, slip casting 68, 98
   Cover 284, 289, 294
      Matching 116, **117,** 228
   -Resistant 197, 199, 213–4, 216
Slump test 44–45
Slumped glass 84
Slurry 168, 226–7
Smart fabric, carpet 295
Smelting 157, 167–9, 171
Smolder test 284
Soapstone 57, 271, **C-68**
Soda 97
Soda-lime glass 82–3
Sodium bicarbonate and sulfide 169, 193
Soffit framing **256**
Soft floor coverings 195, 216
Softwood 105–6, 110, 113, 119, 121, 208
Solar cell 87
Solder 166, 169, 171
Solid plaster partition 134
   Surfacing 180, 187–8, 270–1, 275, 276
   Wood 202, 204, 228, 278–9
Solution dyed 217, 189, 293, 300
Solvent 178–9, 184, 212, 278
Sound absorption 11, 74, 129, 290
   Barrier ceiling tile 257
   Damping 121

-Grade veneer 113
Transmission coefficient (STC) 86, 209
Southern yellow pine 202, Appendix
Soy 112, 219
Space frame 263
Spalled 34
Spandex 189, 292, 294–5
Spandrel glass 86
Spar 241
Specular 167
Spence's plaster 129
Spinneret 176, 299
Spirit 241
Spline butt **281**
   Ceiling 256
Sponge rubber cushion 220
Sponged paint finish 240, 280
Spontaneous combustion 243
Spring, Marshall 282–3
Spruce wood 119, 207, Appendix
Spun–bonded web 299
   Lace fabric 299
   Silk 293
Square-edged planks and tiles 203, 257, 259
Stabilizer 177
Stain, staining 96, 106–7, 243, 278, 280,
   C-28
   On concrete 200, 240
   On wood 205–6, 240, 253
   Resistant treatment 296–7
Stained glass 255
Stainless steel 149, 153, 155–6, 158, 160,
   161, 162, 168, 170, 228, 262, 270,
   277, 292
Stair component 60, **62,** 120, 156, 188,
   206, 211, 213, 265
Stamina wood 112
Stamped concrete and metal 152, 200,
   256–7, **258, C-66**
Stannic oxide 171
Staple, staple-down installation 204, 209,
   257, 282–3, 296
   Fiber 287
Starching 296
Statuary bronze 165
Statue of Liberty **160**
Steel 80, 133, 138, 149–50, **152,** 154–8,
   159–60, 166–7, 170–1
   Frame construction 151, 231, 234
   Products 252, 262, 279
Stencil 37, 96, 205, 207, 301
Sterling (British) 120
Stile 228
Stone 53, 130, 139
   Circle, medallion 60, **C-14**
   Countertop or partition 268, 277
   Engineered 271
   Finish, edge, tumbled 59, 61, 276
   Floor and wall tile, mosaic, panel 116,
      195, 198, 200, 231–2, **234**
   Precious, semi-precious 103, 150

Stoneware 98–9
Store ceiling finish 248
   –Bought cabinet 265
Stove 156, 269
Strapwork 127
Strata 55
Straw bale, strawboard 112, 121–2, 129,
   228
Stretched-fabric system 236, **237,** 262
Strié 280
Strike-off and screed finish 47
Stringer 110
Strip terrazzo installation 201
Stripping 280
Structural ceramics 97
   Lumber 110
   Steel 161, 269
   Wood panels 118
Stucco 40, **116,** 125, 128, 132–3, 138,
   140, 146, 184
Styrene butadiene 176, 185, 214, 211, 219
Subfloor 110, 120, 204, 206, 212–3, 216,
   218–9
Sueding 192
Sugarcane 112
Sulfur, sulfuric, sulfide 31, 84, 146, 161,
   164, 166, 168
   Dioxide gas 145
   Hexafluoride 16
   Oxides 31, 85
Sullivan, Louis 151
Sun-dried brick 63, 64, **66**
Suspended ceiling 80, **247,** 258–9, 254,
   256
Suspension grid 257
Sustainable 12, 110, 112
Swirl finish **49**
Synthetic 175, 183, 211, 212, 243, 279
   Fabric, fiber, rug 188, **190,** 191, 192,
      217, 220–2, 244, 287, 290, 293
   Gypsum 130, 141
   Leather and suede 291, 294
   Resin 232, 241
   Rubber 199, 213, 220, 288
   Sealer 214
Systems furniture 284

T

3-M 193, 297
Table, tabletop 84, 96, **104,** 281
Tackable wall surface 236
Tackless nail strip 218, 220
Taffeta 291, 294
Tailings 169
Taj Mahal, Agra, India 54, **C-13**
Tannin, tanning 193
Tapa cloth 298–9
Tape 141, 144, 173
Tapestry 221, 298
Tarnish 155, 170

Tar 158
Tasar 289
T-bar 161
Teak 103, 202, 272, 278, Appendix
Technical ceramics 98
Tedlar 178
Teflon 177–8, 193, 297
Tegular edge 259
Teijin Ltd. 294
Tell Mureybit 125
Tellurium 168
Tempered, tempering 81, 86–8, 90, 92, 96, 153, 244
Temporary finish 297
Tenacity 285
Teotihuacan, Mexico 37, 128
Terneplate 171
Terrazzo 34–5, **36**, 201, 272, 275, **C-9, C-10**
Tesserae 77
Tetrafluoromethane 16
Tex 287
Textile 140, 173, 284, 292
    Coating, finish 178–9, 184
    Dyeing, pigments 300
    Fabrication methods 299
    Nylon 179
    PET 191
    Wallcovering 235
Texture, textured 2, 88
Thermal barrier composite panels 184
    Capacity **16,** 60,
    Conduction 82
    Finish 59, 199
Thermochromic 292
Thermoplastic 177–9, 184, 290–1, 293
Thickset and thinset ceramic tile **196,** 230–1
Thin brick 72
    -Coat plaster 129
Thinner 238
Tie anchor **65**
    –Dyeing 301
    Flooring 195, 209
    Wall 72
    Wire 62
Tigerwood 202, Appendix
Tile Council of North America (TCNA) 100
Tile, carpet 218
    -Ceramic 97, 99
    Countertop 272, 275
    Floor 181, 212
    Glass 272
    Hollow 73
    Linoleum, rubber, vinyl 213–4
    Plastic 178–9
    Stone 62, 232,
Tilt-up concrete 39–40
Timber 110–1

Tin, tin oxide, tinplate 84, 97, 149, 155, 164–5, 171–2
Tinted film and glass 91, 94, 96–7
Tiny Tim radio **176**
Titanium dioxide, powder 84, 96, 149, 171–3, 245
T-joint 159
Toilet partitions 60, 277
Toluene 158, 184–5, 214, 220
    Di-isocyanate (TDI) 283
Tongue-and-groove 119, 141, 202, 204, 208–10, 212, 253, 281
Topcoat 107, 138, 213, 238
Tortoiseshell 103
Town, Ithiel 54
Toxicity Characteristic Leaching Procedure (TCLP) 278
Transitional cotton 288
Translucent materials, translucency 41, 83, 86, 95, 185, 229, 244
Transmittance 81
Transparency 81, 83, 229
Travertine 58, 200, 271, **C-18, C-19**
Tree cross section **105**
Trevira **180,** 192
Trex 122
Triacetate 189, 287, 293–4
Trinity Church, Boston 55
Trivalent chromium 167
Tropical hardwoods 111, 279
Trowel finish **49,** 129, 138, 199, 209
True bronze 165
Truss 116, 161
Tub-shower unit 177–8
Tuck pointing 32
Tufa 40
Tufted carpet 216, 218, 222, 297
Tugendhat House 151
Tulip wood 103, Appendix
Tung oil 241
Tupperware 182
Turkey, Turkish, Turkoman, Turkmenistan rug 221
Turpentine 160
Tuscan Grill, Waltham, MA 139
Tussah 289
Tweed 293
Twist **107,** 109
Two-way slab 251
Type 6 and Type 6/6 nylon 179, 218
Type I, II, and III wallcovering 215, 233
Type X 132, 140, 224, 256
Tyvek 191

U

U.S. Customs House, Washington, DC 54
U.S. National Institutes of Health 158
Ultraviolet (UV) 37, 81, 177–9, 181, 185, 188–9, 205, 237, 271, 287, 289, 291

Curing 206, 208, 210
    Fading 244
    Resistance 255
Underlayment, concrete or pad 50, 218, 220–1, 206, 209, 231
Unglazed ceramic tile 198
Union Station, Washington, DC **137**
United States Green Building Council (USGBC) 15
Universal design 5, 6–7, **9**
Up-the-bolt application 283
Ur, Iraq 63
Uranium 84
Urea-formaldehyde (UF) resins 112, 119, 210
Urethane finish 50, 72, 112, 211, 214, 243
    Modified alkyd resin 241
Uruk, Iraq 63
Uzbekistan rug 221

V

Vacuum-metalized 167
Vanadium 84, 172
Vapor barrier 178
Varnish 107, 113, 117, 125, 155, 184, 205, 241, 243, 253, 279
Vat dye 300–1
Vaulted ceiling 250
Vaux-le-Vicomte 127
Vegetable dye 300
    -Tanned leather 193
Veining 271
Velvet, velveteen 291, 299
Veneer, bamboo 211
    Base 132,
    Concrete coating 200
    Matching 116,
    Parquet 208
    Plaster 129, 132, **143, 144,** 225, **255**
    Plywood 112–3, 114, 268
    Stone **6,**
    Thin brick 68
    Wood 101, 103, 106, **107,** 113, **114,** 115, 117–9, 121, 208, 228, 237, 254, 279
Venetian plaster 138
Venturi, Robert 65
Vermiculite 129, 131
Versailles Palace 78, **79,** 103
Vertical louver blinds 244

Vicuña 287, 293
Villa Rotonda 127
Villa Savoye, Poissy, France 42, **43**
Vintage linoleum floor **212**
Vinyl, vinyon 110, 113, 121, 176–9, 181, 185, 192, 215–6, 219, 288, 294
    Asbestos tile (VAT) 214–5
    Chloride 185, 234
    Composition tile (VCT) 214, 216, **C-58**
    Fiber 288
    Finish or coating 140, 212, 230, 236, 245, 259, 257, 291
    Flooring 195, 211, 214
    Laminated fabric 263
    Wallcovering 224, 229 , 232–4, **235,** 278 film 234, 291
Virgin wool 290, 293
Viscoelastic fluid 181
Viscose rayon 176, 192, 291, 293
Vitreous 198 coating 168
Vitruvius 64
Voile 288, 293
Volatile organic compounds (VOCs) 13, 19–21, 74, 111, 120, 155, 181, 185, 201, 208, 210–1, 220, 234, 238, 242–3, 271

W

Waferboard 112, 119–20
Waffle slab 251, **252**
    Cloth 299
Wagner, Otto 79, 151
Wainscot 130, **228**
Walk-off mat **195**
Wall anchor 234
    Base 202, 216, 240
    Cabinet **267**
    Cladding, finish, treatment 180, 188, 293
    –Hung granite countertop detail **269**
    Liner 232, 237
    Painter **239**
    Panel, partition 156–7, 173, 176, 189, 228
    Tile trims **232**
Wallboard facing paper 140–1
Wallcovering 138, 144, 178, 181, 185, 232, 236, 289, 299
Wallpaper **23,** 128, 130, 185, **234,** 255
Walnut wood 102–3, 109, 202, 272, 278, 280, Appendix
Warp, 297–9
Warping 107–109, 112–3, 147, 186, 237, 265, 272, 274, 282
Water 43
    –Based finish 243
    Features 46–7

Glass 82
    –Jet finish 199
    –Needled fabric 299
    Pollution and waste 45, 193, 278
    Recycling, use, 17, 121
    Repellant 297
    –Resistant 225, 296
Wattle-and-daub 101
Wax 50, 118, 120–1, 125, 160, 166, 168–9, 193–4, 205–6, 241, 270, 274, 279–80
Wear layer 211, 214–5
Weatherbest 122
Weatherstripping 208
Weave 284
Webbing 283, 290, 294
Weft or woof 297–9
Weld, welding, weldability 156, 159–60, 163, 166, 172
    Puddle 159
    Wire **41,** 132, **133,** 262
Wenge wood 202, Appendix
Werkbund Exhibition, Cologne, Germany 64
Wetting agent 238
White coat 129
    oak 202, Appendix
    pine 207, Appendix
White-metal finish 155, **C-49**
Whitener 296
Whitewares 97
Whitewash 116, 125, 128–9
Whitfield, Nathan Bryan 129
Wicker 279–80 rocker **281**
Wide-flange (W) beam 161
Wild silk 293
Wiley, Ralph 177
Wilkinson, William 37
William and Mary period 103
Willow 279–80
Wilson's disease 168
Wilsonart 275
Wilton carpet 217, **218**
Window 78, **80,** 86, 88, 176, 265
    Blind 185
    Film 244
    Frame 122, 149, 162, 165, 182
    Screen 177–8, 184
    Sill 188
    Treatment 162, 178–9, 185, 244, 289, 291–4, 299
Wire, wired cloth 161
    Glass 91, **92,** 93
    Mesh 262, 269, 283
    Rope 161
    –Tie anchor system 232
Wood 99, 175, 184–5, 192, 213, 216, 220, 276, 287
    Base 184

    Ceiling 254
    Certified 272
    Composite 106–7, 111–2, 118, 122, 186, 278
    Countertop 269
    Door **C-29**
    -Fibered plaster 129
    Finish and filler 105, 107, 113, 208, 241
    Flooring, decking 195, 202, **203, 205, 206,** 253
    Furniture 279, 281
    Subfloor 212
    Substitute 215
    Toilet compartment 277
    Treatment 278
    Veneer 113, 237
Woodwork 116, 265
Wool 219–10, 286–7, 290, 292–3, 295, 299–300
    Carpet, rug 216–7, 221
    Fiber, blend 222, 290, 293
Workability 2
Workstation 188
Woven-wire 132, **133,** 262
    Carpet 216
    Leather 297, **298**
    Pile fabric 299
Wren, Christopher 64, 103
Wright, Frank Lloyd 64, **67, 104,** 130
Wrinkle resistance 296
Wrought iron 156, 279
Wyzenbeek test CHECK 284

X

X-ray protection glass 88
Xylene 184–5, 220

Y

Yard lumber 110
Yarn 284–5, 296 dyeing 299–300
Yellow birch wood 202, Appendix
Yiftah El, Israel 29

Z

Zinc 142, 149, 155, 164–5, 169, 173, 270
Zirconium 96
Zebrawood 103, Appendix
Zodiaq 271, 275